10/91   3026143   AR1095VN   52.95

D0118933

KNOWLEDGE ENGINEERING

*Knowledge Acquisition, Knowledge Representation,
the Role of the Knowledge Engineer, and
Domains Fertile for AI Implementation*

KNOWLEDGE ENGINEERING

Knowledge Acquisition, Knowledge Representation, the Role of the Knowledge Engineer, and Domains Fertile for AI Implementation

Dimitris N. Chorafas

VNR VAN NOSTRAND REINHOLD
New York

Printed in the United States of America

Van Nostrand Reinhold
115 Fifth Avenue
New York, New York 10003

Van Nostrand Reinhold International Company Limited
11 New Fetter Lane
London EC4P 4EE, England

Van Nostrand Reinhold
480 La Trobe Street
Melbourne, Victoria 3000, Australia

Nelson Canada
1120 Birchmount Road
Scarborough, Ontario M1K 5G4, Canada

16 15 14 13 12 11 10 9 8 7 6 5 4 3 2 1

Library of Congress Cataloging-in-Publication Data

Chorafas, Dimitris N.
    Knowledge engineering: knowledge acquisition, knowledge
representation, the role of the knowledge engineer, and domains
fertile to AI implementation: a text prepared for Van Nostrand
Reinhold/Dimitris N. Chorafas. —Fully rev. ed.
        p.   cm.
    Includes bibliographical references.
    "November 1989."
    ISBN 0-442-23969-6
    1. Artificial intelligence.   2. Expert systems (Computer science)
3. Knowledge acquisition (Expert systems)   I. Van Nostrand Reinhold
Company.   II. Title
Q335.C488   1990
006.3—dc20   90-32211
                                                                        CIP

"Thinking is those mental processes we don't understand."

Alan Turing

Contents

Preface

In the future, working with computers will be more like working with people. Machines will understand and respond to human speech and will even recognize the person addressing them. This is one of the practical results of work in artificial intelligence (AI).

While it is easier to communicate with intelligent machines than with dumb ones, as we have done during the last forty years, it is also clear that we need computer scientists who are versatile in the new art and science of *knowledge engineering*. This book is addressed to this subject:

- *Who* is a knowledge engineer?
- *How* does he or she practice knowledge engineering?
- *What* is involved in knowledge acquisition?
- In *which ways* is knowledge representation being done?
- *Which* are the tools at our disposal?
- *Why* is it necessary to do prototyping, modeling, and testing?
- *Why* should we pay special attention to human windows?

This book is written for computer professionals but also for majors in related fields—physics, mathematics, engineering, economics, linguistics, psychology—who plan to enter the field of knowledge engineering. It is practical and down-to-earth, not theoretical; it is also enriched with many applications examples.

The text is substantiated by the necessary background: the scientific infrastructure of knowledge engineering. Science and technology play a major role in our lives. One point on which there is general agreement is that key to problem solving is the availability of know-how that we can effectively exploit. This is the goal of AI research and implementation.

To provide practical examples from fields in which knowledge engineering has been successfully put into practice, the book is enriched with three chapters on applications (15 to 17). From robotics to intelligent databases and polyvalent networks, the implementation of AI enables us to perform more functions with greater accuracy and better know-how than was previously possible with classical software. And because expert systems can collaborate with conventional programs, AI constructs can be integrated with day-to-day operations.

Knowledge engineering is reaching the stage of maturity where it is becoming useful, practical, and cost effective in the industrial and business worlds. Companies are looking to this field for solutions to their problems. These opportunities, in turn, are fueling hardware and software development. AI is thus becoming a lucrative field for properly prepared, aggressive companies and individuals.

This is the background for current predictions. It is believed that in the 1990s the field of knowledge engineering will be more important and more profitable than traditional computing. If we plan for the future, which we should, we must realize the need for training in this new technology of engineers, mathematicians, and physicists, as well as graduates of business administration, economics, linguistics, and psychology. Time is pressing.

This present book aims to meet this training objective. Through a flexible, low-keyed presentation stressing the fundamentals of AI thinking rather than complex mathematical formulas, it leads the reader through the main phases of his future work as a professional.

Part One addresses the issues most closely associated with knowledge engineering. Chapter 1 profiles the knowledge engineer and the domain expert. Chapter 2 explains the process of knowledge acquisition. Six different methods are presented, each with specific examples.

A major decision for an expert system builder is how knowledge is to be represented. Chapter 3 addresses this issue. Casting expert knowledge in an AI construct is a challenging task requiring a methodology and tools. The methodology rests on prototyping, modeling, and testing and is outlined in Chapter 4.

The tools are expert systems shells, whose acceptance is becoming widespread. In Chapter 5, shells are classified and then three specific examples are given, followed in Chapter 6 by a discussion of *second-generation* expert systems shells and in Chapter 7 by ways and means to evaluate the shell and the AI product.

Another area of growing importance is man–machine interfaces. Enhanced through agile expert systems, such interfaces become *human windows*, as Chapter 8 explains. They are the channels through which *multimedia* information is obtained, interpreted, and assimilated into the framework of the interaction between the user and the intelligent machine.

Knowledge engineering will be successful not only if we possess the basic background but also if we are able to proceed with *value differentiation*. This is the subject of Part Two, whose theme is polyvalent. Chapter 9 discusses the role of *supercomputers* in AI, and Chapter 10 addresses the developing discipline of the *mathematics of uncertainty*.

This emphasis on value differentiation is based on the belief that the presentation of tools and methods for knowledge engineering would have been incomplete without reference to the computer power necessary to handle the new intelligence-enriched constructs. It is as if supercomputers (non-von Neumann, fifth generation computers) have been designed for AI implementation. Some of the most imaginative ongoing projects focus on handling the mathematics of uncertainty, which will be an indispensable part of AI in the years to come.

Chapter 11 introduces the reader to objects, metaobjects, metalanguages, and meta-knowledge, which underpin the new mathematics. The concept of *meta* is very important in AI. By focusing on the *inference engine* and its environment, Chapter 12 introduces the concept of predicates but also elaborates on the functions to be supported and the roles to be played by an operating system.

Chapter 13 contrasts the services provided by a *knowledgebank* to those of a *database*. Chapter 14 then elaborates on the implementation of multimedia databases and provides practical examples, including voice integration, text understanding, and office document architecture.

The last three chapters of Part Two concentrate on applications. Chapter 15 documents the role of AI in computer-aided design: from solutions which can now be provided to the thorny input problem, to the effective management of electronic images. It also includes optical storage as an example of multimedia.

Knowledge engineering contributions in robotics and computer vision are the subject of Chapter 16. Polyvalent networks interconnecting thousands of computers, including practical examples from network implementation in financial institutions, are the main focus of Chapter 17.

The Appendix presents a program for training knowledge engineers. Finally, a Bibliography of 200 works is included to help the serious researcher in his or her work.

This textbook is introductory, written in a *simple, easy-to-follow, comprehensive* manner. There are no complex mathematics and no special prerequisites. Each term is defined when introduced, with a reference to the chapter where it is further elaborated. This makes it easier to comprehend the issues covered and makes the basic nature of this work more attractive.

The book presupposes no a priori knowledge of knowledge engineering subjects. It is structured around a fundamental unifying presentation, of which concepts, definitions, rules, qualitative models, and specific examples are the evident expressions.

Let me close by expressing my thanks to everyone who contributed to this book during the extensive research which led to its development. I am particularly indebted to Professors Tibor Vamos and John A. Campbell, who kindly agreed to read and comment on parts of the manuscript. A long list would be necessary to name all of my colleagues who contributed insight and foresight. Dianne Littwin was instrumental as senior editor and Helen Greenberg paid great attention to the fine print of the editing job. Eva-Maria Binder did the artwork, typing, and index.

Dr. Dimitris N. CHORAFAS
Valmer and Vitznau

KNOWLEDGE ENGINEERING

*Knowledge Acquisition, Knowledge Representation,
the Role of the Knowledge Engineer, and
Domains Fertile for AI Implementation*

part 1

METHODS AND TOOLS OF KNOWLEDGE ENGINEERING

1

The Knowledge Engineer

Keywords

knowledge engineering · knowledge engineer · user acceptance · reasoning · knowledge representation · knowledge acquisition · rules · interactive usage · knowledge utilization · know-how · tools · principles · prototyping · planning · requirements · symbolic reasoning · problem solving · metaphors · Organization Department · system analysts · experts · problem solution · creativity · availability · internal testing · deep modeling · qualitative · quality control · versatile output · possibility theory · decision support systems · problem definition · programming work · testing and maintenance · design review · production rules · fault model · rule maker

1. INTRODUCTION

Knowledge engineering is the process of building artificial intelligence (AI) constructs. Task-specific knowledge is an integral but identifiable part of the effort. It reflects an expert's know-how, which must be captured, analyzed, and transformed into rules. This is what the knowledge engineer is asked to do. Yet, knowledge engineering is still an art rather than engineering. We are finding our way, working to develop a methodology and to structure a discipline.

As we will see in this chapter, the knowledge engineer needs many qualities and a great deal of background information. Today, most knowledge engineers are not really *domain experts*. Instead, they are interviewers of other experts. Nevertheless, a knowledge engineer should build his skill on expert knowledge in the field in which he works.

The knowledge engineer must be able to do research on available knowledge. He must be able to perceive other expert knowledge, *understand the detail,* and express it in rules, frames, scenarios, and logic programming. He must build *causal models* using the knowledge of other experts.

A causal model is at least two-dimensional. It includes cause and effect as well as the underlying rules. The knowledge engineer must be able to formulate his knowledge in terms of cause and effect and then express it mathematically. That is why the writing of rules, frames, or scenarios is so important. The real world in which we live is far more complex than the one dimension many people use in their daily work. Furthermore, the work of the expert involves *uncertainty.* Not everybody realizes this fact, but it should not escape the knowledge engineer's attention. For this reason, the knowledge engineer should master all aspects of qualitative decision making. He must know not only the background but also how to apply

1. knowledge banks
2. domains
3. rules
4. induction, deduction, and abduction
5. logical structures
6. heuristics
7. system research
8. cognitive sciences
9. experimental design
10. human windows[1]
11. system evaluation
12. user acceptance.

User acceptance requires *reasoning* rather than the simple implementation of systems and techniques so familiar in traditional data processing chores. Without user acceptance, even the best AI project will fail. When we design a system and even after we test it, we have accomplished only the first step. A logical system grows through usage; one which is not used decays.

Vital to user acceptance is the ability to integrate the AI project with traditional technology. Such integration should take place all the way from original specifications to user training, as indicated in Figure 1-1. The knowledge engineer should not only be aware of this fact but should also demonstrate it by putting it into practice.

Even the knowledge engineer must be trained to do the 12 tasks just outlined in an able manner. Unfortunately, few programs today address these issues. Nor are AI project directors careful in selecting personnel. Quite often knowledge engineers are nothing more than system analysts paid three times as much. No wonder so many AI projects don't reach a fruitful conclusion.

---

[1] The term *human window* is not standard but it is being used consistently throughout this text. A human window is an agile, user friendly, and forgiving (of enduser's errors) man-machine interface. It is upkept at state-of-the art, for instance today emphasizing *visualization.* Human windows are discussed in detail in Chapter 8.

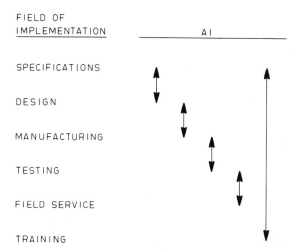

Figure 1-1. We must integrate AI with traditional information technology. In doing so, we should revamp the different steps we have traditionally followed and automate their execution.

There is also the issue of personality. Great architects and designers are both masters of their art and adept communicators. While it is not only helpful but absolutely necessary to take courses in knowledge engineering, in the end it is the individual's personality, imagination, and ability to communicate with professional experts and users that are crucial.

2. PROFILE OF A KNOWLEDGE ENGINEER

The object of *knowledge engineering* is the development, production, and distribution of intelligence through man-made systems. Knowledge engineering is the applied science aspect of AI. The challenges range

- from knowledge *acquisition*
- to *knowledge representation,* that is, the development of *rules* and
- the facilitation to be provided in the *interactive usage* of these rules.

The last factor is known as *knowledge utilization.* Our focus is on *know-how* and its transcription into intelligent machines.

The work of the knowledge engineer is defined by an AI project the way it has been described. This work extends from conception to implementation. While, as a designer, the knowledge engineer may at times resort to informal methods, even rules of thumb, the policy should be that of using good methodology and emphasizing detail. "Great events are the product of small details," says Donald T. Regan.[2] The knowledge engineer should use his know-how and background to establish a methodology which ensures abstraction is

---

[2] "For the Record. From Wall Street to Washington" St. Martin's Press, New York, 1988.

approached, structured, and given a particular context. This is the basis on which he must work. He will often lack complete specifications or an explicit knowledge source giving clear-cut answers in a fully satisfactory manner.

The interaction of the knowledge engineer with the domain expert in order to develop the AI project will help increase the engineer's know-how and maturity. Through practice, he will establish reasoning methods and policies on how to handle facts and rules. His expertise will grow by successive knowledge intake. This cannot be done quickly. What's important is that he remain active and gain experience.

In their work, both the knowledge engineer and the domain expert should remember that all powerful engineering tools can be dangerous. AI *is* a mighty engineering tool, and it should be used with caution. This statement is valid whether we talk of applications in manufacturing, in banking, or in any other domain.

I have used the word *tools*. The knowledge engineer is a tools developer. He does not only interview the domain expert to find out how a particular task is performed, leaving system implementation to others. He is *involved from the initial design through the final delivery* of the AI system itself.

The duties of the knowledge engineer vary, depending on the size, scope, or nature of the project and the organization. Therefore, an a priori definition of what knowledge engineers do is not realistic, nor can it be done in the abstract without paradigms. The problem is to create them.

Since describing is not enough and defining should be the goal, Table 1-1 summarizes the profile of the knowledge engineer.

The *physicist's method* is a good example of the methodology the knowledge engineer should follow. There is also much to gain by converting and refining methods from the physical sciences and applying these methods to the *logical sciences* of knowledge engineering.

Key to the physicist's method is the use of general postulates, or *principles*. We will consider this subject in Part Two. From these principles, the knowledge engineer can deduce conclusions. Hence, his work falls into two parts:

1. He must first discover principles through interaction with the domain expert.
2. Then he must draw conclusions from them.

Once this is done, inference follows on inference. Most importantly, this process often reveals relations which may extend well beyond the area of reality (domain) from which the principles are drawn.

TABLE 1-1. Profile of a Knowledge Engineer.

1. Mastery of information technology or appreciation of it and mastery of one's professional field
2. A focused professional attitude in his or her daily work
3. Decision style (conceptual and/or analytical thinking)
4. Willingness to develop one's career
5. Hard worker
6. Open to new ideas—flexible
7. Ability to work under stress
8. Ability to collaborate with others and to communicate

The following examples of AI constructs (expert systems in this case) demonstrate how closely AI work approximates the physicist's method:

1. *Prospector* helps locate minerals. Developed at SRI, it asks questions about a region's geologic formations and then gives advice on where minerals are likely to be found. Prospector accurately predicted the location of a molybdenum deposit worth millions of dollars in Washington State.
2. *Dipmeter Advisor* analyzes logging data to determine the dip, or tilt, of geologic formations. To gather knowledge for the system, researchers observed one of the company's top field engineers at work for six months. Schlumberger, the company which developed it, says that the system can already match the performance of some newly trained human interpreters.

Now researchers are planning to *combine* AI with advanced *graphics capabilities* so that computers can create pictures and maps of unseen underground formations. They are also beginning to explore some AI applications outside oil-field services—for instance, new ways to give a computer knowledge about complex man-made systems, such as electronic circuits.

These results demonstrate that in the utilization of computer power, we have evolved well beyond classical data processing, which is basically a massive job of handling data. We have moved into the domain of knowledge. What is missing is the fundamental approach to knowledge-intense systems. Until this approach is developed, the role of the knowledge engineer starts with queries about methods and rules, intepreting the expert's answers to questions with respect to *knowledge as such* and *the method of knowledge presentation*. Subsequently, the knowledge engineer does the following:

1. Integrates the expert's answers into the growing knowledge bank.
2. Draws analogies to help the expert structure (or remember) important aspects of *his* own knowledge in the application domain.
3. Provides counterexamples which seem to violate the expert's hypotheses.

The interview of the domain expert should not be one way, it should not be conducted with records being kept in a manual form nor should it consist of conversation alone. From the start, it should be computer based. Whichever fourth-generation language *shell*[3] is chosen, *prototyping* should be the goal of the interview.

In his architectural work, the knowledge engineer should account for all of the resources available to him. From the very beginning of an AI project, all life cycle phases should be accounted for, as Figure 1-2 documents. *Planning* is an integral part of a good project.

In AI work, the planning premises are developed when the *requirements definition* is done. Given the vital importance of this subject, planning and requirements definition are treated at the end of this chapter in "6. Planning the Expert System: A Case Study."

In his deatiled work, the knowledge engineer will use symbolic reasoning. *Symbolic* rather than numerical operations characterize cognitive activities such as

---

[3] *Shells* are defined and discussed with specific examples in Chapter 5. Second generation shells are presented in Chapters 6 and 7.

- problem solving,
- forecasting and planning, and
- induction, deduction, and extrapolation

While *problem solving* is the knowledge engineer's top skill, general approaches must be supplemented by know-how specific to a given domain.

The knowledge that the knowledge engineer has, gains through research, or acquires by working with the domain expert should be translated into metaphors. *Metaphors* are ways of describing what the computer does, in contrast to what people do. They are used in alluding to action, such as making an inference, sending a message, or providing an interface with common technology.

While metaphors come into play in the development cycle, their role starts at the very beginning, as a perspective a knowledge engineer brings to an AI project is most important. When people without the appropriate perspective, or metaphors, try to create a system, a skewed project will often be the result.

Since the machines which we employ are much less powerful than memory-based reasoning would require, specialization is the key to success. Ten, fifteen, or twenty years ago, general systems were built and specific elements were added for different domains. Such systems failed. Success stories, by contrast, resulted from the insight that specialization pays off.

Within the field of specialization, the focal point of a knowledge engineer's method should be the refinement of task expertise. Two different types of knowledge must be learned to perform this job well:

1. The domain knowledge used by the reasoning process.
2. The reasoning process itself.

In other words, refinement of any type of knowledge requires an explicit representation of the know-how that can be examined, structured, recorded, evaluated, and changed over time.

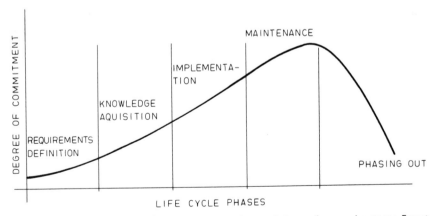

Figure 1-2. The life cycle of any software construct can be seen in terms of successive stages. Expert systems are no exception to this rule.

Since developing an AI system to perform an expert's task means organizing a body of knowledge well enough to represent a domain expert's reasoning, it is proper to take a look at the expert. The reasoning process cannot be better than the man who does it or contributes to it his know-how.

3. EXPERTS[4] AND THEIR CHARACTERISTICS

Over three decades of computer applications practice, when management disliked someone or a supervisor was confronted with an employee who did not know or did not wish to produce, the garbage bin has classically been the so-called *Organization Department.* Worst yet, these people were labeled *system analysts* or used as *experts* of a certain domain studied for DP implementation.

This practice did not enhance the reputation of the Organization Department in the eyes of other departments of the firm. It also had disastrous effects on the resulting data processing applications. High costs, errors, delays, and failure to satisfy end-user requirements were some of the better-known results.

The second major error has been inflexibility. Typically, data processing software is a one-time effort, written in a given environment and remaining there. Time and again, we rediscovered the wheel. This was the mainframe concept, which has by now developed such deep roots that it still flourishes.

There was, of course, a change for the better; this came with the development of the personal computer. Commodity software became the rule, starting with word processing packages and moving into spreadsheets. Finally, integrated software and fourth-generation languages produced a radical change in the computer environment.

Commodity software is not only more economical, it is also thoroughly tested (alpha and beta tests).[5] Most importantly, the really successful packages are produced by people with ingenious ideas, that is, the best domain experts in their field. That's precisely the kind of expertise we need when we develop AI constructs.

Like integrated software, the AI construct would (or should) spread throughout the organization. It should operate in every area where the work falls into a specific domain. There is, however, a difference. My experience (and that of many others) indicates that the AI construct should not be bought. It should be developed in-house, and the *best experts* should be used in its realization.

Every company has some first-class domain experts; otherwise, it could not remain in business. It is precisely one of these people who should be responsible for the development of the AI construct. Furthermore, since the domain expert's work will influence the entire organization, it is vital to choose the person with the greatest expertise.

This being the case, who are the people with the best *expertise* in a given field of endeavor.

---

[4] While this section focuses on the domain expert, let's not forget that it is also applicable to the knowledge engineer. After all, he too is an expert in the knowledge domain.
[5] For a definition of alpha and beta tests, see D.N. Chorafas, *Fourth and Fifth Generation Languages,* McGraw-Hill, New York, 1986.

While some criteria vary by domain, several traits are dominant across the industry and can be discussed as such. An individual is considered a domain expert if he has

- a large knowledgebank in the form of facts and rules,
- strong experience in his domain, though the extent of that domain can be relatively limited, and
- individual experience generally not found in the domain or beyond what is generally available.

The mental process of this person is generally too complex to be described through algorithms. Yet, this typically unstructured knowledge enables the domain expert to choose promising problem-solving strategies. The *problem solution* is our goal.

An important characteristic of the domain expert is a self-correcting attitude. If his problem solution strategy is unsuccessful, he goes back to the point of failure and tries an alternative course. This is precisely what the majority domain experts are doing.

One aspect of the domain expert's work is the networking of minor judgments in order to reach a major judgment. The other aspect of his work consists of the facts, which rest largely on his observation of prevailing conditions.

Studies on the characteristics of domain have repeatedly found that they

1. have a highly developed perceptual ability
2. can conceptualize interdependencies and changes in sequence,
3. have the knowledge and the skill to develop an integrated picture of the project,
4. pay attention to detail,
5. break down complex problems into their essential elements,
6. are able to deal with trade-offs and conflicting goals,
7. know when to avoid inappropriate strategies,
8. correctly estimate the accuracy of inputs,
9. establish criteria to prioritize alternatives,
10. have a strong sense of responsibility,
11. are able to make decisions,
12. are responsive and adaptable, and
13. have a high tolerance for stress.

A domain expert must also have *creativity*. This is a complex quality because it requires an integrative personality as well as conceptual capabilities.[6] The creative process is not well understood, though hundreds of books are written with the word "creativity" in their titles. We do know that creativity requires experience, imagination, and the ability to concentrate. It thrives on challenge. The AI project in which the domain expert would participate is a challenging proposition.

Both the knowledge engineer and the domain expert should appreciate that the impetus for ideas and discoveries is generally the solution of significant problems. If the problem is

---

[6] See D.N. Chorafas, *Membership of the Board of Directors*, Macmillan, London, 1988.

trivial, it will not retain the expert's interest. If it is too complex, it will not achieve a satisfactory conclusion.

The last statement is particularly true when the organization enters the AI field. For this reason, I advise the use of brainstorming sessions to uncover all organizational problems amenable to AI solutions. Once this is done, I classify such problems into four quartiles in terms of difficulty.

The best results are obtained by discarding the upper and lower quartiles, at least temporarily, and concentrating on the two middle ones. The following additional criteria must also be used in making the final selection:

- *Relevance* of the project to the organization.
- *Availability* of internal domain experts.

AI constructs should not substitute for available know-how. Their goal is to make such know-how—if it exists—more accessible to the entire organization.

To judge the knowledge of the organization's domain expert, we should recall that such knowledge typically has three main components:

1. Facts.
2. Rules used in judgment.
3. Procedural issues (how to go about).

Procedural issues are based on experience: association, analogies, hypotheses, reasoning, and intelligent choices. Many of the rules typically concern fuzzy logic, that is, in heuristics. Facts are reflected in the organization of collected experience.

But there are also problems with experts. While they may work in the same domain, they are rarely if ever in agreement. Therefore, it is wise to use one, *the best* domain expert, as a consultant in the development of the AI construct, rather than several experts at the same time.

The opinion of other experts should also be asked, but during the *internal testing* phase of the AI system. While the knowledge engineer retains full responsibility for his construct, it is always a good practice to test the essence of the decision process (hence, the logical concept behind the rules) against the opinion of others. We will return to this issue when we talk about testing procedures.

A second problem with domain experts comes from their main asset: *the domain expertise.* Often, while such experts are first class in their field, they know nothing about other disciplines. Yet, the resulting AI construct should be a communicating engine with interdisciplinary characteristics that can be integrated into a larger system as needed. The knowledge engineer should be able to fulfill this integrative mission.

Unfortunately, domain experts do not have many attributes in common. A study done on this subject with a statistically valid sample produced the results shown in Figure 1-3. Sixty attributes were identified in one domain expert—the large majority being job specific. They were shared by a second expert from the same domain, but a third expert was found to have just 30 of them; a fourth expert had 20 and a fifth had only 10; the 14th through the 20th experts shared only one attribute with the balance of the sample.

This is an important finding that should be kept in mind. The lack of communality in the

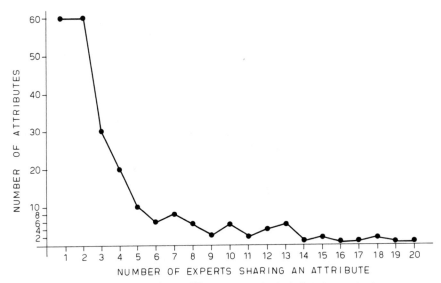

Figure 1-3. Domain experts not only use different personal criteria but also rarely share common attributes. This conclusion was reached by a study on this subject.

attributes of domain experts will not necessarily show up during knowledge acquisition, but it will certainly be mainfested when the AI system spreads throughout the organization.

Still another problem with domain experts is that they are not always able to state their thoughts in a concrete form. They know the facts and the rules, but they cannot always express them.

It is the job of the knowledge engineer to help the expert do so, as we will see in the following chapter, when we talk of knowledge acquisition. It is also his job to organize the domain knowledge and to formulate, in a logical, well-structured manner, the decision rules the expert employs in making judgments.

4. DESIGN KNOWLEDGE
AND THE
AI CONSTRUCT

We have said that knowledge engineering today develops domain-specific, rule-based systems.[7] These systems, like humans, can cope with incomplete and uncertain information. Ambiguity-tolerant software is a new and practical AI implementation in industry.

Part of the power of an AI construct is that it works with equivocal data but produces valid judgments. This is the core of the process which is enabling the development, production, and distribution of intelligence through man-made systems.

Like any other man-made system, AI constructs are subject to a design discipline. Design

---

[7] Though by the mid-1990s, memory-based reasoning may be the dominant type.

knowledge should focus on *deep modeling* following the principles we use with complex physical and logical systems. In contrast to a shallow model, which exploits global databases, a *deep model* consists of mathematical laws. These provide the background and underline the solution. We should, however, remember that we are not talking of classical mathematics but of *qualitative* approaches that permit deviations from steady-state conditions. Therefore, it is not enough to define physical behavior or simply to construct a descriptor for the physical system.

Unlike quantitative solutions which are based on mathematics, qualitative approaches may be weak descriptors of a physical system or of an engineering construct, but they can be strong descriptors for business and managerial systems.

For a physical system, the strong descriptor is quantitative. This is not necessarily true in management. The manager may say, "more or less," "I would rather recommend," "there is no evidence this might happen, but it is not impossible." A managerial answer is not necessarily black or white. Most often it includes tonalities of grey; it may be vague or reflect uncertainty. Knowledge engineering allows for such responses, while they are inadmissible in classical engineering.

Design knowledge is very important, and it must permeate AI work. As an example, a construct designed for diagnosis must start by defining:

- fault conditions.
- normal conditions, and
- deviations from normal.

Design knowledge must base judgments on acceptable data but must also provide for corrective action. It should also forecast catastrophic consequences and account for them.

The stochastic model of a *quality control* (QC) chart exemplifies this situation in Figure 1-4, $\bar{\bar{x}}$ stands for a mean value tendency (the mean of the means of the QC samples). The upper and lower control limits are shown. They are within the range established by engineering tolerances.

The reader with a background in mathematical statistics will appreciate that variation is inherent in any process. Deviation from the mean value is unavoidable—and while it is commonly labeled as an *error*, it is a beneficial error in the sense that we can use it to correct our process:

- When the sample means $\bar{x}_i$ are *quantitatively* expressed,
- Their plotting gives the *pattern* of the process itself, which is *qualitative* in character.

Hence, as Dr. John von Neumann had aptly suggested, an *error* is not something strange, destructive, or unwanted; it is our means of developing control procedures. This is what the domain expert in quality control will do when he observes the pattern of deviations from the mean value, particularly when the trend reaches the upper or lower control limits.[8]

A production process is *in control* if the means of the QC samples ($\bar{x}_i$) fall within the control limit range. But statistical QC theory says that if three consecutive $\bar{x}_i$ means move

---

[8] See also D.N. Chorafas, *Statistical Processes and Reliability Engineering*, D. Van Nostrand, New York, 1960.

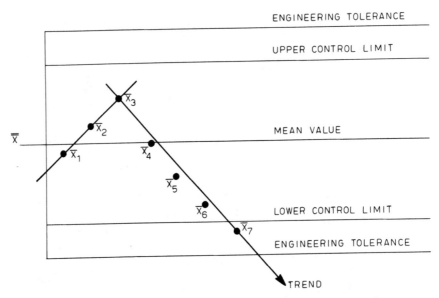

Figure 1-4. A statistical quality control chart is helpful in visualizing the variation inherent in a process, as well as in identifying developing trends. AI projects can greatly benefit from the visualization provided by such charts.

up or down, they establish a trend. The possibility is high that the fourth mean will break the QC limit, therefore moving out of control.

For the moment, let's leave this know-how in the background. Suppose that the knowledge engineer works with a quality engineer to develop an expert system for the automatic detection of deviations. In this work, they must establish fault conditions and normal conditions, as well as defining deviations from normal. That's precisely what the foregoing example did.

In the design process, the AI construct for quality control must be enriched with direct access to encoded knowledge useful for automatic generation of explanations, debugging, maintenance, and extension. It can also be equipped with knowledge components able to assist in teaching humans or other AI constructs. The problem with teaching is that we have almost no knowledge about teaching expert systems. However, in terms of design, we can use the principle of versatile output. For instance, the tutor must have:

- a wide range of instructional actions,
- a number of teaching tools—to be selected according to the situation, and
- mastery to detect learning in its pupils.

A Socratic-type dialogue can be used to advantage. Learning by discovery falls within the current state of the art.

Teaching can be done by example, by analogy, by generalization, and by specialization. By embodying expert knowledge and applying it to make useful inferences, the AI tutor can lead its pupil to learn the statistical QC process. This design has a number of basic characteristics that distinguish it from conventional programs. These characteristics will now be discussed.

1. Attention must be paid at the design stage to ensure that tutor and pupil perform well. We do this by applying expert rules in a relatively efficient manner to reach acceptable solutions. The QC example is ideal because, like a well-behaved AI construct, it *bases its reasoning process on symbol manipulation.*

2. *Knowing* something involves a symbolic representation of facts: QC knowledge. A wealth of experience in statistical QC permits us to describe precisely, and in detail, the basic principles of this domain of interest and to produce intelligent explanations of the reasoning process.

   - The tutor must be capable of reasoning about its own knowledge and reconstructing inference paths for explanation and justification.
   - The pupil must be able to formulate the problem and to convert its tion into an internal representation.

   Furthermore, QC is a rich domain including interpretation, diganosis, prediction, monitoring, planning, and controlling.

The paradigm can now revert to the design of a procedure for knowledge acquisition, a subject discussed in the following chapter with the help of the expert, the knowledge engineer defines goals. Goals are the answers that the AI construct will produce. The knowledge engineer also defines the questions, that the system will ask the user in order to generate primary evidence.

As in the case of tutor and pupil, between the questions and the goals is a whole network of interlinked propositions. They represent the domain expert's arguments. The logical links between the propositions are the rules, weighted by factors of logical necessity or logical sufficiency, that make one proposition depend on another.

The design perspective should account for the fact that in its implementation, the AI construct will ask the user questions. However, unlike traditional computer programs, it will accept qualifying answers such as *maybe* or *highly likely*—not only *yes* or *no*. Qualifying answers change the values of variables associated with each of the propositions and goals. This, too, should be reflected in the design.

Design considerations should also account for the fact that the domain expert's reply to a specific knowledge elicitation question may establish a *pattern.* At this point, the knowledge engineer may select a new proposition as a *hypothesis,*[9] and then develop more questions to test the hypothesis. Eventually the logical process threads its way along a path in which the range of possible conclusions is progressively narrowed. This, too, is a design perspective.

An essential part of some expert systems is the inclusion of probabilities, weights of evidence, and subjective utilities in the database. These are particularly difficult to acquire from experts. There is a fundamental human unease and unfamiliarity with precisely quantified probabilities even among professionals in the sciences.

Extracting precise values is a delicate and laborious process. This is another way of saying that qualitative approaches are not only welcome but also necessary. It is unwise to press or induce the expert to give values if he later turns out to have little confidence in them or if the values given differ on different occasions, depending on the wording of the question.

---

[9] A *hypothesis* is a tentative statement made to lead to the investigation of facts or the solution to a problem. As such, it is subject to testing and verification.

In these cases, and they are many, *possibility theory* rather than probability theory should be used.[10] The choice is not always evident, and to a great extent, it is part of the design premises regarding the AI construct. Other design premises include

1. representing interactions between subproblems,
2. formulating constraints as problems to be solved,
3. incorporating rules for discovering interactions between subproblems via constraint propagation,
4. deriving sufficient information from the interchange of constraints (least commitment, opportunistic expansion),
5. deciding on explicit metalevel problem-solving operators to reason with constraints,
6. using heuristics to make choices even when there is otherwise no compelling reason to do so,
7. retracting guesses as necessary when an unresolvable problem is encountered,
8. taking existing knowledgebanks and adding networks for expressing new knowledge and rules,
9. creating, modifying, or deleting various nodes and arcs in a networking structure, and
10. choosing a grammar-driven command language to prompt endusers.

The knowledge engineer may decide to refine the facts, states, and rules prior to proceeding in the collaboration he has with the expert; determine an initial set of generator constraints from data; or combine data and constraints to generate candidate structures. He may fix abstraction levels for solutions (plans) and/or complete a solution at one level and then move to the next level below.

Design involves planning premises. Knowledge engineers do hierarchical planning by first devising a top-level plan based on the key aspects of the problem. They then refine this plan by considering aspects of the problem that are successively less critical, though important enough to be elaborated.

5. PREREQUISITES FOR
AI PROJECTS

One of the first concepts that the knowledge engineer should learn is that the AI construct needs a starting reference. For instance, in a point system for loans,[11] the project begins with the generation of points. Let the AI system collect the points and sum up a reference number. The method to be used can be written as rules. In a loan, the point system provides *some of the knowledge we need to capture knowledge.*

---

[10] See Didier Dubois and Henri Prade, *Possibility Theory*, Plenum, New York, 1985.
[11] Properly organized banks use a point system in granting loans. The client is given points for his quality history, work situation, loan payment habits, ability to repay, and so on.

When the AI project is undertaken, the bank may already have programmed the point system on its computers. Hence, there is valuable information in the database. This is one more reason why integration of the AI project with the firm's existing computers and communications operations is so important.

If AI is to transform the use of human intelligence, we must build constructs which have the capability to do so. The knowledge engineer should never think that he starts his work from scratch. His task is *to add greater sophistication to the existing environment*—not to reset everything at the point zero.

Connecting the AI system to classical data processing is a *must*. This requirement for AI constructs is as valid as it has been over the last 10 years of *decision support systems* (DSS) and infocenters. Figure 1-5 demonstrates this sense of continuity.

Those of us old enough to remember how the information systems field developed since the early 1950s will recall that for about two decades (the 1950s and 1960s) applications were made in discrete islands, with no significant connections among them. This is the way classical DP has worked and, for many (unfortunate) companies, still does.

The concept of *integration* started to develop in the early 1970s. Many innovations led to the need for integration: distributed data processing, database management systems (DBMSs), DSSs, and, above all, the realization that computer applications *are* interconnected. Networks have been instrumental in forcing this integrative approach on user organizations.

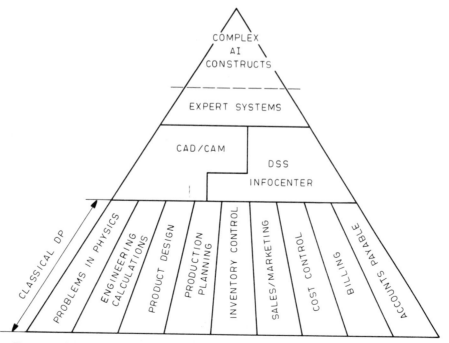

Figure 1-5. Only integrated systems are of value to the enduser. They should operate online, be interactive, and permit users to capitalize on existing computer applications, whether classical DP or DSS.

A similar statement can be made about workstations as personal computers made power available at an affordable cost and placed it at the user's desk. At the same time, managers and professionals required information that classical DP could not provide. Throughout the 1980s, this was done through infocenters, while the DSS solutions of the 1970s developed into the more sophisticated expert systems.[12]

Another innovation which has led integration is computer-aided design (CAD) and computer-aided manufacturing (CAM). As engineering applications expanded and factory floors became automated, we came to realize that we could no longer deal with discrete islands of computer applications. Computer-integrated manufacturing (CIM) became a necessity.

Tables 1-2 to 1-6 show the results of a study made to compare the three regions of computer applications in a given organization: classical DP, infocenter/WS/DSS, and expert systems. Five functional areas were tested and the results are outlined as follows:

> Table 1-2 Necessary know-how
> Table 1-3 Communications expertise
> Table 1-4 Database skills
> Table 1-5 Processing
> Table 1-6 Programs and tools

While this study is not meant to be exclusive, it does provide a good indication of how disciplines focusing on the implementation of computers and communications compare.

Let's notice that classical DP can be enriched with expert systems frontends to extend the life of the software and make it more user friendly. This applies to all areas from basic software to applications programs. IBM, for instance, has written YES-MVS[13] to frontend with an AI construct its strategic operating system.

It is not only a legitimate task of knowledge engineering (and of knowledge engineers) to connect AI systems to the existing computers and communications assets of the firm; it is a

TABLE 1-2. Basic Comparison: Necessary Know-How.

Classical DP	Infocenter/WS/DSS	Expert Systems
1. Raw Data	1. Facts	1. Facts, states, values
2. Hard data	2. Soft data	2. Hard data, soft data
3. One rule (the algorithm)	3. Few rules	3. Many rules
4. Procedure by application (but no overall methodology)	4. One methodology	4. Several methodologies
		5. Self-learning
		6. Knowledge bank

---

[12] In this book, we will use interchangeably the terms *workstation* (*WS*) and *personal computer* (*PC*). More precisely, WS will stand for a networked PC. The alternative classification of a WS as a more powerful PC is as PCs become more powerful all the time. See also D.N. Chorafas, *Applying Expert Systems in Business,* McGraw-Hill, New York, 1987.

[13] YES stands for Yorktown Expert System.

TABLE 1-3. Basic Comparison: Communications Expertise.

Classical DP	Infocenter/WS/DDS	Expert Systems
1. Batch	1. Interactive	1. Interactive
2. Offline capability	2. Online only	2. Global online
3. Realtime update	3. Realtime update	3. Update and deferred
4. Response time 5–7 seconds	4. Response time 1–2 seconds	4. Response time immediate (1–2 seconds) or deferred
5. Long turnaround	5. Very short turnaround	5. Short turnaround
6. Input interfaces and associated problems	6. Direct user input enriched with online access	6. User interactivity enriched by global database
7. Several errors permitted	7. No errors permitted	7. No errors permitted

TABLE 1-4. Basic Comparison: Database Skills.

Classical DP	Infocenter/WS/DDS	Expert Systems
1. Sum of files	1. Infocenter database	1. Global database
2. DBMS requirement recent	2. DBMS a prerequisite	2. DBMS a prerequisite
3. Data orientation	3. Text and data, as well as voice and image	3. Knowledgebank is key
4. Detailed contents	4. Synthetic contents	4. Synthetic and analytic
5. Very large volume	5. Small volume	5. Global capability
6. Field, record, file	6. Infopage presentation	6. Interactive dialogue; Esystem asks questions
7. Access by program or DBMS	7. Menu access	7. Interactive exchange
8. Data-oriented presentation	8. Graphics-oriented presentation	8. Text-oriented presentation
9. Quantitative	9. Quantitative and qualitative	9. Qualitative
10. Access rather general	10. Restricted access, closed user group (CUG)	10. Intelligent access

TABLE 1-5. Basic Comparison: Processing.

Classical DP	Infocenter/WS/DSS	Expert Systems
1. Predefined	1. Ad hoc	1. Predefined, but rapid development
2. Procedural	2. Nonprocedural	2. Heuristic
3. 3GL, 4GL	3. 4GL	3. Shells, Lisp, Probg, 3GL
4. Rather general	4. By management function	4. Very specialized
5. Nonexistent human window	5. Icons, graphic tablet	5. Very strong human window
6. Programmer asks computer for output; computer responds in detail	6. Enduser asks computer; computer responds through menus and infopages	6. Computer queries enduser; enduser responds
7. Long development time	7. Short development time	7. Short development time

TABLE 1-6. Basic Comparison: Programs and Tools.

Old Classical DP ("Stone Wheel")	New Classical DP ("Wooden Wheel")	Infocenter/WS/DDS ("Automobile")	Expert Systems ("Jet Transport")
1. System analysis through personal interviews	1. Packages	1. Horizontal WS	1. Shells
2. Discontinuity	2. Prototyping	2. Prototyping	2. Prototyping
3. Cobol	3. DBMS/4GL	3. Enduser 4GL	3. Lispoid or 3GL
4. Poor documentation		4. Computer-assisted and updated documentation	
5. System testing in parallel		5. Selected sites; alpha, beta tests	
6. No user training	6. Intensive user training	6. Two-hour to 3-day user training period	6. Short user training period as necessary

must. Efforts to avoid connectivity should be censored by management—though it is also true that the classical DP department itself is not always ready to cooperate with the AI project(s).

Whether we add an intelligent frontend to existing applications or develop an AI construct in a newly defined area of implementation, a knowledge engineering methodology underlines four phases of orderly systems work:

1. *Problem definition.* This includes the concepts we have defined about strategy, structure, and the evaluation of degree of difficulty, as well as the major choices to be made. The framework of the subsequent project is part of this phase.
2. *Knowledge acquisition.* We have spoken of the knowledge engineer, of the domain expert, and of their degree of expertise. The knowledge engineer should look beyond the queries and answers to a formalized description and the formatting of the obtained knowledge.
3. *Programming work.* As the appropriate chapter will show, the knowledge acquisition phase should lead to prototyping. Prototyping is the interface between knowledge engineering and programming. Shells should be used for prototyping. The next task is evaluation, followed by optimization. The final phase is programming, using C, C*, Lisp, Prolog, or another language.
4. *Testing and maintenance.* Testing should be intensive during the first months and steady throughout the period of usage. It should lead to the creation of a self-learning environment. Testing costs money; we should benefit from it in more than one way.

One of the basic things these four phases have in common is the need to direct our efforts toward the establishment of integrated methods and tools. Another common requirement is management's involvement in planning, monitoring, and controlling the methods and processes of AI projects.

Knowledge engineering is not black magic. Nor should projects be hidden from management's control. To the contrary: management should be kept informed and should follow projects closely in terms of

1. progress,
2. investments in money and personnel, and
3. the project completion and implementation timetables.

One of the prerequisites in AI design is clear breakpoints for *design review.* Several design reviews should be done from start to finish, preferably in a semiformal manner so that they not only control but also identify bottlenecks, eliminate dead ends, and offer advice.

The investment an AI system requires is in direct proportion to the time needed for completion. No universal answer should be given to the query "How long should development take?" The answer is situational. It depends on the following:

- The problem, its extent, and its complexity,
- Previous experiences in the domain that can be applied to the current project.
- The quality of the knowledge engineering skill the organization possesses; *the greater the AI skill, the briefer the time.*
- The culture of the organization, including recorded long delays by the DP department.
- Management controls: on the budget, on timetables, and through design reviews.

It appears that the time an AI project takes is nearly independent of its urgency. In fact, this is so with one exception: The *more urgent* a project is, the *longer* it tends to take. In addition, the *larger is the team* of knowledge engineers and experts working on the project, the *longer* it will take. Experience has taught us that these factors are inversely proportional. We don't gain time by adding more people to a project; we lose time.

Since knowledge engineering resources are scarce in any organization, a stringent timetable is recommended. Unlike classical DP projects, which often range from chaos to uncertainty, AI projects can and should be kept under control. A small team is highly recommended. Morgan Stanley's *Plumpicker,* one of the best shallow expert systems designed to search large databases, took two specialists over six months—hence one man-year—to completion. This brings up a question: "What's the size of an AI construct that we should consider as a limit?" In a business or industrial environment, the answer can be given in one word: *manageable.* But what does manageable mean?

Five years ago, I heard in a conference that "any expert system that takes less than one week is trivial, and any that exceeds six calendar months of effort is unnecessary." Does this sound unlikely? Not necessarily. For five years, I have been following this guideline in planning AI projects, and it has given first-class results.

Furthermore, unlike old-style DP projects, which were often very large and had to be completed in order to be implemented, with expert systems and other AI constructs, implementation can be done:

- step by step or
- module by module.

There is no need to delay implementation while waiting for the full system. As the AI construct develops module by module, the components that are ready can be put into operation. The originally specialized knowledgebank also enlarges its rule base and, in certain cases, its domain.

6. PLANNING THE EXPERT SYSTEM: A CASE STUDY

Management decided to set up Project A in a domain where it had the best people. The criterion for decisions was a good set of knowledge. But management also wanted this construct to represent a deeper understanding of the domain, not just a collection of "pattern → action" rules corresponding to the problem-solving heuristics of the expert.

The task of Project A was to interface engineering and manufacturing through an intelligent engine. The Engineering Department had seven years experience with CAD, and though the laboratories were scattered geographically, they used as uniform a system of representation as possible. For the expert system in development, the preferred form of representation was production rules.

As stated by management, the goal of the expert system in design was to provide an intelligent facility by which

- designers could explain their conclusions to manufacturing engineers,
- manufacturing personnel could query the engineering database for details, and
- valid coordination could be provided through AI support in making design changes and analyzing their impact on production schedules and inventory buildup.

In the past such coordination required a substantial body of empirical, unstructured knowledge and intermittent communications. Management wanted the coordination problem to be solved using causal or mathematical knowledge.

Production rules was the chosen method for the kernel in the following form:

Condition 1/Result 1
Condition 2/Result 2
      etc.

This condition/result chain was extended to verify all premises. If the AI system did not find answers internally, it had to query the user.

But the system was projected to grow beyond its kernel. The architecture of this expanded mode was to include a wider range of cognitive functions than the largely predetermined, system-directed problem solving of the kernel. This system incorporated, for example, the ability to shadow the user's problem solving, interrupting only when a possible error was noted. It also included the ability to learn automatically from mistakes.

This implementation was projected to make the AI construct a *fault model* that was able to account for differences between the expected and actual operation in engineering/ manufacturing coordination. This is known as a *discrepancy detection* approach.

By explicitly characterizing faults as models of causal interaction and organizing them in terms of interactive complexity—engineering/manufacturing as a function of design changes—the AI construct aimed to diagnose faults in coordination which are beyond the reach of other methods. Furthermore, causal knowledge was to be compiled into a diagnostic problem-solving structure in a way that allowed it to attack all problems within its scope as effectively as an explicit model.

Several challenges came up in the planning phase. They were considered as opportunities to make choices. One of them concerned the trade-offs between facts, states, values (domains), and rules. As the appropriate experimentation documented:

- If the domain is large, the structures (rules) are simpler, but proper definition of the domain creates more work for the knowledge engineer.
- If there are rules, there is more work for the domain expert and more detail is required in describing the decision process; however, the description of the domain requires less work.

Thus, in a knowledgebank, the number of rules and the size of the domain of knowledge (facts, states, values) can be optimized. More precisely,

1. If there are *few rules,* then *a large domain of knowledge* is necessary.
2. If there are *many rules,* then *a small domain* is needed.

In terms of design, large domain knowledge demands a great deal of definition and access to global databases. However, it also creates the possibility of using *episodic memory*[14] as greater computer power becomes available. Fewer rules are handy in developing a *rule maker,* thereby automating knowledge engineering work and helping the user better understand the AI structure affecting his profession.[15] By contrast, if the number of *facts/states/values* is *limited,* then more rules must be made available to describe in detail *the method a professional* uses to reach his conclusions and justify them.

In this context, one aspect of project analysis is the examination of what is generally viewed as a simple *deep* versus *superficial* distinction in the level of reasoning. This led to a better understanding of the territory that lies in between. Knowledge engineers were able to map this territory by listing several knowledge structures at differing levels of compilation. Three alternatives were considered:

1. Textbook type
2. Pattern matching
3. Knowledge pattern and problem solving.

The *textbook type* is defined as a situation for which the problem solver can find a solution in a textbook or in the company's own procedures. Engineering and Manufacturing departments have a collection of such ready-to-use pieces of knowledge. The problem with this approach is that it becomes combinatorily too large for the domain. Hence procedures are limited to the most frequent or most important situations.

---

[14] In an episodic memory data is kept as it comes into the database, in the form of values, events, or episodes (happenings). Data is not manipulated into intermediate stages and stored again, because such manipulation will be done ad hoc, when necessary; it will be executed in realtime through supercomputers
[15] Rules and laws must be very few, very clear, and very precise, says *Cita Solaris.*

Pattern matching, particularly partial pattern matching, is not new. It has been used in many first-generation expert systems. Here, instead of the totality of the problem solving situation, only portions are recognized and partial solutions are collected by using relatively simple rules. This does not exclude the possibility that further portions of the situation can be recognized and the total solution synthesized after several handling cycles.

The *knowledge pattern* approximates generic problem solving. Deeper knowledge of the domain is analyzed in terms of the role it plays in problem solving. Subsequently, this knowledge is compiled in specialized structures tuned for problem solving. Emphasis is on compiling knowledge in a form ready to be used for a class of problems of a given type. This was finally the method chosen for AI projects.

Performance considerations made the difference. Performance in an interactive AI environment is important to the success of an application. Project A required a considerable amount of resources. It was therefore important to understand the performance implications of the new application, from creating and testing the knowledgebank to the enduser's running of the consultation facility on a regular basis. These are factors that a knowledge engineering discipline should support.

2

Knowledge Acquisition

Keywords

knowledge acquisition · judgment · experience · intuition · development databank · inference engine · metaknowledge · understanding of knowledge · knowledge network · functional requirements · technical architecture · knowledge engineer · knowledgebank · cross-domain · recorded session · therblings · work sampling · recognition · uncued recall · action descriptives · record protocols · artificial problems · comparative case analysis · domain structures · applied experimental psychology · written procedures · knowledge protocol · causal model · inductive reasoning · database · experimental design · World KB · text understanding · discovery systems

1. INTRODUCTION

AI systems perform a wide variety of tasks. While they may be more successful in handling some tasks than others, in every case the prerequisite for success is high-grade human expertise. There must be at least one human domain expert who performs the task well, whose expertise will be mapped into the system.

The primary source of the domain expert's exceptional performance is special knowledge, judgment, and experience. But these must be transmitted to the AI construct. Hence the domain expert should be able to explain to the knowledge engineer his special know-how and experience, as well as the methods he applies in solving a particular problem.

We have also said that with current technology the AI construct must have a well-bounded domain of application. The expert must be a specialist, not a generalist. His know-how should be

- focused on a topic or process
- explained in a detailed manner, and
- mapped into the AI system.

This is the process we call *knowledge acquisition.* It results from close collaboration between the domain expert and the knowledge engineer. The task is not easy. One of the problems is the difficulty that experts have in describing exactly *how* they do what they do, especially with respect to their use of *judgment, experience,* and *intuition.*

As a result, knowledge acquisition is a bottleneck—but not as large as it may seem in some projects. In addition, knowledge acquisition has to be supplemented by knowledge representation. Both jobs have to be done well for the expert system to make a useful contribution.

An important approach to knowledge acquisition is *observing* rather than interviewing. A good knowledge engineer will learn by osmosis, not only through queries and answers. *How to do* certain things is the important factor, rather than the details of the field. But the process of doing itself has to be described in detail; otherwise, it cannot be successfully represented.

While knowledge acquisition can be done through interviews, the *best method is to guide the domain expert in building the system himself.* The ability of the knowledge engineer to induce the professional expert to take this self-supporting action would be a hallmark in his career. Nobody knows the business better than the domain expert himself.

More and more instruments are becoming available for delivering (i.e., programming). This is not a task for the domain expert. The expert should think of *his* work:

1. his background
2. his experience
3. the facts he needs
4. their states and values
5. the way he elaborates knowledge
6. the alternatives he considers
7. how he reaches decisions
8. his justifications

(We spoke of the characteristics of domain experts in Chapter 1.)

The knowledge acquisition process falls into distinct stages: getting the relevant facts and associated procedures, refining them and providing linkages, building a prototype, structuring the domain, and extracting the first working model. Also included are debugging and further refining and, most importantly, applying the resulting construct in an experimental situation.

To obtain valid results, each of these steps should be well understood. It is wise to *build a system as soon as one area* (even one example) *of the expert's behavior is understood.* Perform the knowledge acquisition process in a modular manner. It does not have to be monolithic, and it should not be an inflexible undertaking reminiscent of classical DP.

2. PREREQUISITES TO EXTRACTING AND FORMALIZING EXPERT KNOWLEDGE

Knowledge acquisition is the process of extracting and formalizing the knowledge of a domain expert for use by an AI system. Examples of knowledge are descriptions of objects, identifications of relationships, and explanations of procedures. One of the main activities of the knowledge engineer is knowledge acquisition.

Knowledge acquisition involves not only knowledge engineers and domain experts but also *computer support*. Persons with an unsophisticated view of the old DP concepts may believe that more explanation of the nature of knowledge acquisition is needed before computer support can be considered. Nothing is more untrue.

The use of computers to support mental activities is so fundamental a process that it is basic to the process of knowledge acquisition. In reality, we talk of three partners:

- the domain expert
- the knowledge engineer, and
- the computer

The process must be *interactive,* involving all three partners, to provide a significant chance of succeeding. As Figure 2-1 demonstrates, we should work online with computer resources, creating a *development platform* assisted by values in the *database* and by a *shell*. Shells are treated in the following chapter. Databases are discussed in Part Two.[1]

Computers should definitely be used online to help the AI engineer in knowledge acquisition. This is just as valid a method of interviewing the expert as of probing to discover what decision processes he is using. Even when the knowledge expert watches the domain expert at work to discover his processes, he can use computer support to

1. transform his observations into rules about how to do the job,
2. put the rules into a form that the machine can use—for instance, employing shells to construct the system, and
3. show to the domain expert his understanding of the judgmental problem the latter has explained to him through prototyping. This is better done interactively.

Computer assisted or not, the goal of knowledge acquisition is to obtain the skill necessary for the able representation of knowledge. Examples of knowledge representation include *production rules* of the form IF . . . THEN . . . ELSE and *logic programming*. We will cover both of these in Part Two when we speak of the inference engine and its environment.

For now, it should be noted that different representations are suited to different types

---

[1] See also D.N. Chorafas, *Handbook of Database Management and Distributed Relational Databases,* TAB Books, New York, 1989.

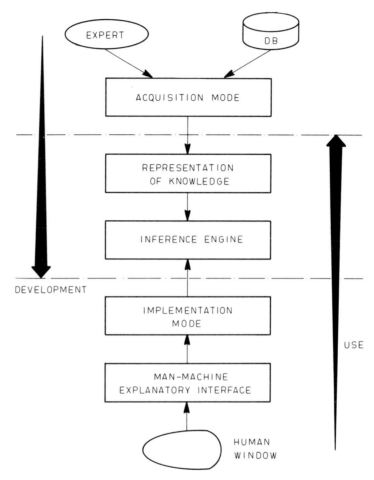

Figure 2-1. There is a common structure serving the development and use of an expert system. This figure shows two ways of approaching such a common structure, depending on the specific purpose.

and uses of knowledge. IF . . . THEN rules lend themselves to the representation of *deductive* knowledge. Typical cases are

- situation, then action
- premise, the conclusion
- antecedent and consequent
- cause and effect

Frames are better suited to the representation of *descriptive* and *relational* knowledge. Such knowledge clusters about or conforms somewhat to a standard pattern—for instance, a description of an accounting procedure or of a decision-making system. Other representation forms such as semantic nets are useful for modeling *classifications, causal* linkages, and so on.

While knowledge representation is the subject of the next chapter, a preview is necessary to give a bird's-eye view of the total job. The next step in the development process is the creation of the *inference engine,* that is, the protocol for navigating through rules and facts/states/values in a knowledge representation scheme.

In order to solve our problem, the inference engine must work through induction, deduction, or abduction. Its real task is to act as *a compiler* of the knowledgebank.[2]

- The task of the inference engine is to select and then apply the most appropriate rule at each step as the AI system runs.
- This contrasts with conventional programming, where the programmer selects the order in which the steps of the program execute at the time the program is written.

In Figure 2-1, three modules succeed one another: knowledge acquisition, knowledge representation, and the inference engine. This is the progression we follow in developing the AI system, which leads to implementation. By contrast, the *use mode*

- starts with the *human window.*
- proceeds with the man–made explanatory interface, and
- reaches the implementation level, therefore the inference engine.

The inference engine will typically be transparent to the enduser, except for the results (advice, justification), which will be presented through the human window. But the inference engine is no *black box*[3] to the knowledge engineer. Furthermore, as experience in AI implementation accumulates, the inference engine becomes no longer a black box to sophisticated users. As a minimum, users can engage in dialogue and ask how the system came to a given conclusion. Sometimes users also understand the sense of the rules.

The sense of the rules is that knowledge representation methods are combinations of (1) data structures for storing information, (2) interpretive procedures, and (3) inferences about stored values. The knowledge representation provides the computer with a description of how the various pieces of information interact among themselves and with the rules which are in command.

Knowledge is not only used in the rules. It is also employed to:

- retrieve relevant information,
- plot a course of action that has not been explicitly programmed, and
- acquire new knowledge.

AI systems may require conventions to represent several kinds of knowledge—knowledge of objects, of relationships, of how events are situated in time, or of how to perform actions. Very important is *metaknowledge,* that is, knowledge about knowledge. It provides the system with *understanding of knowledge,* as well as the ability to fill in missing information.

---

[2] The role and contents of the knowledgebank are fully described in Part Two.

[3] The concept of the *black box* is present in most engineering disciplines. Black boxes are systems whose internal mechanism is not fully opened for inspection, but we know the inputs we can give and observe the outputs we receive.

Metaknowledge guides the AI construct in supplying default values. It helps the construct to acquire further procedural knowledge to work out answers. It also ensures that the expert system can control the lower layers of its structure—the rules, facts, states, and values.

Therefore, a good representation scheme not only accommodates all necessary information and know-how but also pays significant attention to metaknowledge. A valid representation also makes it easy and efficient to make inferences, suppresses unwanted references, and facilitates the acquisition of new knowledge. New knowledge is an instrument for the modification of current knowledge.

The importance of incorporating new knowledge into the expert system has been behind one of the more recent developments in AI: the concept of a *knowledge network*. [4] Universities and industrial firms are working on a knowledge network to ensure that they capture expertise in diverse fields—sales, manufacturing, engineering, customer service—to increase the range of their reach and the quality of the results obtained.

The concept of a knowledge network permits a very flexible strategy of AI systems building, module by module. As stated in Chapter 1, after a given module is complete, it can be immediately implemented, since:

- Once the kernel is completed, subsequent modules will be developed.
- When completed, each subsequent mode will be integrated into the AI system through a knowledge networking approach.

This integrative process facilitates the first and foremost step in knowledge acquisition: *defining the functional requirements*. Functional requirements establish what the AI construct is expected to do. Modularity also makes easier the task of data design to support the system. However, modularity has prerequisites. A *technical architecture* is needed to describe the system's major modules (processes) and how they interrelate. Subsequently, the design must ensure the *finer programmatic interfaces*.

Because of the importance of connectivity, modularity implies the need for extensive testing, which should precede a module's implementation. Modularity offers new opportunities but also underlines the need for imaginative approaches and controlled procedures.

If the AI system is expected to grow over time, as for instance XCON of Digital Equipment Corp., then we need development systems that can control all the activities of the software *life cycle*. Guidelines are set by the use of master planning, architectural perspective, and project management. The mechanics consist of interactive knowledge acquisition, knowledge representation, inference engine development, and therefore, program design. All of these are life cycle elements. For each module, software maintenance should not only be more precise than the general case is today, but also well coordinated.

Thus, while knowledge acquisition is often considered an interviewing process, in reality it is much more than that. It has prerequisites, starting with master planning. It involves decisions about the software life cycle. It requires architectural perspectives. Only when the prerequisites are satisfied can the more detailed work be accomplished in an able manner.

---

[4] For a schematic representation, see Figure 3 in Chapter 3.

3. PROCESSES OF KNOWLEDGE ACQUISITION

We have said that the first challenge is to discover the proper domain expert. This is followed by the knowledge acquisition process itself.

Chapter 1 has outlined the foremost attributes of domain experts. The expert must be able to explain his special knowledge and experience and the methods he uses to apply them to particular problems. In addition, the task must have a well-bounded domain of application. It takes a domain expert a few hours to express his way of working, but is the expert available and willing to be committed as the need arises during development.

Hayes-Roth et al. (1983) suggest that the problem to be handled through AI should be nontrivial but tractable, with promising avenues for incremental expansion. Wellbank (1983) emphasizes that every stage of knowledge elicitation will proceed much more quickly and easily *if the domain expert understands the way the system works.*

The domain expert must not only contribute his know-how but also, at the internal testing stage, should compare the construct's reasoning with his own. When it comes to different conclusions from his, he must identify at what point the AI construct's knowledge is deficient. This will be difficult if the domain expert cannot easily see the path the system's reasoning has taken. The knowledge engineer must also know the expert system well, because he must alter it to act correctly. But it is not enough to think of these issues at the testing phase. They must be considered from the beginning of the AI project—indeed, even before the final selection of a potential application.

Once a domain expert for an appropriate problem has been found, it is necessary to set realistic and incremental objectives and to select the right knowledge acquisition method. Following is a description of the most important knowledge acquisition methodologies currently used.

a. Interviewing

As Figure 2-2 demonstrates, knowledge acquisition proceeds in the following sequence: *expert to knowledge engineer* and *knowledge engineer to knowledgebank.* The knowledge engineer acts as a filter. He also helps to narrow the expert's conceptual domain and to map it into a *heuristic*[5] or other form.

Eventually, when the AI construct is ready and running, a new expansion will take place—this time in terms of the population of users. However, modular systems feature another expansion: in *cross-domain* capabilities.

Interviewing sounds like a simple process; it is not. There are two communications problems between the knowledge engineer and the expert:

- They don't speak the same language.
- Often the knowledge engineer does not understand the expert's field.

---

[5] Heuristics is the kind of reasoning that governs countless everyday decisions. It is not just trial and error; it defines a state of relationship that is likely, though not certain. Thus it accepts vagueness and uncertainty.

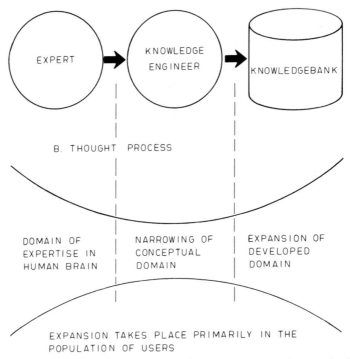

Figure 2-2. The interview for knowledge acquisition is both a communications process involving the domain expert and the knowledge engineer, and a thought process which converts concepts and ideas into rules.

Other problems are more technical:

- Conceptualization of the domain
- Expression of the right rules
- Rule development as a system
- Errors in conceptualization and/or rule expression
- Feedback for validation of the domain and rules
- Disagreements among experts
- Delays in AI construct delivery

Further, every knowledge engineer knows how to ask questions. The right questions don't necessarily come as a matter of course. Some twenty-nine years ago, when I started working as a private consultant, I had an interview with a senior vice president of AEG-Telefunken in location. He sat comfortably in his armchair and said, "Now you ask me the questions." Though I had had interviewing experience with IBM and Booz Allen and Hamilton, it was not that easy.

Many companies teach their consultants or representatives to carry a form with standard questions. This is a poor practice; the results range from average to disastrous. You cannot waste the time of senior executives or top professionals with standard questions. At best, they will lose all interest in the interview. At worst, they will cut you off. *You must engage them in a dialogue*— the Socratic method. My experience shows there are two effective methods.

- "I would like to learn your field of work. Will you kindly explain it to me? As you go, allow me to interrupt and ask some questions."
- "Let me tell you something about artificial intelligence. However, be patient. The field is still in its infancy. As we discuss the subject, tell me where it applies to your work. Also, feel free to interrupt whenever you like and ask for explanations."

About 90 percent of the time, one of these strategies works—provided that the knowledge engineer *masters his art* and *has confidence in himself*. Otherwise, forget the interview; it will not produce results.

The key is to engage in dialogue at a sustainable level. Ask the domain expert for specific cases in his work. As we will see in Section 4, if he is a true expert, he will collaborate. If he cannot provide specific cases, he is no expert.

It is no secret that many AI interviews are done with the wrong people, with the wrong questions, and for the wrong reasons. For this reason, their relatively high failure rate should not surprise anybody. That's the bad news. Now the good news. The use of the appropriate system building tool, typically a shell, of prototyping, and of computer support helps ease some of these problems. But it does not cancel them.

Improvements are possible. Incrementally, this will be the case of the recorded session.

b. The Recorded Session

British Petroleum (BP) tried it, and it seems to work. What BP is doing is to put a petroleum expert in the chosen domain to explain his business to two newly hired engineers. A knowledge engineer does not necessarily participate to the session. The reason for having two young engineers at the receiving end, rather than one, is that a dialogue is more easily maintained. Not everybody is interactive. Young people are often timid. It is expected that two young engineers will sustain teacher–pupil communication better than one.

The whole session is tape recorded in minute detail—including whatever is written on the blackboard, whether text, equations, or diagrams. Speech is also recorded. Detail is very important in this process. Subsequently, BP knowledge engineers carefully examine the session in slow motion. They

- extract everything that is significant in terms of rules and domain,
- restructure their findings,
- make a protocol of queries, and
- put themselves in position to address the expert, starting with a scenario rather than from scratch.

This approach is novel as an AI acquisition methodology but not as a playback method. In 1925, F.B. Gilbreth, the father of motion study, had devised a similar procedure for the analysis of *therbligs*. Therbligs are the basic elements into which workers' motions were analyzed, whether for timing or for dexterity tests. Gilbreth's method (which I used in 1953, at the University of California for my master's thesis) works well. It is surprising what one can uncover in slow playback. Gilbreth's film recording was in black and white. BP's approach is therbligs in color. The process has merits. It edits out some of the noise[6] that occurs in a personal interview.

c. Observing the Expert
in His Work

We have said that the knowledge engineer can learn from the domain expert through osmosis. The methodological exploitation of this process is itself an approach of knowledge acquisition.

If interviews are a good way of defining the expert's work and are quicker than observation in getting information, they may also mislead, giving exceptions as the normal course. Industrial engineering has developed a ratio delay, *work sampling* method. It is based on random observations. A similar process can be applied in terms of work evaluation for knowledge acquisition.

No expert would allow a knowledge engineer to observe him closely all the time. But appointments can be arranged to follow valuable work sessions and take careful notes on the expert's work. If nothing else, this approach may be helpful in refining, through observation, both the interview technique and the results of recorded sessions.

A main benefit of the observation approach is that experts are usually bad at *explaining* but good at *doing*. Quite often, much of what the expert says in responding in an interview is what

- his job description says, or
- he thinks he is doing, or
- he would like to be doing.

That is, he responds by giving information which represents anything except what he is really doing.

Recognition is a reliable way to approach the expert's business. By observing him in his work, the knowledge engineer does not need to ask: "Do you do this or that?" He sees what takes place, and he can be specific in asking questions. An *uncued recall* is vague and misleading.

Action descriptives are the best approach. Observing the expert work, the knowledge engineer has the opportunity to ask: "What do you dow hen this case occurs?" Of course, precise questions require that the knowledge engineer know or at least understand the expert's field. While he works, the expert's activity, skill, and know-how can be recorded through *protocols* characterizing a given field—that is, through signs and rules which are action specific. Such protocols can subsequently be fine-tuned in a workshop session with

---

[6] Noise is any unwanted input. Even chamber music is noise when we wish to sleep.

the expert, exploiting *artificial problems* through case studies to observe the expert in simulated situations.

The important thing is to be active and to take readable notes without missing the essential tasks. *Comparative case analysis* is an active method and helps to elicit patterns, structures, and rules of a given domain.

Steady, properly conducted observations with a sample of experts also provide a good way to answer a question that has bothered knowledge engineers for many years: "Is the knowledge of, say, five experts additive?" Observations have helped to document that the opposite is true: *Knowledge is not necessarily additive.* The question then becomes: "How can we pull together the knowledge from different sources?" The answer is that we need to do far more comparative studies than are available today, and we need to use *applied experimental psychology.*

d. Self-Service Scenario

This differs from the interview by eliminating the middleman: the knowledge engineer. In effect, the expert is interviewing himself. He is doing so with the assistance of the proper support environment (see Figure 2-3).

The proper support environment will, of course, be computer based. It will include a shell[7] and prototyping. Still better is something that acts as a knowledge-based tutoring system or a computer-assisted instruction system. Today several AI-enriched tutoring systems are available, but not in the knowledge acquisition domain. Examples of knowledge-based tutoring systems are programming tutors (BIP, PROUST), an arithmetic tutor (WEST), a medicine tutor (GUIDON), and an electronic circuit tutor (SOPHIE). Those who have worked with these expert systems appreciate them. Those who have not may be saying: "Tutoring systems don't exist and don't merit any discussion."

But to work the right way, the domain expert should have an appreciation of the added functional capabilities of a knowledge-based tutoring system over a standard, computer-assisted instruction system. He must also understand the additional resources required to

Figure 2-3. The domain expert can also act as knowledge engineer in a self-service scenario, as exemplified in this figure.

---

[7] I don't like too many distinctions, such as *tool kit.* They confuse the issue rather than clarify it and often contain contradictory or false claims.

operate with a knowledge-based tutoring system as a means of self-service in knowledge acquisition.[8]

Simpler tools for the self-service process include four environments:

- A knowledgebank editor with stylized English.
- Knowledgebank debuggers with rule checking.
- A computer-based explanatory approach.
- An AI-enriched advisory system.

Some versions of the third environment and practically all of the fourth involve meta-knowledge acting on the rule set.

Waterman said: "The knowledge engineer should not be the domain expert." Indeed, several experiences indicate that the knowledge engineer is not effective in interviewing himself as a domain expert. However, *if*

- there are existing *written procedures* that are *very clear,* and
- what is required from the knowledge engineer is an evaluation capability,

then he can function as a domain expert. We will return to this subject later.

There are, of course, problems with self-service. First, there is much intellectual work to be done by the expert. With few exceptions, only minor parts are done by the machine—thus requiring polyvalence on behalf of the user. Second, this is not always a rewarding experience. Knowledge engineers who did self-service on knowledge acquisition state the difficulties and frustrations the job involves. And Babrow is both an expert programmer (domain) and an expert knowledge engineer.

If the decision is made to proceed with self-service knowledge acquisition and there are good reasons for it, then I would advise the expert to write a *knowledgebank protocol.* Figure 2-4 gives an example. It has seven chapters—three related to the basic phases of knowledge engineering and four dealing with knowledgebank development. For each chapter, there is a procedure. It is written in a few lines, but it should be available interactively through the machine in more detail. This approach is just as valid in facilitating the interview.

e. Writing a Causal Model
for Inference

This method can be helpful provided that causality is easy to identify and demonstrate, which is not always true. If a causal (cause and effect) model can be built, then its availability will facilitate the explanation of rules. A causal model for inference has to be developed in connection with knowledge of the domain itself. As an alternative, it will require an interview (which, as stated, must be online) or the study of well-established procedures which are clearly written, as well as complete, noncontradictory, and well understood.

We have spoken of some of these approaches. A causal model is based on a cause-effect situation which is clear enough to give the knowledge engineer the information he needs to build an AI construct. This knowledge may be contained in *company rules* and *bylaws.* In

---

[8] Self-service in the sense that the contribution of the knowledge engineer is practically automated.

	ITEM	PROCEDURE
KNOWLEDGE ENGINEERING	1. KNOWLEDGE ACQUISITION	1. NEWLY ACQUIRED FACTS, STATES, VALUES
	2. KNOWLEDGE ANALYSIS	2. SITUATION OF EVENT(S) CAUSE OF EVENT(S)
	3. STRUCTURE PLANNING	3. HIERARCHY AND STRUCTURAL CHARACTERISTICS
KNOWLEDGEBANK DEVELOPMENT	4. CONFIGURATOR	4. DECISION ON USING RULES, FRAMES, OR LOGIC PROGRAMMING
	5. PRODUCTION	5. DEVELOPMENT OF AN INFERENCE ENGINE AND A KNOWLEDGEBANK
	6. COMPILATION	6. USE OF A COMPILER AND A PARSER IF LOGIC MACHINE-LEVEL LANGUAGE IS DESIRED
	7. TESTING	7. EVALUATION OF RESULTS, DEFAULTS, DEMERITS, CORRECTION

Figure 2-4. The protocol for the development of the knowledgebank can be divided into two parts which share seven critical steps, from knowledge acquisition to testing.

other terms, the careful study of already existing procedures in the organization provides rich material for the development of expert systems. The knowledge we need is found in them. It must:

- be extracted and formatted,
- not be contradictory, and
- be expressed in terms of cause and effect.

Still the knowledge is available, though at times supplementary interviews may be necessary. Remember that what is *clearly understood* is the best candidate for the development of an expert system. Clearance of loans and evaluation of risk, for instance, is a good area in which to apply such approach for the simple reason that every self-respecting bank has thorough written procedures in this field. The decision process about the loan may be fuzzy—yes/maybe/no—but the procedures are well established. Practically, they are algorithmic.

The knowledge engineer may study the written procedures and develop a causal model.

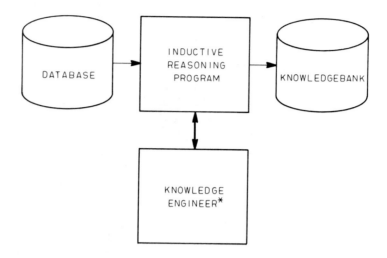

*COULD ALSO BE THE DOMAIN EXPERT

Figure 2-5. This block diagram outlines the approach taken by an expert system project in exploring inductive reasoning through semiautomatic approaches. It requires the collaboration of a knowledge engineer or domain expert.

He does not necessarily need a loan expert for this job. The writing of client profiles or inventory management all examples where this process is feasible.

Tools can be helpful. Typically, they will be similar to those we examined for the self-service scenario—BIP, PROUST, WEST, GUIDON, SOPHIE—but they should be specialized, applicable to the domain for which the causal model must be built.

Skeptics say that tools are not available; that they might be the result of the job to be done—not its preconditions; or that tools have little to do with the process of knowledge acquisition. I have heard all these arguments, and *they are false. If* the job to be done (whether in AI or any other field) is that of the unable being asked by the unwilling to do the unnecessary, *then* the obstructive arguments have their place. Otherwise they are nonsense—just excuses to avoid a job which has to be done. It is no coincidence that EDP has come to mean "emotionally disturbed person."

- *If* you wish to remain an EDPer, *then* forget about AI; it is not for you.
- *If* you wish to revamp your know-how and be professionally active, *then* don't listen to these silly arguments.

If some of the tools you will need are not on hand when you start your first AI project, then develop them. And once yuou develop them, use them. Reusable software is a state of mind, and it is one of the best approaches to get results.

There are many ways of using causality in the process of inference. One variation is known as *inductive reasoning by analysis.* As Figure 2-5 shows, what it means in practice is that data in the *database* are:

- manipulated through an inductive reasoning program interacting with a knowledge engineer and
- subsequently feed into the knowledgebank.

These approaches are semiautomatic. A fully automatic solution is theoretical. There is no available machine to do it, nor is much research being done in this field. Eventually, Fifth Generation Languages (5GC) solutions may be developed, particularly if enriched with memory-based reasoning (MBR), as explained in Chapter 13. MBR has a set of feature which permit it to bypass the need for deep model rules. Rather, as the application develops, the key question will be how to define new features without having the human user at the console or WS using the idea database approach of conceptual definition.

Note, however, that the causal model for inference may be a step foward in self-service scenarios. In Figure 2-5, it will suffice to replace the knowledge engineer with the domain expert, and the AI systems will be developed by career experts rather than knowledge engineering specialists. The next generation of expert systems may be tooled for this approach as their design focuses on causal models and heuristic rules. The approach has merits, and in the coming years it may become a fundamental tool. We will see.

A sound methodology must also be developed for such a solution to become popular. *Experimental design*[9] may provide significant help in knowledge acquisition. We don't just import/export information elements from the database. "Garbage in, garbage out" has been the DP saga for thirty-five years. That's long enough.

f. Fully Automated
Rule Induction

Automatic rule induction is still a research area. Breakthroughs will permit us to generate rules automatically and define domains, but we must still wait for them. Today and for at least the next three or four years, we do not have:

- the technologists,
- the AI constructs, or
- the powerful computers

to obtain a fully automated inference of rules and domains. What many people fail to understand is that it is one thing to go from *data and text to the knowledgebank* and another to go from *the knowledgebank to the AI system.* Breakthroughs may, however, revolutionize this domain of knowledge acquisition from other fields of AI—for instance, from research on natural language translation or from projects on *text understanding.* An imaginative project on text understanding is currently underway at the University of Passau. Its goal is explained in Figure 2-6. A similar project exists at the University of Massachussets.

W. Bruce Croft at the University of Massachusetts and Udo Hahn at the University of Passau are leading projects which it is hoped, will eventually result in breakthroughs. The

---

[9] See Chapter 4.

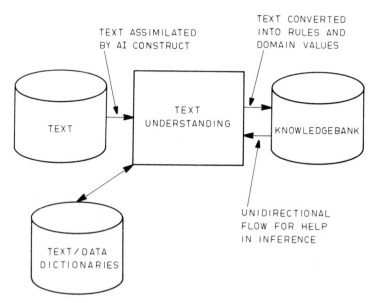

Figure 2-6. Several projects focus on text understanding. The one referred to comes from a leading German university which is fairly well advanced in this area.

same is true of ICOT and ATR.[10] Such projects profit from large-scale, machine-readable and -understandable dictionaries.

Modeling text understanding takes a methodological approach to automatic acquisition of knowledge through text analysis. Natural language understanding processes have been of interest to AI designers almost exclusively with respect to the development of natural language interfaces. The work at the University of Passau documents that another major application focuses on attacking the knowledge acquisition bottleneck of current expert system technology.

The automatic construction of knowledgebanks through text understanding systems is particularly challenging, since major methodological premises in the field of man–machine dialogue do not apply to text understanding. Text analysis has specific requirements, while natural language text understanding is approached in terms of cooperating, lexically distributed processes.

One model which generalizes the concept of word expert parsing is based on

- a purely object-oriented specification in terms of actors.
- a formally sound description of the knowledge representation system it refers to,

---

[10] Institute for New Generation Computer Technology, Tokyo, and the Advanced Telecommunications Research Institute, Science City—both in Japan.

- a domain-independent, highly modularized semantic parser and, most important,
- the incorporation of text structure phenomena in terms of a lexically distributed text grammar.

While such research efforts are well organized and properly staffed, many problems of methodology and approach still need to be solved. It may take five to ten years to do so. Even after solutions are found, research must proceed in applications perspectives including

- resolution of conflicting knowledge
- treatment of time-dependent knowledge
- management of knowledgebank versions and their control

In terms of control, in the Passau project the automatic interview component has not yet been tackled, but progress is being made in connection with the shell and even better results have been obtained in the *advice-taking* module. The *data-to-knowledgebank* work is now complete, and is the text-to-knowledgebank component.

The advice-taking engine transforms natural language statement first to high-level and then to low-level operational structures. One of the difficulties is integration. In AI we still know very little about the interaction of text with data and graphs—which may be very important in understanding the nature of embedded rules.

This is precisely where writing a causal model for inference can be of help. Solution 4 is partly automatic, but it also presupposes integration of a human expert. He may not be needed in the text-to-knowledgebank component, but he is needed in other tasks.

Prior to closing this section, we must mention the contributions that *discovery systems* may make to knowledge acquisition, from AM to Cyrano. To recall the facts, the emergence of Douglas Lenat's AM program in 1976 was met with surprise and controversy; AM's performance seemed to bring the dream of super-intelligent machines to our door. However, no generation of automated supermathematicians appeared. Lenat subsequently explained AM's problems and led the development of Eurisko. Work on Eurisko revealed certain requirements of discovery programs related to explicitness of representation. After Eurisko, the work by Kenneth W. Haase, Jr., at MIT on the discovery program Cyrano revealed more requirements on discovery processes in general.

Able solutions will be coming; there is no doubt about that. But it will take time, and knowledge acquisition requirements are pressing. Happily, we have five methods which are workable if we use them wisely. And they are available *now*.

4. SOLVING THE PROBLEMS OF KNOWLEDGE ACQUISITION

We can synthesize, and hence manufacture, knowledge. But we cannot bypass a vital link in the chain, such as knowledge elicitation. At the same time, since we cannot foresee the future use of the AI system with acuracy, we need to examine a wide range of possible utilizations.

As knowledge engineers, we must look at the opportunity from different points of view. We can annotate each possible scenario, documenting for ourselves and others the possibilities we are examining. As our experience accumulates, we would like the development system not only to keep a record of our scenarios but also to show us how they relate to each other—in practice, showing us a picture of our thought process. We may wish to move from one scenario to another and create new scenarios based on the results of our analyses.

This approach, too, is part of the knowledge engineer's expertise. It is also strongly related to knowledge acquisition. The key is flexibility. Provided that we have agile minds—and the knowledge engineer should have one to be part of the profession—flexibility can be computer assisted. Let's use this opportunity.

In a knowledge acquisition process, flexibility is very important because we know that human knowledge is *not* perfect—neither is it static. It is imprecise, vague, uncertain, and in evolution. The following questions then arise:

- How can we improve our approaches?
- How can we represent the logic?
- How can we remain flexible and adaptable?

Numbers may be out of reach. Symbols may not be enough. Yet, we need both, plus a methodology. This is the way to proceed. But methodology is no half-baked approach adopted for the occasion. Nor can it be adopted in midstream. We have to return to the beginning—and to the fundamentals.

We have mental capacities which, if we understood better the ways the mind works, could be utilized to advantage in a decision environment—and, by extension, in writing AI constructs. Because we still don't understand the human mind well, we usually tune our system to the *individual capabilities* of the decision maker—or, generally, the domain expert. This is not necessarily the best solution, but it is a feasible one. A better solution might be a more general one which fits all decision styles, but we don't know how to develop it. We lack both the concept and the tools. Furthermore, with the exception of super-computers, the machines we use are not powerful enough for sophisticated AI jobs.

That is the reason so often given to explain why, under current technology, AI systems are domain specific. Another advantage of a limited domain is that we are better able to control errors. Yet, errors occur. Among the sources of expert errors is lack of understanding of the following:

1. Trade-offs
2. Proper definition of key variables
3. Suboptimization
4. Correlation between variables
5. Interdependencies
6. Need to decouple the system selectively
7. Connectivity to classical DP applications
8. Variability of user requests as a function of time
9. Impact of time lags in module development
10. Need to revamp and restructure
11. Degree of necessary flexibility

12. Transients, their frequency and influence
13. Possible impact of shock effects
14. Conflicting goals and their resolution
15. Criticisms by nonexperts or even by experts with different opinions

We have said that in the knowledge acquisition phase and more generally, in the development of AI systems, we should avoid people with limited knowhow who poase as domain experts. They are controvesial in terms of their supposed expertise and they cannot be helpful. But at times, company politics make this avoidance difficult. More frequently, in some cases it is not clear who is a *real* expert and who is not.

The best way I have found to overcome this problem is to study the man's reaction. It has been documented that *real experts* are much happier if we can help them eliminate the routine from their business, releasing their time to do creative work. Nonexperts are defensive; they care about the past much more than about the future. Real domain experts have a healthy, open attitude because they have confidence in themselves. They know their strengths (and weaknesses) and have a plan on how to channel their resources in the best possible way. Pseudoexperts take precisely the opposite approach because they are afraid of their own emptiness. Thus, they cling to trivialities.

Real domain experts are easy to work with because, in general, they are open and collaborative. They may not have crisp answers (a true expert rarely has that kind of response), but they know how to organize and express their ideas. This makes the task of the knowledge engineer rewarding—both in regard to what he learns and in the comprehensive way the answers are given to him.

Sometimes it is difficult to distinguish the real domain expert from the pseudoexpert. Yet there are certain criteria which can be used to tell them apart. These criteria will now be discussed.

1. *Resistance to change*

The real expert is not afraid of change and therefore does not react negatively to it. He also knows how to capitalize on change and appreciates that change is inevitable. This statement is significant for personal carriers and also for expert systems and their maintenance. A study by the Department of Defense recently documented an impressive statistic on expert system obsolescence due to domain changes (Table 2-1). The true professional understands this subject; the pseudoexpert does not.

TABLE 2-1. Findings of a Department of Defense Study on Expert System Obsolescence.

Time Frame	Probability of Domaine Change
1 year	50%
2 years	>80%
3 years	100%

2. *Destabilization under stress*

The real expert knows himself and both his strong and weak points. He has confidence in his opinions; appreciates that professional life is not just black and white but has many gray areas; and, when necessary, can live with and thrive under stress. Stress destablilizes the pseudoexpert. His domain is too narrow and cannot withstand wide swings. Yet such swings are part of professional life. Change brings stress to the pseudoexpert, whereas for the real domain expert it provides opportunity.

3. *Lifelong learning*

The true domain experts are always the most eager to engage in lifelong learning. They never miss an opportunity to improve their know-how, and they consider it their duty to train others in bettering themselves. Pseudoexperts have precisely the opposite attitude. They are secretive in divulging what they know because they know so little that they think secrecy will conceal their emptiness. Nor are they keen to learn more or to develop the wide range of faculties exemplified in the 13 points listed in Chapter 1, Section 3, on domain experts and their characteristics (p. 9).

Neil Jacoby, my professor at UCLA, said to me thirty-five years ago: "The best way to hang a bad executive is to give him lots of cord." For more than three decades, I have applied this advice to business, and it works. If modified, it is also applicable in knowledge engineering work.

Another good way of distinguishing real experts from pseudoexperts is to analyze their motivation. Real experts want to see things working early. They want to reduce paperwork, get access to facts, and obtain computer support for their decisions. Pseudoexperts find always excuses for delays and responses to cover up their lack of knowledge. Says Dr. Stephen W. Hawkling, "Some people never admit that they are wrong and continue to find new, and often mutually inconsistent, arguments to support their case."[11]

To summarize our discussion of experts: A domain expert is a professional characterized by certain traits and attributes. He

- is open minded,
- has wide knowledge of his domain,
- possesses extensive experience and excellent learning mechanisms,
- works under stress
- is able to deal with exceptions,
- is not afraid to lose his job if he tells his trade secrets because he knows that he is moving ahead in his profession—but also
- is capable of recognizing the limits of his expertise.

His skills in learning combined with his experience and knowledge equip him with better problem-solving mechanisms than those of the pseudoexperts. Only extensive experience, for instance, permits reasoning by analogy. Also, other things being equal, the expert can express himself more clearly because he has ordered his thoughts.

---

[11] *A Brief History of Time*, Bantam, New York, 1988.

We need orderly thoughts as well as tools for learning; knowledge acquisition *is* a learning process. Learning is gathering experiences in order to better fit behavior to the properties of the environment. Learning denotes adaptive changes in the system in the sense that they enable one to do the same task or tasks drawn from the same population more efficiently next time.

Knowledge acquisition is learning. The formalism for knowledge representation is only a tool, which is needed because acquired knowledge must be represented within the chosen formalism. Humans can learn without knowing our own representation formalism, and an AI construct cannot do so.

In *Public Opinion,* Walter Lippmann talks of a reporter who respects himself and his reader. A reporter, Lippmann says, is an analyst, and an analyst cannot allow himself to have pet opinions or biases. The knowledge engineer is an analyst, and he too must be open-minded.

Knowledge acquisition itself is a process of analysis. It is not the traditional system analysis applicable to DP; this process has been totally distorted after thirty years of mispractice. Knowledge acquisition is quite different from system analysis for DP—even if, in some areas, they shade into one another—but still is an analytic process.

It's important for a knowledge engineer to identify himself with his project. This means more than getting involved. Whenever we start creating a framework to base our beliefs, we must be open-minded. We cannot afford to be dogmatic. "I know one thing, that I know nothing," Socrates said.

3

Knowledge Representation

Keywords

knowledge representation • production rules • accuracy •true value • precision • transparency • conceptualization • objects • events • procedures • metaknowledge • representation • efficiency of representation • propositional logic • declarative knowledge • procedural knowledge • AI construct • structure • inferences • rule convergence • plan • plan repair • blackboard • vague • definite • script • object operations • knowledge sources • intelligent control • preconditions • delete list • add list • data driven • goal driven • forward chaining • backward chaining • strategies • methodologies • specific problem data • event driven • integrating • model • object • inheritance • meta • knowledge about knowledge • hypotheses • control strategies • constraint propagation • monotonic • nonmonotonic • premises • goals • subgoals • sideways chaining • alpha-beta procedure • search algorithms • AI searching • breadth-first search • depth-first search • hill climbing • branch-and-bound search • algorithm search procedure • beam search • mean-ends analysis

1. INTRODUCTION

Knowledge representation is the task of casting a collection of knowledge within the computer. This must be done in a way that permits inferences to be drawn. The knowledge is the result of the acquisition process and typically concerns the real world. The process of knowledge representation focuses on the accuracy of this casting, but also on the richness and diversity of knowledge to be represented. To achieve this, knowledge representation deals with

1. developing mechanisms designed to map properties of real-world objects and events,
2. understanding the structure which permits machine cognition of relationships between people, objects and events,
3. establishing methodologies for modeling of human knowledge, awareness, and beliefs, and
4. making available tools for describing and organizing world knowledge.

While the term *production rules* is sometimes reserved for one type of representation, in this book it is defined in a more general sense. Production rules are a *formalism for exploring and expressing this knowledge so as to enable computers to perform as expert consultants*—and eventually to substitute for human operators. Production rules require methodologies that are able to observe machine understanding, learning, and intelligent behavior in the chosen domain of knowledge. At the heart of the production rule system are the formalisms for describing task areas, as well as the rules of behavior or of the game, such as

- cause/effect,
- situation/action, or
- IF . . . THEN . . . ELSE paradigms.

Symbols and operators combine into structures which include concepts, abstractions, knowledge, facts/states/values, rules, intentions, goals, meanings, and plans. Such structures may be simple or complex. In either case, they have little need for numerical computation. Emphasis is on symbolic (hence, nonnumeric) representation and manipulation.

Knowledge representation follows the process of knowledge acquisition. As underlined in the preceding chapters, knowledge engineering is not just knowledge acquisition. It includes representing knowledge and applying it. At times, this can be done by mathematical modeling or the implementation of a known and applicable heuristic approach.

With reference to the development and use of an expert system, Figure 3-1 relates acquisition and representation to the system itself and to the use of knowledge. The expert system from which this chart comes was designed for library search in an experiment approximating the concept of *idea databases,*[1] described in Chapter 13.

Being experimental, the problem is cast into a number of different choices which lead to a specific representation. Choices are consequential, accounting for the fact that there is no specific theory of representations. Today virtually all knowledge about representation is empirical. This is a different way of saying that representation is not precisely the name of a specific set of solutions. It is a reference applicable to a large group of approaches. Some of these approaches have given good results; others are poorly understood. As often happens

---

[1] An idea database queries are nonprocedural and in general, queries are noncrisp. The user expresses his wish *about* a text or context, and AI software does the search and the presentation.

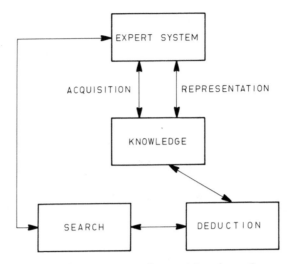

Figure 3-1. The development of an expert system is essentially an interactive process of knowledge acquisition and representation. It involves induction or deduction, as well as search and testing procedures.

in the computer profession, representation also includes a number of issues only slightly related to the main concept, yet necessarily within the larger aggregate of the knowledge engineering effort.

2. CONDITIONS FOR KNOWLEDGE REPRESENTATION

In spite of shortcoming in tools and methods, knowledge representation is the single most important factor in determining how powerful an application we can build with an AI construct. The approach should be fundamental. The language should be versatile and sophisticated, supporting both logical and numeric variables of several distinct types.

The application sets the pertinent variables by querying the domain expert or through some other approach. One of the goals in an application may be theoretical knowledge. Extracting expertise is not necessarily the only antecedent to a representation process. Theoretical and practical knowledge can also be used to enhance each other.

If we need better methods for extracting knowledge from experts, the same can be said of representing it. The goal is to obtain well-defined, objective functions; however the knowledge engineer working on a representation project should keep in mind that a lot of expertise depends on judgment. The trouble with judgment is that most of it is an unconscious process. Hence, it is difficult to state as well as to represent in a precise fashion.

Accuracy rather than precision should be the goal in knowledge representation. *Accuracy* refers to *how close* a measurement (or event) is to the *true value* of a quantity. As the degree of accuracy varies, so does our ability to approximate a true value. *Precision* refers to the clustering of measurements about *their own* average. If they are tightly clustered, the precision is high. Accuracy is more important than precision because of the way our mind works. Brain processes depend on

- response to stimulus
- perception, intake of information
- cognition, leading to thinking (mental processing)
- problem solving through heuristics rather than algorithmic approaches
- memory and recall (or regenerative) capability
- concept formation
- pattern recognition
- selection and classification
- sotrage and retrieval
- conclusion and presentation

Because AI deals with mental and logical processes and problems, issues raised by the choice of representation are relative to *transparency,* with associated ease of inputting, editting, and verification of knowledge. Another key reference is *conceptualization,* which focuses on the abstract view of the problem and its solution, leading to isomorphic mapping through knowledge representation.

Factors affecting our judgment influence and are influenced by facts, values, beliefs, and assumptions. Experiences also influence the way we conceive facts and subsequently represent them. It also affects the manner in which we formulate our rules and then use them.

Since human beings represent knowledge to build an AI construct, these considerations are as applicable in machine intelligence as they are in human thinking. The main variables we try to represent are facts, strings, numbers, categories, and phrases. We also try to represent *objects:*[2] their classes and groups, characteristics, descriptions, and relations with other objects.

Knowledge representation includes *events,* the definition of what objects are involved, pre- and post-conditions, and relations with other events. *Procedures* are another reference. They tell how to do things, how to generate goal-relevant rules and behavior. A crucial aspect of knowledge representation is *metaknowledge.*[3]

Metaknowledge is instrumental in AI, as all problems must be mapped into some form of internal representation which is expressed in a hierarchy of rules. This hierarchy of rules exemplifies the importance of structured approaches and the methods knowledge engineering must offer for differentiating among the various characteristics of a given problem—as well as among problems. The approaches chosen should comprise a versatile and flexible system for passing knowledge back and forth between the user and the AI system and for processing the knowledge within the system. This ability to communicate concepts is the key to

1. mapping the acquired knowledge into a construct,
2. offering worthwhile advice and results for real-world problems, and

---

[2] See Chapter 11.
[3] Explained in Chapter 11.

3. constructing efficient knowledge systems that can run on small or large computers, depending on the problem and the equipment at hand.

The goal is to derive new, focused, machine-readable knowledge from that which is already explicit as a result of knowledge acquisition. The approach must be formal, orderly, logical, open to possible generalization, and featuring metareasoning.

To obtain the wanted outcome, the designer must specify facts and ranges. He may, for instance, set the values permitted for numerical parameters in a range declaration. The number types may include positive integers and both positive and negative floating-point decimals. Alternatively, the designer may use only logical constructs.

The designer should also focus on constraints to logical manipulation. He may declare that number parameters be calculated, or domain properties deduced from rules or asked of the user. Other parameters may be qualitative features that can take any number of specified string values. The designer may see to it that the consultation shell builds a menu of the listed category options asking users for their selections.

In these cases, representation will be written by rules and statements which make up the knowledgebank. Prompting by the system helps the user communicate with the knowledgebank. Several expert systems are limited to the provision of an intelligent man–machine interface. In fact, the word *limited* is not correct. A good human window is of great help to the enduser.[4]

Having accepted both logical and numerical values for knowledge representation, we can say that at least in a numerical sense *representation* as a concept is not new. Since the late 1940s, analog simulation has been used. In the 1950s and 1960s, digital simulation was a focal point. Simulation is a form of representation, as we will see when we talk about prototypes, models, and simulation.

Whether logic-based representation or simulation is used, the goal is the mapping of knowledge. Figure 3-2 exemplifies this statement. In both cases, our goals are

- *efficiency of presentation,* expressed through through the accuracy of our construct—with knowledge represented after it has been acquired
- *effectiveness of implementation*—measured in terms of resources: programmer time, computer memory, and computing time

We have already stated that we also aim at modularity. It makes it easier to change parts of the construct in isolation from the rest without upsetting the other parts of the system.

Logic-based representation typically takes the form of *propositional* (or first-order predicate) *logic.* The advantage of this method is that formal procedures are available. The disadvantage is that many problems are not easily represented in logic.

As stated in preceding chapters, in a rule system *knowledge is represented* as a collection of hypothesis/action patterns:

IF . . . THEN . . .

---

[4] Critics may say that this paragraph has more to do with user interfaces than knowledge representation. In reality, the two issues are inseparable, something that nearsighted people find difficult to understand.

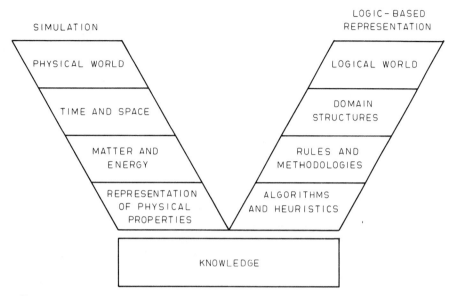

Figure 3-2. Simulation and logic-based representation can be divided into layered structures. In this particular case, four layers are identified for each—and for both of them, the bottom line is knowledge.

The format is of the type

> IF   < hypothesis, condition, structure, test. . . . >
> THEN   < action, consequence, derived structure, result . . . <

We can distinguish two directions of knowledge use:

> IF → THEN

This is known as bottom-up, forward chaining, or the data-driven model.

> IF ← THEN

This is known as top-down, backward chaining, or the rule- or goal-driven approach.

Three types of knowledge can be distinguished:

1. *Declarative knowledge.* This is a knowledge structure resembling a statement of facts, relations, or objects, or alternatively events, rules, or other mathematical expressions.
2. *Procedural knowledge.* This construct is akin to an algorithmic structure. It is expressed as a sequence of commands for action(s).
3. *Metaknowledge.* We have said that metaknowledge is control knowledge. This construct contains knowledge about knowledge. It tells us how to use available know-how. (We will speak much more about objects and metaknowledge in Part Two.)

In principle, the context of implementation may vary. But in a production rule system, the knowledge representation structure will focus on the guidelines we have examined. Remember that no two knowledge engineers use precisely the same approach, and that the knowledge specialist working on any given problem has more than one tool at his disposal.

In some cases, the choice of the tool is situational. In an AI construct written for text understanding, a phrase parameter may permit us to refer to pieces of text relating to the current problem by name. It can be referenced and automatically inserted in any statement. Its value can be set either by asking the user or by proving the conditions of a rule.

Important in knowledge representation is a full set of logical operators that can be used in creating rules in the knowledgebank. Examples are the logical *and, or* operators, the *exclusive or,* and *negation.*[5] As further examples will demonstrate, we can use production rules, frames, a semantic network, Bayesian theory, or possibility theory to construct the motor of the expert system.

Finally, repeated reference has been made to the fact that AI constructs must be interactive. The end user should be able to prod, turn around a session, exchange information, and receive advice during a consultation session, rather than only at the end, when the user has answered all the program's questions. In either case, the system should guide the user step by step through the consultation procedure.

3. CASTING THE KNOWLEDGE AS AN AI CONSTRUCT

An *AI construct* is a *hierarchy of definiens and rules* that enables a system to reason about the *structure* and *function* of things, as well as to make *inferences.* There is always a starting point in this hierarchy. In Figure 3-3, this is called Knowledge 1. The AI construct typically contains many rules or other forms of representation. Not all of them are used to find a solution to every problem. This, too, is shown in Figure 3-3. The principle is that *the greater the rule convergence* within a given application, *the higher the confidence* we can have in the result.

Using the following example of knowledge representation we will develop a simple AI system (in essence, an expert system) for financial analysis and sales/inventory evaluation. We will do that twice:

- The first time, we will use IF . . . THEN . . . ELSE rules.
- The second time, we will use frames.[6]

Let's start with the background. ZETA is a high-technology company that makes compact disc drives for PCs. Sales fluctuate with the PC market and also as a function of competition for disc drives.

---

[5] I suggest the symbols "." for logical *and;* "+" for *or,* "⊕" for *exclusive or;* and (') for negation.
[6] A *frame* graph is structural, describing relationships among defined events as well as between events and actions. Individual topics are thought of as frame-like entities, each slot representing a value within a range.

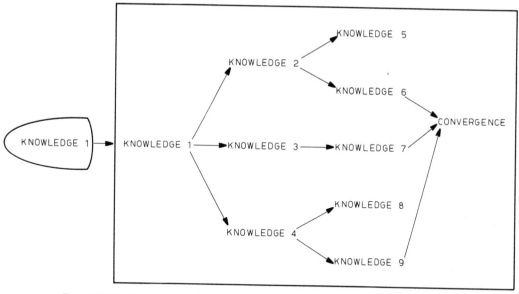

Figure 3-3. The knowledge that the enduser sees in interacting with the expert system is the top of a network of knowledge elements which ideally converge. In the typical case, such knowledge elements are transparent to the enduser.

ZETA sells to two markets:

- OEM for integration into new PCs.
- PC users for machine upgrade.

The company has collection problems, and its inventories are rather high. Furthermore, the board of directors is not certain about the company's standing in terms of leading financial analysis indicators. The following criteria are used in board decisions.

- Return on assets
- Return on sales
- Growth rate of sales
- Growth rate of net income
- Acid test (current ratio)
- Net sales to inventory
- Inventory to net working capital
- Minimum collection period
- Maximum collection period
- Average collection period
- Sales campaigns
- Sales discounts
- Inventory reduction
- Fixed assets on tangible net worth (TNW)

- Net profits on net working capital (NWC)
- Current debt to inventory
- Current debt to NWC

The chairman of the board asks you as a knowledge engineer to develop an expert system for financial analysis and sales inventory evaluation. He wants you to use both *production rules* (logic programming) and *frames*.

As we will see in Chapter 6, the continuation of this problem will require the building of agile man–machine interfaces. The human window must enable consolidation of results and produce responses through natural language. Emphasis must be placed on factors which are most important in producing the observed changes or differences.

Following is the solution to the case study, starting with the first alternative, *production rules*.

Rule 1

IF   industry is high technology
      and return on assets < 20%
      and return on sales < 15%
      and growth rate of sales < 10%
      and growth rate of net income < 5%

THEN   financial status is abnormal

Rule 2

IF   financial status abnormal
      and acid test < 1.5
      and net sales to inventory < 5.5
      and inventory to NWC < 60

THEN   liquidity problem exists

Rule 3

IF   liquidity problem exists
      and minimum collection period > 20 days
      and maximum collection period > 50 days
      and average collection period > 30 days

THEN   collection period is critical

Rule 4

IF   collection period is critical

THEN   recommend action to reduce collection period
        and start a sales campaign
        and sales discounts
        and inventory reduction

ELSE   negotiate new loans

Rule 5

IF   negotiate new loans

THEN   evaluate fixed assets to TNW
          and net profits on net sales
          and net sales on TNW
          and net profits on NWC
          and current debt to inventory
          and current debt to NWC

Rule 6

IF   majority of leading indicators negative

THEN   propose that the board file for Chapter 11

The *frames* solution to the case study is quite simple, particularly after the inference engine has been cast as a logical expression using IF . . . THEN . . . ELSE rules. Figure 3-4 outlines the layout and organization of a frames construct.

4. PLANNING PREMISES IN AI

At one time, writing production rules as described in the foregoing example was synonymous with expert systems development. However, as AI technology has become increasingly geared to handling more complex types of reasoning, bottlenecks may develop in the absence of planning activities. Bottlenecks can also result from the poor quality and limitations of the delivered technology.

In talking about a planning effort, we must distinguish between human-oriented planning and machine-oriented planning. The former is important in the development phase: from knowledge acquisition to representation and testing. The latter is dominant in the implementation process, when the enduser interacts with the expert system. Behind both is the concept of planning.

Some people feel that plans and planning are not a legitimate part of knowledge representation; they are wrong. Knowledge representation is the phase immediately following knowledge acquisition. When completed, the latter process leaves us with a collection of concepts and would-be rules. We have to

- sort them out properly,
- rearrange them in a manner that makes sense,
- plan both the development phase and its structure (human-oriented planning), and
- plan the execution phase during usage (machine-oriented planning).

Only when this process is successfully completed can we proceed with the second part of knowledge representation: writing the prototype using a shell.

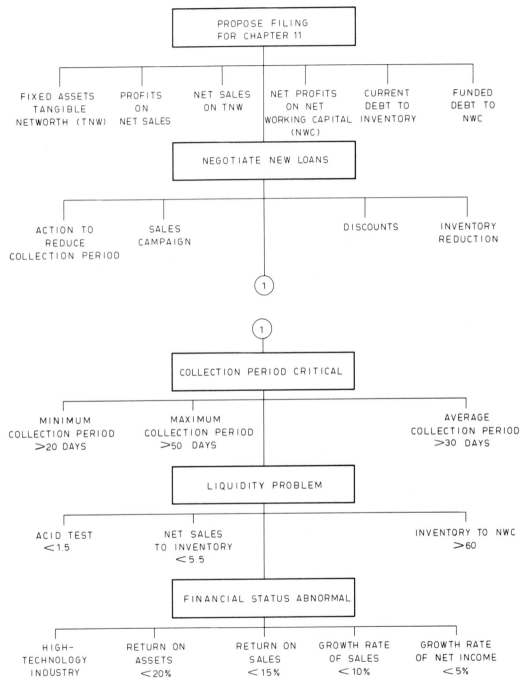

Figure 3-4. Example of a frame structure from a case study on financial analysis and sales/inventory evaluation. Notice that this approach permits a methodological organization of the elements that are part of the final decision.

In AI implementation, planning means several things:

- Breaking the original problem into a collection of subproblems.
- Solving each of these subproblems, perhaps recursively.
- Combining the solutions to form a solution to the original problem.
- Choosing a procedure and a methodology to accomplish this work.

These activities are pertinent to human planning during the process of development. In a machine-oriented sense, during the actual implementation planning permits us to think through a potential solution to a problem before we attempt to solve it. It induces us to examine alternatives and to build detail into potential solutions by using the expert system's facilities.

In AI applications, the word *planning* has also been associated with solving a simplified, hypothetical abstraction of a problem. This helps us discover a plausible outline to guide us in developing the solution.

Planning may often be applicable to knowledge representation. In analyzing phenomena and their representation, the following must be done:

1. Develop strategies for incremental rule acquisition
2. Develop tools for rule acquisition
3. Develop a rule syntax
4. Rule description
5. Effective cross-correlation
6. Efficient programming
7. Testing and debugging
8. Developing an agile consultation facility

While different theories of knowledge representation constitute the basis of day-to-day work, in a system development sense, their existence makes planning even more important. It permits *clarity,* making domains and rules easier to examine and understand. Planning makes feasible greater *flexibility.* Knowledgebank structures are much easier to modify at the planning stage and/or when the proper plans are made for modifications.

In addition to clarity and flexibility, for implementation an AI system must be able to plan a goal-directed behavior. Suppose, for instance, that the construct must achieve goal X, given initial conditions X'. We can represent this situation in abstract state space by stating the following:

- The system is currently in initial state Y', which can be described conceptually by initial conditions X'.
- As a result of goal searching, the system wants to be in the goal state Y. This can be conceptually described by goal X.

With this representation, we know the points of departure and destination for future plan(s). To build a plan, the system requires two kinds of knowledge:

- about the world in which the plan is to be executed and
- about the primitive actions that the systems is able to perform in that world.

The final plan can be defined as a configuration of these primitive actions. The system development process assumes that plan P will lead it from the initial state Y' to the goal state Y through a sequence of intermediate states (S_i).

A *primitive action* is represented as an arc connecting a couple of these states. This is a very helpful notion to understand frames and Petri nets. Figure 3-5 defines the states

$$Y', S_1, S_2 \ldots Y$$

Action A_1 is followed by the action A_2. An effect of A_1 is said to *satisfy* a precondition for starting A_2. Since an action can have a number of preconditions and effects, the plan is a *configuration* rather than a linear sequence of actions. For instance, two, three, or four arcs may be converging toward a given state Z.

Plan execution is important. All plans are built to be executed. Various strategies for planning and execution may exist, offering different answers to the question "How much can an AI construct plan prior to starting execution?" One strategy may be that an AI system (operating in a static world) can build the whole plan and then execute it. However, because the world is constantly changing, the plan may not be proper by the time of its execution. Hence building the whole plan and then executing it may be a bad strategy.

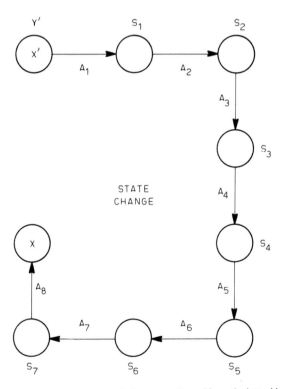

Figure 3-5. Expert system planning is a network of states and transitions, the latter identifying a state change, as explained in the text.

Developing an appropriate strategy of interaction between planning and plan execution is important if the AI system is to behave in a goal-directed manner and be useful in a changing world. Interaction modes may be quite diverse, but such a mode should definitely exist. Most interaction strategies are based on the hierarchical model of planning, which we will discuss in the following paragraphs. They also combine planning and a plan execution strategy. This is important for the reasons we have just discussed.

Just as vital as plans and planning strategies is the notion of *plan repair*. Suppose that something goes wrong with the plan: The results of plan execution differ from those expected by the system. This can be interpreted to mean that part of the plan or the AI system's world model is wrong. If so, the system has to bring the model and the plan in line with the world. To do so, the knowledge engineer and, eventually, the AI construct should be able to

1. monitor the results of plan execution,
2. compare them with expectations,
3. determine discrepancies,
4. define how the world model and the plan should be fixed, and
5. do the necessary plan repair.

These five vital steps demonstrate that goal-directed behavior is a process consisting of planning, plan execution, and plan repair. The feedback look is repeated whenever the AI construct sees discrepancies between the expected, planned behavior and the real results of plan execution in the AI system's world.

Corrective action is based on *rationality,* which imposes a valid, well-thought-out organization of domain and rules, plus feedback for evaluation. Planning helps to determine direction, but control is also necessary. Agile action (and explanation) requires not only that we describe but also that we define facts and rules, as well as approaches to justify decisions. Planning is key to this activity.

We can better accommodate undertainties inherent in real-world knowledge when we plan for them. This is important because the most interesting problems in AI are such that we cannot just start at the beginning and proceed to problem completion. Planning is one response to this difficulty.

We can follow one or several types of plans: *hierarchical, nonhierarchical, scenario based,* or *opportunistic.* The last term is a misnomer. It is preferable to call it a *blackboard* solution.

The hierarchical approach generates a set of AI plans at different levels of abstraction:

- The higher level is more abstract. We often refer to it as being *vague.*
- The lower level is more concrete. Sometimes it is called *definite* or *crisp.*

As in a hierarchical structure (of which we will speak in relation to metaknowledge), each step in a higher plan is based on a lower plan. It imposes constraints on the lower plan, which satisfies the requirements of the higher plan.

Nonhierarchical planning premises create representation problems. Solutions typically contain implicit and explicit components. *A set of states is implicit.* There is an initial state and a final state (the goal). There is also a set of operators; both are explicit. States are represented *explicitly by a set of predicates.*

PROGRAM: HOW TO GET TO WORK IN THE MORNING

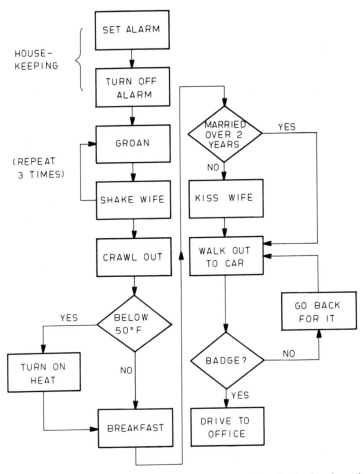

Figure 3-6. Block diagrams were not invented with expert systems. They date back to the early 1950s, at the beginning of the programming effort, as this example shows.

As we will also see in Part Two, scenario planning resembles a hierarchical structure, except that it draws on a library of templates (preestablished plans) for repetitive situations. Also known as *script,* this approach somewhat resembles the emulation of a 30-year-old block diagram for data processing. (Figure 3-6)

An opportunistic plan features a central pool of knowledge called a *blackboard.* A collection of AI programs that can read and write on the blackboard are known as *specialists.* Under the right circumstances, each specialist can create a piece of the plan.

Specialist programs operate asynchronously, that is, independently of one another. This is important because that deadly embraces deadlocks are avoided. But their real significance lies in the fact that specialist programs are the paradigm of *object operations*. We will return to this notion in Chapter 11. The blackboard architecture has four definitive elements:

1. *Entries,* intermediate results generated during problem solving.
2. *Knowledge sources,* independent, event-driven processes that produce entries.
3. *The blackboard* itself, a structured global database that mediates knowledge source interactions and organizes entries.
4. An *intelligent control* mechanism.

The intelligent control mechanism decides if and when particular knowledge sources should generate entries and record them on the blackboard. It may also grant access to the system.

Specialist programs (and objects) act when the proper initial information is present on the blackboard. Subsequently, they leave on the blackboard the plan fragment they produce as a result of their operation. One specialist program recognizes the complete plan and terminates the planner. This structure has been introduced by the expert system Hearsay for speech recognition. Its implementation enables bottom-up design (and hence forward chaining) and island building. As such, it is representative of a data-driven system.

Since cooperative AI systems are becoming more widely used, the concept of the *blackboard* is vital. It is based on the principle that when a system brings a number of knowledge sources to bear on a problem, processes must be developed to share information. Thus, the blackboard method provides a focal point; procedures can leave instructions for, and receive results from, other procedures. The blackboard approach can be specialized so that

- either each procedure has a special location reserved for the messages it sends and receives or
- special locations are devoted to different kinds of tasks, which any procedure can use.

Another way for procedures to talk to each other is by sending messages. This works like the pipe system in Unix.

In the case of specialist action, for each operator three lists of *predicates*[7] are represented:

1. Preconditions
2. Add list
3. Delete list

The *preconditions* are the list of predicates which must hold in order for this operator to be applicable. The *add list* represents the set of predicates which become true once the operator is applied. The *delete list* is composed of predicates which are no longer true once the operator has been applied. These include the preconditions.

---

[7] A predicate, in logic, is that which is affirmed or denied grammar about the subject of a proposition. In grammar, a predicate makes a statement about a clause. (See also Chapter 12, Section 2.) A *clause* is a group of entities forming part of a compound or complex. Clauses may be dependent or independent.

5. DATA-, EVENT-, RULE-, OBJECT-, AND GOAL-DRIVEN SYSTEMS

Suppose that we have written the rules of an AI construct and have done the planning. The rules have to be linked together to form a system. An inference engine is a program's protocol for navigating through the rules and data in a knowledge representation. The aim of this navigating is to solve a problem. The task of the inference engine is to *select* and then *apply* the most appropriate rule at each step as the AI system runs.

Years ago, there were two principal ways in which linkage was provided: *data driven* and *goal driven*. Correspondingly, there were two strategies to ensure the necessary linkage among the system's rules: *forward chaining* and *backward chaining*. We will speak about them in the next section.

Typically, a data-driven approach led to forward chaining and a goal driven environment to backward chaining. The situation is no longer so easy. The number of linkage systems has increased. We now have

- data driven
- event driven
- rule driven
- model oriented
- object oriented
- goal directed, and
- reasoning based on hypotheses.

These are the classes often found in literature. Admittedly, they are redundant, and some of the explanations associated with them are contradictory.

Data driven reasoning yields a problem-solving paradigm triggered by a change in data values. The execution cycle is based on the premise that whenever a data value changes, the AI system scans the set of active rules to find rules whose IF conditions are satisfied by the new value. In this sense, affected rules are added to the system's agenda. At each execution cycle, the THEN portion of the top rule on the agenda is executed. If it changes a data value, it causes more rules to fire and to be put on the agenda. The result is a solution that is easy to trace. It can be mapped in a graph of values as changes occur.

Generally, problem solving which proceeds *from specific problem data* is considered *data driven*. An *event-driven* methodology is similar, except that the situation (or data) is evolving over time. In this sense, data-driven and event-driven reasoning offer some excellent advantages. However, time, when applied as primary problem-solving paradigms, they may yield expensive solutions because of the way in whcih they proceed.

A data-driven approach starts by generating all possible solutions. It then eliminates the unreasonable ones, rating the remaining reasonable solutions and recommending the best one. A syllogism based on a data-driven approach is:

> *If* you have a high fever
> *Then* you are ill.

> You have a high fever.
> Hence, you are ill.

A *rule-driven* approach may feature induction, deduction, or abduction.[8] *Induction* is generalization. The scientist discovers by induction:

> Bubi is a dog.
> Dogs are mammals.
>
> Hence, there must be a class of mammals.

The rule driven approach can lead to sideways chaining.

Deduction elicits the consequences of a given statement:

> Birds have two legs.
> The sparrow is a bird.
>
> Hence, it has two legs.

An inference that proceeds from more to less abstract (more detailed) statements is *model oriented.* A model system looks at all states in a coordinated manner, *integrating* top-level rules with middle- and lower-level ones. This can be achieved by combining states into a tree or by addressing values which are below or above a reference factor. Model-driven AI systems try to model the real world by defining entities, their attributes, and the relationships between entities. This is the function of a model, as Chapter 4 will explain.

Another AI approach deals with objects, attributes, and relationships between objects. For an explanation, we can refer to the database management system (DBMS). A DBMS stores the same attributes for each instance of an entity, and the design of the database is rigid. It must be predefined. An object-oriented AI approach can be flexible and dynamic.

An *object-oriented* knowledgebank can store different attributes for different instances of an object. The attributes of an object that are not explicitly stored can be inferenced when needed. This reduces the need to define a knowledgebank in advance and to adhere rigidly to certain standards.

The *model*-oriented and *object*-oriented methodologies lead to the concept of *inheritance.* Inheritance rests on the attributes of higher-level objects. By defining an inheritance hierarchy, we obtain a *taxonomy.* With this, it is possible for objects to inherit attributes and default values from higher levels in the hierarchy. The concept of *meta,* used to define higher levels of *knowledge about knowledge,* is part of this concept.

One of the advantages of the inheritance method is that if attributes are properly located within the hierarchy, redundancy can be avoided. It is also feasible to supply a detailed definition for lower-level objects without a lot of explanation. Hierarchies of definitions enable an AI system to reason about the structure of things, as well as to make generalizations—and hence, to use induction.

Goal-directed reasoning is basically deductive; it is also a paradigm familiar to conventional programmers, as it works much like a subroutine approach. The goal-directed system tries

---

[8] Induction, deduction, and abduction are treated in Chapter 12, Section 3. The following is only a brief introduction, as we need to define the induction and deduction processes in connection with rule-driven systems.

to determine the value of a variable, X. To do so, it looks for rules of the IF . . . THEN . . . ELSE type that yield a value for X. The IF condition of each rule that yields a value for X is evaluated to see if it is true. It is this evaluation of variables that resembles a subroutine call.

In an execution mode, the goal-directed system chains down until it finds an IF test for which the values are either known or can be found. When they are found, the system starts returning these values up the calling sequence. An example of a goal-driven syllogism is:

> *If* you stand on the ladder
> *Then* you can reach the grapes.
>
> You want to reach the grapes.
> Hence, you must stand on the ladder.

The chaining of value calculations can be compared to the way a spreadsheet works; it uses formulas instead of rules to define values. However, with AI systems,

- variables can have multiple values simultantously,
- the system maintains certainty factors for each of these values, and
- it allows the value of any variable to be unknown.

Reasoning based on hypotheses is a different matter altogether. It refers to a class of problem-solving approaches involving reasoning about future alternatives. This helps to determine the best sequence of steps for attaining a desired result. Reasoning based on hypotheses is proper to all planning premises. It involves generating plans, comparing their effectiveness, and executing. This approach permits us to search breadth or depth in an ordered fashion.

6. FORWARD CHAINING, BACKWARD CHAINING, AND OTHER METHODOLOGIES

The proper way to start the discussion on forward and backward chaining is to ask: "Is there one form of reasoning which can always be used?" The answer is "No." The next question may be: "How do mathematicians think?" The answer is that many mathematicians reason both forward and backward—though they may argue that reasoning backward has a much smaller search tree. We saw this when we spoke of the possible complexity of a data-driven approach.

Still another legitimate question is: "What *control strategies* have been employed with previous AI constructs?" The answers are many and different:

- For AM, the control strategy is to plan, generate, and test.
- R1 is data driven; there is no backtracking; the keyword is "match."
- EL uses forward reasoning, employs guesses when needed, and does relevant backtracking. The basis is priority-oriented, queue-type control.
- Dendral uses forward chaining.
- Mycin employs backward chaining through the rules.

The reference to Mycin is important because of its ability to refine the knowledgebank. It features a facility for interactive assimilation of new knowledge. When the user objects to a conclusion, Mycin walks through the rule tree with him to identify the source of disagreement. The user may modify an existing rule or add a new one. Further, Mycin uses statistical data that it gathers to suggest possible new rules. It also incorporates a method of structuring a person's knowledge about a problem. The construct asks: What is the primary object about which the expert system should offer advice? What are its parts and subparts? What are the attributes of these objects and their possible values? The construct then expects that the reasoning process will try to establish what value the attributes have.[9]

Other control strategies are least commitment (NOAH); constraint propagation and heuristic search (Molgen); event-driven, exhaustive search for each state and state-triggered expectation (VM); and forward reasoning with chaining representations (SYN). There is also a combination of top-down and bottom-up processing (Hearsay II), as well as a network editor and a grammar-driven command language (KAS).

These references demonstrate that there is no unique approach. But there is a need for chaining IF . . . THEN . . . ELSE rules to form a line of reasoning: If the chaining starts from a set of conditions and moves toward an even remote conclusion, the method is called *forward chaining*. Generally speaking, this has characterized the data-driven approach in the past.

Forward chaining is a natural direction for problem solving when data or ideas are a starting point. Hence, it has been used in expert systems for analysis, design, diagnosis, and concept formation. However, forward chaining is not necessarily a single approach. There are at least two techniques: *rules* and *constraint propagation*. Rules enable us to describe both *monotonic* (logical) and *nonmonotonic* (production system type) reasoning. In the former, the application of a rule to a set of descriptions only extends the knowledge bank with new facts. In the latter, modification of old descriptions is allowed. A viewpoint mechanism enables both cases to be handled the same way.

Most forward chaining systems

- *begin with a collection of premises* and
- *combine them* to produce an end result.

In several cases, the choice of direction for the system is made on the basis of how a person would solve the problem: If the conclusion is known or is a goal to be achieved, but the path is unknown, we work backwards. This method is *backward chaining*.

As stated in the preceding section, backward chaining has been the typical solution for goal-oriented approaches. This method performs deductions directed to reaching a certain goal. A goal is temporarily asserted in the knowledgebank as a fact to be demonstrated. Goals can be asserted either by the system, in attempting to satisfy the premises of some rule, or by the user. If a goal has been demonstrated, it is converted into a fact.

---

[9] More precisely, these are characteristics of EMycin.

Most backward-chaining systems are used for diagnostic purposes:

- *They begin with a goal,* for example, a list of symptoms to explain, and
- *try to discover* what premises (conditions) would cause the goal (symptoms) to be true.

Backward chaining is more applicable when a hypothesis or goal is the starting point. For instance, in planning situations, backward chaining works *from goals to subgoals* by using the action side of rules to deduce the condition side of these rules. Mycin, for instance, has predominantly a backward-chaining mechanism. But it is flexible. It can interrupt backward chaining and go to forward chaining—or vice versa.

We can also use a *combination* of forward and backward processing, particularly when the search space is large. Figure 3-7 suggests the usage of both forward and backward chaining to exploit a global database search and deep knowledge capabilities.

There is, as well, *sideways chaining,* also called the *rule value* approach. It uses neither forward nor backward chaining solutions but instead focuses on evidence:

- For each item of evidence, it assigns a value.
- This is the value of this rule in the process of inference.
- Then it first asks the question with the highest value.

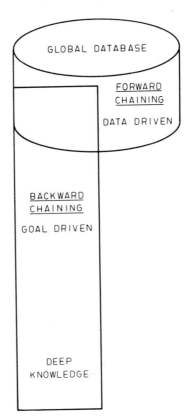

Figure 3-7. This figure is taken from a project which associated forward chaining with global database implementation of expert systems and backward chaining with deep knowledge constructs.

A search is made in the more promising branches to the deeper level. In a nutshell, the *alpha-beta procedure* works as follows:

- when max-position ≤ alpha; alpha cutoff
- when min-position ≥ beta; beta cutoff

In a number of cases, *search algorithms* are very important. The search algorithm that the designer follows may vary from one case to another. *AI searching* can take the following forms:

- *Best-first search.* In this method, the AI system applies a heuristic function to the nodes of a logical network. It does so at each step in order to choose the one most likely to lead to the desired solution.
- *Depth-first search.* The nodes are reached in order from the initial node down in a given path until either the answer is found or the search goes below a predetermined depth bound.
- *Hill climbing.* This method provides an AI system with ways to overcome conditions such as backtracking, trying a path that was declined before, or applying more than one rule before evaluating the result. The construct may do so in order to jump to a different part of the search space.
- *Branch-and-bound search.* At each step, the shortest of the uncompleted paths under consideration is extended one level until a solution is found to the problem.
- *Algorithm search.* This procedure is a refinement of branch-and-bound search. Rather than choosing the shortest path to expand, the estimate of the distance left to the goal is added to each path before expanding.
- *Beam search.* The AI construct proceeds horizontally before moving down a level, as in best-first search. However, in beam search, the path moves down only from the best nodes at each level.
- *Means-ends analysis.* Some search systems use the difference between the goal state and the current state to guide the search. When a difference is identified, a subgoal is generated to eliminate that difference.

The lack of fundamental theories for selecting the best strategy to attack a given problem is partly due to the fact that during the last ten years very few theoretical advances have occurred. Basic research to develop more elegant approaches is relatively lacking, and this evidently affects AI systems development.

4

Prototyping, Modeling, Testing

Keywords

prototype · *conceptual modeling* · *simulation* · *imprecise facts* · *undertainty* · *user-driven design* · *technology-driven design* · *evolutionary prototyping* · *beliefs* · *models* · *qualitative relationships* · *quantitative relationships* · *analysis* · *analogy* · *metaphor* · *syntactic matching* · *experimental treatment* · *inference* · *test of hypothesis* · *producer's risk* · *consumer's risk* · *operating characteristics curves* · *scientific principle* · *variables* · *experiments* · *experimental design* · *Latin squares* · *computation of variance* · *analysis of variance* · *internal testing* · *class nature* · *external testing* · *quality control* · *quality* · *evaluation* · *shells*

1. INTRODUCTION

A *prototype* is an *unproven, imperfect machine.* It is also a very useful platform, as it provides us with a workbench on which we can experiment with ideas, concretize our thoughts, test our design, make rapid modifications, and improve the AI construct we develop. Prototypes are *conceptual modeling* instruments. As such, they relate to all areas of computer science, especially AI, databases, and programming languages. Indeed, conceptual modeling is a topic in itself rather than a secondary aspect of data modeling or digital simulation, though it is closely related to both data modeling and simulation.

Research on knowledge acquisition, the methodologies for knowledge representation, the development of rules, semantic networks, and data abstraction is using an increasing amount of prototyping. Prototyping is also used for the integration of results—and is thus part of knowledge representation. However, there is no general agreement on what is meant by a prototype. Some people consider mere screen and report mockups a prototype. Others mean a simulation where data can be entered, fed back, and manipulated. Mockups and simulations can be valuable, as they give much better indications than paper layouts and charts. But they miss the full potential benefits of prototyping.

In contrast to traditional DP, the AI prototype supplies a rapid solution to the whole or a part of the problem—at a cost. The cost is machine cycles, but a good prototype can be delivered early in the process of development. Experience teaches that at that stage it is often necessary to have a view of the application. A good prototype is

- small enough to implement,
- large enough to impress,
- cheap enough to get funded, and
- urgent enough to get a commitment.

Successive incremental prototypes provide another benefit: The AI system can be put into use far earlier than conventional DP programs. For instance, a carefully constructed expert system can be useful even at the 30% completion level, provided that a working prototype is available. This is particularly true of the human window of the AI system. The user interface is an environment that permits effective designer–user dialogue in a quasi-natural language. We should pay attention to it. Lessons learned about screen and report presentation can easily be extended to the whole system. We can use the prototype to draw conclusions about system performance, operability, and feasibility.

Depending on the implementation, the prototype may come close to real data, real processing, and real screens. It is a full system. However, it is very inefficient in terms of processing—and therefore in machine cycles and in response time. In other cases, the prototype may be a less than complete real system. This rests on Pareto's law, the 80/20 rule that 80% of operational requirements will be met by 20% of the system.

A major benefit of fast prototyping is that the AI system is able to demonstrate its potential usefulness (and limitations) before a lot of resources have been committed to it. A project that clearly will not produce the required return on investment can be stopped before it becomes very costly. Another benefit of prototyping is the ability to focus on tools. To develop design specifications for an AI project, we need tools that allow us to establish and maintain an effective dialogue with the knowledgebank, the global database, and other computer resources.

As emphasized throughout this book, it is vital that the AI construct maintain an online, interactive link with other computer applications. Hence, the prototype should be designed to account for interactions at the user–host, host–node, switching node, and other interface levels. It should also be constructed in a modular manner so that the prototype can be altered easily without affecting the other layers of the communications system.

Today, valid and useful expert systems are typically networked. The communications engine itself may be subject to prototyping. If so, the model program should focus on data links and transport activities, on session and presentation control, channel throughout, channel traffic, mode-dependent transmission delays (message or packet), expected length of various node queues, reliability and availability, delay/throughput, and other traffic characteristics. We should be keen to prototype the network and the AI constructs which run on it.

The preceding discussion underlines the fact that AI prototyping should not be limited to the level of a simple logical construct. It is the whole project, rather than only its motor, which should be considered—with each critical problem being modeled and then solved. No system is better than its weakest link.

2. PROTOTYPING AS A DESIGN TOOL

Prototyping is a natural tool for AI application development. Prototyping concepts have long been used in engineering. As software development is a form of engineering, the concept should be transferable.

We have spoken about knowledge acquisition and representation as means of obtaining specifications, and in Chapter 2 we emphasized the need to employ online tools. Many experts don't describe their know-how until they have gained experience with the finished system. Prototyping is intended to involve the expert in the development process from the beginning—doing so in an optimal way when the system is online and interactive. With prototyping, expert-generated ideas about rules, features, and functions are incorporated into a working model. The model itself is a system. As the expert responds to the model and the way it works, improvements can be made.

Does the last statement confuse the difference between *prototyping* and *modeling,* as well as the implementation of one or the other? People who function as pure theorists and have never developed real-life systems would say "Yes." Unfortunately, they miss the point: Between these two concepts (and their implementation) there is really no difference.

A model is a working system typically developed for prototyping reasons. It permits simulation of a system:

- Preoperating it,
- pinpointing its strengths and weaknesses,
- and correcting it quickly and inexpensively.

A simulation is a working analogy. When we have two systems, one of which can be mapped into the other, we use the simpler system (model, prototype) to study the more complex one, learn from experiments, and immediately apply what we have learned. This is why, when it is ably used, prototyping is a valuable approach; ultimately, the model becomes a close representation of what the expert does. In this sense, prototyping functions as an aid in rapid development—as well as acting as an interactive design tool.

The most effective way to get commitment for an AI project is not to carry out an interminable and absurd feasibility study, but to create an prototype of a possible application and show how it works. *Rapid prototyping* can win acceptance. However, it should be kept in mind that the prototype is not necessarily a suitable base on which to build a well-engineered and usable commercial product—though the temptation to throw away the prototype and start anew is just as wrong.

The process of prototyping in AI is explained in Figure 4-1. It starts with facts, states, and values. *Facts* and *states* create the *domain; values* are recorded in connection to such facts and are typically called *data.* Our goal is to model a situation by idealizing it. Hence:

- Phase 1 of prototyping is data abstraction.
- Once we have abstracted data, we apply a heuristic tool (Phase 2).

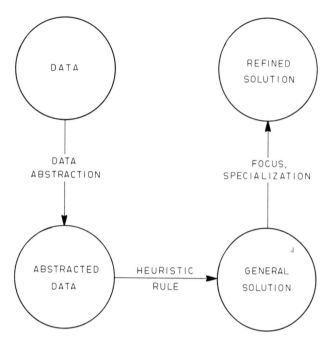

Figure 4-1. Simulation and expert systems have a methodological infrastructure, as can be seen by comparing this figure with Figure 4-2.

- The implementation of heuristic rules leads to a general solution.
- Subsequently, we operate on this heuristic solution using focusing and special-ization.
- The result is a refined solution.

As underlined in the preceding paragraphs, prototyping a heuristic approach has a strong resemblance to *simulation.* Therefore we can apply nearly three decades of experience to the simulation domain. The resemblance is shown by comparing Figures 4-1 and 4-2.

The simulation process in Figure 4-2 starts with the real world, which is subjected to a process of abstraction. The result is an idealized model which uses algorithms rather than heuristics. An algorithm is a precise description of the computational process leading from variable input data to desired (information) results. The simulator may also be a heuristic or a probabilistic model. Through extrapolation, interpolation, or some other process, we obtain the results of the experiment. Often, it is a very good approximation and, as stated, it serves as a useful design tool.

Because of the benefits of this method, prototyping is being increasingly used, particu-larly in relation to frame-like objects. Other prototyping applications center on inexact reasoning:

- Bayes' theorem,
- empirical approaches such as belief/disbelief, and
- new theoretical approaches ranging from possibility theory to Shafer's belief theory.

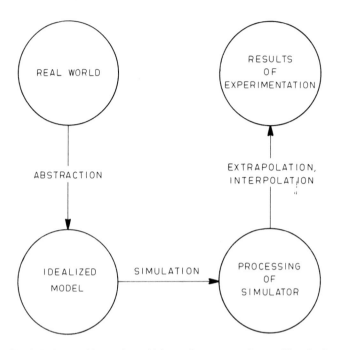

Figure 4-2. Simulation is a working analogy which permits us to experiment without having to build a new physical model every time we change our hypothesis. Simulation can enrich heuristic rules but can also serve as a complementary module to heuristic solutions.

Possibility theory can express *imprecise facts* as well as *uncertainty*. Some projects with goal-oriented prototypes have introduced the concepts of concurrent statistical sampling to produce timely and efficient analyses of the simulated events. The simulator collects only those data that are relevant to the current questions. As soon as the simulator completes the relevant computations, a desired results is being produced. Usually the simulator will be run a statistically significant number of times to provide a sample of observations.

Once we have developed the prototype, what next? The prototype can, among other things, be a superbly effective channel of domain expert–knowledge engineer communication. Together these experts can do a formal review of the prototype and document the lessons learned.

It is relatively easy to just demonstrate the prototype. But

- a one-way process fails to obtain and exploit expert feedback, and
- the prototype review must be two way, including structured documentation.

Figure 4-3 shows the contribution of the feedback system, which provides well both quality and accuracy. There is value in getting feedback in time to be able to use it and build AI systems reflecting it, rather than obtaining feedback when the final version is installed. At that point, it is too late and too expensive to make changes.

We will talk about AI system testing at the end of this chapter. A prototype is itself

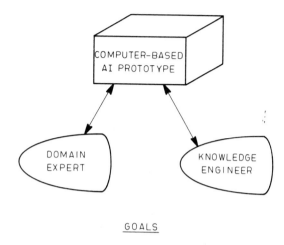

GOALS

1. MODELING: ABSTRACTION, CONCRETIZATION,
                PREDECISION

2. TESTING: SYSTEMS STRUCTURE, INFERENCE
                MECHANISM, FUNCTIONALITY, HUMAN
                WINDOW

Figure 4-3. Modeling and testing are different goals, but both are served by computer-based prototypes and can be exploited by the knowledge engineer and the computer expert.

subject to testing. The prototype review process needs to be well organized and can become a major logistical exercise.

Prototyping supports a concept of *user-* rather than *technology-driven design,* which should be the cornerstone of AI constructs. Keep in mind that a prototype is not a theoretical system. It is a working model which can be implemented on the machine for the environment for which it has been conceived.

Provided that prototyping is specific to the job, and not a generality, the advantages include the following:

1. Interactive development
2. Short implementation timetables
3. What you see is what you get (WYSIWYG)
4. High-quality end product
5. High productivity of domain experts and knowledge engineers
6. Easy domain expert–knowledge engineer communication
7. Able use of human resources

Though it is not free of cost, in the long run prototyping provides a feeling of involvement and saves time by helping to debug the projected AI system. It both clarifies the critical dimensions of the problem and increases satisfaction. Involvement and participation greatly improve the developer–user relationship.

When we prototype an application, we learn its parameters. We also know what resources are available and, since we have started putting the proper tools in place, chances are good that the prototype itself will tell us how long it should take to develop the system. Thus, through prototyping, we create a sense of control and ownership on the part of both domain experts and knowledge engineers—though for different reasons.

The transition from prototype to operational system can be handled in two ways. Some projects throw away the prototype, keeping the system dictionary, which contains the real investment of the prototyping effort. The result is the need to rebuild. It has the benefit of avoiding compromises on requirements that result from keeping or slightly changing what was done in the prototype. Starting afresh leads to better systems, and that is exactly what is required for successful operations.

By contrast, many AI projects prefer to modify and extend the prototype, modifying it toward the final system. This saves work already done but can lead to design compromises. Organizations which upgrade the prototype to a fully functional system talk of *evolutionary prototyping*. This method can be entirely appropriate for one-shot AI systems, but it is not appropriate for commercial environments.

There is another major factor to keep in mind. It is based on two different but related subjects:

- the shell in which the prototype is written.[1]
- the machine on which it runs.

Many companies use symbolic machines (Symbolics, TI Explorer) for prototyping. Such machines are expensive, and by now obsolete. Typically, they cost upward of $100,000. We cannot afford to give such expensive equipment to every professional who will work with the AI system. Either the AI construct should run on a personal WS on a dedicated basis or since the PC is networked it should use a supercomputer server for number crunching.

A similar point can be made about shells—the typical prototyping tool. As we will see in the next chapter, the better shells run on larger computers. Shells at the WS level may have some of the characteristics needed for prototyping, but not the full power. Therefore, for portability reasons, rewriting may be necessary. When this is so (and I am only speaking of WS), then the choice of C as a programming language is advisable.[2]

Even if reprogramming proves necessary, the prototype of the AI construct has many benefits. The original domain expert, as well as those who will test it, sign off a specification that they understand, having seen it in operation. This specification consists of words backing up a picture, rather than words attempting to describe an unseen program, as is the case with typical DP methodology.

---

[1] See Chapters 5, 6, and 7.
[2] The choice of using shells on a WS, but accepting a slower response time vs. reprogramming in C, depends on the type of application as well as the number of systems to be installed in the organization and the expected payoff. Generalizations are meaningless and can be dangerous.

3. THE CONCEPT OF
MODELING

Modeling AI includes the treatment of such apparently unscientific concepts as *beliefs* and *purposes*. This is important to prototyping on at least two different levels: (1) for better understanding of logical inference systems and (2) in modeling as such, which is a recurring issue when different aspects of AI projects (particularly man–machine interfaces) are considered.

For reasons explained in this chapter, it is crucial to develop testable models. However, not every logical phenomenon can be reduced to a testable form or subjected to an intelligent behavioral criterion, since neither our concepts nor our tools are yet quite ready for focused modeling in the AI domain. Testable models are designed implementation in the physical sciences. An explanation of modeling in the sciences in general is therefore important.

We have said that prototyping is modeling. A *model* is a statement of a law of behavior. Within the phenomenon that the law of behavior is supposed to represent, we should expect the model to predict future real-life situations. That is the concept of experimentation. It remains valid

- if these situations are governed by the mathematical law used in model F and
- if the population of values (data) does not change significantly to make the model invalid.

The major *challenges in developing models* are to conceptualize the idealized form, understand the sense of approximation, and distinguish the relevant parts from the irrelevant ones. It is also necessary to separate the significant effects from the insignificant ones, summarize and/or discriminate if the same reason accounts for more than one result, and translate quantitative data into qualitative information. The ultimate challenge is to apply the experimental results to real-world situations.

Inasmuch as it involves abstraction and identification, interpreting is modeling. Figure 4-4 presents a reference model with data structures from computer-aided design (CAD). It involves geometric modeling, product data definition, a graphics kernel, picture transformation, and man–machine interactive module. The interpreter acts as a shell. CAD without modeling support is inconceivable.

In CAD as in AI projects, the goal of mapping is to transform a *base domain* into a *target domain*—for instance, mapping engineering design into manufacturing processes or mapping manufacturing processes into field maintenance action. Similarly, a financial model is a representation of the activities of a business in terms of *qualitative* and *quantitative* relationships. Such a representation reflects the key variables of the business, of the economy, or of subsets thereof. The use of a financial model helps us to understand the financial consequence of possible decisions. It also controls past activities. The equations comprising such models form part of the knowledgebank. Users benefit from two sorts of explanations:

1. about the model itself, and
2. about the results of the model.

CONSTRUCTIVE SOLID GEOMETRY

BOUNDARY REPRESENTATION

CALLS FOR PRIMITIVES OR BUILDING
BLOCKS

THE APPROACH FOLLOWS THE CONCEPT
OF STICK-TOGETHER SURFACES

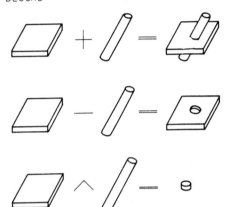

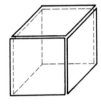

WE DEFINE A NEW PRIMITIVE THROUGH
BOOLEAN EXPRESSION

Figure 4-4. A reference module with finite elements from CAD. Notice how graphics modeling can be achieved through boolean expressions.

Similar statements can be made about other decision support systems (DSSs) for management. Modeling enhances the goal of DSS, which is to assist in *analyses* related to decision-making tasks: forecasting, planning, directing, controlling, reporting. The same can be said of expert systems, but at a higher level of sophistication.

In all these examples, modeling is necessary. This is particularly true when a combination of human judgment and automation can effectively use one or more procedures which have already been implemented:

- "what if" analysis
- ad hoc analysis
- monitoring of business operations
- global information access and analytical queries

Because the user expects first-class service, prototyping is increasingly including non-procedural approaches. While the cycle shown in Figure 4-5 remains valid, the challenge becomes one of solving logical problems by analogy to past AI problem solutions. This challenge can be phrased in two short sentences:

- Find the analogies.
- Match them.

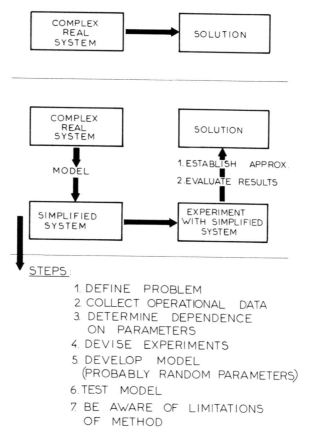

Figure 4-5. When we are unable to go from the complex real-life system to the solution, then we use a model, which is a simplified system, and experiment with it to reach the solution.

The term *analogy,* as used in this context, refers to the similarity between base and target, source and object. Analogy leads to a *metaphor* which can be applied in:

- knowledge representation,
- syntactic matching and graph matching, and
- mapping and interactive mapping.

It makes little difference if knowledge is represented in the form of hierarchical (tree) structures or object clustering for purposes of pattern recognition, natural language understanding, loan evaluation, medical diagnosis, or engineering system configuration. But while computational analogies are necessary, they are not enough. With many AI projects we also need syntactic matching.

Syntactic matching is a term with several implementation references, including matching nodes (tree isomorphism); deviations from high quality; judging similarities between nodes;

and background knowledge in matching trees and forests. Among the problems we face in syntactic matching are:

- time and cost
- multiplicity
- inconsistency
- the worst case.

Positional association and translation are required to achieve a syntactic matching application. At the current state of the art, there are no real formal specifications. Analogy is empirical, and matchers use heuristic criteria.

Whether in CAD, in finance, or in DSS, the acid test for the matcher is:

- Definition of tolerance and
- Definition of acceptance/rejection

We have seen an example from quality control with charting in Figure 1-4. The concept is portable, and the message is that we have tools for these processes: mathematical statistics. Statistical experimentation should be seen as basic in AI. The three main features of the scientific method are

1. the performance of experiments,
2. the drawing of objective conclusions from experiments, and
3. the construction of laws to simplify the description of the conclusions of large classes of experiments.

The *old* approach in science distinguishes between theoretical and empirical solutions. The *new* approach distinguishes among three alternatives: theoretical, experimental, and empirical—with emphasis the last. *Experimental treatment* is the combination and testing of the experimental factors which must be compared. Experimental results are reported in terms of frequencies, mean, standard deviation, analysis of variance, correlation coefficients, factorial analysis, and tests of the hypothesis.

Just as design is portable in many diverse domains, so is testing. The object is to ensure that the end product conforms to the original specifications:

- If the specifications are the result of the domain expert's thinking, know-how and decision making, then the product to be tested is the result of knowledge acquisition.
- If the specifications are the outcome of knowledge acquisition, then the product to be tested is knowledge representation. It can occur in stages, from methodology to mapping into the machine.

To test successfully, we need inference. The term *inference* had been used in science long before it was applied to AI projects. While inference is achieved through a number of statistical tools, the term is used particularly in connection with the testing of hypothesis: *We test a decision made against the actual situation.* For instance, the actual quality of a manufactured product (acceptable/unacceptable) can be tested against the decision made (accept/reject).

We have said that a hypothesis is a tentative statement. The *test of a hypothesis* rests on six well-established rules:

1. Define the communication system.
2. State the level of acceptability.
3. Perform N (random) trials.
4. Classify each trial as a success or a failure.
5. Count the number of failures.
6. Select the decision on the basis of a (statistical) rule.

As Figure 4-6 demonstrates, we have four quarter spaces defined by the null hypothesis (H_0) and the alternative hypothesis (H_1) under conditions of the actual situation and the decision made. If in a quality control application the decision is H_0, then we reject a lot which should have been accepted. This is known as *producer's risk* or Type I error. By contrast, if we accept a lot when we should have rejected it (decision H_0, actual H_1), then we have a *consumer's risk* or Type II error. There are also two quarter spaces where the decision is correct. In either case, an inference has been made.

This statistical quality control plan is known as *operating characteristics (OC) curves*. It is a powerful tool in AI and is particularly applicable where an outgoing quality level and a lot tolerance percentage defective can be established.

In science, whenever we reject, we do so for good reasons. Hence, we are fairly sure of what we do. When we accept, our action is motivated by the fact that we have no reasons for

		DECISION MADE	
		H_0: ACCEPTABLE	H_1: NOT ACCEPTABLE
ACTUAL STATE OF QUALITY	H_0: ACCEPTABLE	CORRECT	ERROR
	H_1: NOT ACCEPTABLE	ERROR	CORRECT

H_0: THE INSPECTION LOT IS OF ACCEPTABLE QUALITY

H_1: THE INSPECTION LOT IS BELOW ACCEPTABLE QUALITY

Figure 4-6. The test of a hypothesis is one of the most basic procedures in mathematical statistics as well as in knowledge engineering. Any such test regards the null hypothesis, H_0, vs. the alternative hypothesis, H_1.

rejection. We are less sure of what we do. Acceptance is *only tentative*. This should be kept in mind in every testing situation. The *basic scientific principles* are as follows:

> *If* the experimentation indicates that something is erroneous,
> *Then* I have evidence that it is erroneous.
> *If* experimentation indicates that something is *not* erroneous,
> *Then* I have *no* evidence to determine whether it is erroneous or correct.

This looks like an AI construct; that is no coincidence. Let's repeat the premise to ensure that it is well understood. The philosophy of testing is portable among disciplines, and we are far more sure when we *reject* than when we *accept* a hypothesis, a fact, a process, or an object.

4. LEARNING EXPERIMENTAL DESIGN

Alan Rowe is correct when he insists that teaching only the mathematics of knowledge engineering is the wrong approach. Not only does the knowledge engineer need a well-rounded background to do a valid job; the heart of his work has to do with *variables,* and therefore with *experiments*. The teaching of knowledge engineering, Rowe says, must include applied experimental psychology and experimental design.

Let's return to the fundamentals. AI systems involve variables, sometimes many. Variables can cause trouble. Because of their interaction, the situation can get out of hand. To control a large number of variables, statistics offers us the discipline of *experimental design*. I have not applied it to AI, but have done so several times with engineering problems. Let's follow a complete example with *Latin squares*.

Consider four different designs for a dial. We want to evaluate them for readability, so we have four persons read each dial—a total of 16 tests. Suppose that each reading is to be made under four conditions of lighting. To get every possible combination, we now need 64 measurements. In addition, several sets of data may be required for representative results. Obviously, some method of reducing the number of measurements without forcing us to rely on mere guesswork would save time and money.

Latin squares provide just such a method. Their name is derived from an ancient puzzle: How many ways can Latin letters be arranged in a square table so that each letter appears once and only once in each row and column?

Setting up a Latin square is only one step in this variables-handling procedure. It is followed by two standard statistical techniques:

1. To compute the variation in readibility caused by the experimental conditions.
2. To decide which conditions should be considered important in the final design.

The Latin square method can be applied to a wide variety of design situations.

To express the foregoing example in terms of a definite design problem, suppose that the four dials represent proposed designs for aircraft altimeters: straight horizontal scale (II), straight vertical scale (V), round dial (R), and semicircular dial (S). They are to be read by

TABLE 4-1. Design for a Latin Square
Implementation.

Lighting	H	V	R	S
		Dials		
I	W	X	Y	Z
A	Z	W	X	Y
B	Y	Z	W	X
L	X	Y	Z	W

four pilots (W, X, Y, Z) under four lighting conditions: high (I), above average (A), below average (B), and low (L). By experimenting, we hope to determine what effect dial design, lighting, and pilot have on accuracy of reading when the same reading time is allowed.

To program the experiment, we draw a gridded square with a row for each condition of lighting, a column for each dial design, and letters for the pilots assigned to cells in the square by one of several techniques (Table 4-1). To prevent their reappearing in a row or column, the letters are simply rotated one step as the rows are filled in from top to bottom. Another method is to use a table of random numbers. There are 576 possible arrangements of letters for a 4 × 4 Latin square and 161.280 for a 5 × 5 square.

A basic assumption with Latin squares is that the experimental conditions are indeptndent of each other. That is, dial design and astigmatism of the operator may affect the accuracy of the reading, but it is assumed that they have no dependent effect on each other. This assumption allows us to eliminate many combinations because row and column treatments balance; no letter appears twice in any row or column. Thus, 16 tests take the place of 64, with little sacrifice of statistical reliability.

With the Latin square as a guide, a dial reading is taken for each combination of pilot, lighting, and dial, and the percent error is written in the appropriate space. Columns and rows are summed at the bottom and side. Readings are repeated several times to avoid stray errors. And to reduce the "learning effect," altimeters are set differently for each reading.

A glance at Table 4-2 reveals some informative trends. Lighting seems to have the greatest effect on error. But how much effect does it have, and what is the assurance that this is not simply a chance effect? In another example, the trends might not be so clear-cut

TABLE 4-2. Experimental Values from
the Latin Squares Test.

Lighting	H	V	R	S	Sum
			Dials		
I	1.2	1.3	1.8	2.1	6.4
A	0.9	1.1	2.0	1.6	5.6
B	1.9	2.4	3.6	3.6	11.2
L	3.6	3.2	5.4	4.6	16.8
Sum	7.6	8.0	12.8	11.6	40.0

or the square might be so large that trends would be masked. Statistical analysis, then, is the only way of coming to a final reliable conclusion. The analysis has two parts: *computation of variance* and *analysis of variance*.

Variance is a statistical computation that shows scatter about the mean: how individual values spread out from the average. The *mean* is the arithmetic mean:

$$\bar{x} = \frac{\Sigma x_i}{n}$$

where x_i is the value of each reading and n is the number of readings. But simply adding plus and minus variations from this mean will always give zero. *Variance* is computed by squaring the variation from the mean for each reading, adding the values together, and then dividing by the number of readings less one:

$$s^2 \frac{\Sigma(x_i - \bar{x})^2}{n - 1}$$

This is more commonly written

$$s^2 = \frac{\Sigma x_i^2 - \dfrac{\Sigma(x_i)^2}{n}}{n - 1}$$

because it does not involve actual computation of the arithmetic mean.

The denominator, $n - 1$, is called *degrees of freedom (df)*. To illustrate the meaning of this statistical term, assume that a series of 10 variables ($a, b, c, \ldots$) have a fixed mean value, 5. Any value can be chosen arbitrarily for 9 of the variables, but the 10th cannot be picked at random. There is only one value for the 10th variable that can cause the mean to be 5. Thus, there are 9 degrees of freedom—one less than the number of variables.

For convenience, the numerator of the variation equation is computed first. The sum of the squared values of all 16 entries in the table is

$$(1.2)^2 + (0.9)^2 \cdots + (4.6)^2 - \frac{(40)^2}{16} = 26.38$$

This is followed by summing for columns and rows, but now it is the sum of each column and row (not of the entries) that is squared and then divided by the number of readings it represents:

Dials (columns)

$$\frac{(7.6)^2}{4} + \frac{(8.0)^2}{4} + \frac{(12.8)^2}{4} + \frac{(11.6)^2}{4} - \frac{(40)^2}{16} = 4.9$$

Lighting (rows)

$$\frac{(6.4)^2}{4} + \frac{(5.6)^2}{4} + \frac{(11.2)^2}{4} + \frac{(16.8)^2}{4} - \frac{(40)^2}{16} = 19.0$$

And choosing values from the table for *pilots:*

$$\frac{(10.5)^2}{4} + \frac{(10.2)^2}{4} + \frac{(8.5)^2}{4} + \frac{(10.8)^2}{4} - \frac{(40)^2}{16} = 1.12$$

The values for the column-and-row sum of squares are subtracted from the total sum of squares to give the residual sum of squares. This is the scatter that represents experimental error:

$$26.38 - 4.9 - 19.0 - 1.12 = 1.35$$

Each sum of squares has 3 degrees of freedom (4 variables); the total sum of squares has 15 degrees of freedom (16 variables). The residual degrees of freedom is $15 - (3 + 3 + 3) = 6$. Standard statistical practice is to show values for the sum of squares and degrees of freedom in tabular form for convenience in further computation.

The sums of squares in Table 4-3 measure how much each experimental condition causes variation from the mean reading error. They show, for example, that lighting causes the most variations—a sum-of-squares variation of 19. From this, it might be concluded that changes in lighting have more effect on reading error than either of the other two experimental conditions. But what is the probability of this much variation occurring by chance?

Analysis of variance is, in part, an investigation of this chance effect. Before performing the experiment, a level of significance ( ) was chosen. This value sets a limit for allowable variation about the mean. If, for example, a level of $\alpha = 0.05$ (commonly used in statistical experiments of this kind) is chosen, it means that variations with less than a 5% possibility of occurring by chance will be accepted as meaningful variations. Thus, there is a 5% possibility of being wrong (simply a chance variation that is not so meaningful) and a 95% possibility of being right.

Statistical tables are available that give values that can be compared with sum-of-squares values. Suppose that $\alpha = 0.05$ and we wish to find what variation is meaningful at an 0.05 level of significance. The ratio of lighting sum of squares to residual (or error) sum of squares, divided by corresponding degrees of freedom, gives an F ratio of

$$\frac{19.00}{3} \times \frac{6}{1.35} = 28.13$$

The statistical tables give an F ratio of 8.94 for an α of 0.05, where there are 6 degrees of freedom in the numerator and 3 degrees of freedom in the denominator. Thus, any ratio of 8.94 has only a 5% possibility of occurring by chance and any ratio larger than 8.94 has less than a 5% possibility of being wrong by chance.

We conclude that lighting variation is significant because a variation of 28.13 has less than

TABLE 4-3. **Variation in Lighting Caused by Experimental Conditions.**

	Squares	df
Dials (columns)	4.90	3
Lighting (rows)	19.00	3
Pilots	1.12	3
Residual (error)	1.35	6
Total	26.38	15

TABLE 4-4. Variation in the Other Variables.

	Sum of Squares	df	Mean Square	F Ratio	5% Ratio
Dials (columns)	4.90	3	1.63	7.25	8.94
Lighting (rows)	19.00	3	6.33	28.13	8.94
Subjects	1.12	3	0.374	1.66	8.94
Residual (error)	1.35	6	0.225		
Total	26.38	15			

a 5% probability of happening by chance. The other experimental conditions are examined the same way (Table 4-4).

Most statisticians agree that a level of $\alpha = 0.05$ is sufficient to judge experimental effects which are *significant,* while a level of 0.01 is commonly referred to as *highly significant.* However, choosing a very low level ($\alpha = 0.001$) not only decreases the possibility of judging chance effects as significant but also increases the possibility of neglecting a truly significant variation.

The experiment shows that lighting in this example is the only experimental effect causing a significant variation in reading error at the 5% level. Remember experimental design when you are analyzing domain variables.

5. INTERNAL TESTING
OF AN AI SYSTEM

We have said that one of the major advantages of prototyping is testing and evaluation of the AI system. While validation has attracted a certain amount of attention, evaluation has not yet been properly addressed. Yet a sound theory exists: Feedback can provide the needed infrastructure.

A feedback process enables evaluation whereby the comments serve as a basis for iterative refinements of the AI construct. I call this process *internal testing.* Domain experts help determine the *accuracy* of

1. the embedded knowledge and
2. any advice or conclusions that the system provides.

Evaluations by other experts who will be the users also help determine the *utility* of the system—that is, whether it produces useful results, the extent of its capabilities, its ease of interaction, the intelligibility of its responses, and its reliability.

Feedback theory may be of assistance if we know how to apply it. We can introduce an expert system component into the feedback loop. The approach works best if we test module by module. Serious testing should start at the level of the first module and then proceed to cover the whole prototype. Validation can be made by playback, subjecting the values of parameters to a formal statistical test, feeding values back into a system to study behavior and measure discrepancies. Metrics is important in validation.

Statistical tests are effective only if objective have been decided; the boundaries of the systems have been determined; and the domains have been correctly classified. In seeking algorithmic solutions, the *class nature* of the algorithm should be observed. Other requirements are that

- the pertinent variables have been chosen,
- the hypothesis of interaction has been formulated, and
- a decision has been made about what constitutes passing the statistical test of the parameter value.

Testing a system means defining the system, stating the hypothesis, and selecting a typical portion:

- Random sample
- Representative part
- Model construction

The next steps consist of the experiment, observing and recording the results, and subjecting the results to a (statistical) test. Finally, one decides, on the basis of the test's outcome, whether the system is or is not operating (constructed, functioning) at an acceptable quality level.

Model testing is not a new discipline. We know from engineering that the most useful models will be constructed by those who

- know the actual system and
- have the background to describe it and evaluate it.

The main purpose of comparing a model and a real system—in this case the AI prototype vs. the domain knowledge and the expert's rules—is to show that we can match the behavior of an existing system. We also know from engineering that even if designed by an expert, a model needs to be tested.

Evaluation is not the same as validation. *Validation* is the determination of the correctness of the software produced by a development project. It focuses on the user's needs and requirements. The validation process analyzes software to determine the extent to which it performs the logical functions it is intended to do. Evaluation focuses on the *accuracy* of the software, though it may also concentrate on utility. Validation asks whether the correct problem was solved. Evaluation measures accuracy and usefulness.

Evaluation not only is a different process from validation, it is also subjective as well as objective. We are looking for gaps in knowledge—among other things, missing constraints. Rules may turn out to be applicable in the wrong circumstances, or they may overlap. If so, they will lead to inconsistent or redundant conclusions. A conflict resolution system must be built, because in an AI construct, rules interact in unexpected ways. During evaluation, we should also account for the fact that at some stage new rules can be added to several parts of the construct. The knowledge engineer must account for this eventuality, which has a probability nearly equal to 1.0.

The possible future addition of new rules to the construct affects both validation and evaluation. For validation reasons, whenever a change is made to the construct, it must be propagated throughout all parts of it. The knowledge engineer must find all the associated changes that are necessary. There is no better way to assist him than by maintaining computer documentation online. The knowledge engineer should never lose his understanding of the knowledgebank as a whole.

Subtle and hidden assumptions concealed in the order in which rules are listed should be brought under control. When this is done, changes to the rule base have effects which can be foretold. Otherwise, such effects cannot be foreseen.

A proper test of developed AI constructs should definitely involve domain experts other than the one who acted as consultant. That ensures logical debugging. Testing should begin early to obtain maximum feedback from the experts.

Evaluation is useful in determining whether the AI construct is meeting its requirements. It helps identify those issues that deviate from the original statement of goals. It can also help provide suggestions for refinement in

- the inference engine,
- the explanation facility, and
- consistency checking.

Logical debugging should take place following knowledge acquisition, after the first prototype (breadboard model) is done but prior to full knowledge representation. It is impossible to test the AI system for all combinations of its rules after it has reached a considerable level of complexity.

Logical debugging makes sense because, after the first prototype is done, there is a shift of key in the knowledge acquisition process. The expert can more easily supply the knowledge that should go into the system, since it is now embodied in a way we can observe and criticize. This approach to development through incremental testing of functions is demonstrated in Figure 4-7.

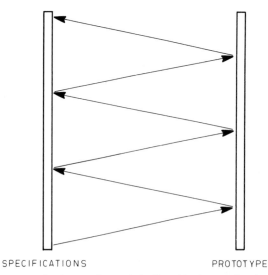

SPECIFICATIONS   PROTOTYPE

Figure 4-7. Expert systems development is greatly facilitated by the use of an interactive prototype which permits the incremental testing of different functions and modules, as well as of the final construct.

The testing done by the knowledge engineer should be paralleled by that of the domain expert. There is no reason why, if we add a new rule, all rules currently in the construct will work. We must check them regularly—and, whenever possible, automatically.

Logical bugs and faulty reasoning must be traced to their source. New knowledge that has already been chosen must be put into the structure without generating an unwanted behavior. The knowledge engineer must actively seek out deficiencies in the knowledge-bank to avoid contradictions and lack of coordination, or inconsistent or redundant conclusions.

The AI system's *constraint mechanism* can provide assistance. Constraints are a good way to *specify* and *supervise* relations. They help guarantee control—for instance, by revealing inconsistencies in assumptions.

The AI construct should know where the user is in his *input* and *goals* even if the user himself does not. That is another area where internal testing can be instrumental, supplementing what the constraint mechanism should do: Use the other expert's test to prove consistency.

A Mycin evaluation demonstrated 75% *correct* answers when contrasted to the answers of other experts. Is this score high or low? To answer this question, we need one more statistic. When other experts judged their peers on their opinions, they found many wrong opinions. As a result, Mycin's grading rose significantly. The fact remains, however, that, as I suggested in my book on expert systems,[3] most of the AI constructs built so far have not been rigorously tested. Maybe they perform well, but there is no evidence of component tests and subsequent deep system evaluation.

Yet, we know too well that testing is one of software's weak points. This has been the issue which (unfortunately) has highlighted software development for over thirty years. These problems are now compounded by the need to do conceptual debugging—the process of evaluation. While it is true that this field is new and that most AI projects have so far been experimental, it is no less valid to suggest that there should be better ways of testing for completeness, consistency, and acceptability to endusers, as well as evaluation and validation. In general, software projects have demonstrated that the type of evaluation acceptable in research environments is not good enough for actual operating conditions when the programs written are used in hundreds or thousands of copies—which should be the goal of AI developments.

6. FORMALIZING EXTERNAL TESTING PROCEDURES

There is a great difference between the one-shot experimental project, computer software designed to run for production purposes, and a *programming product*. The one-shot experimental project concerns the designer, his laboratory, or the company he is working for. But this is not a marketable product.

---

[3] D.N. Chorafas, *Applying Expert Systems in Business,* McGraw-Hill, New York, 1987.

A computer program designed for production purposes must be thoroughly tested. It also requires first class documentation. Never purchase commodity software with either defective or incomplete documentation or no evidence of thorough testing—at both the component and system levels.

The testing of a program designed for production runs is a trifle compared to that needed for a programming product. For AI constructs as the industrialization of knowledge, high software quality should be a *goal*.

We have said that evaluation involves logical comparison of the conclusions on a repetitive inference basis, keeping other variables equal. This way the internal consistency of the methodology can be checked, albeit in a way which is not separated from the rules. But who can ensure that this process has been performed?

The answer is: very careful drafting of the *contract*. Remember that with AI contracts, their rules and domain facts/states/values, no test can be done for omission. Therefore the tools have to be very clearly specified. This situation is not limited to contracting external to the organization. The term *external testing* refers to any test external to the AI development team. In this sense, a test done by the *quality control* department of the communications and computers organization,[4] is considered external testing.

Consider the following example from classical DP. In a symposium on software engineering (New York City, 1976), a representative of the Department of Defense (DOD) stated that a line of code for weapons systems cost, at the time, $50. Assuming a ten-year life cycle, maintenance costs amounted to $4,000—or $400 per year, nearly an order of magnitude more than the development cost.

The causes may not be evident, but there are good reasons for this amazing statistic. After the software is tested and given ready status, the weapon system is deployed in hundreds or thousands of copies throughout the world. Bugs show up and maintenance (i.e., patching) has to be done immediately, hence locally.

As a result, in 1976 DOD devised a new policy: external testing for full quality control assurance. It also budgeted for external testing more money per instruction than the development cost—though the latter included a large sum for internal testing. Let us note this policy.

Like weapons systems software, the developed AI construct will be deployed in hundreds and thousands of copies. It is true that prior to delivery and distribution, the AI construct will have passed formal alpha and beta tests. But is this enough? We want the AI system to be delivered on time, within budget, and to perform efficiently. But such criteria, while necessary, are not enough. We also want to be sure that the AI construct will perform its specified functions. Hence, we must

- first specify these functions contractually,
- then ensure conformity to specifications.

In this situation, precision and *detail* are paramount. *Quality* is built at the drafting board. Otherwise, the software design may be hard to understand and difficult to modify, difficult to

---

[4] Provided that it has the skill and know-how required to do such test. Simple experience with classical computing/DP software is neither sufficient nor warranted.

use, or easy to misuse. It may also be unnecessarily machine dependent or hard to integrate with other programs running in the organization.

A thorough evaluation with the right set of criteria will reveal these potential problems only when the specifications are properly written at the start and contractually accepted by both parties. What are the practical and theoretical problems we should be aware of in an evaluation?

1. Ability to reason with uncertain information.
2. Missing knowledge.
3. Inconsistency in results.
4. Incomplete or incoherent justification.
5. Human window questions.
6. Passing the test of sensitivity analysis.
7. Logical structure of decision problems and possible impacts of each alternative.
8. Ability to suggest values to decision makers in case the user lacks part of the data.
9. Knowledge to evaluate the expected utility for each alternative.
10. Exits to permit easy integration with other ongoing applications.

Some of these issues have been handled ably by AI constructs, but in general, designers have not paid enough attention to them. "We don't really know how to do it," said an AI project leader about half of the items in the preceding list. When one hears this statement, one knows how the project will end.

It is true that some of the problems in this list are difficult, but they are not insoluble. In a close world it is relatively easy to deal with missing information; however, most AI constructs operate in an open world.

Mycin assumes that anything it does not know is not real. That is a false assumption. The expert system should have the ability to

- ask valid questions and
- update its hypotheses according to the answers it gets.

On the other hand, a Mycin-type assumption simplifies testing, making it easier to consider the most likely result. For instance, the outcome with the highest probability is easier to calculate when the factors and outcomes are a smaller finite set.

For practical reasons, serious testing should start with the level of the selected inference method. There are different lines along which such testing can be carried out:

1. *Perform logical comparison of conclusions derived from consecutive runs.*

Consistency is controlled in a way that is not separated from the rules. Constraints should also be evaluated.

2. *Evaluate the most likely result.*

For instance, evaluate the outcome of the highest probability based on the hypotheseis. This may involve scanning through the knowledgebank, looking at an expert's reaction or a contention system, playing the devil's advocate. *If experts disagree, tag the rules.*

3. *Prove what is wrong with the AI system.*

In other words, do conceptual validation prior to evaluation. What kind of understanding does the expert have that the AI system lacks? Have all the processes that should be there been incorporated? Have we developed more rules than are necessary?

4. *Do a system theory test.*

Are we sure that none of the rules contradict each other? Do they define a complete system? Would Euclid have been satisfied with the system of rules?

5. *Validate the human window.*

Questions/answers, a comprehensive mode of asking/replying, and presentation of conclusions are examples of such tests. However, they are not the only ones. Human-centered questions include:

- How should the AI construct's advice be related to the ongoing job?
- What is the response to "how" and "why" questions?
- What is a satisfactory explanation?
- What is the deeper explanation based on rules?
- What is the meaning and procedure of evaluation?
- How important is divergence from opinion?

Here we enter subjective terrain. Remember that both humans and AI systems are sometimes unavoidably fallible. It is also possible that not all errors are serious. This is a major contrast to DP in such applications as billing, payroll, or engineering structural studies.

When it comes to a matter of opinion, we must focus on the persons. How do we evaluate an expert? The answer is evaluation rather than software validation procedures addressed to

- software robustness,
- program portability, and
- quality of documentation.

In these cases, it is the engineering of the software, not of the rules which is the issue. Methodology, structure, rules, hypotheses, inference methods, information elements, human windows, code, databases, and communications should all eventually be included in our tests. We will return to this subject after we have spoken of *shells*.

5

Shells and the Development Environment

Keywords

shells • interpreters • knowledgebank • linguistic solutions • AI languages • standard and hybrid languages • AI environment • programming environment • model-based systems • rule-based systems • model-based reasoning • rule-based reasoning • class • worlds • garbage collection • tell-and-ask language • inheritance algorithms • multiple uses • multiple users • design scratchpad • test-case generator • knowledge units • hypothesis • process • rules • icons • detail • default values • equilibration • system testing • cooperative approach

1. INTRODUCTION

We have discussed the merits of prototyping. We now need the tools to do it. Such tools must be computer based and fit the development environment in which we are working. This is the reason for shells. *Shells* are knowledge-based, higher-level programming languages designed and used in an AI-oriented environment. Typically, they are useful as domain-independent tools. They

1. offer prototyping capabilities, some to a greater extent than others.
2. make an implicit commitment to one method of reasoning and—in some cases—one way of handling uncertainty, though the newer generation supports more than one method.
3. provide tools (subroutines) which help avoid the need to program standard features.

4. assist in reducing development time by a substantial factor and, in some cases,
5. are valuable for learning about AI systems relatively easily.

Now let's see what shells are not meant to do. Some people believe that using a shell makes AI system building easy. This is not necessarily so. It is one thing to avoid repetitive work and another to delegate the heart of the AI construct to the shell. The shell automates the routine work—not the core business.

Other people believe that shells are helpful in prototyping. This is true. But let's not forget that some shells are committed to only one form of representation—for instance, frames. At times, we need a repertoire of shells to deal with a variety of problems—though second-generation shells do offer multiple paradigms.

What the shell does is to establish the structure of the domain. This may work well for one project, but it may not be so for the next one. Shells tend to be designed for a specific class of problems, though vendors typically forget to specify which one.

Still other people believe that shells are simple and fairly cheap learning tools, as well as invaluable methods for building serious AI systems. This is an overstatement, particularly the second half.

We have said that shells are domain independent, *not* that they are universally applicable tools. They provide a fixed choice of representation. What we need to add is that

- they are not general enough for most complex applications, and at the same time
- they have a relatively high overhead in terms of computing cycles, though they do save human labor.

There is nothing amazing about this statement if we recall that shells are *interpreters*. They are good for people who must

- do prototyping,
- learn on AI systems, or
- accelerate timetables.

However, they are not necessarily production tools unless we talk about one-shot expert systems produced as demonstrators or for esoteric jobs which will not be repeated in more than one copy.

Shells have their partisans who think that they are *generally* the preferred environment for production and delivery. This may be true in a university environment, but not for business applications.

One of the criteria for the development of expert systems is the plurality of their usage. AI constructs are useful in industrializing know-how: We pick the brains of a top domain expert, map it into an expert system, and distribute the product in hundreds of copies throughout the organization. In this situation, we will surely not invest the extra cycles the shell will consume by acting as an interpreter. We will use the shell for prototyping and, after thorough testing (internal as well as external), rewrite the expert system in a lower-level language, for instance, C. Indeed, for this reason, some second-generation shells compile into C.

What has just been said should not be interpreted to mean that AI shells have no place in our environment. They are valuable assistants, and many of them constitute well-rounded fourth- and fifth-generation languages. Even the use of machine cycles may be somewhat less important—but only up to a point. With AI products running on WSs, we cannot forget the machine cycle issue even if the WS become more and more powerful.

We must also keep in mind that the same knowledge may be used in two different ways by two different interpreters. As we know from software engineering, two different interpreters can result in somewhat qualitatively different behaviors during program execution. This may not be very important in classical DP, but it is crucial in AI systems.

No doubt the contribution of shells could be enhanced if it were possible to convert from interpretation to compilation. This way, it would be rational to keep the AI program written in a given shell as source code for maintenance and use the object code at the WS level. That is what newer shells tend to do.

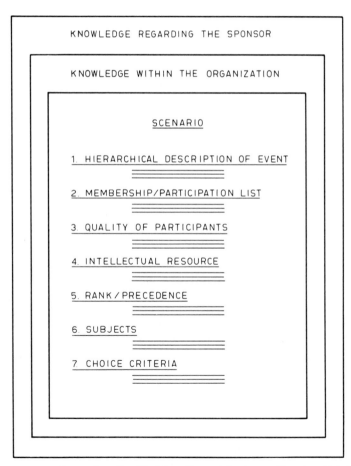

Figure 5-1. Example of scenario writing. The internal layered structure and its external interfaces are identified.

Software engineering specifies that the purpose of a compiler is conversion. In this case, it converts a high-level English form of knowledge into a compact form which can be efficiently run on smaller computers. Another function of the compiler is to check the content of the knowledgebank for syntactic correctness and consistency. In doing so, the compiler will identify any errors with a message which should allow the error(s) to be easily located and corrected.

In conclusion, we can define shells as toolkits of components enclosed in system commands. If we compare the structure and content of a shell to those of a contract for a given project (Figure 5-1), we see that there are two layers of system commands regarding knowledge of the sponsor and of the organization. Then the scenario starts. Its chapters correspond to the shell tools.

Shells help an increasing population of users put together expert systems and, more generally, AI constructs. The problems are

- runtime efficiency,
- choice of the shell, and hence of the environment, and
- generality of usage.

Correct choice also involves availability of explanation and interaction facilities. We benefit from shells because they help speed up development and make prototyping feasible.

In this chapter, KEE (Section 3) will be used as an example of the conceptual base and infrastructure of a frame- and model-oriented shell. BRAINS (Section 4) will be the testbed of a rules-and-frames shell. With the same opportunity, commands, utilities, knowledge-bank structure, and inference engine, the mechanics will be demonstrated.

2. CLASSIFICATION OF AI DEVELOPMENT TOOLS

Historically, the first ideas regarding the use of system commands in AI came with *OPS*[1], designed by Carnegie Mellon University in 1978. The first commodity shell on record is *AI/X*, made available in 1980. This was followed by *EMycin* (empty or essential Mycin), and *Mycin* has given rise to a whole family of shells: Puff, Sacon, Drilling Advisor, Teiresias, Guidon; while Kas, Sage, AL/X, and Micro-Expert were developed from *Prospector*.

APES and ESP[2] are Prolog-based developments. Among a growing number of shells we distinguish Nexpert Object, CLIPS, AION, KBMS, Knowledge Craft, ExSYS, KES, LOOPS, SRL+, Voras, BRL, M1, S1, Reveal, Microprolog, Prometheus, Expert-Ease, Timm-PC, Rulemaster, Human Subset Language (HSL), Inferno, and Omega. Without doubt, in the mid-1980s the most popular shells were KEE[3] and ART.[4] Both frame-

---

[1] Official Production System, by Carnegia-Mellon University.
[2] Made in England. It is not to be confused with the Japanese ESP, which is a language.
[3] Knowledge Engineering Environment by Intellicorp.
[4] Automatic Reasoning Tool by Inference Corporation.

based ART has a second generation version: ART-IML which we will examine in Chapter 6. Also in Chapter 6 we will review Nexpert Object (the most popular expert system shell today as well as AION, KBMS and some first class developments by the GTE Laboratories.

The late 1980s saw the emergence of second-generation shells which capitalized on the experience gained with first-generation shells earlier in the decade. The Inference Corporation, the maker of ART, worked with NASA to develop CLIPS. It then converted CLIPS into ART-MIM, where IM stands for "Information Management." Both CLIPS and IM are covered in the following chapters.

Capitalizing on years of experience in the development of expert systems, the second generation of shells brings together powerful mechanisms is encapsulate

- *knowledge,* more precisely, what to know, and
- *processing tools* which permit users to do something with the acquired knowledge.

They allow not only knowledge engineers but also domain experts to modify the language interactively from different directions. This functionally is essential to reduce the knowledge acquisition bottleneck by giving domain experts direct access to development chores connected with the expert system.

Second-generation shell design is based on the principle of using a knowledge-based tool for knowledge design, thus performing a self-service, problem-solving task. The interface and other facilities are provided to help the problem-solving effort and, at the same time, make better use of the domain expert's knowledge.

As I mentioned in a preceding chapter, I do not make a distinction between shells and toolkits, because such a distinction is merely academic. By the same token, I do not call shells an *environment,* reserving this term for a different definition. The AI literature is filled with differences in interpretation, but generally a development environment is much larger than that of a shell. The following definitions are stated in terms of infrastructure and tools:

1. *Knowledgebank.* We will speak about this in Part Two and show that it includes the domain (facts, states; the values in the database); the rules; and the methodology or methodologies. Eventually, it becomes the learning mechanism.
2. *Shell.* This is characterized by the system commands of a domain-independent structure, but also by other tools (such as human window constructs) and many utilities. The main purpose of a shell is prototyping.
3. A *range of linguistic solutions* halfway between a shell and a programmed language. OPS 5, by Carnegie Mellon, is at the top of that range; Rosie, by the Rand Corporation, is closer to the AI language level. Figure 5-2 shows the difference between Lisp-based languages and OPS.
4. *AI languages.* Basically they include Lisp and its dialects, and Prolog and its descendants (ESP, parallel prolog, flat concurrent prolog, guarded horn clauses).
5. *Standard and hybrid languages.* C and Basic are good examples of the standard type; C* refers to parallel C; L/1 (by IBM) is a hybrid combining PL/1, Lisp, and Prolog.

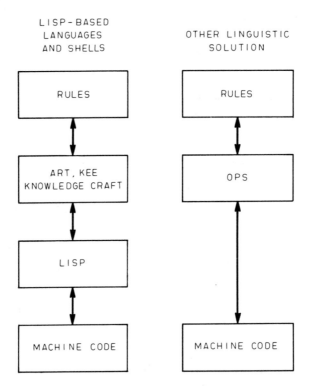

Figure 5-2. Some of the shells are Lisp based. The rules or frames they support and the commands they integrate compile into Lisp. But this is not the only approach. An alternative solution is used by OPS.

6. *AI environment.* This consists of pieces which can be put together like a Mecano (kit of parts). It provides a shell but also a full range of other tools, some of which may be specialized. Others are of a general utility nature, but as shells envolute, they cover a great deal of what an "environment" is supposed to provide.

In this sense, a *programming environment* supports inference mechanism(s), database access, natural language dialogue interfaces, procedural interfaces, explanation facilities, and so on. Applications are not necessarily included in an "environment," though the recent trend is toward doing so.

An "environment" becomes a complete expert system only when the appropriate domain knowledge is added by the knowledge engineer. Thus, buying a shell does not automatically produce an AI system solution; the same is true of "environments." Shells are tools that provide knowledge engineers and other users with the ability to capture, interpret, and distribute expertise. They may help solve more complex problems than those solvable with, say, an AI language, but they do not eliminate the need for knowledge acquisition and representation.

TABLE 5-1. Characteristics and Requirements of Shells.

1. Constructive, analysis, mapping, configuring, and diagnostic capabilities
2. Natural language interface, selection, categorization, and object orientation
3. Integration with DSS, planning, simulation, and classical DP applications
4. Icon and graphic processing, agile, user-friendly man–machine interfaces

The knowledge engineer must provide the knowledge representation and control capability which can cope with the demands of the evolving AI system. He must also support the conventional software needed for the interfaces of the system, including the external database interface. Using the shell, the knowledge engineer should ensure, from the time of early prototype development on, a highly configurable human window. He should provide the definition relationships, declarative control, and knowledge bank construction. He must also be responsible for network programming—connecting to external databases that provide external language interfaces, and so on.

Table 5-1 lists the requirements for and characteristics of shells. While originally most offerings did not have a layered structure, the newer releases do. An example is KEE 3.0, which we examine in the following section. Another example is Knowledge Craft.[5]

Shells should be evaluated for adoption in terms of their capabilities in serving us high-level programming tools with their utilities and handlers. They are designed to help turn knowledge into expert advice. Still, the knowledge engineer must establish the logical associations between the rules. The shell provides a language for building the knowledge man–machine interface, compiler, value checker, and runtime generator.

Shells are written for declarative rather than procedural programming, but as linguistic constructs they may be in transition. Two main forms of design philosophy are *model-based* and *rule-based* systems.

Model-based[6] *reasoning* is the term used in AI to describe an approach to problem solving that involves building and analyzing an explicit computational model. This model may reflect the structure, principles, and behavior of a system. Since the knowledge represented in models is explicit, it is easily accessible to other facilities.

Part of the challenge of modeling is that it requires a representation language expressive enough to describe the system of interest. It should do so in sufficient detail to support problem solving while minimizing the work of translating a conceptual model into its computational analog structure. There are two issues to consider when using *rule-based* reasoning: predictability and speed. Close-loop systems often include processes which require that an action be taken within a specific period of time. The problems come at this point. The number of possible combinations of a large rule set may make it unsuitable for operation within specific time constraints. Metarules and constraints help control the amount of time consumed by any particular rule chain. Another issue is that of unpredictable behavior.

---

[5] By the Carnegie Group.
[6] Not to be confused with the discussion on models and prototypes presented in Chapter 4. The sense used here is much more limited; it is oriented to a frame presentation.

No solution is ideal, and shells reflect this fact. Furthermore, within a few years, AI systems may undergo major changes, this time moving from

- rule-based memory to
- episodic memory[7], where domain information will be stored in very large databases as events or episodes to be retrieved and manipulated through heuristics, algorithms, and very large computer power.

The structure, utilities, appeal, and general implementation of shells will have to follow such a trend if it develops.

Proponents of shells say they are worth using, since they

- impose a design methodology,
- limit the ways in which an AI construct might be developed, and
- provide a quick method of developing a functional prototype, if the problem can be represented by means of the shell.

Even if the problem cannot be represented by means of the shell, valuable information on the characteristics of the problem can be gained and applied in choosing an adequate tool for another approach. However, not too much time must be spent finding out that a shell is inadequate. As stated in Chapter 4, the initial functional prototype should be done on a simplified version of the problem. This is not even a compromise.

AI constructs are developed incrementally, each cycle of development ending with the need for a reconceptualization of the problem. This way, further progress can be made. Starting with a limited problem definition rather than a large one makes it more difficult to overrun the bounds of the initial conceptualization.

The system's interfacing and explanation facilities are also useful in saving time. They can ease the task of tracing errors or misunderstandings in the knowledgebank. Using a shell also improves the quality of AI constructs by providing a debugged environment in which to concentrate.

Not everybody is convinced of the need for shells. Some knowledge engineers maintain that they are useful for organizations with few AI specialists trying to produce a demonstration on a well-defined problem. Then they add: "If you have ideas of your own and notions of what you shoul do, shells may become a hindrance. You need a broader range than the one they support."

In the Introduction, we also said that the knowledge engineer should not forget that shells have disadvantages. For instance, an added interface layer may require its own resident interpreter; the shell itself is a more general tool in an AI field based on specialization. Different projects in the organization may choose different shells, leading to a proliferation of programming languages.

Another limitation of AI tools is that, with few exceptions, advanced media are available only on larger, expensive machines. This precludes their use by many potential users with PCs. Yet it is often demanded that the final system be delivered on a PC.

---

[7] See also Chapter 13.

Users of PC-based AI tools must either restrict their choice of application to the limited power of the available WS or abandon their chosen tool and invest in more expensive equipment. This is particularly the case when their application outgrows the WS in size or complexity. Hence, there is a clear need for tools which are compatible across a wide range of machines.

The next question is: "What is the cost effectiveness of shells?" The answer starts with the savings in the time of knowledge engineers and domain experts. It follows with the financial picture: AI languages (Lisp, Prolog) can be obtained for $90. But the Symbolics machine they need costs $120,000. So, as far as the development environment is concerned, shells are more cost effective than programming at the language level, though it requires more computer power.

Not everybody agrees with this statement. Some argue that Prolog has been shown to be a powerful language for prototyping and implementing AI applications. This argument is based on the power of logic programming techniques and focuses on technical features, not necessarily on cost/effectiveness during the development cycle.

Precisely for cost/effectiveness reasons, in selecting a shell you must make sure that it does not have a multiplicity of features that swamp the user and require a correspondingly long time to learn. Also, because of the needed machine cycles, it is better if the shell has fewer features, but those it provides should be both powerful and in an easily understood form. Furthermore, the shell should not require very expensive specialized hardware to run on, and it should be compatible across a wide range of machines.

3. KEE: EXAMPLE OF AN EXPERT SYSTEM SHELL

KEE features a frame-oriented representation language containing facilities for describing objects and classes of objects in the domain being modeled. An object or a class is represented by a frame. The frames are linked together to form taxonomies. The description of a class contains two kinds of attributes:

- those that describe the class itself, hence *own* attributes, and
- those that describe each member of the class: *member* attributes.

Each object in the knowledgebank can be a member of one or more classes. An object inherits the member attributes of the classes of which it is a member. Those inherited attributes become own attributes of the member.

Classes may be subclasses (specializations) of other classes. Every member of a subclass is also a member of the larger class. A subclass inherits the member attributes of its classes as additional member attributes.

"Personal computers" may be a *class.* They have *own* attributes "small" and "serial" and *member* attributes "size" and "processing type." Computer A may be a member of both "personal computers" and "assets owned by Mary." Computer A would acquire *own* attributes "size" and "processing type" from the description of "personal computers."

But "personal computers" are also a subclass of "computers." It has the specialization "PC." Other characteristics belonging to the larger class "computers" will be inherited by the subclass "PC": "input," "output," "memory," "stored program," "need for power supply," and so on.

KEE also considers a class to be an object. In this manner, the description of a class can indicate the classes of which the class itself is a member. The class inherits *own* attributes from these "classes of classes" of which it is a member, just as any other object does. This ability to represent classes of classes is used to provide adaptable features. For instance, each class description is expected to have a method for determining whether a given object is a member of the class. A general membership-testing method is inherited by each class from the "class of all classes" frame. A user can provide any class with an individualized membership test by overriding the inherited general method in that particular class.

KEE also has facilities for describing object attributes. Each attribute is represented as a slot in a frame, and a slot can have multiple values. Menu entries are provided to support the addition, removal, and replacement of individual slot values.

Knowledge engineers access the KEE subsystems to tailor the construct. KEE also supports an evolution of its representation, acquisition, and problem-solving modules as they are expanded.

A frame-based approach permits association of behavioral information with object descriptions. Behavioral information is in the form of Lisp procedures (or classes of production rules). The behavior is invoked by

- sending a request to the object or
- accessing or changing an attribute of the object.

This is the sense of object-oriented programming. It allows much of the information in a program to be stored *declaratively* in frame structures. We talk about objects in Chapter 11.

The object-oriented approach is the kernel of KEE, as indicated in Figure 5-3. The frame subsystem features slots that are synonymous with attributes. The rule subsystem consists of reasoning over frames. Apart from common windows, the graphics subsystem supports KEE pictures (object-oriented graphics primitives) and active images.

Pop-up menus, multiple windows, graphs, pictures, and switches can be activated by objects and by a mouse. There are bit-mapped, user-defined icons, which provide a method of communicating the prototype through an agile man–machine interface.

Demons are represented as a frame but are attached to the slot. They fire on warning. "What if" questions in keywords permit us to compare different states. The assumption-based truth maintenance subsystem (ATMS) allows us to monitor consistency and equilibration.

The new version, KEE 3.0, extends the capability of KEE to incorporate creation, exploration, comparison, and merging of *worlds* that represent alternative situations for a problem. KEE worlds can also be used for checkpointing simulations, saving interim states as worlds.

When a fact is asserted in a world as a result of the firing of an inference rule, ATMS shares the rule's premises as a justification for the assertion. If the premises subsequently cease to be true, then the assertion will be withdrawn in all worlds. The ATMS also maintains lists of facts that cannot simultaneously be true in a consistent world. In this manner, it reduces the search for a problem solution by preventing the merging of worlds which contain contradictory facts.

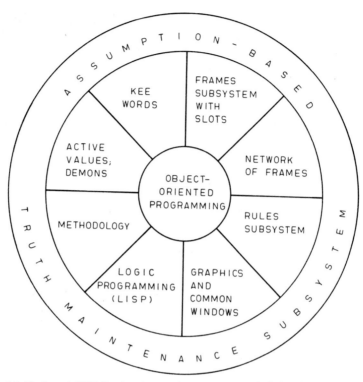

Figure 5-3. The kernal of KEE, like that of many other expert system shells, is object oriented. The outer layer is an assumption-based, truth-maintenance subsystem.

The periodic reclamation of memory when running Lisp-based applications is called *garbage collection.* This becomes important once information elements enter a knowledge system. KEE provides a garbage collection facility. If the required response time for control actions is much larger than the time needed to do background garbage collection and knowledge system analysis, there should be no problems with real-time control. However, certain strategies may be used to minimize the impact of this Lisp operation. They include:

- using a machine with continual background garbage collection capabilities,
- designing the application to reduce the use of memory-hungry functions such as window creation,
- compiling the code, and
- off-loading low-level computational processes to conventional machines where appropriate.

The shell also features a logic-based *tell-and-ask* language for asserting facts and for retrieving them from the knowledgebank. Some applications may involve storing and retrieving numerous relationships, such a *above* and *below,* among objects. If the knowledge engineer wishes to represent those relationships in a lattice (to facilitate consideration of the transitive properties of the relationships), he can do that by including in his assertion and retrieval methods knowledge of the lattice and its properties.

Further, the reasoning facilities of KEE make it feasible to draw deductions from the facts and rules in a knowledgebank. Methods include the *inheritance* algorithms and the deductive retrieval functions associated with each *tell-and-ask* expression form. The production rule facility augments the assertion and retrieval of facts, allowing the shell to respond actively to an assertion by applying rules that have a premise matching the assertion. The rule system is activated

- by supplying a rule class when calling the tell-and-ask assertion and retrieval functions or
- by directly calling the rule interpreters in active values attached to slots.

The production rule language uses tell-and-ask for the premises and assertions of rules. Rules can contain negations, disjunctions, and arbitrary Lisp s-expressions[8] as either premises or assertions.

- A backward-chaining interpreter is available for deriving answers to queries.
- A forward-chaining interpreter is available for responding to new facts and simulating actions.

Rule premises and assertions can contain variables so that rules can be written to apply to any member of a class of object. Rules are represented as frames so that they can easily be grouped into classes. When a rule is entered into the system, it is translated into an internal form that can be efficiently processed by the rule interpreter.

Finally, it is important to emphasize a facility which has been added to KEE. It derives from the *model-based* reasoning feature[9] and enables AI system developers to build multiple applications around a single model. It permits AI applications to expand toward *multiple uses,* and *multiple users.*

The principal function of one implementation, for instance, is to provide support for a diagnostic expert system by simulating more than 20 faults. The model also simulates 10 automatic testing and fault correction procedures. This model acts as a *design scratchpad* in the knowledge acquisition process. The knowledge engineer

- first constructs his concept of the system,
- then generates expert system rules by systematically examining each component of the model displayed in the knowledgebank graph.

He first asks, "What faults can occur at this component?" and "What are the observable symptoms of the fault?" Next, he embeds simple Lisp programs in each breakable component to create a *test-case generator* that automates fault simulation. This speeds up expert system debugging.

The model in reference provides support for graphic interfaces that reflect three different perspectives on the system. First, a schematic diagram represents the system engineer's

---

[8] Any legal Lisp expression is an s-expression, including a single atom, though most programmers tend to use atoms and s-expressions as different categories.
[9] Intellicorp calls it MBR, but this form can be confused with the *memory-based* reasoning we discuss in Part Two and consider on several occasions.

perspective. It ensures access to fault-simulation functions. Faults can be introduced through the mouse on a schematic component, selecting from a pop-up menu of options.

Second, a monitor panel represents the system operator's perspective, using various gauge and meter images to report the values of component attributes.

Third, an expert system control panel maps the perspective of the diagnostic expert system developer. It includes images for initiating, displaying, and reporting the results of the reasoning process.

These three references access the same core model. Each selects different pieces of information (and uses different display formats) to present a slice of the model. This can be done because of the availability of general-purpose graphics facilities that exploit the model structure.

4. BRAINS, THE SHELL WITH PRODUCTION RULES AND FRAMES

Developed in 1984 by Toyo Information Systems (TIS), the licensee in Japan of KEE, BRAINS[10] is a shell which includes frames, rules, classification modeling, and pure production rules. It is written in Lisp and supports the following dialects: Common Lisp, Zeta Lisp, UTI Lisp, and Franz Lisp. In contrast to other shells, it works under the following U.S. operating systems: MVS, VM/CMS, VMS, and Unix, as well as on the following operating systems from Japanese vendors: OS4/FA, OVIS/S, VOS3, and AOS.

In the production rule operation of BRAINS, rules are grouped into *knowledge units* (*KU*). These are applied under the control of a main execution sequence. Any KU can activate any other KU.

Each rule is provided with certainty factors. Inference works in both backward and foreward chaining. Explanation features like rule trace, back trace, and printouts of the rule tree support the user in the reasoning process. The user interface features graphics with a mouse and mouse-activated menus. As a development tool, it includes

1. rule-based system commands
2. a knowledgebank compiler
3. a knowledgebank loader
4. a justifier/explainer
5. an identifier of values (true/false)
6. a flash for unknown information elements
7. an equilibrator (weeding out contradictions)
8. a test data maker
9. a hypothesis tester (for incompatibilities)

Certainty factors are shown. The user can obtain an explanation through the presentation mode command.

---

[10] BRAINS is not available in the United States. It is a successful Japanese shell and a good example of generalized second-generation AI tools. The fact that it was not invented here should never take precedence over rationality.

Known as SUPERBRAINS, the 1987 release contains all features, like production rules, certainty factors, and backward and forward chaining, but also

- frames for knowledge presentation,
- facilities for an explanation of the relation between frames, and
- inspection functions that display the rule history conflict set, internal data, and frames.

The entering and display of data depend on the computer SUPERBRAINS is run on. On mainframes, the user interface is not as sophisticated as on Symbolics. The latter uses the standard menu system, whereas on the mainframes a command language is employed.

An interesting implementation of BRAINS, and, for that matter, of AI in general, is in *quality control circles*. Their aim is problem solving using the intelligence of a small community—for instance, the workers on a production floor or the employees in a bank's branch office. Quality control circles are a Japanese adaptation of American brainstorming sessions. They focus on a specific topic and permit a free exchange of experiences leading to problem identification and solution. Japanese banks, for instance, use quality control circles to uncover problems concerning the market appeal of new financial products but also related to the capability of bank employees to understand them and sell them to clients.

The aim of one application of AI in quality control circles was to structure expert knowledge, integrating the know-how of several persons, and to distribute it within the firm. Employees could query the knowledgebank on the basis of their own know-how and experience.

The knowledgebank itself was converted into C language code. When this code was compiled, the resulting object code has been small enough to fit into a PC. For instance, a knowledgebank with about 500 rules can be converted into executable code that fits within 640 KB of RAM. Though slower on a PC, execution speed is still acceptable compared to that of a nonconverted system.

Micro portability is, of course, most important.[12] BRAINS' Translator, an optional feature, allows one to transport the expert system one has built on a mainframe or special symbolic machine to microcomputers. Translator processes the BRAINS knowledgebank and converts it into C language. Other development tools include

1. a system command (rule based),
2. a knowledge bank compiler,
3. a knowledge bank loader,
4. a knowledge bank reference (explainer)
5. data values (summary of),
6. data contradictions,
7. hypothesis contradictions,
8. unknown data flash, and
9. a test data maker.

Items 6 to 9 operate after inference. The standard compiler converts to Lisp.

---

[12] In its new release, KEE can run on a PC for some of its features, but it must be connected to a VAX for number crunching of other code.

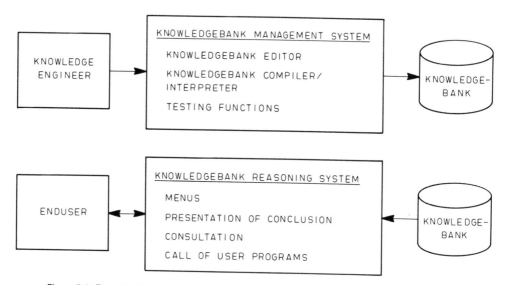

Figure 5-4. The role of the knowledge engineer and that of the enduser can be quite different, though both interact with the knowledgebank. This figure shows where the difference lies.

Figure 5-4 shows two interaction methods and the supports provided for each; one is from knowledge engineer to knowledgebank, the other from knowledgebank to enduser. Figure 5-5 shows a tree structure for a sample expert system using BRAIN facilities.

As Figure 5-5 demonstrates, BRAINS consists of three main sections:

1. ***DATA DEFINITION
2. ***PROCESS DEFINITION
3. ***KNOWLEDGEBANK

The object of ***DATA DEFINITION is to define conclusions and findings that will be used to draw the conclusions.

The first subsection (**HYPOTHESES) defines possible outcomes or conclusions which are labeled by *TAXONOMY. It can also contain *INTERMEDIATE HYPOTHESES and *TREATMENTS, but the sample expert system does not use them.

The second subsection (**FINDINGS) defines questions that need to be answered to reach the conclusions. Four types of questions can be used:

*CHECKLIST	Allows the user to select all "yes" answers
*MULTIPLE CHOICE	Allows only one of the many choices
*YES/NO	Requires either a Y or an N answer
*NUMERIC	Requires the answer to be a number

The sample expert system uses only the *CHECKLIST and the *MULTIPLE CHOICE questions.

The object of ***PROCESS DEFINITION is to define input generated by another

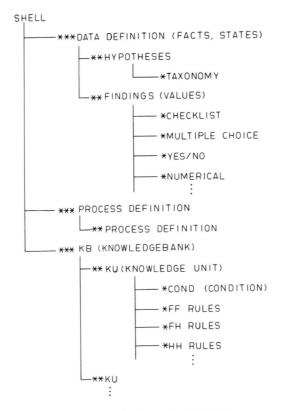

Figure 5-5. Example of a shell-based expert system program.

system where facts or findings are automated. We will omit a detailed explanation of this section here.

The **KB (knowledgebank) deals with rules which are used to draw conclusions. Its sections consist of one or more **KU (knowledge units). Each **KU begins with a *COND, which is used to decide if the **KU is appropriate. If the *COND is true, then the *KU is applied. In *KU, three types of rules are available:

> *FF RULES
> *FH RULES
> *HH RULES

*FF RULES define a relationship between two facts, such as *"If it is sunny, then it is daylight"*:

$$F(RAINING, T) \Rightarrow F(CLOUDY, T)^{13}$$

---

[13] A $\Rightarrow$ B means IF A THEN B.

*FH RULES define a relationship between a fact and a conclusion. Also, a number is used to indicate a confidence level from 0.0 (absolutely not true, impossible) to 1.0 (absolutely true, possible).

*HH RULES state a relationship between two or more facts and conclusions. They have an IF . . . THEN format:

```
IF
     condition
*THEN
     rule-1
     rule-2
         .
         .
         .

 *END
```

If necessary, a REFER command is available. The consultation mode is nearly natural language (NL).

As stated in Chapter 4, when more than one rule results in the same conclusion, the confidence level of the conclusion becomes higher. BRAINS uses a certain algorithm to compute the final confidence level.

The structure of the knowledgebank is shown in Figure 5-6. The consultation mode includes *why* and *how*. It features explanations of conclusions; shows the tree structures of inference (both forward and backward); and, upon request, lists the commands of the knowledgebank.

A certainty factor is also shown. Users can get *Explanation* using the PRESENTATION MODE command.

Transparent to the user, the inference engine works in five planes, as shown in Figure 5-7. The top two layers feature the plan of treatment and conclusion. The next two layers are dedicated to intermediate hypotheses. The object of the bottom layer is representation of the situation (domain, facts, states, values). Commands are available for man–machine interfacing. Examples are:

DX	Lists the conclusion action
EXP	Explains which rule(s) the system used to reach the conclusion
SUM	Summarizes the questions and their answers
RULE	Lists the details of the rule described in response to the EXP command
REF	Allows any statement in the expert system to be reviewed
FIND	Redisplays the specified question(s) and answer(s)
WAR	Lists contradictory rules
UNK	Lists questions which were answered as U(nknown)
RED	Edits (makes changes to) the specified rule
EXEC	Executes the expert system from the beginning
FIX	Allows the answer for a specified question to be changed

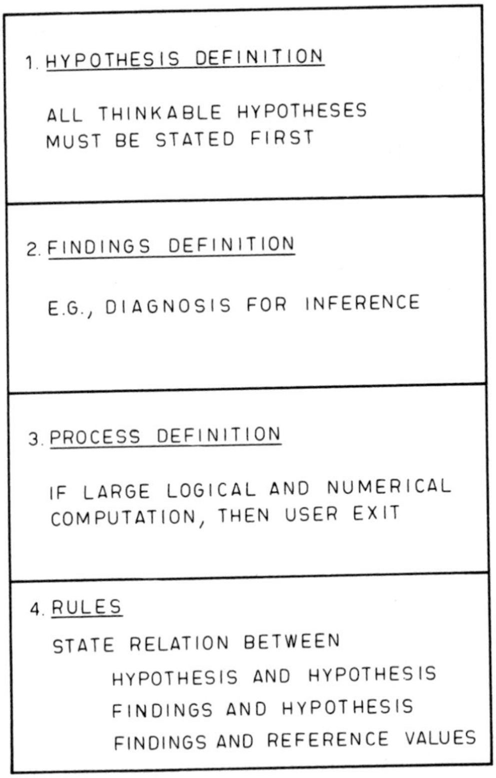

```
┌─────────────────────────────────────────┐
│ 1. HYPOTHESIS DEFINITION                  │
│                                           │
│    ALL THINKABLE HYPOTHESES               │
│    MUST BE STATED FIRST                   │
│                                           │
├─────────────────────────────────────────┤
│ 2. FINDINGS DEFINITION                    │
│                                           │
│    E.G., DIAGNOSIS FOR INFERENCE          │
│                                           │
├─────────────────────────────────────────┤
│ 3. PROCESS DEFINITION                     │
│                                           │
│    IF LARGE LOGICAL AND NUMERICAL         │
│    COMPUTATION, THEN USER EXIT            │
│                                           │
├─────────────────────────────────────────┤
│ 4. RULES                                  │
│    STATE RELATION BETWEEN                 │
│       HYPOTHESIS AND HYPOTHESIS           │
│       FINDINGS AND HYPOTHESIS             │
│       FINDINGS AND REFERENCE VALUES       │
└─────────────────────────────────────────┘
```

Figure 5-6. The knowledgebank, too, can be presented as a layered structure. The upper layer consists of hypothesis definition, and the lower layer consists of the rules the knowledgebank contains.

KEEP	Saves the expert system with changes, if any
HELP	Provides a HELP message
HOW	Queries the system

SUMMARY refers to values of fact finding. DATA VALUES treats true/false questions. If the same findings are true in one case and false in another, they will be revealed as contradictions. The same is true of hypotheses. UNKNOWN DATA is shown to the user in form of questions.

At the end of inference, by using the UNKNOWN DATA command, the shell identifies which data were unknown. Then the inference is repeated; the results may be different.

The MAKE TEST command permits testing of the system with user-supplied data. The data provision is

- *based on hypotheses.* The inference engine will ask questeions, while
- data may be input from external files and databases.

One of the limitations is the management of the global database. BRAINS has no embedded database access functions; hence, it is necessary to write needed routines. One AI application did so and was attached online to IBM's DB2.

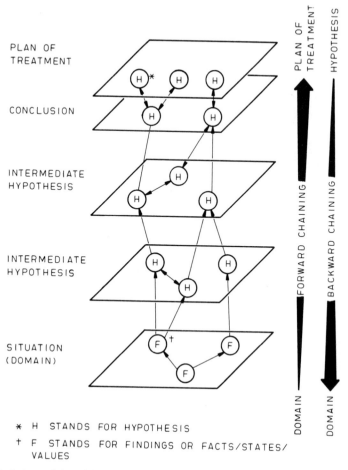

Figure 5-7. An integral view of the inference engine, from plan of treatment to domain, and vice versa. The approach works in both ways, depending on whether the methodology is forward chaining or backward chaining.

5. EXSYS[14]: A SHELL OFFERED AT THE PC LEVEL

We have said that BRAINS compiles the developed AI construct into C language, which can be run on the PC, and that the 1986 version of KEE can be run partly on a PC but needs maxicomputer backup (for instance, VAX). Neither KEE nor BRAINS is an expert system shells designed for PC-level development work.

---

[14] For Expert System Development Package, by EXSYS Inc.

But there exist affordable shells which run easily under MS DOS. Evidently, the smaller the machine cycles, the less the complexity and sophistication of the shell. PC-based shells are in no sense a free lunch, paying bottom prices and getting top results. Yet, they have their place in the market. An example of such a shell is EXSYS.

EXSYS is written in C language. It uses IF . . . THEN rules, not IF . . . THEN . . . ELSE. While practically anything that can be expressed in IF . . . THEN . . . ELSE rules can also be written in IF . . . THEN rules, more rules are needed. On the other hand, IF . . . THEN rules execute more quickly.

EXSYS can cell external programs and pass data back to itself for analysis. This is done by writing data to a disc file which EXSYS automatically reads.

- Data can be passed for multiple variables or
- an external program can be assigned to a particular variable and called only when the value for that variable is needed.

Through the use of external programs the user interface can be customized. In some applications, front-end programs have been written to assist the human window and pass all necessary data to EXSYS. In addition, the results of an EXSYS run can be directed to a disc file for processing by another program.

The EXSYS knowledgebank uses straight text presentations and asks multiple-choice questions. The user can add comments and send messages at the beginning and end. There are however, two drawbacks: lack of graphics and lack of input flexibility.[15]

The shell's editing module creates the rules, conditions, and alternatives that make up an expert system.

- It has features designed to help keep track of the flow of logic and options in the system.
- It prompts the user to provide the data it needs to set up an application.

The use of color and screen design is helpful in displaying the established rules and conditions.

In application development, the screen is divided into three sections. The left side displays IF, AND, and THEN. The right side shows alternatives and conditions that can be recalled, scrolled, expanded, and edited. The bottom of the screen displays prompts. It indicates the commands available at the particular functional level at which the user is working.

EXSYS has a *change and rerun* command which, at the end of a run, allows all of the information the user gave the program to be displayed. The user may then change any of his answers and rerun the program, with the rest of the answers held constant. In this case, the shell displays both the previous probability value for a solution and the one based on the new assumptions. This feature permits expert system constructs to be developed and tested without much difficulty.

EXSYS supports numeric variables and trigonometric, logarithmic, exponential, and

---

[15] Remember that this is a PC-level, low-cost package.

square root functions. Expressions can be tested with =, >, <, >=, <=, and <>. Variables can also be assigned values in the THEN part.

The editing program allows the user to review and change the contents of the knowledge-bank. The review and revise functions are helpful. The editing module links to the run-time module so that the user can try out changes as he makes them.

The shell makes it possible to initialize a variable and use it to keep running trials. The value of the variable can be displayed with the program's conclusions at the end, and the shell explains how the value was reached.

EXSYS permits the user to add notes and explanations telling other users why particular conclusions were drawn. It is also feasible to specify the probability that a conclusion is correct. The user can set the probabilities within an application according to one of three sets of conditions. The first simple set of conditions permits the user to set all choices to a value of either 0 or 1.

- This means that there is no *probability* involved.
- The first rule that has all of its IF conditions met draws the conclusion stated in its THEN section.

The second set of conditions makes it feasible to set choices on a value scale from 0 to 10. In this system, which is the one most often used, the values 0 to 10 permanently decide the conclusion. These values are the equivalent of absolutely *yes* or *no*. The values of 1 to 9 represent degrees of confidence ranging from probably not to probably so. These values are averaged over all of the rules to select a final choice.

With probabilities, there is also a provision for reaching two different conclusions from two identical sets of conditions. In addition, probabilities can be combined. These features make EXSYS practical for applications which require such an approach.

In some cases, the user can give a set of answers that could eventually lead toward two different conclusions. Then the shell continues to ask questions to determine if the conditions could possibly lead to another conclusion. Should two conclusions be possible, EXSYS evaluates the probabilities assigned to each set of rules. It then selects the most likely alternatives.

A rule editor allows the rules to be run as they are created. This avoids the need to use a separate text editor, which has several disadvantages. With an embedded editor, the user does not need to switch programs to run his rules and then switch back for corrections. He can remain in the run mode and (at the press of a key) return automatically to the editor.

An embedded editor also makes it feasible to put a qualifier in once; after that, it is recalled by number or by another method. The rule editor also automatically checks all new rules as they are entered against the existing rules for conflicts. Any conflicts discovered are displayed to the user for correction. Hence, equilibration is supported.

6

Second-Generation Expert Systems Shells

Keywords

> *ART-IM • information management • C • Unix • truth maintenance • expert systems • pull-down menus • dialogue • hypertext • global database • Cobol • 5GC • DP • language • CLIPS • shell • rule-based • syntax • debugging aids • quality assurance • integration • extendability • communications links • interactive development • online help • Nexpert Object • Bechtel • financial control • rule format • prototype • hypothetical reasoning • rule editor • hypotheses • classes • properties • visual thinking • Nestor Learning Systems • neural networks • Aion development system • knowledge definition language • KBMS • AI Corporation • SQL • inverse inheritance • GTE Laboratories • IDA • CALIDA • Compass • Prophet • case-based reasoning*

1. ART-IM BY THE INFERENCE CORPORATION

The Inference Corporation is the author of the Automated Reasoning Tool (ART), which in the 1980s was one of the two best-selling expert system shells in America. Introduced in 1985, ART was used in such outstanding AI constructs as credit card handling at American Express, forex auditing at Chemical Bank, and fraud control of medical claims by Lockheed. It is now employed by 300 companies in about 700 different operating versions. One of the users, NASA, has developed a dialect of ART for real-time implementation known as

CLIPS[1], which has recently been converted by Inference into a programming product and is marketed as ART-IM, where IM stands for "information management."

ART-IM is written in C. One of its advantages is that it is only 10% of the size of the original ART and works four times faster. The current version runs under MS DOS, MVS, and VMS (under development). The original ART (but not IM) runs under Unix. Inference projects that for ART-IM there will be a run-time Unix version in C.

ART-IM incorporates a comprehensive, rule-based technology that saves development time and costs by allowing the software expert to concentrate on capturing knowledge and permitting the expert system tool to focus on how and when to use the knowledge. Rules can be added, deleted, and modified independently of any other rules in the expert system. This makes it possible for the developer to incrementally evolve and enrich the expert system's knowledgebank.

A basic premise is that most rules in practical business applications describe relationships between objects, and these relationships change over time. ART-IM can match patterns across multiple objects through rules. This pattern-matching feature gives developers the ability to design real-world expert systems.

The technology of ART-IM is based on a forward chaining, data-directed approach. It includes representations for

- objects,
- relationships, and
- rules with dynamic inheritance.

Dynamic inheritance adds power to the system by allowing rules to look at incoming data and influence the processing. Object-oriented approaches increase the quality of knowledge representation by permitting developers to attach multiple distinguishing characteristics to describe important properties of an object.

ART-IM also has *a truth maintenance* facility to keep conclusions in the knowledgebank *accurate and consistent*. This facility is programmable, so that a developer has complete control over what rules represent logical inferences.

- If some conclusions are based on certain facts and the user changes one of the facts, ART-IM automatically deletes all the conclusions that are no longer justified.
- If the user has specified several entries to an expert system and then realizes that one of the entries is wrong, he can change any previous input and the expert system will immediately revise and update the whole situation under its control.

ART-IM features an interactive debugging environment. It saves development time by allowing developers to trace the knowledgebank in order to control and monitor the state of an application at any given point without recompiling. Experienced developers have the option of using the *ART-IM Studio,* a flexible text editor in ART-IM's development environment.

---

[1] See Section 2.

The Studio allows the user to look at any conclusion that the expert system has reached, automatically showing all data and rules that were employed to reach that conclusion. If an error appears in the system, developers can automatically access the knowledgebank source files, bring them up in the editor, and point to the rule or object that needs to be changed. The development environment features pull-down menus, dialogue boxes, overlapping windows, hypertext on-line help, and a mouse.

ART-IM is based on the principles of a data-directed architecture. In contrast, most traditional languages require developers to structure and sequence rules manually before they can be applied to the problem-solving process. In a data-directed architecture, the data cause rules to be selected and applied. In other words, the data are in control, and eventually this saves development time and costs.

In summary, the developer can focus on capturing the knowledge while the AI tool decides how and when to apply it. As the expert system receives data from sources such as files, databases, other application processes, or users working at terminals, the data are passed through a systems integration layer and are automatically converted into an internal form in the knowledgebank. They are also translated into the internal form chosen.

It is precisely this feature of ART-IM that makes it a good tool for *global database integration*. During a meeting in Los Angeles on May 24, 1989, Dr. Alexander D. Jacobson, chairman and CEO of the Inference Corporation, mentioned that American Airlines is trying to solve integration problems involving disintegrated databases and it is currently faced with a polyglot collection of computer systems that grew out over the years and must now be integrated into service application areas. This is precisely the case of more than 90 percent of large industrial and financial organizations today.

A feasibility study in this area by Inference shows that able solutions will significantly automate the process of accessing data. Today the large majority of corporations have difficulty collecting data from distributed databases and integrating them; *this is an urgent problem which must be addressed immediately.*

- The solution goes well beyond PC-to-mainframe approaches.
- The AI shell must be able to do the work without manual intervention by the developers.

Several meetings between American Airlines and Inference have taken place to establish specifications. They have agreed that a solution can be found and that a system will be available about 12 months after the project starts.

Finally, ART's integration architecture permits its native commands to be called by IBM recovery utilities, making feasible deep integration—that is, hybrid systems: AI cooperating with current DP and fully integrated into Cobol code. The architecture also permits the restructuring of Cobol programs through ART prototyping. This may be released more quickly than IBM's Repository system and might prove to be a better solution.

A specific example may be useful. The Ford Motor Corporation (an investor in ART) has rewritten its *Warranty System,* which was available in Cobol but had aged, had become very tangible, and cost too much to maintain. This practical application of an AI shell to classical DP problems demonstrated that, in contrast to Cobol, the development time was 30% less and in maintenance, the staff was reduced by a factor of 3.3 (two people instead of seven).

Impressively, CPU time with Warranty was the same as with the old Cobol code. ART compiles into Cobol, but as an alternative, it can also compile into C.

The application done at Ford used 5GC, employing rule-based language for classical DP rather than building an expert system project. The prerequisites for successful implementation were

1. a *language* which is highly expressive in a business sense
2. the ability to incorporate the *conventions* of current programmers to permit human migration, and
3. an emphasis on *cost/performance* from development to maintenance.

"You cannot sell a system which needs special machines or too many cycles of current machines," said one of the executives participating in the meeting at Intelicorp. WS and general-purpose computers are better solutions for expert systems, and the same is true of hybrid systems. We should always be on the alert for systems which can enhance our productivity.

2. THE CLIPS EXPERT SYSTEMS SHELL

Developed in 1986, with its 4.2 version released in mid-1988, the C Language Integrated Production System (CLIPS) is a shell for developing expert systems. It is designed to allow AI research, development, and delivery of different computers and operating systems (MS DOS, Unix, VMS) from PCs to Cray computers. CLIPS is supported by COSMIC, which was established in 1966 by NASA to provide a central office to collect the software developed under NASA funding, transferring it for reuse by industry, universities, and government agencies.[2]

CLIPS is a forward-chaining, rule-based shell. The program contains an inference engine and a language syntax that provide a framework for the construction of expert systems. It also includes tools for debugging an application. Like ART-IM, CLIPS is based on the Rete algorithm, which enables efficient pattern matching. As facts are asserted either prior to or during a session, CLIPS pattern-matches the number of fields. Wild cards and variables are supported for both single and multiple fields.

- The syntax allows the inclusion of outside (externally defined) functions written in a language other than CLIPS.
- The CLIPS code can be embedded in a program such as a simple subroutine call.
- However, CLIPS is not very powerful in graphics, a crucial component of visualization.

CLIPS supports a valid rule syntax with free-form patterns, single- and multifield variable bindings across patterns, and user-defined predicate functions on the left-hand side (the IF, or antecedent) of a rule. Since it is completely integrated with C, users may define and call

---

[2] COSMIC is located at the University of Georgia Athens, GA

their own C functions from within CLIPS. This capability enhances the building of coupled numeric-symbolic constructs, one of the characteristics of second-generation expert systems.

The shell provides an interactive, text-oriented development environment, *including debugging aids*. NASA is using CLIPS to model an intelligent fault management system for the space station's radio link to earth. This link must retransmit audio and video reports 24 hours a day at over 300 megabits per second. In this setup, CLIPS

- continulusly monitors oncoming signals for impending failure,
- isolates the source of a possible failure, and
- produces a recommendation for solving the problem.

CLIPS is also helping space shuttle mission planners schedule radar tracking stations to support shuttle missions. By examining preflight information to schedule the radars optimally, *the AI construct has decreased the time required to perform this task from two weeks to two hours*.

CLIPS has also been used by NASA to control teleoperated robots. A group at the Langley Research Center has designed an expert system that converts high-level task commands into the 50 to 600 specialized menu commands required for even the most elementary construction tasks.

- A family of expert systems written in C enhance manual control, overseeing inputs provided by a human operator to prevent them from confusing or contorting the robot.
- Alternatively, an operator can either override or further assist the expert system as it guides a robot.

Another Langley application uses CLIPS in a program that integrates graphics, databases, and a knowledgebank as part of a structural design system. This program helps select the best structure to support point loads in two dimensions.

At the Marshall Space Flight Center, an expert system that arranges mission manifests for Spacelab missions was developed in CLIPS. Goddard Space Flight Center researchers use CLIPS for ground support systems that perform *fault isolation and diagnosis in communication links*. CLIPS has also been employed at Goddard to develop an expert system that performs *quality assurance and data integrity testing of files* from the Spacelab output system. This is an impressive range of applications.

NASA has used Inference personnel in developing CLIPS. In 1984–85, NASA became an important customer of ART. A year later, NASA required a solution leading to the possible implementation of space stations, where a very high level of automation is fundamental to success. During this operation, NASA added functionality to ART and implemented CLIPS.

Two of the key features of CLIPS are *integration* and *extendability*. It can be embedded in procedural code, called as a subroutine, and integrated with languages other than C, such as FORTRAN and ADA. It can also be extended with the addition of user-defined functions.

Another feature of CLIPS is the *interactive development environment*. On the IBM PC and other machines, CLIPS provides an interactive, text-oriented development capability including *debugging aids, online help, and an integrated editor*. An interface with pull-down menus and multiple windows is supported on the Macintosh. The input/output router provides a flexible intput/output system that permits nonportable, machine-specific interfaces to be layered on top of CLIPS while preserving the portability of the shell's kernel.

By using the rule compiler, knowledgebanks may be compiled into turnkey executables. CLIPS comes with *all* source code, approximately 25,000 lines of C, which can be modified or tailored to meet a user's needs. A utility aids in verification and validation of rules by providing cross referencing of fact relations, style checking, and semantic error control.

Multiple-field variables add a simple list-processing capability to CLIPS, and several functions are available for manipulating them. However, multiple-field variables can slow down execution if they are used too often.

Rules can be constrained through the use of functions and predicates or through user-defined variables. A comprehensive extended math system is available for users who have complex problems to solve. System memory is the most important limitation on the number of patterns and functions contained in a rule. Firing a rule can

- assert new facts into the fact list,
- call user-defined functions,
- handle input and output,
- perform mathematical functions using the basic or extended math package, or
- make system calls.

Rules and facts can be entered interactively from the prompt. Created within the editor, they can be quickly inserted into the knowledgebank and executed. The development context is very similar to that of many LISP systems.

CLIPS' windowing requires a mouse. It is quite easy to use, but it seems to slow execution.

One of CLIPS' key points is its extendability through user-defined functions. An elaborate input/output router system lets programmers develop a wide variety of interfaces and attach them to CLIPS. The router uses logical names and a system of input/output priorities that permits users to develop their own interfaces and establish a priority for each.

The design of CLIPS is characterized by three elements:

1. a global data memory or fact list,
2. a knowledgebank containing all the rules, and
3. an inference engine.

Programs written in CLIPS consist of rules and facts. Since this shell is *data driven,* the fact list contains the data that will stimulate execution. Building a fact list is a simple operation, and the software includes a number of powerful utilities for data manipulation.

Rules can be either typed directly into the shell or loaded from a file of rules created using a word processing package. Rules follow the familiar IF . . . THEN pattern and are defined using LISP-like syntax. CLIPS attempts to match the rules against the facts in the fact list; if the pattern of a rule matches, the rule is activated.

With this function, CLIPS begins to resemble a neural network. Activated rules are placed on an agenda which

- is ordered by the shell in terms of increasing priority and
- fires the rule with the highest priority.

After a rule fires, a certain amount of refraction time is required before it fires again. It is feasible to consider using the shell as an environment for neural modeling. In fact, integrated neural net technology is employed in expert systems developed by NASA for search and retrieval purposes.

In its current offering, CLIPS includes a mathematical library. COSMIC also markets other software packages, including graphics, engineering, aerodynamics, and physics programs, at fair prices. The price for CLIPS is $500 on the PC or Vax Series), with another $124 for the documentation.

3. THE NEXPERT OBJECT SHELL

For reasons of diversification, the Bechtel Power Corporation—one of the largest construction companies worldwide—has branched into AI projects, expert systems shells, and associated AI consulting. Addressing itself to this field, the Bechtel AI Institute has branches in San Francisco, London, Tokyo, and Singapore.

The expert systems shell marketed by the AI Institute is called *Nexpert Object*. It is a general-purpose expert systems shell which is fast becoming the market standard for second-generation shells; 6,000 licenses have been sold in three years. Nexpert Object is an entry-level tool, user friendly and therefore good for quick starts, and with a valid user interface. Minimal AI experience is needed to employ it. It

- is well integrated,
- supports a shareable image,
- features calling standards for the operating system it uses
- provides DBMS interfaces, and
- has a good price/performance ratio.

We will see in Chapter 7 how Lockheed evaluates this shell, which it considers the best on the market. Bechtel has also achieved the following expert systems applications with Nexpert Object:

1. *Contract Advisor*

This runs on Machintosh II and produces very complex contrasts involving *engineering procurement and construction*. Through an agile windowing application, queries can be asked by the user about

- projects,
- partnerships,
- legal requirements,
- issues involving clients,
- approaches to verification,
- methods of payment, and
- bonuses.

The Contract Advisor expert system is an "assistant to." It produces the draft of a contract and features integration of Nexpert and word processing routines.

2. *Insurance underwriting*

This is a key implementation area. The expert system focuses on insuring *new* car drivers by

- screening credentials,
- using public databases for information, and
- providing policy guidelines.

It is now being extended to include renewal of insurance policies.

3. *Financial control*

One of the banks collaborating with Bechtel in the use of Nexport is Security Pacific. Said a Bechtel executive in regard to this project: "One of the most worthwhile results we got with expert systems is incremental development."

4. *Client receivables*

This is a financial application provided for a major industrial company. It tracks outstanding accounts (receivables), controls the amount and timeliness of payments, and settles balances on the account. Another financial expert system implementation internal to Bechtel focuses on *visualization*. All the results are given graphically—typically through the enduser's WS. As one executive commented: "We are in no way able to present such complex output in tables."

These examples show the range of applications supported by knowledge engineering design. Nexpert Object

- handles rules, patterns, and reasoning premises in a nonmonotonic manner,
- assists in knowledge acquisition and provides a graphic development environment, and
- assures database links and delivery to the enduser for whom the application is intended.

Nexpert Object is an expert systems tool which helps create representation and reasoning mechanisms. It is based on the principle of *knowledge design,* reflecting the ability of domain experts to be fully involved in the construction of a knowledgebank. For this purpose, it allows computation of chunks of knowledge, giving the domain experts direct access to the system.

Nexpert makes feasible hybrid systems with the capability to integrate programs written in Cobol, PL/1, and C, calling on them through the Execute command. The overall structure is shown in Figure 6-1. Around the kernel functions are the

- knowledgebank,
- programming language,
- human window, and
- gateway.

The gateway links the system to external programs. The human window links it to the end users and supports internal graphics capabilities. The gateway and the human window together help bring entities from multiple environments into an object structure.

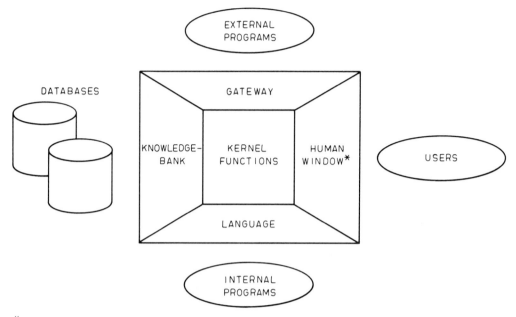

*EXPLAINS AND SUPPORTS GRAPHICS

Figure 6-1. The architecture of this shell, and its integration with its environment, are explained. Kernel functions are endowed with linguistic support, knowledgebank-building capabilities, a gateway to external programs, and a human window.

The *augmented rule format* provides properties such as

- forward symmetry,
- backward symmetry,
- rule access to inference mechanisms, and
- procedural attachments.

Any rule can be processed either forward or backward, according to the structure of the knowledgebank. Nexpert is based on objects similar to frames or schemata, leading to the notion of patterns.

The shell provides the ability to reason about facts involving patterns. The latter are descriptions of instances or classes to be sorted out of the object base.

Object organization is important, since an object in Nexpert is an *instance* or a *prototype* and, hence, a structured description of an item corresponding to an entity in the real world. Objects are created either

1. by using a special object editor or
2. directly from the incremental compilation of the rules in which they are used.

An object can be created at any time in the processing cycle. It is subsequently compiled incrementally. Every object has a name and belongs to one or several classes. It may also have components (subobjects).

For any given object, its class is a generalization. By applying the *inheritance principle,* a subobject shares properties defined by the object with which it is associated. This is a strong point of this shell.

Dynamic inheritance makes it feasible to implement real-time applications, with objects participating fully in the reasoning process. It is possible to inherit methods written in a conventional programming language.

Inheritance relationships constitute parameters stored in metaslots, the descriptive elements of object or class properties. Among the metaslots of a property are the *If Change.* They describe methods to be applied whenever the value of a given property is modified. *If Change* and *Order of Sources* are inheritable.

Objects and their links to other objects or classes can be created or modified by rules and/or by object metaslots where they apply. *Rules can address these objects through pattern matching.* A *Create Object* function is basic to transforming database query results into data structures about which the system can reason. States of inference for a given set of variables can be stored as object structures (or hierarchies), thus *permitting hypothetical reasoning.*

Bottom-up editing permits us to define objects with their properties prior to editing, thus providing *degrees of freedom to the knowledge engineer.* Top-down editing permits objects to be edited from the top level to the bottom, first describing top-level classes and then subclasses down to instances.

Through its interactive editors, *Nexpert offers a declarative way of solving conflicts,* permitting the knowledge engineer to

- control the direction of processing and
- establish priorities in focusing attention.

This allows both the ordering of subtasks, in backward and forward chaining, and *system control including priority of processing.* This, too, is an interesting property offering good programming possibilities.

An expert system built through Nexpert Object can reason either from facts (hence, forward chaining) or from goals (backward chaining). The latter type of reasoning corresponds to a goal-driven behavior in solving problems as the expert system navigates through the knowledgebank, discovering relevant rules and goals.

The support of nonmonotonicity is important, as experts use more than textbook knowledge, experiential learning, or their intuition. They also *refer to their previous conclusions,* gearing their reasoning to different hypotheses. True domain experts and knowledge engineers are also able to act in the presence of

- uncertainty and vagueness,
- incomplete information, and
- sudden contradictions

The ability to reason based on past inferences, as well as to make default assumptions that overcome incomplete knowledge, is the characteristic of nonmonotonicity. This is supported by Nexpert Object.

Through this facility, the system keeps track of logical dependencies established by means of *direct* or *assumption-based reasoning.* This reasoning, in turn, makes the expert system aware of the reasons leading to given conclusions. It can also cope with

- changes which introduce a contradiction into any condition which has been previously evaluated,
- resetting of a hypothesis made to reevaluate portions of the reasoning path, and
- the treatment of uncertainty associated with online information.

Graphics capabilities are incorporated at different levels. Graphic tools run as object-oriented facilities permitting users to integrate different devices. These facilities are available on all machine environments supported by Nexpert.

The user can obtain information on any item; it is presented through pop-up menus. *Rules* and *objects* structures are displayed and edited in a graphic, spreadsheet-like *rule editor. Data, hypotheses, classes,* and *properties* are listed in the *notebooks* of the *encyclopedia.* A *network* illustrates the notion of *visual thinking.*

The Network is an automatically created graphic representation of the knowledgebank and its control. Two Networks display

- rule structure and
- object structure.

The Network facility acts as a dynamic, automatic *browsing tool.* It permits deductive and evocative navigation through the knowledgebank. The Network also permits users to trace the reasoning of the system during processing, thereby providing explanations as required.

The concept of *hybrid solutions* is itself very important. Nexpert structures can be controlled by an external program. A program can

- initialize Nexpert,
- load a knowledgebank,
- start the inference engine,
- interrupt a session,
- resume an interrupted session, or
- reset the inference state.

Basic control commands are also available in the programmatic interface(s). External programs can investigate the working memory of Nexpert; access the list of all the hypotheses, objects, and so on; and ask for the status and value of any data or hypothesis—thus providing significant flexibility. A program can also

- change the inference state of Nexpert by suggesting a new hypothesis,
- change the values of certain data elements,
- generate new objects, and
- modify structural relationships between objects and classes.

These facilities are very important, as integrating a new technology—such as expert systems—into an existing environment allows the latter to access the new component and benefit from its services, regardless of tasks and domains. The AI library of Nexpert Object ensures that expert systems structures can be accessed from other processes and written in languages such as C, FORTRAN, Cobol, Ada, and some assemblers.

Nexpert is written in C and operates on IBM mainframes under MVS[3] and VM; DEC Vax VMS[4]; Unix running on Sun, Apollo, HP, Vax, IBM RT, and other WSs (including X Windows); OS/2 and MS DOS 386-based machines under Microsoft Windows (with 640K or more of central memory board); Macintosh Plus, SE, and Macintosh II. The runtime system is available on this SW/HW with character or graphics terminals. Knowledgebanks are compatible across the different platforms.

Database links permit Nexpert to access data stored in external files or databases. The expert system can retrieve data from the database and write the results of its reasoning into the database. Alternatively, it can create a new file. *Databases may be large and are managed to provide data integrity in concurrent environments.* Information elements can be accessed or produced by other applications. Data can also be edited with existing packages running on PCs.

Finally, there are user exits able to accommodate other products, such as neural networks. Nestor, Inc., is the company represented by Bechtel Power for that purpose.

Nestor's initial commercial product was *NestorWriter,* which allowed a computer user to enter handwritten text into the DP machines through a PC with a data-entry tablet. This product requires no programming and *adapts to the user's personal style of writing.* It has been developed for commercial settings where handwritten paperwork creates problems involving

- quality,
- timeliness,
- productivity, and
- cost.

A follow-on product to NestorWriter was the *Decision Learning System* for the financial services market. It is designed to be used for *predictive modeling* in such applications as underwriting and securities/portfolio management.

Another product, the *Nestor Learning System (NLS),* has been made available to users through the *Nestor Development System (NDS)*[5]. The latter provides access to the former for the development of solutions in complex pattern recognition or signal-processing applications. A parallel effort embodies NLS in a hardware computer architecture characteristic of neural networks.

The effective use of neural networks in solving financial and industrial problems is a new trend. While some applications seem feasible, certain users are unhappy because neural networks cannot document their opinion with rule-based expert systems.

Several companies are working on this problem. In part, it arose because small firms with connectionist projects did not have the money to develop justification capabilities similar to those available with rule-based supplies. Besides, neural networks should be seen as a niche market, with the resulting products finding their best utilization not as a monolithic approach but as coprocessors.

---

[3] DB2 has been supported as of July 1989.
[4] Requires VMS 4.4 and higher, as well as a GPX color station.
[5] An interface between Nexpert Object and NDS is being developed.

4. THE AION
DEVELOPMENT SYSTEM

The Aion Development System (ADS) is an expert systems shell built by the Aion Corporation and *dedicated to an IBM environment.* It can be delivered in MVS/TSO, MVS/Batch, CICS, IMS, VM/CMS, and on PCs under OS/2 or MS DOS. Particularly designed for TSO, Batch, and XA, the ADS/MVS features native access to DB2, VSAM, QSAM, and Teradata DBC/1012, as well as external program interface to data in other formats. Business graphics are featured on GDDM-supported displays.

Originally projected for backward chaining, Aion now features both methods (backward and forward), including hypothetical reasoning. An object-oriented capability will soon be released.

The shell permits developer-defined steps for high-level, goal-oriented program control. It offers procedural control options for specifying the order of knowledgebank execution, and features segmentation for improved performance and maintenance of completed applications.

Memory resource management is provided for both PC and mainframe operating systems. An expert system built on a WS platform can be moved to a supported operating system on a mainframe without change, thus permitting the use of a WS for development.

Aion's *Knowledge Definition Language (KDL)* specifies the underlying logic of an application. It provides for object representation using parameters, rules, types, messages, reports, graphs, processes, functions, states and vocabularies. Data representation is done through

- predefined data types, and
- user-defined record structures.

Predefined types include string, boolean, date, time, integer, floating point, packed decimal, zoned decimal, fixed decimal, list, and set. User-defined types can include any combination of these, as well as *constraints on values.*

Both frames and rules are supported. A whole application can be written in this dual environment. Aion features an integrated report-writing language with automated formatting and retrieval of data. There is also a text editor for message creation, with extensive formatting support and *customizable edit interfacing.*

Useful features are the explanation and help facilities for developers and endusers, in addition to help text. The knowledgebank provides syntactic and semantic error checking. There is a *runtime debugging monitor* with breakpointing, full tracing, and audit support.

Other features include cross referencing of all knowledgebank objects; knowledgebank segmentation for multiple developers; and *edit and runtime passwords for system security.* Also available is a knowledgebank backup and retore facility to maintain system integrity, as well as support for regression test cases.

There are two ways to deliver an application. The first is *through an interpreter.* This is a runtime operation which, as in all systems, consumes many cycles. The second is *by means of compilation.* This is done in Pascal and constitutes Aion's high-performance option.

The application at the Kundenkreditbank in West Germany a CitiCorp subsidiary, has been written in the Aion shell and is integrated with other real-time routines addressed to retail clients. It currently supports 440 concurrent users on the mainframe. Among banking implementations in the United States written in Aion are those for credit analysis (consumer, corporate) and legal requirements connected with loan processing.

Other expert systems applications using the Anion shell have been developed by the insurance industry for claims processing and risk analysis.

The Aion expert systems shell has been particularly applied to manufacturing:

1. Cost containment[6]
2. Help desk
3. Process control
4. Factory scheduling operations
5. Scheduling and distribution of shipping orders and auto routes
6. File Management

On the negative side, Aion has so far not addressed global database issues. For this reason, applications involving intensive database activity rely heavily on IBM DB technology, particularly SQL.

5. KBMS BY THE AI CORPORATION

The Knowledge-Based Management System (KBMS) is the new product of the AI Corporation. It integrates *Intellect,* an earlier tool of the same firm which dealt with agile man–machine interfaces. KBMS aims to provide a capability for global database management, but strictly within an IBM SQL environment.

An essential feature of KBMS is its inference engine. It offers paradigms of reasoning:

- forward and backward chaining,
- object orientation, and
- hypothetical reasoning.

Another basic feature, *call-in,* provides the ability to invoke KBMS rules from another program, especially one written in Cobol. The ability to call commands in a database is a characteristic of all second-generation AI tools.

The same is true of natural language programming. Today this capability focuses on English commands that generate program statements. KBMS does so in SQL, the essential feature of Intellect. The facility of using natural language querying after consultation allows users to probe as deeply as they want to discover why the system did what it did.

Full screen interaction is a major advantage in man–machine interfaces. As Larry R. Harris has commented during our May 1989 meeting: "Today, everything takes place on a two-dimensional screen, but Cobol I/O is still one-dimensional, line-oriented. So we had to build a tool to allow the design of two-dimensional screens."

---

[6] An expert systems application by the U.S. operations of Northern Telecom which evaluates change orders.

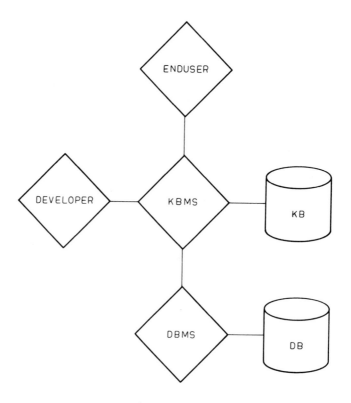

SYSTEM INCLUDES 4GL CAPABILITY

Figure 6-2. Functional liaisons by the shell KBMS. The latter acts as a kernel enriched with communication commands to help the developer, manage the knowledgebank, interface to a DBMS, and assist the enduser.

Figure 6-2 exemplifies the KBMS functional liaisons with developers and endusers, as well as knowledgebanks and databases. Among the special features being supported are conflict resolution and pattern matching. Pattern matching permits developers to establish binding procedures so that the programmer does not have to code the sequence in advance. This pattern then applies across the database. The shell permits its user to handle logical AND and logical OR operations effectively, but not fuzzy sets. Only crisp queries can be asked.

The KBMS shell permits the writing of simple IF . . . THEN . . . ELSE rules. Though no specific limit to the number of rules to be handled has been mentioned, the system seems to be at its best with rather simple structures. However, many queries can fit within its frame of reference.

The inference engine establishes *binding on multiple scenarios* and makes them valid networkwide. As stated, it uses object-oriented approaches as its basic working mechanism. Hypothetical reasoning permits users to choose among two or more alternatives.

The process of extracting common elements weeds out repetition in the rule base and puts it in the object base—which is more easily maintainable. The AI Corporation describes this as *inverse inheritance*.

Evidently, KBMS cannot be evaluated in the abstract. Valid references require:

1. definition of the existing hardware and software environments to which KBMS is applied,
2. comparison with other second-generation AI tools, particularly those able to manage distributed databases intelligently, and
3. implementation perspectives and associated evaluation with real-life applications in order to focus on applicability.

6. SHELLS AND EXPERT SYSTEMS AT THE GTE LABORATORIES

The high-technology laboratories of General Telephone and Electronics (GTE) are very active in AI. Though many of the expert systems developed there are oriented to telephony (like the Compass and Prophet AI constructs), significant results have also been achieved in other areas, like securities and intelligent databases. For instance:[7]

- An experimental system has been built for securities management.
- Particular attention has been paid to network diagnostics and facilities management.
- A knowledge-based expert systems shell (IDA) has been developed for global database management.
- An AI application using this shell integrates databases under VMS (Vax), Unix (Sun), MS DOS, Symbolics machines, and Xerox operating systems, as well as mainframe environments.

CALIDA stands for *California Intelligent Database Assistant*. This is the name of the expert system solution which has been successfully applied in integrating databases of dissimilar structures, including the handling of database semantics and domain integrity. Two basic database structures have been addressed:

- SQL-oriented relational databases, presently run under Oracle and DB2,
- Hierarchical-sequential files, organized at two levels of reference with records of varying length.

While this expert system is not a programming product, and has been primarily written for GTE implementation, it has been successfully applied, to judge by the results. Within the GTE environment, the results are extremely impressive.

IDA is the *best solution* I have seen so far in the integration of distributed databases. Its first practical implementation, CALIDA, has been done in an applications-oriented sense,

---

[7] Also impressive are the expert systems *Compass* and *Prophet* for network diagnostics.

providing Southern California GTE with significant benefits. "Networks are distributed and databases need cooperative expert systems mechanisms," said Dr. Gabriel Jakobson, associate director of GTE labs.

GTE Labs employs 600 people, in contrast to the 10,000 at Bell Labs. Given this disparity, two policies have been established in subject selection for R&D at GTE:

1. Focus on an able choice of subjects.
2. Adopt a high-risk/high-return orientation.

Research on *knowledge-based systems* employs 25 professionals. Three areas have been singled out:

- Implementation of expert systems
- Database research
- Machine learning

Proper analysis led to the conclusion that the implementation hardware should include PC,[8] Vax, Sun, and Symbolics; mainframes were excluded. A second policy decision was that all resources must be networked.

Working on the leading edge of computer science, researchers at GTE Labs have developed several new programs, including the following:

- The Local Area Network Design Assistant (LANDA), an interactive, intelligent tool for assisting in the design of local area networks using a given set of customer specifications.
- The Generic Business Modeling System (GBMS), a software tool for business modeling regarding information systems, including the engineering of databases.

We have already mentioned IDA and CALIDA for the aggregation and management of distributed databases, as well as *compass* and *prophet* for network administration, diagnostics, and maintenance.

Both rule-based and non-rule-based expert systems are being developed. The latter rest on cases which have been found through practice to offer broader constructs than those supported by rules. This is the *case-based reasoning approach.*

At GTE Labs, a significant contribution has been made by the development of a system that demonstrate that AI works. This is the story of SEC 144. Developed together with Northeastern University's (Boston) Center for Computer Science and Law, the Securities Expert Consultant for Rule 144 of the Securities Act of 1933 has been designed with the following *user profile* in mind: a small law firm that needs to advise a nonaffiliated client concerning restricted securities selling.[9] The expert system SEC 144 answers two questions:

1. Can the nonaffiliated owner of restricted securities sell these securities?

---

[8] Both IBM compatible and Macintosh.
[9] Similar work on legal compliance in the securities industry is being done at the University of Massachusetts and the University of Texas.

2. If the nonaffiliate can sell the restricted securities, how many shares can he sell?

With 50 rules worked out by one knowledge engineer and one domain expert over a *one-month period,* SEC 144 is a simple expert system which

- can be used as a demonstrator
- and can also be combined with another expert system at MIT, which is said to be operational, to form *a legal assistant for litigation.*

SEC 144 states *how many* securities of a certain type can be sold and *when.* For instance, if a nonaffiliate has owned the restricted securities for three or more years and has not been an affiliate of the issuer for the past three months, there are no restrictions on selling the securities. But if a nonaffiliate has beneficially owned the restricted securities for less than two years, then they cannot be sold.

For beneficial ownership between two and three years, the restricted securities can be sold if a number of conditions are satisfied. The process of determining the number of shares that the nonaffiliate can sell is called *aggregation.* When a nonaffiliate sells restricted securities, the quality that can be sold is the maximum of

- 1% of the shares outstanding,
- the average weekly volume of trading in the restricted securities reported on all national exchanges and/or through the automated quotation system during the four weeks prior to receipt of the sell order, or
- the average weekly volume of trading in the restricted securities reported during the four weeks prior to receipt of the sell order.

The expert system advises that according to current legislation, the maximum may be reduced by previous sales by the nonaffiliate over the past three months. The maximum may also be reduced if the restricted securities were acquired in a special situation—for instance, as a gift. In a special situation, sales of the same class of restricted securities by the original owner reduce the number that can be sold by the SEC 144 client.

This is only one example of the responses the expert system gives, as observed during the demonstration at GTE Labs. The important point is that legal expert systems are feasible and can make a significant contribution to the process of compliance with laws governing securities trading and banking activities.

7

Requirements for Valid Shells and Case Solutions

Keywords

second-generation shells • hybrid capability • portability • multifunctionality • intelligent databases • DBMS • open architecture • connectivity • fast prototyping • multiparadigm • visualization • enduser • response time • project management • expert systems • R&D • extendability • interfacing spreadsheets • integrative ability • performance • survivability • commodity • AI construct • icons • equilibration • computer-aided software engineering (CASE) • hype • open interfaces • heuristics • development cycle • reverse engineering

1. INTRODUCTION

While today the adoption of second-generation shells seems to be indispensable, not every structure brought to market can fit a company's objectives in developing second-generation expert systems. Therefore, I start by outlining a set of overall prerequisites for shell selection. These have crystallized out of discussions I had with knowledgeable executives in the United States, England, and Japan in 1989.

The prerequisites for shell selection are as follows:

1. *Hybrid capability,* the possibility of integrating with current code in DP through open subroutines at either the source code or object code level (preferably in C).
2. *Upward and downward* compatibility, from MS DOS (and eventually OS/2) through Unix, VMS, VM, and MVS—without inordinate demands for memory at MS DOS level.
3. *Portability to parallel computers* as the processing environment changes and supercomputers become the pivotal point of the landscape.

4. *Multifunctional approach* covering rules, frames, and scenarios, but also newer approaches such as fuzzy sets and neural nets, or at least those that accept and integrate specific tools for that purpose.
5. Support of *different methodologies,* such as forward and backward chaining and blackboards, and adaptability to newer ones as they develop.
6. Ability to *implement human windows,* including intelligent graphics and the whole range of *visualization* functions.
7. Reasonable *simplicity* so that endusers other than computer specialists can work with it on their problems.
8. *Intelligent database features* to make it feasible to exploit a global distributed database of incompatible data structures.
9. Ability to *work with different DBMSs,* particularly relational ones (DB2, Ingres, Oracle, Informix, Unify) but also networking (IDS) and hierarchical ones (IMS and others), as well as the possibility of developing toward *object* DBMSs.
10. *Networking functionality,* with emphasis on both local and wide areas, working in a fully interactive manner.
11. Membership in *open architectures* and integration into custom-made ones without excessive interfacing.
12. At the *chip level,* support for Intel 286, 386, 486, and i860, as well as other (RISC) designs and the chip lines of Motorola and Nippon Electric Corp. (NEC).

Evidently, it will be very difficult to find an expert systems shell that satisfies all these criteria at the same time. These should merely be considered as *guidelines whose purpose is to help focus the search for the best alternative.*

Some characteristics of shells are more important than others—for instance, spanning *different architectures,* handling *different DBMSs, connectivity,* and *visualization.* In the last analysis, if we cannot find a shell which can do most of these things in an able manner, then we may have to custom-make a solution by adding some necessary routines.

Keeping the list of shell characteristics in mind, I believe that the test to be done in order to identify the appropriate shell should consist of a relatively simple program to be coded through alternative AI tools under investigation in order to evaluate

1. fast prototyping
2. simplicity of programming
3. ease of learning and easy to use
4. short development time
5. multiparadigmatic capability
6. runtime efficiency on the PC
7. visualization capabilities
8. visualization as judged by the enduser
9. online connection to databases
10. interfacing to different databases and DBMSs
11. integration with existing facilities

12. interfacing to DP programs
13. resources used in development
14. ability to run on conventional hardware
15. portability and deliverability
16. quality of connectivity
17. accuracy of the AI construct
18. response time

It is from this perspective of critical factors that expert systems shells must be considered, and it is quite clear that no expert system shell or any other computer-aided solution which may be under consideration should be chosen without thorough testing. This must take the form of an experimental design:

- Two expert system projects should be developed and run.
- This should be done with both shells, but on the same PC.
- They should have exactly the same functional specifications, including database access.

The criteria outlined in the preceding paragraphs constitute a consensus among executives in leading industries and financial institutions with experience in expert system development. It is wise to test thoroughly prior to making a commitment, as the outcome of these tests will be the basis of advanced software development for the next five to seven years.

2. LEARNING FROM THE EXPERIENCE OF OTHER ORGANIZATIONS

To facilitate the performance of the tests which must be made in order to provide documented answers to key evaluation questions—thus establishing which shell should be selected—I have sought the experience of leading specialists in this field. The opportunity occurred at the Third International Symposium on AI and Expert Systems, which I co-chaired in West Berlin from June 12 to 16, 1989. Two specialists, both with experience in testing expert system shells, participated in this discussion, and their advice has been appreciated: Dr. Kent Bimson, director of Lockheed Aircraft in charge of project management, and Prof. Dr. Tibor Vamos, director of the Automation Laboratory of the Hungarian Academy of Sciences.

Lockheed has found that complex project management for avionics and space projects cannot be effectively done by using classical tools, such as PERT and the critical path method. More powerful approaches are neceessary, and only AI can provide them. Enriched with AI, project management software uses a knowledgebank to circumvent the complexity of control functions. If we view the generation of control activities as a search process, then the job of the knowledgebank is to limit the search. The alternatives at each point in the search space form the branches of an AND/OR goal tree.

- Nodes of such a tree combined (through a logical AND operation) with a common parent must all be satisfied before the parent is satisfied.

- Nodes associated through a logical OR operator with a common parent can satisfy the parent independently by their own solution.

This is the simple schema. Much more complex approaches are used in project management through AI constructs. Knowledgebanks serve to prune structures in two ways. First, nodes can be replaced, along with all their descendants, by a complete solution to the subproblem specified in the knowledgebank. Second, sections of the tree can be pruned if available knowledge specifies the impossibility of a solution in these sections. Such a knowledgebank must be structured so that the information it contains applies in a large number of possible instances.

Lockheed has developed a number of expert systems for project management, including an enterprisewide product. Their design and implementation have required a test of expert systems shells almost every two years to take advantage of the best technology. Said Dr. Bimson: "Old shells which run only on Symbolics machines will never be able to integrate into the real world. We now appreciate that we have to support an integrative capability."

The latest test done by Lockheed included ART-IM and Nexpert, the best current shells available in the United States today. Nexpert was chosen. While the criteria of Lockheed are not necessarily the criteria of every other firm, some references are valid to all cases, as, for instance: "We have to be able to say: 'This is another tool, integrative with what we had so far. It is not a different environment'." Lockheed is only one reference and since the results of other tests should be of significant interest to everybody, Table 7-1 summarizes what Dr. Bimson has found.

The tests of expert system shells done by Prof. Vamos at the Hungarian Academy of Sciences were *generic*. The following are the criteria that these tests defined as being crucial. They are not very different from the criteria suggested earlier:

1. R&D invested by the originator company to support future developments
2. Ability to do effective distribution at the end-user level
3. User friendliness of the shell and its output
4. Extendability of the shell primitives
5. Interfacing to C, dBase, and spreadsheets
6. Range of supported operating systems: MS DOS, OS/2, Unix
7. Runtime operation and associated response time
8. Able graphics capability or interface
9. Agile use of windows
10. Integrative ability with classical DP

Lockheed also considered the fact that the Nexpert Company deals strictly with development; marketing is done by other corporations, such as Bechtel Power. This division of functions enhances the ability of the developers to concentrate on new features.

The tests conducted by the Hungarian Academy of Sciences demonstrate that ART is more oriented to developers. Nexpert Object is better from the viewpoint of the enduser— particularly the everyday user. At the same time, one of the conclusions reached at the Third International Symposium on AI and Expert Systems is that in the 1990s "the everyday user will be the vital point of reference—much more important than the developer. We must train the enduser to do his own development work for simple expert systems—and we

TABLE 7-1. Evaluation of Nexpert and ART-IM by Lockheed Aircraft in Terms of Adoption.

Nexpert	ART-IM
1. *Portable* between different operating systems	Not so easily portable, because uses different windowing in the function of the operating systems X windows and MS windows; in new operating system environment, windowing must be redone[1]
2. In terms of *functionality,* allows better domain control	
3. Facilities *embedded* for activating and deactivating rules	
4. Provides ability to build in *control structures*	
5. Runs *Hypercard*	
6. The August 1989 release has *multivalued slots*	No multivalued slots featured; this is critical
7. Faster in *performance*	Slower than Nexpert but better than other shells
8. *Cleaner* development environment	More complex than Nexpert
9. More *efficient* in development work	
10. Easier for the *enduser*	
11. Fully integrated *graphics*	
12. Statistically based constructs available	
13. Supports the ability to develop *explanation systems* on variance, as well as deviation reports	
14. More intelligent decision support than its alternatives	
15. Provides infrastructure for *knowledge acquisition*	
16. *Good survivability;* 50% of new expert systems being built are Nexpert	*Good survivability;* Inference Corp. is now the second largest developer of expert system shells
17. Is *communications oriented* and designed to be an interactive tool	
18. Provides better *hybrid systems* capability	
19. Can be called from other environments as well as call other environments, permitting the user to optimize the choice of code (call-in, call-out)	

[1]ART is supported under Unix, which is not yet true of ART-IM. This is the reason for this reference.

should have the tools to achieve such goal." This statement sets the stage for the work to be done in advanced information systems development during the next few years. It establishes the direction for the leading companies, as well as the goals they plan to reach in AI implementation.

Solutions must be not only farsighted but also comprehensive. Therefore, before describing second-generation expert systems shells and their functionality, we should look at the broader subject of computer-aided software engineering—its scope, mechanics, basic tools, and expected benefits.

3. TESTING THE SHELL AND THE COMMODITY AI CONSTRUCT

Sections 5 and 6 of Chapter 4 focuses on internal and external tests of the AI system. As stated at the conclusion of that chapter, the discussion was not exhaustive. Having presented the subject of shells and the reasons why they should be subjected to thorough evaluation, we now return to testing.

Let's start with a real-life example of the support shells and value that added facilities can provide for testing. At NASA, the Requirements Engineering Automated Development (READ) system was developed with the use of the Knowledge Engineering System (KES). The goal of READ was to determine the software functional requirements for command management activities of NASA-supported satellites.

Expert systems such as READ offer a sound first cut of satellite functional requirements in about thirty minutes. By contrast, the more classical procedure takes three to four months, with meetings held once or twice a week. READ also standardizes the requirements language for future satellite command management systems. It has been validated through backcasting and mapping by analogy.

Shell support for testing procedures is closely related to the facilities it provides for

- tracking at the user's command,
- representation (including graphics and color),
- easily identifiable interfaces, and
- logical debugging aids,

Knowledge engineers often find it very helpful to draw an emerging inference net on paper in order to show the domain expert how the system is progressing. An easily understandable presentation has advantages in use as well as at the debugging stage. Users are able to reassure themselves that the AI construct's conclusions are sensible and that new knowledge can be added easily as it becomes available.

In practically all applications, comprehensibility to users is important, and *icons*[2] make an effective human window. A complex contingency in an AI system presented as a set of rules is not very useful. A graphic presentation is much better. In the *Dipmeter Advisor,* for

---

[2] An icon is a representation of a familiar object, typically a graphic one.

instance, the interface is graphic, and it has proved invaluable in testing and user acceptance. Many knowledge engineers emphasize that the assertions and rules comprising an inference network are easiest to understand when presented in graphic format. Thus, graphics appears to be an excellent medium for situations which otherwise require many lines of text. But while presentation is important and is closely related to shell facilities, it is only part of the total test picture.

After the prototype is done through a given shell, the larger test picture should consider the many users who may add validation routines regarding information elements (domain), rules, and responses. The majority will do so unconsciously, as very few of them understand the intricacies of the AI structure. But all of them will carefully look at the system to see if it presents an effective human window.

The technical aspect cannot and should not be overlooked. How many systems, for instance, have traps to catch users who make changes to rules/or other parts of the knolwedgebank? The answer is: "Very few." Yet, traps are an important part of the construct. If the shell does not provide them as a matter of course, they should be added by the user organization. Nobody ever said that shells are perfect. We should examine the tools we use prior to using them.

The same is true of standard facilities used for testing data. Not only the shell—or any other development tool—should incorporate testing. In addition, standard "test cases" are needed, many of the qualitative, logical nature.

Similarly, the typical answer to the question "How often does one know if the system works or does not work?" is "Rarely." This, however, does not mean that a system test is not important. To the contrary: It is *vital,* and facilities for doing it should be provided by the shell.

The ease with which user organizations adopt AI development tools without really knowing what they need is surprising. Companies do not buy payroll software that does not work, yet they do not establish rigorous standards in purchasing an expert system or any other AI construct.

The preceding discussion is not relevant to shells alone, though shells are especially important because they are used to develop other systems. If there are deficiencies in the linguistic interface, the AI constructs that emerge from the shell will get them by inheritance. The preceding discussion, however, is valid for the full range of AI systems currently on the market. For the benefit of knowledge engineers who are or will be considering them for possible purchase, here is some advice on what to look for.

1. Take smaller modules, which are easier controllable, and test them individually to see if each of them fits the recommendations of the domain expert.

Even if you wish to buy a larger AI system, ask the vendor to modularize it. Small modules are controllable. They don't have to be treated as a black box. We can look into them and understand what they contain.

2. Use the AI system itself to assert its semantics, syntactics, and pragmatics, giving an error signal if something goes wrong.

If this cannot be done, then the system *is not for you.* An AI construct will be able to do what it is supposed to do only if test procedures are built into the system.

Let me further stress that *detail* is important; generalities are not enough. Embedded test procedures should include all *default* values and associated situations. They should also be subject to a comprehensive, user-friendly presentation.

3. Make sure that every module contains the necessary *editors* to do consistency checking. Every module should be subjected to *equilibration*.

If the shell you are using does not have the needed tools, then you must develop them. Remember, however, the penalties in performance for external routines. They were discussed in connection with EXSYS.

I consider equilibration more important than debugging, but debugging also is necessary. Relevant debugging aids include various kinds of trace and break facilities. The latter are useful for followup on significant actions of the system while it is running—for instance, when a rule is being tried.

We have also spoken of break facilities. They allow users to make modifications and continue the computation. For example, if the conditions of a rule are not satisfied, but the knowledge engineer wants to see what would happen if they were, he can change the contents so that the conditions are satisfied and then continue the computation.

4. AI constructs can present security risks. If classical DP application programs can be illegally manipulated, so can AI systems—with much more disastrous results.

To face this challenge, it is necessary to bring into the test procedure the organization's DP auditing department, appropriately extending its functions and responsibilities. Like quality, security should be embedded in the AI system at the drafting board. The DP Auditing Department must confirm that this is the case. Let your DP Auditing Department use *their* imagination.

5. Since the AI community as a whole has not yet come up with a standard methodology for AI system testing,[3] you should develop your own. But in every organization, there should be one, and only one, official AI system testing methodology.

There is no doubt that we need a methodology for *system testing*. And to succeed, we need a methodology which extends over all phases of engineering—from acquisition to representation, prototyping, and the use of shells and other linguistic constructs to internal and external testing. In addition, valid methodology should be based on a *cooperative approach*, one involving end users as well as domain experts and knowledge engineers. Endusers will build upon AI system expertise using their skills. Hence, they should be part of the testing process.

If this can be achieved, then the AI system will not only be tested but will also be accepted much more easily. We should never forget the issue of user acceptability. At the bottom line, it will make or break the expert system.

---

[3] Sections 5 and 6 of Chapter 4, as well as the present section, describe my policies and those of colleagues who contributed to them.

Criticisms by endusers ensure that the AI construct comes up with a variety of opinions. Endusers have their own opinions. Performance is based upon opinions. (For this reason, some companies evaluate developed expert systems through panel meetings prior to distributed through the organization for applications usage. Thus, the endusers who will be the expert system's owners must state what, in their judgment, constitutes a good system, a bad mistake, and an acceptable test. This will greatly enhance the dynamics of testing and will also create a useful precedent for the future.

4. COMPUTER-AIDED SOFTWARE ENGINEERING (CASE)

CASE is one of the most important subjects in the U.S. financial, manufacturing, and distribution industries today. CASE stands for "computer-aided software engineering," but every person who makes, buys, or uses fourth-generation languages seems to have his own definition, making it difficult to agree upon a meaning. The very term fourth-generation language has been corrupted by misuse through its assignment to totally unworthy products.

The proper fourth-generation language allows endusers to say what they want rather than how to do it. This permits an application to be developed in simple English-like statements, or parameters, with a focus on agile, user-friendly interfaces—and, hence, human window facilities.

One significant advantage of a fourth-generation language is that it has much of the basic coding already built in, and another major part can be automatically generated. This means that programming takes less time and is less complex. Maintenance is also a key issue. At the Mellon Bank, CASE tools are selected on the basis of reducing program maintenance by 50% or more.

We need powerful tools to build new software because, with the languages of the 1950s and 1960s, which are still popular, it is hard to write complete specifications. Yet:

1. The *complexity* of the problems we are faced with has tremendously increased.
2. The *business requirements* are changing very rapidly.
3. There is *plenty of exaggeration* and missing information.

Still companies look at CASE as the means for improving programmer productivity. Executives of the Bank of America, for instance, mentioned during a May 1989 working meeting in Concord, California, that the majority of their 1,000 programmers today work on interactive development using CASE tools. While this practice started several years ago, only since the beginning of 1988 had the bank moved aggressively to interactive software development using CASE.

Figure 7-1 demonstrates the philosophy of the Bank of America in the transition from conventional programming languages through fourth-generation languages to expert sys-

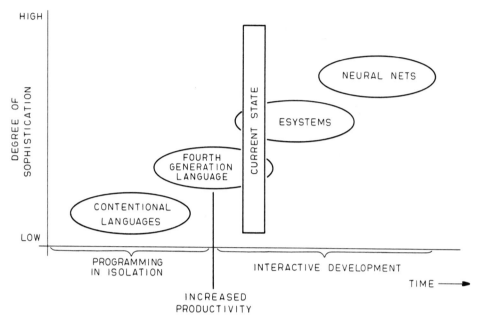

Figure 7-1. Linguistic developments will have a much greater impact when they integrate in an agile manner with online distributed databases. This facility was very low with conventional programming languages, has improved with fourth-generation languages, is still better with expert systems, and is expected to be at its best with interconnected neural networks.

tem shells. The role of online access to distributed databases is underlined. The immediate objectives of CASE are to[4]

- *minimize* staff *retraining*
- *maximize reuse* of the existing development environment,
- select only *proven products* and vendors, and
- adopt only tools with *open interfaces.*

Crucial to this strategy is the ability to address all target platforms from PCs to mainframes. The Bank of America is betting on the personal WS for the future.

Management has stated that so far it is pleased with the PC development tools it selected, their prototyping ability, and the demonstration features of the tools. Internal business clients at Bank of America have been impressed by the development speed and the CASE tools' ability to produce logical specifications. The bank is now looking for standardized code created by the Telon Code Generator and further programmer productivity gains from the

---

[4] Among the selected tools are Excelerator, MicroFocus Workbench (a PC-based component), and Telon code generator (on the mainframe).

use of a multitechnology programming environment. However, there have been a few mismatches, for instance:

- failure of Telon to take advantage of full SQL capability and
- incomplete transportability of Excelerator specifications into code generators.

However, even with these reservations, both Excelerator and Telon *save time.* They shift development to the frontend at the WS level, where it belongs. There is productivity to be gained. The weakest part is lack of integration among vendors.

Nevertheless, in general, conventional approaches are most applicable to problems that are primarily deterministic. There is one and only one correct solution to look for, and it deals with problems which are algorithmic in nature. The path to this solution is known in advance.

But this is hardly the world in which we live today, and it is the negation of the banking world of the 1990s. Hence, we need tools with which we can skillfully manipulate problems that have the following characteristics:

- They are *nondeterministic* in nature, possibly fuzzy. There may be more than one acceptable answer; the database queries are not crisp; both hard and soft data exist.
- *Their solution is heuristic rather than algorithmic.* The path between inputs and outputs is not known and must be searched for intensively.

The leading American financial institutions are sensitive to these new specifications. At the Mellon Bank, when an information technology tool is announced, a team of its specialists examines the programming product for *efficiency.* Attention is also paid to future developments in programming. Said Dr. George Di Nardo, Executive vice president at Mellon during our mid-1989 meeting: "We believe that in three to five years the programmer as we know him today will be gone. The work will be done strictly at the program specifications level."

CASE tools aim to address this program specification level, but just selecting and using a tool is not enough. The programmers have to be made more productive, and the computer system as a whole has to be run more efficiently. Some banks use a carrot-and-stick approach. The Mellon Bank gives a "reward" for inefficient programmers. It is called "the pig of the month," and those who qualify for it have to wear the pig's hat.

But the bottom line is what counts, and when it comes to the selection and use of the CASE tools themselves, many experts find it difficult to differentiate CASE from fourth-generation languages. They admit that the dividing line between the two is unclear, and is becoming increasingly uncleard:

- Essentially, CASE is a computer methodology that lays much of the groundwork for programming.
- It does not change the basic methods used to program a computer; it simply speeds them up.

Critics say that most of the currently available CASE tools are nothing more than a waterfall model of software development enriched by media commonly used by developers. Many of the tools capitalize on the fact that errors found in requirements analysis and design specification are much easier to correct than errors found later in the software development cycle. This has led to the policy that computer-aided software engineering must

1. provide leverage in the software project requirements analysis,
2. help improve the design specification phase, and
3. potentially, generate code automatically from the software design specification.

Using this line of reasoning, special-purpose code generators should be included in CASE tools, as should of project management software. Code analyzers, performance evaluators, computer configuration management, and also code restructuring tools are part of this group.

This support should be geared to the profile of the programmer/analyst—someone who is able to reengineer procedures, do nonprocedural programming, and produce predevelopment specifications. Based on these specifications, the code itself should be automatically generated and compiled.

Several things must be done in order to get results:

1. *Culture change.*
2. *Able tool* selection
3. *Retraining* of programmers and analysts
4. *Reverse engineering* approaches
5. Valid solutions to *data modeling* problems

Data arrive in many different ways. We have to streamline them and make them homogeneous in order to reduce redundant data and improve the efficiency of their handling.

Data-modeling methodologies, user inferface, and screen design approaches are an integral part of CASE. This is equally true of

- Real-time analysis,
- Evolutionary delivery,
- Attribute specifications,
- Software reuse, and
- Metrics.

However, no known system so far supports all of the features necessary for a complete methodology, nor is there general agreement about what a good methodology should be.

Some CASE tools do offer facilities (but not universal methodologies) for data modeling and realtime control design. Somewhat more popular are user-interface design tools. More recent market introductions include expert system design capabilities either through their own shell or via the incorporation of one that is generally available. AI constructs and hybrid systems capability are becoming integral parts of CASE.

In this sense, CASE tools help automate the most tedious portions of designing, modeling, and specifying a system. They also underline the reusable aspects of software, particularly those routines that appear repeatedly in many different applications. Call-in and call-out facilities ensure that they are preprogrammed so that they can be called up when writing a customized program.

5. FROM CONVENTIONAL PROGRAMMING TO EXPERT SYSTEMS APPROACHES: THE CHALLENGE OF REVERSE ENGINEERING

Whereas the early CASE tools of the 1970s, like Project Isdos (PSL/PAS) at the University of Michigan, focused on system analysis, newer offerings employ an increasing amount of AI. This is happening, first of all, in response to users' requirements. But it is equally true that classical approaches simply cannot solve the developing challenges—for instance, *reverse engineering.* Yet, by many accounts, reverse engineering represents the future. As Dr. Di Nardo commented: "All Chief Information Officers should concentrate on the ability to extract both information elements and procedural or nonprocedural commands from their repository of data assets and their programming libraries. From then on, a graphics specifications system should automatically create the new programming environment."

Conventional programming cannot achieve the expected result because *conventional approaches were not designed for reverse engineering.* Classical programming is based on the following notion:

Program = statements + variables

These variables are typically integers, real numbers, and characters. The statements specify what to compute but not what to decompute, and this is what is currently needed. Reverse engineering of lines of code is necessary to prune and restructure current program libraries, as well as to help reduce the crippling amount of program maintenance that is now necessary. As long as we keep on spending 70–80% of our human resources on maintenance, we will never be able to do what the user needs.

In contrast to classical programming approaches, rule-based systems are both more flexible and better focused:

Program = rules + object definitions

The objects include facts, states, values—and goals. The rules specify what to infer. Hence they reflect the way professionals think and make decisions.

Another fact to be noted is that successful expert systems can only be built in close collaboration with a domain expert who is an enduser. When we move the programmer to the enduser level, he is better aware of the job being done. He can also comprehend that if he keeps on asking for changes, he will never have the new applications he wants in order to be competitive.

To improve upon what it has already achieved by using the approach described in the preceding chapter, the Bank of America set for itself the following objectives for the next few months:

1. *Measurement.* Extend the implementation of metrics, collect additional time/ effort data, compare them, and decide on improvements.
2. *Quality appraisal.* Monitor the accuracy of generated code, as well as the quality of the overall effort.

3. *Support.* Enhance ongoing product support for pilot projects through better use of all tools.
4. *Integration.* Ensure a common presentation of all development tools. Focus on product integration within the bank.

The management of the Bank of America Systems Engineering (BASE) Division is always searching for improvements. For instance, Telon was tested to generate DB2 reporting applications after custom code had to be written because of weaknesses found in DB2.

To help improve the collaboration between software developers and endusers, the Mellon Bank has designed a *programmer workbench*[5] in which has been embedded

1. electronic mail between developers and endusers
2. a number of CASE tools
3. structured programming methodology
4. data analysis tools and standards
5. online access to the database administrator (DBA) and the databases
6. word processing graphics for documentation
7. other utilities, such as a scheduler
8. media that track the programmer on productivity

Mellon claims that the Workbench, its tools, and its associated methodology have been responsible for increasing programmer productivity by more than 10% a year; this is a realistic goal. Clearly, improving programmer productivity and sharply reducing program maintenance requirements are critical issues to a bank which has millions of lines of code to manage and many more to develop. This is the reason for using the best technology available.

The Dai-Ichi Kangyo bank in Japan today has 22 million lines of code. Mellon has 200 applications systems with 20 million lines of code. UBS has nearly 18 million lines of code in Switzerland and more than 20 million lines worldwide. One reverse engineering system enriched with AI might be enough to do the needed renewal job.

The Workbench has paid significant dividends to Mellon, and Dr. Di Nardo emphasized that the bank had to develop it themselves because neither IBM nor any other vendor could come up with a satisfactory system. Apart from greatly assisting programmers and analysts, it automates the DBA job,

- providing *file* design approval online,
- easing file comparisons,
- simplifying observance and control or standards,
- speeding up development time tremendously, and
- improving the chance of developing reusable code.

Said the executive vice president of the Mellon Bank: "We believe in reusable code, and we need a fully integrated database no matter if it runs under IMS, DB2, or other DBMS."

---

[5] A Wang VS 300 connected to IBM mainframes through TSO.

At Mellon and many other leading financial institutions, emphasis has also been placed on the able support of *human windows*. Studies have documented that managers and professionals do *not* want to have presented to them *knowledge* and *information*

- in different and novel ways or
- in a variety of incompatible formats.

They want to see the presentation the way they are accustomed to work in their daily practice, and expect systems can help reach this goal. I consider AI constructs as instrumental both in peer-to-peer communications and in visualization. In fact, they are the so far missing link.

AI-enriched approaches are vital because graphic user interfaces for WS applications are difficult to build without rules that simplify the implementation process. In the background is the fact that not all user interfaces have to look alike. It is therefore desirable to

- maintain a consistent watch across applications, and
- be sensitive to the fact that users often have different preferences.

Customization is important in getting user acceptance of the system. One user may prefer pop-up menus, while another may insist on icons. Our tools must allow a broad range of interface styles and must be customizable on a per-user basis. To help create customized interfaces, developers should consider the following questions:

- Which main classes of interfaces should be supported?
- What constitutes a good set of programming abstractions for building such interfaces?
- How can the enduser employ an interface, given these abstractions?
- Is practical experience a guide to developing user interface tools?
- What can we learn from past practice?

User interfaces need not be purely graphic. While today many application designers prefer iconic interfaces because they believe that novice users understand pictures more readily than text, recent research suggests that *excessive use of icons can confuse the enduser* with unfamiliar symbolism. A textual interface might be more appropriate in a given context. The choice of graphic or textual representation should favor the clearest alternative, but user interface code should be object oriented. Objects are natural for representing the elements of a user interface, as they support their direct manipulation.

Objects provide a good abstraction mechanism, encapsulating states and operations. *Inheritance* makes extension easy. Hence, AI concepts dominate a human window design. Compared with procedural implementation, user interfaces written in an object-oriented language are significantly easier to develop and maintain.

Organizations with experience in agile human window design have come to the conclusion that interactive and abstract objects should be separate. It is important to distinguish between *interactive objects,* which implement the interface, and *abstract objects,* which implement operations on the data underlying the interface. Separating user interface and application code makes it possible to change the interface without modifying the underlying functionality, and vice versa. This also facilitates customization by permitting several interfaces to the same application.

In a number of valid human interface solutions, objects are composed of clauses which define common strategies for arranging components to fill the available space. Base classes present communication protocols for all objects in the hierarchy. Composition classes define the additional protocols needed for operations, such as inserting and removing elements, and for propagating information through the composition.

These considerations are far removed from the concepts addressed by classical programming. Not only can the able development of human interfaces benefit greatly from expert systems (and also be assisted by the primitives of expert system shells), but this discussion also helps document that unless we change our culture and our approaches to information systems design, we are condemned to total ossification.

6. DEFINING AI FUNCTIONALITY: A JAPANESE EXPERIENCE

Classical system analysis and programming methods build applications through a series of independent steps: User requirements are translated into a system analysis. This analysis is turned into specifications, which are then converted into detailed designs, subsequently written in code, and finally tested for implementation. The result is a long, costly development cycle aggravated by increasing maintenance requirements.

With the most modern CASE tools, and, more specifically, expert system shells, specifications are directly translated into application prototypes that are reworked until they are ready for production delivery. This developmental approach employs the components of a knowledgebank and an inference engine, storing a set of variable, rules, actions, relationships, and goals for subsequent usage.

Newer approaches involve *object-oriented programming*. This methodology is an extension of database concepts and involves

- *factoring of knowledge*, that is, rules, to validate data derived from application programs, and
- storage of such knowledge, together with the data, in the form of objects.[6]

Rules or procedural code can be attached to objects, so that whenever the object's value is changed, deleted, created, and so on, the rules will automatically be executed. For example, attaching data validation criteria to a data object eliminates the need to code the validation procedures into each program or application that uses the data. Instead, the validation procedures are stored with the object itself.

---

[6] An *object,* in AI terminology, is a logical grouping of facts and is the cornerstone of knowledge-based systems.

Throughout the development process, editors provide immediate testing and debugging feedback. At runtime, *the inference engine*[7] automatically controls the execution sequence of the application. It processes the roals in the knowledgebank, using the most efficient path.

But there is no question of returning to the stereotypes and the ossification of classical DP. For this reason, at the beginning of this chapter I outlined a number of requirements which must be met for an able choice of an expert system shell. The Japanese too have worked on similar processes, and in reaching their conclusion they emphasize the following qualities:

1. *Low cost* of both development and runtime versions, including the cost of the machine platform.
2. Ability to run on *conventional* software and hardware, and particularly on the WS.
3. *multiparadigmatic,* that is, the ability to handle objects, rules, frames, and scenarios.
4. *Portability and deliverability*—an expert system built in one environment but able to move into others worldwide.
5. *Fast execution* on the engines on which the AI construct runs—hence, practically written in C.
6. *Hybrid solutions* through interfacing to other programs ranging from classical DP to integrated software and office automation.

All of these requirements are valid for CASE tools as well, particularly today when there are alternatives from which to choose. In fact, the better alternatives are offered by independent vendors rather than by mainframe providers.

Keep in mind that whatever we do should show a verified trend toward greater maturity and lead to impressive productivity gains. Nearly two decades have passed since software engineering was first advocated. Although some useful techniques and tools are now available, in most organizations software engineering is not widely used.

The problems of achieving high software reliability and steady productivity increases in software production still remain serious. New, powerful ideas do not seem to have appeared through the classical media, hence the high expectations for the knowledge engineering approaches for making a breakthrough in software development.

One of the most laborious and difficult tasks associated with the implementation of a complex computer-based system is the development of its software. But we rarely appreciate that we need to take important steps to ease this process. If we wish to be rational in doing analysis and programming work, we must develop specification models that are

- general enough for system abstraction and design but also
- sufficiently precise to synthesize executable computer code.

At the same time, we must investigate a wide range of other significant issues. These range from improving environmental support for the software development process to aiding the development and implementation of reusable software.

---

[7] See also Chapter 12.

In Japan, the *AI Center* (jointly operated by ICOT and the Japan Information Processing Development Organization) did a thorough study on the impact of AI technology. The results, which included 203 Japanese organizations, show that among the many probable application areas of knowledge systems, DP-type *software development* is given high priority by Japanese users. The responses are seen in Table 7-2.

Based on these statistics, OKI Electric did a subsequent study which identified a number of domains where AI tools can be of great service in the more classical DP sectors. The following has been reported:

1. *Application of the business domain knowledgebank*

System engineers of a large software house, the subsidiary of a Japanese securities company, work to construct a knowledgebank from bulky volumes of securities business manuals. This is considered useful for teaching software engineers about their application domain and, most importantly, for requirement analysis.

2. *Guidance system for problem solution*

Japanese companies are keen on adopting problem analysis methodology—hence, a sort of CASE—for clarifying system specifications. This work is often conducted as a group discussion, where the role of a highly qualified instructor/leader is critical. A current AI project is based on the premise that a guidance system toward problem solution, realized by assembling the know-how of experienced instructors, would be very useful.

TABLE 7-2. Expert System Application Areas for the 1990s as Seen by Leading Japanese Financial and Industrial Organizations.

Application Area	No. of Responding Companies	Typical Examples of Projected AI Applications
Design	31	Interface to CAD; system configuration support; materials selection
Software development	27	Automated programming; software design support; software reuse; reverse engineering
Diagnosis	26	Troubleshooting of power devices; plant diagnosis, including measurement; network diagnosis
Forecasting	21	Prediction of market trends; sales planning
Decision support	18	Corporate strategy; analysis of trends in forex and securities; judgment on loans
Control	15	CIM; robotics
Embedded systems	14	Troubleshooting; compliance control
Computer-aided instruction	10	Teaching high-technology subjects; computer-based training
Miscellaneous	39	Investment advising; assets management; tax advisory; information retrieval; automatic translation

3. *Guidance system for using tools*

The goal to integrate various software tools which are currently used in the organization. An AI-enriched approach:

- helps in selecting appropriate tools for the user's specific purposes.
- shows how to use them, and
- provides advice when trouble arises while using the chosen tools.

In effect, this is an automated help desk solution. The approach blends computer-aided software engineering concepts with expertise embedded in AI rules.

4. *Software design support system*

A Japanese project focused on software design activity as the process of transforming specifications into detailed descriptions. The approach consisted of building a knowledge-bank consisting of transformation knowledge based on the best expertise available. This turned out to be rewarding, especially when the process was performed following a specific design methodology, such as Jackson's method or Warnier's method. The researchers also noted that today there already exist similar systems that do not explicitly apply knowledge engineering approaches, leading to the concept that even partial introduction of knowledge-based solutions can be quite effective.

5. *Standard inspection and evaluation system for software development*

A knowledge-based approach has been developed in Japan that guides the software engineers' activities in accordance with established standards. It also evaluates the quality of products produced at each work step in terms of the rules set by the standards.

6. *Guidance system for reusing software components*

In Japan, as elsewhere, software reuse by accessing a software component library enhances productivity. A considerable effort is underway to construct such libraries. Questions concerning this approach are as follows:

- What kinds of components should be stored?
- How should they be structured?
- How should they be retrieved?
- How should software be synthesized from these parts?

Knowledgebanks are employed to answer these questions. Other interesting projects include project management, as well as knowledgebanks for maintenance of software and for tracking software supplied to the users.

OKI technologists also conducted another survey. They distributed questionnaires to 100 software engineers and researchers selected from an inventory of authors who wrote papers on the subject of software engineering or the effect of AI applications on software. The main query concerned *past attempts and future plans of*

- expert system development and
- software processes in general.

TABLE 7-3. Current and Projected Expert Systems by Functions and Phases.[8]

| Function | Phase | | | | | | | |
	Requirements Analysis	System Design	Programming	Testing	Operations	Management	Other	Total
Analysis					1	1		2
Diagnosis				1	6	4		11
Instruction	1	6	5	1	1			14
Guidance	4	8	6	3	6		1	28
Design		7	7	2				16
Control					5			5
Prediction						5		5
Planning				1		7		8
Others	4	2	1	2			2	11
Total	9	23	19	10	19	17	3	100

[8]Statistics based on answers to a questionnaire administered in Japan.

One out of three respondents referred to knowledge system development for general software processes. The responses included

- a cost estimating expert system for software development,
- procedure generation for an image processing expert system, and
- a software design support expert system.

In terms of future prospects, guidance-type systems and tools for the design and coding phases were considered most intently. Table 7-3 presents, in matrix form, the statistics obtained, by phase of the software development process as well as by function.

In both the United States and Japan, some of the most important reasons why leading information technologists look at AI for support are largely connected to the able development and use of more powerful tools. They include

1. discipline in software development,
2. verification of specifications and code,
3. security in operation,
4. a close look at any changes during maintenance, and
5. issues relating to liability due to software.

8

Developing and Implementing Human Windows

Keywords

knowledge delivery systems • human window • natural language • metasystem • learning system • metaphor • object oriented • metaconcept • input media • mouse • viewport • viewport management • physical windows • logical windows • browsing • border • title • commands • scrollbars • justification • multimedia • document handling • multimedia documents • uncertainty management • plausible inference • office document architecture • query specification • plausible inference • conceptual query • exact match • partial match

1. INTRODUCTION

The integration of AI constructs and natural language solutions leads to efficient *knowledge delivery systems*. These are long overdue. In over thirty-five years of computer practice, we have not been very successful in designing human interfaces. This situation may now be changing.

Developers mimic what people do when they strive to create new types of displays—in both a physical and a logical sense. While many problems must still be solved, we have developed a concept of a human window and of its need. The *human window* is a tutorial dialogue method. It guides man–machine communication in two important ways:

1. It structures the dialogue.
2. It provides a homogeneous interface, yet one that is adaptable to the user.

The art of making human windows is new, but its importance is so great that AI scientists that suggest about 40% of our resources should be channeled to interface development.

Some say that this statistic is no longer valid because today there exist standard human windows. This argument is false. For ease of use, the human window has to be customized, consistent, and comprehensive. In the Dipmeter Advisor, 42% of the code is devoted to the human window. This interface is graphic, has tested well, and has gained wide user acceptance. Able man–machine interfaces have extended portability.

Window design must involve more than a mouse and pop-up menus. It is often suggested that a valid approach is a natural language system that permits concepts to be

- easily defined and
- applied to one another in any combination based on the user's request

A good natural language system determines how to combine formulas based on the particular wording of a sentence. Interfacing must be provided in a form that end users will be able to master, in a context that can be maintained through the dialogue, and, if possible, corporatewide.

Yet, there is no evidence that natural language alone will suffice. For able, lasting solutions we must focus on

- primitives,
- multimedia interconnect, and
- multimodal interfaces.

Multimodal interfaces include textual means, pointers, menus, advanced graphics, touch, speech, and vision. All the senses should be involved. Speech recognition and synthesis are part of the system. We must, for instance, provide access via telephone to the AI construct for consultation.

Multimedia interconnect methods includes voice, image, text, data, and graphics. A transparent database search is part of the system, as is vision interface to other knowledge-based systems. We should not forget that over 70% of sensory input and 50% of energy consumption are connected to vision.

A good user interface should be incorporated from the prototype stage on. To facilitate development of the AI construct, design specifications should pay full attention to all the needs of the enduser. Starting with a high-resolution screen (1 megapixel or more), windowing primitives must support the ability to create, fill, move, reshape, and overlap. There should be good editor routines and tools designed to adapt the system to the language of the user's choice.

Logical and physical windows (see Section 4) can be defined to be larger than the screen itself if looked at through viewports. This is what we did in the past: pan and scroll quickly through large amounts of screen information with full color control and use of graphics character sets. Yet we know that much more will be necessary in the future.

Solutions should be tested using the tools available in applied experimental psychology. Designers of human windows need to know about

- perception and cognitive,
- dialoguing,
- problem solving,
- explanation criteria, and
- phrasing in a comprehensive but compact way.

Work must also be done on usability characteristics and determinants such as enduser training, environmental factors, and virtual hardware and software design. Human window criteria can be improved by testing projected approaches through person-to-person interaction. The effects of various tools and techniques on the organization must also be studied.

2. CHOOSING A NATURAL LANGUAGE SOLUTION

The question is often posed: "What is natural language processing?", followed by another query: "Why is it important?", and then by a third one: "Is it really difficult?" Interest in these questions is justified by the fact that an important theme in AI research an implementation is the man–machine interface and the quality of communication it can support. This has much to do with user understanding and effective techniques of expression.

Natural languages are in marked contrast to formal programming languages such as Lisp, Prolog, Basic, Pascal, or C. The latter were designed to be easily understood by computers. Pascal and C are intended for the specialized task of expressing algorithms. Lisp and Prolog deal with list processing and data structures. Heuristics address complex information-processing jobs.

Research on natural language understanding by computers is one AI field. Understanding the computational mechanisms that underlie the use of natural language is the objective of computational linguistics. The latter is a science at the juncture of AI philosophy, and psychology that aims to

1. understand how humans communicate,
2. improve man–information communication skills, and
3. help develop machines with human-like communications capabilities.

The first goal, to understand how humans communicate, is a scientific goal. When properly pursued, it helps us understand ourselves. In fact, while all of us think of ourselves as experts in the use of *our* natural language, we have only vague notions of the mental processes involved. A clearer insight into the essential nature and functioning of such processes might enable us to be better communicators. We can also train others in language skills more effectively.

Current improvements in man–information communication skills do not attempt to solve the problem totally. Rather, they make it much easier to build up incrementally an effective man–machine interface. For instance, natural language database querying allows interactions at a much higher level of sophistication than was previously possible.

So far, developers have been able to provide a self-contained interaction that gives the information the user needs to solve his problem. In this sense, natural language is used incrementally to define the rules in English rather than in a formal rule language of the classical computer programming solutions. Today's natural language systems like Intellect (developed by the Artificial Intelligence Corporation) and Broker (by Cognitive Systems) permit us to

- move from simple to relatively complex questions in plain English.
- validate the system's understanding of the query, and
- receive instant responses.

The ability of computers to understand natural language increases their accessibility and flexibility. Natural language is therefore a basic goal of fifth-generation computer projects. Such Japanese projects aim to develop natural language computer systems. The British Alvey[1] project made man–machine interfaces the goal of one of its key divisions.

Researchers in these projects agree that a logic programming framework is most suitable for implementing natural language processing. The basic mechanism of logic programming is unification, whereas that of natural language understanding is pattern recognition. Figure 8-1 demonstrates how a real-world image can be converted into an idealized form, mapped in a basic features list, and, through symbolic representation, described by natural language. In this sense, natural language approaches can be viewed as a method that enables man–information communication in a form that does not require us to learn new linguistic skills. This can be accomplished by

- providing the computer with linguistic knowledge and processing abilities and
- establishing a mechanism that makes it feasible to communicate in the user's own culturally learned language.

Note that this form may be either visual or oral. There is no unique solution for handling natural language.

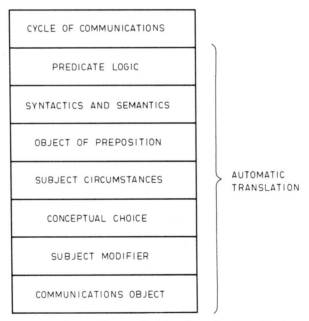

Figure 8-1. Any AI application can be conceived in a layered schema. This figure presents the example of automatic translation, dividing the expert system approach into eight layers.

---

[1] The British Alvey project has been financed by the government to promote research on knowledge-based systems and man–machine interfaces in the UK. The name comes from Dr. Alvey, who suggested the need for such a project to the Prime Minister.

Research in natural language is one of the oldest fields of AI, indicating that the limitations of the present communication methods have been appreciated for some time. The premise is that a program written by the enduser in a natural-language system is likely to be perceived by the enduser as more efficient (often substantially more efficient) than a classical query program—though it may be inefficient in terms of machine cycles. This is so because the user is unlikely to take full advantage of the indexes, hierarchical data design, and other facilities of the DBMS. By contrast, a valid natural language interface will try to optimize. The result is often quite efficient. At worst, the only additional "cost" of natural language over formal querying is in the translation from English to the formal query program.

Nevertheless, the popularity of this approach may be short-lived. More generic solutions focus on massive progress in the area of natural language understanding and generation, with the aim of providing comfortable, practical, human-engineered interfaces. Generic approaches are expected to make priceless breakthroughs with the next generations of computer-related aids.

Research on natural language processing has goals well beyond database query and machine translation. Promising applications include text selection and text understanding. Text generation is important in expert system interaction, as well as in machine translation and speech applications.

For about thirty years, machine translation has been an AI effort. At first, it appeared to be simple, involving a multilingual dictionary, simple rules of syntax, and enough computing power to make it work. The result has been failure due to wrong assumptions. The first language translation projects supposed, erroneously, that we can do an adequate job of translating without understanding the text. Today, however, developers appreciate that it is not sufficient to understand the text. We must also understand

- the cultural environment in which the text is generated and
- the object environment to which it is mapped.

Text generation is an important but difficult area. Prerequisites include understanding the goals and knowledge of both ends of the communication; selecting the parts to be exchanged in order to satisfy both sets of goals; and converting this knowledge to a linear form with an appropriate structure. The AI construct must decide how much information to put in each sentence, select and compose anaphoric[2] references, introduce interesting variety, and decide where and how to rely on indirect linguistic acts. The resulting program must be able to retain the human recipient's interest and attention, p roviding a knowledgeable way of talking to him or writing for him.

Knowledge of a natural language is closely related to knowledge of the cultural environment in which this language originated and is used. This goes far beyond natural language processing per se—that is, the development of a new technology based on the useful paradigm of logic programming, though such a paradigm is basic to the AI approach. A broader approach calls for

---

[2] Anaphora processing is an algorithmic approach to the handling of pronouns and nouns.

1. cultural definition,
2. discourse analysis,
3. text understanding, and
4. the electronic supports to be used by the knowledgebank for machine translation.

Only in the narrow sense can the search for meaning be restricted to words, as with keyword systems; to common phrase patterns, as with pattern matchers; to systems which develop meaning from an electronic dictionary; or to a parser of a given syntactic structure. Many sorts of problems are arising in the broader context. Such problems range from cultural representation to syntactic ambiguity and from semantic meaning to referential constructs. They involve pragmatic considerations but also external task knowledge, and they touch on both direct and indirect acts.

In spite of these problems, natural language reasoning may soon replace today's expert systems. This will happen if research provides results which are both culturally acceptable and fully interactive—in short, if endusers become convinced of the wisdom of natural language solutions.

3. CRITERIA FOR DESIGNING MAN–MACHINE INTERFACES

The goal of man–machine interface design is to place more emphasis on the effective communication between the enduser and the machine expert in those tasks where man needs assistance—more specifically, on communication between the enduser and the information handled by software and hardware. This emphasis focuses on what computers should do rather than on what they can do or are currently doing.

Research on man–machine interfacing shows that advances in enduser interface technologies, such as natural language understanding, must be complemented by strategies that make information systems cooperate actively with their users. Personal WSs should

- understand fragmentary and ambiguous requests,
- present meaningful rather than just literal answers,
- deal effectively with exceptional situations,
- guide the user through complex dialogue sequences, and
- adapt easily to changing requirements.

Able solutions require in-depth theoretical analysis, construction of prototypes, and empirical evaluation of cooperative interfaces. Such interfaces may be local at the WS level, but they may also address distributed databases, image processing systems, and other systems—AI constructs being a vital example.

Practically all recent research has attempted to overcome some of the limitations of older approaches by using knowledge-based systems. However, to benefit from AI usage, we have to understand past limitations as well as accomplishments, raising questions and challenges for the future.

Criteria defined as crucial in human window design include rapid iteration around the dialogue cycle, reasonably simple dialogue specifications, parametrically chosen interfaces for a given application, uninterrupted and immediate access to full functionality, and minimum constraints on possible forms of dialogue performance. Controlling logging and replaying of user input are also important, as is the ability to compare potential alternative designs by means of rapid iterations.

Simple specifications are a key component of the dialogue. So is the ability to make rapid changes, allowing users to design interfaces without extensive training. Multiple interfaces to a given application are important in serving users of different cultures and backgrounds, as well as for understanding the effects of specific design features on performance.

In the laboratory, techniques such as intelligent window management, intelligent graphic displays, and DWIM (do what I mean) are becoming almost commonplace. In daily practice at the WS level, iconic interfaces and toolboxes have set some standards of user friendliness. New approaches for adding intelligence to the user interface have been developed, and others are being studied experimentally. All of them have strengths and weaknesses with respect to the enduser.

While practically everyone believes in the need for user-friendly solutions, there is no general agreement on how to approach the issue and what to emphasize.

- Some researchers consider plain English the most user-friendly approach.

This includes not only the user's commands to the machine but also assimilation of information, presentation of the response, and guidance toward a decision. Linguistic constructs are a valid solution, helping the user communicate with the machine.

- Other researchers emphasize the importance of an interface which graphically represents results all the way to the inference network, showing the path of reasoning followed by the system.

They suggest that this interface is helpful not only in building AI constructs but also in providing an explanation facility—perhaps more effectively than the common English sentence. Not only the ancient world used icons; many languages today still do so.

More fundamental human factors research has shown that there is no one best method of presentation and communication that guarantees a comprehensible approach. Any method can be well or badly designed. The best solution depends on what the user is trying to find out or do. In fact, there is much more scope in interface design, now that bit-mapped, windowed displays are widely available in the market. Few systems in the future will be hampered by the lack of graphic presentation, and many systems will include natural language solutions.

The most successful approaches will be modular. A prime motivation in choosing these solutions is that it allows the behavior of man–machine interfaces to be modified independently of the application. This raises the questions of how, when, and by whom changes to the human window can be effected.

One evident answer is the dialogue designer, but it is not necessarily the best. Another answer is the user (if he is knowledgeable enough). A third, equally valid answer is a *matasystem* which monitors the user's behavior and adapts the interface accordingly. This is particularly valid in the case of *learning systems*.

Metasystem solutions encompass the area of intelligent user interfaces and can be universally seen as desirable, though there is evidence to suggest that users perform more effectively, at least with text-based systems, when they are allowed to choose their own names for system commands. Adaptive man–machine interfaces can ably complement problem-solving routines, leading to a different type of programming than we have been accustomed to using with computers.

A particular area of interest in man–machiner interaction is the control of processes involving the user in an open loop whereby he makes decisions on the interface. Such acquired knowledge has been subdivided into skills, with rule-based and knowledge-based divisions.

- Skills are subconscious.
- The rule-based approach is used with tested, conscious solutions.
- The knowledge-based approach is used to deal with situations and requires conscious reasoning.

Whether user actuated or through system self-learning, adaptive interfaces can be best described as *metaphors for man–machine communication*. In fact, there is a much closer relation between the human window and the knowledgebank than is generally believed. As Figure 8-2 demonstrates, each element in the human window maps some of the rules in the background. There is a connection with an existing system (DBMS, DSS, CAD) that supports distributed processing between the WS and the host. The human window commu-

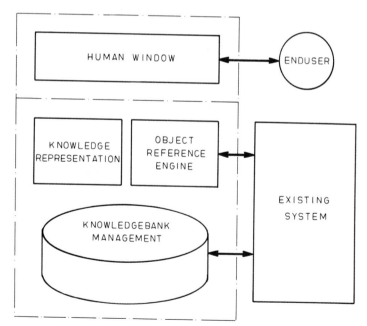

Figure 8-2. Hybrid solutions require an efficient interconnection between the expert system and the existing system, as well as between the expert system and the enduser who wishes to communicate both with the new construct and with the existing application through the human window.

nicates knowledge via natural language, while object representation and knowledgebank management are ensured by appropriate routines.

For nearly twenty years, designers of man–machine communications set up interfaces which were friendly to them and assumed that they would appear so to users. Man–machine interface designs were also based on folklore and hunches, and the literature on man–machine interfacing was rarely consulted. One remedy to this problem has been to involve the user in the design process. However, this does not guarantee success, since users often do not understand man–information interaction capabilities or their own preferences.

Proper interface design involves symbolic systems, color, spatial composition, animation, and sequencing. Such approaches are applied to the design of icons, windows, menus, cursors, help, mail, and other utilities. Emphasis must be placed not only on English-type communication but also on using color effectively, with diagrams to help transfer mental models. Establishing a grid for spatial layouts; limiting hierarchical distinctions of type fonts, gray values, and line weights; carefully grouping logically related items; and considering alternatives to the *metaphor*[3] of the messy desk are other examples of factors to be considered in the design of the human window.

Modularity permits separation between dialogue and application, as well as within the dialogue component: management of the display, of input and output, and of mapping application functions. Metaphors make feasible rapid dialogue definition and flexibility in defining the dialogue, as well as consistency between applications.

Metasystem concepts allow the designer to use a high-level language for dialogue specification. Further assistance may be given by adding dialogue-level primitives not only for interfaces but also for managing the dialogues produced.

4. INPUT MEDIA, VIEWPORTS, AND VIEWPOINTS

The preceding sections referred to metasystems[4] and showed how useful they can be in an interactive dialogue with a global database. As Figure 8-3 suggests, such dialogue requires both explanation and knowledge acquisition facilities—as well as a significant amount of knowledgebank support.

The developers of PSI and SIMPOS have stated that as far as human window design is concerned, an object-oriented solution is an effective means of reducing the work of specification and implementation. Though one of the drawbacks of this approach is the overhead due to its dynamic execution, such overhead is admissible when the system is running on a powerful personal WS. In compensation, it provides a flexible and extensible system for a good interface environment.

In fact, for the optimization of SIMPOS, its developers redesigned and recoded the supervisor and the window system. This reconstruction was quite easily done (in a few

---

[3] A metaphor expresses what machines can understand in contrast to what people understand. In biblical terms, a metaphor is an allegory.
[4] The meta concept is explained and documented in Chapter 11.

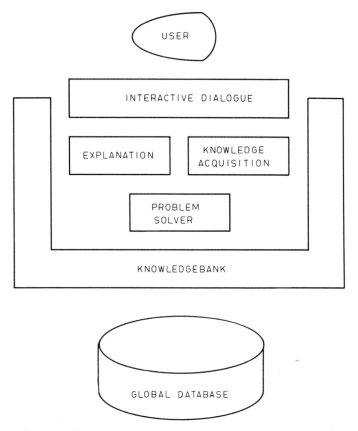

Figure 8-3. The interactive dialogue supported by expert systems should not be limited to the acquisition module, the problem solver, and the explanation/justification routines, but should also reach the global database—the latter being an increasingly important requirement.

weeks), without much effecting on the rest of the system, because of the modularity of the object-oriented approach. At the same time, the firmware group of PSI improved the microinterpreter and implemented object-oriented calls and slot accessing firmware.

These examples show the close coordination and interaction necessary to improve a logical construct—and to design it in the first place. When the machines used as WSs are not supercomputers, solutions have to be simpler, always considering the capabilities and limitations of current input media.

The most common method of input is a keyboard. Most of its keys are letters or numbers. Function keys are different; they are labeled *Crtl* (Control), *Alt* (Alternate), and *Del* (Delete). There are also arrows to move the cursor onscreen, *Return* and *Enter* keys, and so on.

Generic commands or primitives are a small set of commands that can be used throughout the system. Examples are *move, copy,* and *delete.* Each command performs its intended functions in the same way, regardless of software the type of object selected. In many cases they are primitive, and, like explanation facilities, they should be seen as desirable features of a shell.

The facilities provided by a consultation shell can improve upon an implementation scenario. For instance, the ESP Advisor[5] consultation shell provides interactive access to the knowledgebank, allowing the expertise and information to be inspected and used in a conversational style. To do so, the Advisor has a set of commands which permits the internal operation of the shell to be examined and questioned. There is also an online help facility, which, as the name implies, provides the use of the appropriate commands. The latter include

EXPLAIN—explains the question
WHY—asks why the question has been raised
WHY advice—asks why the last piece of advice was displayed
HOW—asks how the parameter was proven
SHOW—displays the current parameter
VOL—volunteers information before certain questions are asked
CHANGE—changes answers to previous questions
HELP—helps with command X
TRACE—traces the reasoning process
PRINT—prints the advice and information
LOG—logs the consultation session in a file
SAVE—saves the consultation on disc
STATUS—displays the status of established parameters
RECAP—summarizes the advice or information displayed so far
HELP user—displays the user's commands

However, even if assisted by shell primitives in terms of man–machine interaction, keyboards are awkward, slow, and tedious. It is faster to enter data using a *graphic tablet* if the input environment can be so structured. Another possibility is the *mouse* that points to a menu window. A still better alternative is a vocal recognition device.

Whichever solution is chosen, in addition to the core activity of managing the windows, the window manager has to handle the input devices. Input may be directly viewed on the screen through a viewport. Activities may update a large virtual window, of which only a small section is visible on the screen. This visible part is the *viewport*. It limits the viewing space of an activity which may perform actions outside it.

Viewport management requires procedures for updating the viewport's size and scrolling its contents. It also makes feasible a distinction between *physical* and *logical windows*.

- A physical window displays one or more page(s) of a document which can be manipulated logically.
- Logical support should definitely include a multiwindow manager able to *scroll* up, down, left, and right; *command windows:* insert, delete, shrink, expand; and *turn pages:* next, previous, by one, two, or three or more steps.

---

[5] Not to be confused with the Japanese ESP, which is a language, ESP Advisor was made in England by Expert Systems International.

The capabilities of logical support allow the *browsing* of documents under user command. Browsing, in turn, is helpful in running menus and makes feasible the handling of embedded applications.

Each window also has a *border* which encloses the viewport, separating one window from another. The border may include a *title, commands,* and/or *scrollbars.* Window management must therefore offer the ability to create and update the title and commands; set scrollbars and commands on and off; and highlight a border component for user feedback.

Window management also matches screen designations with appropriate windows. If the window manager is used by more than one process, it must provide mutual exclusion for the sharing screen and its windows. Window management also permits the screen to be shared by several windows which may overlap, implementing procedures for creating, destroying, and updating the location of a window.

Utilities are necessary to manage the content of the viewport. This content may be composed of text, data, and simple graphic objects. For each, procedures must be offered for

- painting,
- updating subsequent to a user action,
- pointing, and
- highlighting for system feedback.

Window handling involves moving a window to a new position; changing its size; or shrinking it to (or expand it from) a title header.

A screen-sharing policy must be established. For instance, overlapping of windows may be prevented, or the topmost window may be designated the active one. Current activity switching can have side effects. For instance, the menu windows of a disabled activity may vanish, or those of an enabled one may appear and its main window will come forward.

More sophisticated than the viewports, AI-based mechanisms enable users to handle different views of the knowledgebank, providing a mean to represent changes in the AI construct or the subject being modeled. They also make it feasible to modularize and factor portions of knowledge.

As implemented in at least one system, assertions made by the user belong to a specific *viewpoint.*[6] A deduction can be performed in a viewpoint, though complex deductions may span several viewpoints. Logically, such viewpoints are sets of statements. They contain the assumptions made by the knowledge engineer or enduser. In the Omega shell, for example, viewpoints are organized in a structure which corresponds to the inheritance relations between them. Multiple inheritance is permitted. The underlying assumptions include all facts asserted in the viewpoint itself and in the other viewports from which it inherits.

One advantage of an object-oriented viewpoint mechanism is its ability to accommodate many varied views, and hence the configurable interaction techniques that users can tailor to their liking. By providing functions that let the enduser pick up the elements of the layout

---

[6] Viewpoints are not part of the user interface in its limited sense, but they are a component of man–information interaction.

and move them about as needed, the object-oriented viewport eliminates the need to develop a priori multiple versions to satisfy hypothetical cases. Ad hoc solutions are far more effective. This is particularly important for the design of flexible, open-ended, problem-solving environments. Unstructured exploration *is* inefficient in its use of time and computer resources. On the other hand, closely directed approaches do not allow endusers to explore all topics of interest if they are denied control of the interaction.

During a personal meeting, Ken Haase, of MIT, suggested the use of an automatic explanation system that examines objects or collections of objects—for instance, objects which describe a particular domain or representation of language—and generates a structured English explanation of them. This explanation and description are designed to help endusers introduce themselves to the domain or language. The system's analysis tries to extract salient features and use them as an organizational focus for explanation.

With such a knowledge-intense explanatory system, a user can merely point to a collection of units and type. *Explain this* to acquire a structured explanation including whatever special observable structure the objects possess. The resulting structure is a hierarchy of explanations, each level of which sorts out the *objects over* one of a number of possible relationships. Such relationships are akin to structural slots of a given explanation.

The knowledge-based explanation process takes the set of objects being explained and generates a partition of it for each structural slot. The resulting partitions (one for each structural slot) are compared, and the slot whose partition contains the largest subgroups is then selected as the focus of the explanation. The intuition this supports is that the organizational focus for an explanation of some objects should be the relation which organizes them into the biggest chunks.

Further, for each subgroup in the partition selected, a subexplanation is generated whose relevant objects are the elements of the subgroup and whose structural slots are inherited from the original explanation. The explanation structure produced by this process may be passed to a text generator, a graphic exploration, or a theory-making mechanism that tries to classify regularities in the shell's structures.

One advantage of such a consultant system is that interactive explanation facilities can be provided with an AI construct as an aid to its operation—for instance, financial simulation or the debugging and testing of engineering design.

An interface program would not prevent the designer from communicating directly with deep levels of the system, but it would provide a means of showing exactly what, for instance, the CAD tools in use are doing. Such a system might also ensure automatic knowledge elicitation as part of the interface, so that the information design methods being created by the developer or the enduser could be made explicit, evaluated, and possibly incorported into the system.

5. DIALOGUE THROUGH A HUMAN WINDOW

Sections 3 and 4 suggested a rich arena for the representation of information focusing on man–machine interaction and on AI-assisted explanation facilities. The same is true of the retrieval of inforamtion, an issue elaborated in Section 6. But prior to retrieval, we need interpretive efficiency, which is typically provided by a dialogue system.

Man–machine implementation of dialogue systems is not new. Query modes are representative of this approach, which has its roots in conversation. Ordinarily, we communicate when in each other's presence and in the presence of the things talked about:

- We speak about things, and point to and look at them as well.
- We use gestures even when discussing abstractions.

By adding explanation to the query, AI makes this approach more powerful. It can be used to frontend elder applications, extending their life cycle. It can also be employed to make a new construct user friendly.

A very simple example of frontending is HAL, a linguistic interface to Lotus 1-2-3. It replaces the traditional menu line by a space for typing English commands. For example:

- "Print this" is a print command for the table in which the cursor resides.
- "Profits $= 0.1 \times$ Sales" automatically formats the profit column to look like the sales column.

Then it fills those cells in which a number belongs. The transition from novice to expert user of a spreadsheet is made easier, as the user needs no particular training to recognize the command tokens. He enters English words directly, a process which is often more efficient than input techniques suited to naive or causal uses.

This approach can be used in a variety of processes: eliciting knowledge, elicitation, receiving and giving advice, interpretation of raw data, browsing, and teaching. It can be employed in CAD for specific aspects of the generation of layout, simulation, and testing, as well as in financial modeling in communication with the simulation software.

In Chapter 4, Section 5, we considered the case of a company which structured an expert system for financial evaluation. Returning to this example, suppose that after the original demands (1 and 2) are satisfied, the chairman asks for a user-friendly human window. This human window should produce explanations by tracing down the tree of dependencies among the variables in the expert system. Specifically, the response to a *Why* query must be an analytical evaluation of the factors which are important in producing the observed financial results. The explanation should help the user understand the operation of the system, pinpointing factors whose significance may not be readily apparent. The natural language summary must enable the user to check for logical errors and detect critical factors. The chairman also wants to receive warning messages from the expert system. Here is a sample dialogue produced by the human window:

Why did Acid Test go down?

Acid Test went down because current liabilities increased.

This result was only partially offset by increase in current assets.

Acid Test = Current Assets/Current Liabilities

	T1[7]	Amount Change	T2[7]
Current Ratio	2.90	-1.60	1.30
Current Liabilities	XXXX	XXXX	XXXX
Current Assets	XXXXX	XXXXX	XXXXX

Continue Explanation

Current liabilities went up because of short term loans payable and taxes payable.

Current Liabilites = Accounts Payable + Salaries
Payable + Taxes Payable
+Short Term Loans Payable

Short Term Loans Payable T2 Period were as follows:

Company	Amount
XXXX	XXXX
XXXX	XXXX
XXXX	XXXX

Taxes Payable T2 Period were as follows:

Location	Type of Tax	Amount
XXXX	XXXX	XXXX
XXXX	XXXX	XXXX
XXXX	XXXX	XXXX
XXXX	XXXX	XXXX
XXXX	XXXX	XXXX

[7] Time period 1, time period 2.

At the senior management level, the details of human factors design are twice as important as those of most other man–machine interfaces. Since the primary purpose is to make dialogue specification and implementation easier, we must provide a good dialogue interface to the enduser. Dialogue primitives must be capable of encouraging communication and understanding. Computer prompts are a valid approach to communications. During personal meeting at Oxford Alex Goodall developed the following example:

Computer: Which of the following symptoms best describes the
problem?

1. Engine difficult to start
2. Engine overheats

  3. Gear shift problems
  4. Break problems
  5. Poor stability and steering
  6. Lights do not work

  Enter the number of the relevant option

Operator: 1

Computer: First check that there is fuel in the tank and that the
             fuel valve is switched on.

             You would be surprised how often people make these
             simple mistakes.

Computer: Is there fuel flowing into the carburetor?

Operator: No

Computer: You should first check and clean the fuel tank cap air
             vent which may be clogged.

             The air vent is provided in the tank cap to supply
             gas smoothly to the carburetor.

Computer: Is the fuel tank cap air vent clogged?

Operator: No

Computer: As the fuel tank cap air vent is not clogged it is
             most likely that the fuel cock or filter is clogged.

             The fuel cock filter will collect impurities and so
             should be periodically checked and cleaned.

This is a simple version of a diagnostic program. More sophisticated constructs have been
developed by automobile manufacturers and distributed to their dealers and service stations
to help in diagnosing problems.

  The human window of a diagnostic expert system is very similar to the Goodall example.
Its infrastructure is shown in Figure 8-4. In the background can be a global database on

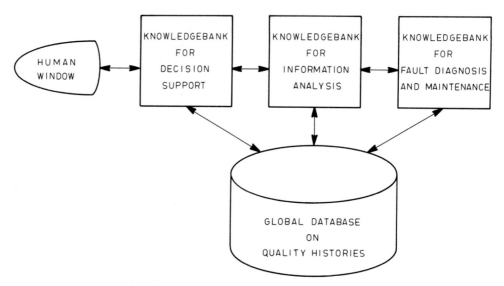

Figure 8-4. A number of knowledgebank modules can be grouped together and interconnected with global databases. This example comes from an expert system implementation in quality control and reliability engineering.

quality histories or a local database. Apart from the human window software, the three main blocks of the AI construct are rules for

- decision support,
- information analysis, and
- fault diagnostics and maintenance.

The decision support subset is an explanation facility which gives the user the reasons for a decision persented by the AI construct. For instance, after examination of an investment problem outlined by the end user, the decision may be: *Don't buy the asset.* The justification of the decision may be as follows:

- Terms of the investment are unfavorable.
- The cost of money is too high at this time.
- Alternative possibilities offer a better return on the investment.

Justification is one of the stronger means of establishing the respectability of expert systems among users. It should be written not only comprehensively but also in a convincing manner.

When we spoke of forward chaining and backward chaining, we also said that the AI construct provides justification through backtracking—that is, by examining which of the rules have fired. It is these rules which are presented to the user to justify the decision.

In conclusion, the design of a human window should be based on human factors. Some of the requirements facing human factors researchers have been developed over many years of experience in designing and using a range of laboratory systems to investigate a variety of interface dialogues. In the past, this required complex software with large sets of functions. Today AI constructs have simplified the job and have provided valuable user interface management tools.

6. ENDUSERS' ACCESS TO MULTIMEDIA DOCUMENTS[8]

A study done in the Netherlands in the early 1980s has demonstrated that only one out of three documents required by management can be located at the first search. For some documents, up to seven consecutive searches are necessary. A similar study done in 1985 by Bankers Trust showed that only 35% of the time of managers and professionals is productive. The rest is taken up by trivia and administrative chores. As a result, a five-year plan was established in high technology to reverse this ratio, making 65% of the time productive—that is, essentially doubling managerial and professional productivity.

In 1982, Staal Bankiers, of Rotterdam, employed 70 people; in 1985, 200. Of these:

- 40% were in marketing.
- 60% were in back office support.

Then the bank engaged in an ambitious program with computers, communications, and DSS. The goal for 1988–89 was to reverse the ratios:

- 60% in marketing.
- 40% in backoffice support.

This would mean 0.66 back office persons for every front desk/marketing officer. Sanyo Securities has reached this ratio: 0.6 back office people for every front desk marketing officer (vs. 2.0 back office individuals at Merrill Lynch) through a thorough automation of functions. Most importantly, this successful implementation rests on AI constructs.

These statistics and management problems show that the task of establishing a valid man–information interface does not end at the human window level, regardless of how valuable the latter is. Past problems with old-fashioned queries did not arise at the human interface level alone; they included weak solutions with database searches and led to long response times.

As stated in Chapter 3, modern, dynamic, online systems require fifth-generation computers and AI in order to be successfully implemented. Able man–information interfaces imply *multimedia* and place emphasis on *document handling*. Able, AI-assisted solutions to document handling are an important ingredient in the coming era of intelligent information systems.

Classical solutions to the document-handling problem have failed both at the man–machine interface level and at the search mechanism level. We have seen the AI contribu-

---

[8] One reviewer commented that the discussion did not deal with "interfaces." The argument was nearsighted and missed the difference which exists between *interfaces* and *human windows*. The end user does not care about EDP terminology; what he wants is solutions.

tion to the human window. Now let's examine some fundamental productivity situations with *multimedia documents leading to memory-based reasoning.*

Multimedia documents have different inference mechanisms associated with the different text/data types. A framework of plausible inference should allow users to interpret and combine the probabilities arising from various comparisons. *Uncertainty management* concerns

- the type of document,
- logical structure/contents, and
- retrieval criteria.

The retrieval process should be regarded as a form of *plausible inference,* the plausibility being quantified by some probability or possibility measure. Older retrieval mechanisms, including those associated with WS query, were data oriented. This situation, too, has changed. We must consider the information elements to be

- stored
- downloaded
- received, and
- retrieved

between machines. Such data structures (i.e., text structures) must be normalized throughout the system. But *the retrieval mechanism will follow heuristic approaches*—which, incidentally, produce much richer results than stochastic ones.

This situation is a far cry from the concepts of the past in regard to office automation. Emphasis is now placed increasingly on an *office document architecture.*[9] Uncertainty will become a characteristic of office studies of the future. It will also be a basic ingredient in managerial and professional productivity. This was both the evidence and the conclusion reached at the April 1987 National Bureau of Standards (NBS) Symposium on Office Automation in Gaithersburg, Maryland:

- The basic concept is that of database search under conditions of uncertainty.
- The hypothesis is that a database search which is vague and stochastic gives *much better results* than a crisp, precise search.

This is not only a totally new concept, alien to classical DP; it is also the way to the future.

There are reasons for uncertainty in querying. With certainty, only very limited goals can be achieved. *Partial match* attributes are based on the probability of matching. They can have preferred and acceptable attributes of different levels of importance: high, medium, or low. One approach is to associate quantitative references with these qualitative levels and then compute the overall score for a document. Another approach uses qualitative *plausible inference.* This is the sense of idea databases.

Conceptual querying is the cornerstone in an idea database—for example: "Find all pages, including the concept I underlined," or "Find reports that contain a table with a caption about sales."

---

[9] See also Chapter 14, which focuses on the office document architecture.

The new theory treats *retrieval as inference* and assigns two types of attributes:

1. *Exact matching:* keywords, date, author.
2. *Partial matching:* text, string, graphics, audio, image.

Partial matching involves uncertainty in the retrieval process and, hence, plausible inference. A plausible inference framework applies to the entire document or to specified sections of it.

The networks being developed today must be increasingly document oriented, not only for transport but also for storage and retrieval. This requires far greater sophistication than that supported by the data interchange architecture/data content architecture. It is necessary to handle compound electronic documents from creation to their destruction.

Proposed as a recommended standard by ISO, the office document architecture[10] involves both

- office document models and
- the concept of *uncertainty in retrieval.*

Uncertainty is related to the query rather than the document itself. Documents have types, logical layout, and structures. Such type/layout/structure definitions are constrained by standards. Standards include (1) the need to describe the range of document structures permitted by the standard and the relationships between logical and layout views of a document, as well as (2) the means for ensuring that the standard(s) is (are) enforced.

From human window design to document search, a modern system architecture should not only incorporate current notions but also project future requirements and provide for an able response to them. This is another good reason why AI is so important in the computers and communications solutions we are adopting today.

---

[10] Explained in Chapter 14, Section 5.

part 2

VALUE DIFFERENTIATION

9

Supercomputers and AI

Keywords

decidability · *fifth-generation computer* · *single-system image* · *one logical network* · *idea database* · *computer epochs* · *hypercubes* · *cache* · *synchronization* · *degrees of freedom* · *objects* · *non–von Neumann computers* · *symbolic computation* · *deductive retrieval* · *data-level parallelism* · *local area network* · *logical environment*

1. INTRODUCTION

An amazing device was discovered in 1900, in an ancient ship wrecked off the island of Antikythera, but was decoded only in 1955. This device, dating to the first century B.C., was apparently designed to perform the dual function of an astronomical clock and an analog computer. As such, it constitutes the first evidence of man not only thinking in terms of mechanization but also providing a specialized tool to do this job.

Man continued to work on his tools, and calculating devices were always in his mind. Leonardo da Vinci (1452–1519) came close to making one. Yet, it was only in 1666 that Sir Samuel Morland provided a significant advance in the design and engineering of computing devices with the invention of a trigonometric calculating machine. Wilhelm Schickard's machine (1623) and Leibnitz computational device (1673) also deserve a place in this pantheon. The wheel-based empire of Leibnitz was able to do multiplication and division.

A few years earlier, in 1642, Blaise Pascal (1623–1662) had built some elementary machines to assist in the computation of taxes. His device performed addition and subtraction. Pascal and other mathematicians pondered the problem of reducing routine computing to a mechanical function, at the same time increasing the speed and accuracy of the work.

The story of Charles Babbage's attempt to construct an analytic engine is too well known to be repeated. However, his work, which occurred between 1830 and 1840, provided significant insights regarding computer development roughly a century later—when components and engineering techniques developed to the point where computers (the way we define them today) became feasible.

Punched card accounting and computing equipment began in the 1890 U.S. census, though punched cards had been used several years earlier to control the weaving of complex patterns on looms. After 1890, the development of bookkeeping and adding machines proceeded at a rapid pace.

The first equipment capable of performing a long sequence of operations was developed in 1939 at Harvard University in collaboration with IBM. Known as Mark I, the Automatic Sequence Controlled Computer, it was completed in 1944. It was an expression of the mechanization-rationalization-modernization movement of the late 1930s.

There was a precedent to the making of this computing device. In 1936, Alan Turing wrote a paper on the design and limitations of computing machines, and the *Turing Machine* was born. That same year, Konrad Zuse asked the German War Ministry in Berlin for enough electronics equipment to build a computer for which he had the plans. His request was refused, the decision stating that a computer was not essential to the military effort.

During the same period, E. T. Brewster made the then heretical assertion that the human body was a machine. It was a vastly complex machine, he asserted, many times more complicated than any machine ever made by human hands—but still, after all, a machine.

- Yes, the body was living; hence it did not look like a machine.
- But at another, more detailed level of reference, it was determined in a machine-like fashion.

Alan Turing properly phrased the problem: "What will be the most general kind of machine that deals with symbols?" We have the answer today, slightly over fifty years after this question was asked. It will be a fifth-generation computer[1] enriched with AI.

2. GOALS OF SUPERCOMPUTER IMPLEMENTATION

We often fail to appreciate the size of a growing population. Some 60 million computers exist; more than 35% of them were shipped in the last two years. The value of the worldwide installed computer base approaches $600 billion. Assuming a twenty-year software life cycle, programming investments in U.S. corporate data centers (1960–89) are far in excess of $1.3 trillion.

Growth in applications requirements and in user expectations puts current computer solutions under stress. The reasons will now be discussed.

---

[1] As with Babbage, the 1946–50 contributions to computer design by von Neumann, Eckert, and Maughly in America and Turing and Williams in England are too well known to be repeated. The emphasis on Alan Turing is justified by the fact that both in 1936 and in 1952 he was the first person to speak about AI concepts.

1. *Storage capacity.*

Most major organizations now feature over 1,000 gigabytes (heme, over 1 terabyte). Some are planning for 2 to 4 terabytes by 1992–93. It is impossible to manage such a colossal database capacity by classical, so-called von Neumann-type computing. At the same time, database size has outgrown what can be done through classical database management systems (DBMS)

2. *Processor power.*

Many organizations feature 100 to 200 million instructions per second (MIPS) with an impressive 50–60% rate of increase per year. The need for cycles will grow even more rapidly, given the demand for power by AI. In addition, both central resources and personal computing require impressive power improvements to handle AI constructs. Current computer architectures have reached their limit in terms of further growth.

Already a number of industries are installing supercomputers in order to face fast growing requirements for number crunching. Wall Street has joined the user population with the major investment banks and securities houses installing supercomputers in order to maintain their competitive edge. Another reason is cost/effectiveness. One benchmark has shown that the cost of a mainframe with vector processing vs. a hypercube solution is 47.5 times higher.

3. *Continuous, nonstop operation.*

Theoretically, tandem, for one, is achieving such an operation through a parallel processing solution based on a von Neumann-type architecture. Practice, however is a different matter. Both in a robot-run factory and in banking operations, we now need a twenty-four-hour, seven days per week dependable nonstop realtime service. This requires not only a new architecture but also different components and autonomously operating devices.

4. *Single-system image.*

Networks dominate large-scale system configurations. The better-known industrial, business, and financial organizations—such as the Fortune 500—today have many networks in operation. They also know that they can no longer integrate them physically. *One logical network* is the goal, and this must be achieved by AI approaches and fifth-generation machines. One logical network is very important for communicating databases. Global access is a commanding architectural concept. Database splits slow system growth and make the use of the information elements uneven.

5. *Increasing use of AI.*

This implies developments which require both the available computer power and the global database to be accessible online. The architecture of an AI-oriented machine is different from that of von Neumann-type computers, as Figure 9-1 demonstrates.

Fifth-generation computers are knowledge processing systems designed to support intelligence-intense modules concerning specific areas of human expertise. They also feature sophisticated problem-solving and inference functions, as well as human-oriented input-output in the form of natural languages, speech, and picture images.

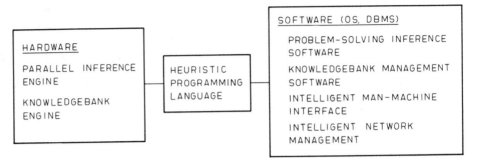

Figure 9-1. A heuristic programming language interfaces between the hardware of an inference engine and the software running on it. Four basic fuctions of this software are identified.

In systems, knowledge is often represented in terms of IF . . . THEN rules of the form

IF	hypothesis 1	and
	hypothesis 2	and
	. . .	
	hypothesis n	
THEN	action 1	
ELSE	action 2	

where, if all the conditions are true, then the implication is true, with an associated significance factor. This structure is most closely matched by logic programming as a computational model. Statements are relations of a restricted form called <clauses>.

Execution consists of a suitably controlled, logical deduction from the clauses that form the program. Fifth-generation computers are designed to operate in a way based on logic, as illustrated in this example.

The architecture of fifth-generation computers exploits the tremendous advances that have been made in microelectronics. The parallelism which they feature uses that potential. Logical operations—not computing—are the key. Logical structures will dominate the new computer generations.

The design of the fifth-generation computer is aimed at exploiting the brain's strengths: *parallelism* and *intelligence*. AI approaches and symbolic processing suggest a largely parallel style. An *idea database*, which we will examine in proper chapter, works through a combination of AI and parallel processing. Parallelism and intelligence indicate the way programs will be done in the future.

A logic-type orientation in machine architecture provides important software advantages. Knowledge handling is the goal; when this is achieved, the problem of knowledge delivery will have been solved.

The architecture of non-von Neumann-type computers differs markedly from that of their predecessors. ENIAC was built at the Moore School of Engineering in Philadelphia in the middle to late 1940s. Almost at the same time, two computers were built in England: one by

A. VON NEUMANN COMPUTER

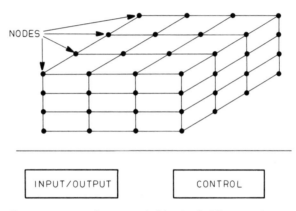

B. NON-VON NEUMANN COMPUTER

Figure 9-2. A von Neumann computer is composed of the classical five parts: input, output, memory, ALU, and control. A non-von Neumann machine differentiates between processing (reduction activities) and the input/output and control functions. This example comes from a hypercube architecture.

F.C. Williams at Manchester University,[2] the other (EDSAC) by M.V. Wilkes at Cambridge University. These were stored-program machines structured approximately as shown in Figure 9-2A: precisely the von Neumann architecture.

First-, and second-, third-, and fourth-generation computers follow this architecture, though they differ in other characteristics:

- First-generation computers were made with vacuum tubes. Interestingly enough, ENIAC features 18,000 tubes, but it did operate successfully.

---

[2] Which established the cathod ray tube (CRT) technology for high-speed storage (Williams tubes).

- Second-generation computers replaced the vacuum tubes with transistors but maintained the structure of the first generation. From the second generation on, developments were also marked by software progress: languages, operating systems, DBMSs, and communications routines.
- Third-generation computers featured two improvements: first, upward compatibility was achieved, as exemplified by IBM's 360 series; and second, and more important, the focal point of the architecture became the memory, with the arithmetic-logical unit (ALU) relegated to the level of an internal peripheral.

This was the beginning of a major shift in computer structure but also in the concept of the computer itself. While we usually talk of computer generations, it would be more precise to refer to *computer epochs.*

The years 1935 to 1968 were characterized by the design of *faster and faster* machines. A new goal dominated the following decade: to produce *smaller and smaller* machines. Minicomputers made feasible distributed information systems. They also ushered the fourth computer generation.

- The basic characteristic of the fourth generation is its smaller size. First, at the end of the 1960s, came the minicomputer, followed at the end of the 1970s by the microcomputer. Fourth-generation computers also brought advances in design such as pipeline organization and vector processing.

By 1978, with microcomputers (PCs), the motto became *cheaper and cheaper.* Up to 1987, the goal was to produce the same architectures, but smaller and cheaper. These were variations of von Neumann architectures—though new solutions began to appear.

The aim of fifth-generation computers, expected to last until the end of this century, is to be *newer and newer.* With this will come an increasing amount of AI implementation and a radically different architectural concept.

Figure 9-2B shows a non-von Neumann architecture: a *hypercube.*[3] Its implementation is exemplified in the *Connection Machine.*[4] Processing takes place in the interconnected nodes. Each node has

- a logical and an arithmetic unit, and
- an associated nonaddressable, high-speed memory that operates like the *cache* in von Neumann-type machines.

The computer is a network of thousands of nodes. The smallest Connection Machine features 16,384 nodes; the next size contains 65,536. CM-2 reaches a peak capacity of 10,000 MIPS and a sustained power of 2,500 MIPS.

Information transfer in the Connection Machine ranges from 2 to 3 gigabits per second (GBPS). There is no need to segment the program; the operating system takes care of that. If data structures contain fewer than, say, 65,536 elements, the Connection Machine makes

---

[3] Defined in Section 3.
[4] Built by Thinking Machines of Cambridge, Mass.

the assignment directly. If it contains more, the system moves in virtual mode, simulating a larger number of processors.

In a virtual processor mode, the Connection Machine can easily support up to 1 million processors. Data handled by the system may be as few as 1 bit or as many as thousands of bits. For picture processing, 1- to 8-bit values are common. For numeric processing, 16- to 64-bit words appear most frequently. Language processing values, such as words and sentences, can vary from a few bits to thousands.

3. THE ARCHITECTURE
OF HYPERCUBES

The hypercube is an example of a fifth-generation computer. This architecture is known as *Boolean hypercube* (or *cosmic cube*). It was invented by the Parallel Processing Project at the California Institute of Technology (Caltech). The major goal of the Caltech project was to develop the capability of concurrent processors, that is, computers which process many instructions simultaneously. Advances in hardware technology and software development have led to this aggregate of processors, with microprocessor nodes arranged at the corners of multidimensional cubes.

Many problems of interest can be mapped easily onto this architecture, and it is currently feasible to match and exceed the performance of vector supercomputers. The original (Mark I) supercomputer consisted of 64 nodes, based on the Intel 8086/8087 microprocessors. This computer has been operational since 1983. Caltech also built the Mark II hypercube, with increased memory and communication capacity, as well as its successor, the Mark III. This machine, based on the Motorola 68020 processor, has been operating since 1986.

The architecture permits an n-dimensional cube, where n is any number. One-, two-, and three-dimensional examples are given in Figure 9-3. There are 2^n processors, each linked to n of its neighbors. This represents a good compromise between reducing the distance that signals have to travel and keeping the number of links manageable. Such machines allow gradual expansion up to supercomputer power at competitive prices.

Thus, the term *hypercube* refers to an aggregate of microcomputers at the nodes. Hypercubes combine a binary number of processors in an n-cube dimension which defines the communications paths. The computational units are expected to grow as systems become more complex. Hypercube processors have *only local memory. There is no shared memory.* Processors communicate by sending messages along the connections between them. On a hypercube with 2^n nodes, a message can be transmitted between any two nodes by passing it along n links. *Synchronization* occurs by the availability of data and messages:

1. The number of links between processors is fairly small.
2. In an n-dimensional hypercube each processor has n neighbors and therefore n links from it.
3. We can double the size of a hypercube by adding a second hypercube of the same size, connecting processors with the same index in both hypercubes.
4. Topologies can be embedded in the hypercube. We can embed rings, grids, and trees as neighboring points are allocated to neighboring processors.

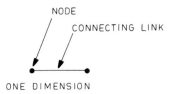

ONE DIMENSION

TWO DIMENSIONS

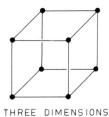

THREE DIMENSIONS

Figure 9-3. Hypercubes can be one-, two- or three-dimensional. The 3-D is more characteristic of a hypercube architecture and provide the possibility of interconnecting paths between the farther-out edges.

Cube manager utilities include load kill (a message), wait, send/receive messages, a determine queue dimension, a probe, and a system log. Node identification, a system clock, a node clock, and an exception handler are other necessary modules.

The guiding principle of the Caltech project has been the development of interesting applications on the hypercube. Targeted are scientific or engineering problems with many *degrees of freedom*. The purpose of hypercubes is not to solve small problems more efficiently, but rather to attack large problems that currently cannot be solved at all. This is accomplished by assigning a subset of these degrees of freedom to each processor in a way that matches the physical nature of the problem. For example, each processor may be assigned a subset of a grid. Boundary conditions are handled by communication with adjacent processors. It may be shown that efficiency is a function of the ratio of the processor speed to the communications bandwidth.

The Flat Concurrent Prolog (FCP) Matrix Multiplication is an example of a simple program distributed over a concurrent engine: the Intel Personal Super Computer II (iPSC).[5] The program first establishes a mesh-connected virtual machine on the iPSC. Then the elements of two $n \times n$ matrices, which are initially in a single processor, are distributed across all the processors. A product calculation is performed at each processor node, and the data are contained in a distributed structure.

Process mapping is achieved by a simple programming notation that moves processes dynamically between processor nodes. Streams between processes are used to transfer both data and other processes in a manner similar to the one we will describe in Chapter 11. In one application, the complete program for the virtual machine was only seven FCP clauses long; such a program is a simple, high-level specification, with relatively little concern for execution on a parallel machine.

Communication primitives in the basic iPSC system provide for message exchange:

1. *Global broadcast,* sending a message from one node to all others.
2. *Global operations* and commutative arithmetic operations, such as *sum* or *maximize,* with contributions from each node.
3. *Global concatenation,* collecting messages from each node.
4. *Meshes,* providing each node with left/right or north/east/south/west neighbors.
5. *Long messages,* transmitting messages larger than 16-kilobytes.
6. *Sparse global send,* sending and receiving with selected subsets of nodes (narrowcasting).

The cube itself features the computational nodes and their interconnect capability. It is supported by a message-passing, node-operating system. An Ethernet link from all nodes connects to the cube manager. The cube manager provides a development environment; it executes host processes, collects and presents results, and derives the interface to remote systems.

The hypercube example helps dramatize the concurrent processing capabilities of non-von Neumann computers:

- A conventional mainframe features a 10^0 = one processor.
- Classical multiprocessing solutions have 3 or 4×10^0 = three or four processors.
- Coarse-grain parallel computers such as the Teradata Database Computer exhibit 10^2–10^3 processors.
- Fine-grain parallel computers like the Connection Machine have 10^4–10^5 processors.
- The human brain has 10^{12} processors.

Today the best example of fine-grain parallelism, the Connection Machine, has a 10^7 difference in the number of processors compared to brain functioning. But each switch of the brain works slowly, at a rate of 10^2 per second (or 10^{-2} seconds per switch). Hence, in

---

[5] Designed and produced by Intel at Beaverton, Oregon, iPSC is a hypercube architecture. Interestingly enough, the word *personal* is featured in its name.

the human nervous system, the number of *bits per second per system* (*BPSS*) is 10^{14}. The processors of the Connection Machine work at a rate of 10^{-6}–10^{-7}. With 10^4–10^5 processors per engine, fine-grain parallelism has 10^{10}–10^{11} BPSS.

The difference between natural and man-made systems today is 10^3–10^4. Given technology's advances, this gap will be closed prior to the year 2000. Recall that in Chapter 1 we stated that by that year we expect to have android brains with approximately the capacity of the human brain.

4. MACHINES FOR SYMBOLIC COMPUTATION

The other aspect of fifth-generation computers is *symbolic computation*. It is useful in a wide range of implementations, from natural language to robotics, expert systems, and the management of very large databases. The first generation of symbolic computation engines has been oriented to expert systems implementation; the next one will focus on distributed memory and messaging systems. Such systems must feature *uniform processing*.

1. Text, data, and graphs,
2. programs,
3. metadata, and
4. object data

should be handled in a uniform manner. *Deductive retrieval* is another requirement. When the amount of knowledge is large and the knowledgebank has to be shared, the difference in quantity often entails a difference in quality.

Significant software developments must proceed hand in hand with hardware breakthroughs. In fact, the best way to design a modern computer is to start with the software and then design the hardware. This pattern is in direct contrast to past practice. Earlier, because hardware developed rapidly, supporting software—particularly the operating system—took 10 years to be established.

Rapid software developments are very important for two other reasons:

- Standardization will be lower in the future than it was in the past—in spite of optimistic predictions of the opposite.
- Increasing hardware power will sharply reduce the implementation time lead.

Figure 9-4 focuses on the latter subject, comparing memory-based reasoning to the now established rule system in AI. With the hardware featuring giga instructions per second (GIPS) rather than MIPS, the time required for implementation shrinks. It is no longer necessary to write rules in an AI context. We depend on a memory of episodes and machine capacity for retrieval and system development.

The way the computer is programmed changes as well. A programming language is a design tool and a vehicle for human communication. Programming involves not only giving instructions to a computer but also creative thinking. This is particularly true in AI. Because of the AI contribution to future computerized offices, programming will become a common, fundamental, and primary task, along with "writing." Those who intend to make good use of

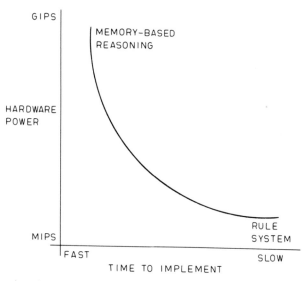

Figure 9-4. If we have hardware that is able to process giga instructions per second (GIPS), then we can use memory-based reasoning approaches. If the hardware processes in mega instructions per second (MIPS), then rule-based systems are more advisable.

computing facilities in their intellectual work will be required to personalize their computer. AI programming approaches are

1. nonprocedural, declarative, and therefore easy to use,
2. equipped with database management interfaces, especially for relational databases,
3. involved with a significant amount of logic programming—but are also
4. useful for developing distributed processing and databasing systems.

Eventually, with fifth-generation computers, the principal programming style will be knowledge programming, a further evolution from logic programming. This will involve constructing a model or a program while accessing a number of knowledgebanks. The approach involves describing declaratively the logical relations and conditions of the problem to be solved instead of specifying the procedure to be used.

Future programming styles, including those listed below, will probably bear a greater similarity to

- writing or composing a book, and thus to literate programming styles.
- doing engineering design work, and hence to prototyping in executable specification languages; and
- developing AI constructs through object-oriented programming approaches.

Fifth-generation computers should not only account for but also be adaptable to these programming style requirements. AI programs frequently require a large address space. This is an advantage because it allows the program to address many locations without requiring the hardware or software to do a lot of context switching, which would slow down processing. Also, processing is simpler, cleaner, and faster if the address space is large.

In other words, whereas conventional computing excels at solving problems that can be expressed in numerical terms and which lend themselves to repetitive, algorithmic solutions. AI technology deals with solving unstructured problems, interpreting information, using experience, and dealing with uncertain or incomplete information. Myriad techniques will be developed to address these problems.

Knowledge is represented as symbols, which are used to map real-world objects and properties associated with them. These symbols can be linked together, using structures such as networks or graphs, to represent such relationships at hierarchy and dependency. The hierarchical relationships among these symbols are established by using the symbolic operators for associative purposes.

Only powerful machines can successfully handle with symbolic computation a subsecond response time. These machines have to be dedicated: one man–one computer WSs. The term *crayette* has been coined to indicate the attempt to put a Cray computer's power on a WS.

The now classical microprocessor lines (Intel, Motorola) cannot satisfy such requirements even with the steady progression that brought the microprocessor from the Intel 4040 model of 1971 to its 1988 version of relative sophistication: Intel 80386, Motorola 68020/30. Then came the more powerful 1989–90 Intel i486 and i586, as well as Intel's RISC microprocessor—with similar developments happening at Motorola.

- *The i860 RISC microprocessor is extremely fast.* Intel has reduced the cycles per instruction (CPI) time of the i860 to a fraction of that of other known chips and plans to feature it in hypercube architectures (iPSC-III).
- *The i860 is highly integrated.* It includes both data (8K) and instruction (4K) *cache units,* as well as a cache controller and other peripheral functions that in the RISC versions of other manufacturers are located off the chip.

Integration gives the i860 an additional speed advantage, since any time a principal system task can be incorporated directly on the central silicon chip, system speed is enhanced. Furthermore, the i860 is one of the few processors that handles 64 bits of information at a time. (The only other chips that offer this capacity are a semicustomized one used by Apollo and an early-stage Fujitsu/SPARC implementation.)

Intel's RISK chip is object-language compatible with the 386 CISC and the 486.[6] It is designed to work in conjunction with the traditional 386 and Intel's new 486 by using the same memory paging methods. At the same time, research is underway to respond to the power requirements for symbolic computation. First, very large system integration (VLSI) promises to provide more than 1 million components for a few dollars, as current prices are bound to drop. The basic building blocks will no longer be gates or multipliers, but units capable of specific tasks such as speech synthesis, probabilistic reasoning, and so on.

---

[6] The i860 is *not* machine language compatible to the i386 and i486, as a January 1990 conference with Intel helps document. Compatibility will be assured at a higher linguistic level.

Built-in intelligence will be the rule—with increasingly higher kilo logical instructions per second (KLIPS). Second, expertise will be mapped in hardware. An expert system on a chip is being tested at Bell Laboratories, being used to control a robot arm. The chip is intended for applications requiring realtime responses, such as missle command and control, robotics, and manufacturing operations. It uses fuzzy logic techniques and is therefore suitable for applicaitons where data are not precise.

The robot arm application is on a customized transistor chip, including 16 rules in ROM, a controller to manage the movement of bits through the chip, and an inference processor. AT&T claims that the system is significantly faster than AI constructs in software because the operating instructions are written into the chip's circuitry rather than retrieved from external memory. Also, the use of fuzzy logic reduces the number of rules required for the system to act on problems. The researchers claim a chip speed of 80,000 fuzzy logic inferences per second (KFLIPS).

Hitachi has designed a microprocessor that processes AI programs very rapidly; Micro-Prolog, Lisp, and Smalltalk programs are being handled 20 times faster than on a common chip. The AI 32 has been conceived as a slave processor which, in cooperation with a common microprocessor and a special micro, is operated for the administration of the knowledgebank and database. Although the AI 32 serves especially the processing of AI programs, it also handles interrupt requests, guides input/output behavior, does paging, and initiates the actual working phases. The new engine is conceived in a way that makes it easy to develop AI software for it, helping to bridge the semantic gap which is frequently the impediment between logic programming languages and the basically primitive architecture of von Neumann-type computers.

With time and experience, off-the-shelf knowledgebanks with thousands of rules will appear. While most current applications use only a few hundred rules, easily stored on a single chip, the experience which will be gained through implementation will result in increased requirements.

Chip vendors are working to develop intelligent building blocks for AI systems. In the earlier example of the expert system on a chip Bell Laboratories estimated that they can achieve 64 rules by using all the chip's capacity and, 256 rules by moving to 1.25-μm fabrication technology. Several chips can be interconnected.

Eventually, AI systems on a chip will become transportable and marketable—comparable to books and software. They will represent knowledge in an organized but adaptable manner; support knowledge in terms familiar to endusers; employ user-friendly interface functions; exploit available methods of reasoning; and integrate with existing applications as well as with newer, more sophisticated reasoning methods.

5. THE MULTIPLE FUNCTIONS OF PARALLELISM

AI applications have created problems without a pure logical or numeric perspective. They include both *logic and arithmetic* subproblems. Furthermore, they are ill understood and poorly defined. Nevertheless, they can be handled by AI—a task that would have been impossible with classical DP. But we must be very cautious in the way we proceed to solve problems. It is not only heuristics we need but also

- technology transfer and
- computer literacy.

Both are basic in putting a *cultural change* into effect, and a cultural change should be the first objective of an AI implementation. As many companies have found, automation supported by knowledge-based systems that affects all levels of the organization produces a cultural change which proves irresistible.

This situation is welcome, as it justifies a large part of the investment in AI and fifth-generation computers. Conversely, if there is no cultural change today in the company, then the company will not be able to survive in tomorrow's highly competitive, knowledge-intense market.

I discuss fifth-generation languages and AI under the same heading because, as experience has shown, they are closely related to one another. AI is a concept, and therefore broader. The fifth-generation computer is an object, and hence is more contained within the AI domain.

In Section 2 we said that the design of the fifth-generation computer is aimed at exploiting the brain's strengths: *parallelism* and *intelligence*. AI approaches and symbolic processing suggest a massively parallel style. Within this perspective, a parallel model links several

- inference processors,
- complete engines, and
- secondary memory devices

in a network. The processor is an inference machine which acts as a unification entity. Network and hierarchical memory are integrated.

In a fully parallel mode of execution, all processing elements handle the same program. Each element operates on the contents of its own memory. Data-level parallelism uses a single control sequence—hence, a single program—and *executes it on all data simultaneously.* For instance, to operate on the whole data set at once, the Connection Machine has a distinct processor for each data element:

- a network of, for example, 65,536 individual computers (nodes)
- handling an equal number of messages in random pattern,
- each computer with its own 4,096 bits of memory.

These 65,536 nodes are interconnected through a massive communications system. The *Router* operates at 500 MBPS.[7] The *operating system* supports networking. The *languages* are C* and *Lisp (the asterisk stands for parallel version).

IBM conceives of fifth-generation computers as a separation of function: input/output, communications, and application processing. A high bandwidth is provided for interconnec-

---

[7] Remember that the physical line capacity is 2 to 3 GBPS.

tion. Shared memories are conceived for interprocessor communication and for isolating processors from input/output communications.

Central system services ensure locking, journaling, and recovery. Evolution of the operating system ensures that all processors are interconnected. However, we must differentiate

1. the *switching chip* (mesh) for the high bandwidth and
2. *local area network* solutions.

IBM's work on the mesh (Figure 9-5) is MVS oriented. Also using the mesh approach, the Japanese Institute for New Generation Computer Technology (ICOT) works with PSI/SIMPOS (as we will see in the next section).

In all these solutions to parallel processing through fifth-generation computers, the goals are a high bandwidth, support for alternative pathing, enhanced availability, high capacity, and extended add-on capabilities. In various ways, these goals reflect AI requirements, as the important criterion of AI programs is interconnection.

Expanding on the concept of interconnection, the key components of fifth-generation computer developments are the cache at every node; the possibility of using commodity microprocessors; the orientation to personal computing; the drive to parallelism; and emphasis on communications. Databasing plays a key role, including virtual memory (VM) approaches. The need for more power and the handling of logical constructs underline this effort. A key task is to offer fifth-generation computers at affordable prices and, at the same time, support steady innovation.

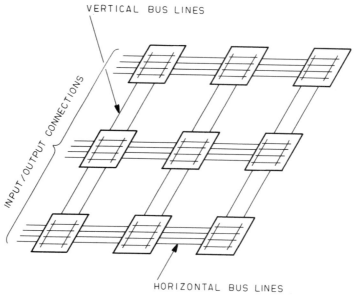

Figure 9-5. An alternative to hypercubes for new-generation computers is mesh-type interconnection, as shown in this figure.

The question is sometimes asked: "What is the difference between hypercube fifth-generation computers and array processors?" The answer is that the Connection Machine and Cray computers do not deliver the same power. Not only is the hypercube architecture much faster, but the supported facilities are different. The Cray computer is more effective as a number-crunching arithmetic calculator. The Connection Machine excels in situations involving event change—and, hence, reasoning.

Current computers, including supercomputers, do not distinguish between data of different types. They generally operate with sequences of simple bytes without specific recognition. This fits simple data processing (and number-crunching) requirements but not those of sophisticated applications. At the same time, simple von Neumann-type designs are subject to an increasing number of software errors. In fifth-generation computer-oriented (non-von Neumann) architectures, such errors are recognized and corrected at an early stage by the machine. This is the process of equilibration.

One of the goals of fifth-generation computers is to correct a tight spot of classical architecture known as the *von Neumann bottleneck,* which is created between the faster CPU and the slower main storage area. We gain speed if we reduce and number of

- instruction accesses, which are typical of a general purpose computer, and
- data accesses, which characterize direct processing by a von Neumann computer.

The first step helps to reduce about two-thirds of instruction access, the second about two-thirds of data access. This leads to a different kind of parallel processing than is usually conceived. Programmable registers, logic programming concepts, and the capacity for direct processing of AI intermediary code make the fifth-generation computer the engine for future problem solutions.

6. PSI, THE JAPANESE FIFTH-GENERATION COMPUTER

PSI stands for *personal sequential inference* engine. It is a fifth-generation computer and the brain-child of ICOT. We will follow this development as an example of the effort involved in fifth-generation computing.

In terms of planning, the ICOT project has been divided into three stages:

- The *initial stage* (1982–84) emphasized technological elements. The outcome has been PSI and ESP,[8] the programming enviornment.
- The *intermediate stage* (1985–88) focused on the fundation of fifth-generation computer systems, using knowledge, software, and hardware from the initial stage.
- The *final stage* (1989–91) produced a prototype parallel fifth-generation computer system, completely integrating all results obtained up to this point.

---

[8] Extended Self-Contained Prolog.

As previously noted, the first letter of PSI stands for *personal.* The goal of the initial stage was to produce a machine able to handle AI constructs at the personal WS level. The premise was that WS power requirements will continue to expand and that these requirements cannot be satisfied by classical computers.

Both logic orientation and processing capacity will become a problem when AI functions are included as a *matter of course* in the terminal systems. Hence, there is a need for a fifth-generation computer solution able to handle such requirements beforehand.

The second letter of PSI stands for *sequential.* This is a sequential inference engine which has been working (when released in 1984) at the 30- to 40-KLIPS level. Since then, efforts have been made to produce an engine that works at the 100- to 200-KLIPS level.[9] For instance, CHI (by NEC) is a personal sequential inference engine of higher performance: about 300 KLIPS. Such developments rest on the premise that knowledge processing requires 10^3 greater amount of computation.

As stated in the preceding section, in machine design we *gain speed* if we reduce the number of instruction accesses and eliminate most of the data accesses. We also improve *program quality* if errors are recognized and corrected by the machine. This has been the guideline in PSI development.

At the same time, attention has focused on the *logical environment* of the engine. A kernal language, KL-O, was developed with object-oriented features added to Prolog. PSI was built through KL-O and its successor, ESP. Extended ESP is an object-oriented programming language.

The operating system for PSI is Simpos,[10] written in ESP. KL-1 (and eventually KL-2) are different developments with guarded horn clauses (GHCs), a parallel Prolog version.[11] A relational database machine (Delta) was constructed as a first step in developing a knowledgebank engine.

PHI-2 is one of the changes made in PSI in the 1984–88 periods. It combines into one module a layered logical structure including

- an inference machine (PSI),
- dedicated hardware, and
- auxiliary (disc) memory.

The dedicated hardware performs associative keyword *searches of knowledge.* Retrieval and update efficiency are improved through metaphors and the implementation of a *knowledge compiler* with a knowledge server and a predicate server.

CHI[12] is another development based on PSI. Like other inference engines developed in Japan, it is an outgrowth of the fifth-generation computer systems project, providing

---

[9] ICOT also has a parallel PSI project known as PIM; it works on a mesh basis. Another project network. PSI 2 through a local area network and servers.

[10] Simpos stands for *sequential inference machine operating system.* SIM was the name of PSI in the initial phase of the ICOT project.

[11] The role of GHCs will become apparent when we talk about knowledgebanks.

[12] CHI stands for cooperative high-performance sequential inference background machine. It is a commercial product of NEC.

TABLE 9-1. Comparison of CHI and PSI.

Factor	CHI	PSI
Execution speed	200–300 KLIPS	20–50 KLIPS
Central memory	100 megawords	16 megaword
Cache	16 kilowords	8 Kword
Word	32 + 8 bits	32 + 8 bits
Control	Structure data copying	Structure data sharing
Chip	1 megabit	256 kilobits
Execution mode	Back-end	Stand-alone
Clock	180 ns	

- a sophisticated, intelligent processing environment
- for a wide range of applications and development tasks.

CHI executes 5 to 10 times faster than the major conventional, large-scale mainframes. It also offers unparalleled flexibility in developing and processing A-I applications.

Table 9-1 compares CHI to PSI. Note the improvements which have been made. Note also that whereas the original PSI version was a stand-alone machine, there have been successful parallel PSI projects. One project aims at networking about 100 PSI engines. Of these, 30 are on a local area network and the others are distributed. Another project aims at tightly coupling PSI, starting with four engines. A mesh solution has been chosen. The ultimate aim is to integrate the sequential machine into a parallel processing system.

Some of the Japanese applications of their fifth-generation computers are connected to robotics and artificial vision; others are used for machine translation. AI-enriched automatic translation has as its goal an integrated multilingual approach which participates in every stage of processing, including voice input, editing, printing, and voice response. Specific targets include vocabularies, a translation accuracy of better than 90%, and a total translation cost of less than 30% the human cost. To achieve these goals, research focuses on cultural analysis, grammar rules for various languages, multilanguage terminology banks, and special WSs for translation purposes.

The development of intelligent programming systems is another attempt to increase significantly software productivity and reliability. Subgoals range from the implementation of logic languages and an automatic programming system to a complete software development consultation facility.

Research in this area is also expected to contribute to the design of software and hardware cooperative problem-solving mechanisms and parallel inference engines. In such an aggregate, independent but interconnected inference systems would collaborate in solving a single problems.

During the next five years in the United States, Japan, and Europe, the majority of computer installations will still be of the von Neumann type. However, such installations will increasingly feature specialized graphics processors, speech recognition devices, realtime translation capabilities, and advances in robotics. Inference engines and knowledgebanks will be at the heart of most new developments. Projected for the middle to the late 1990s, autonomous intelligent vehicles are considered to be the test beds of sixth-generation computers.

10

The Mathematics of Uncertainty

Keywords

true • false • necessity • belief • unknown object • additivity axiom • cognitive process • possibility theory • possibility logic • decision field • fuzzy logic • linguistic categories • domain dependent • context dependent • uncertain data • empirical approach • theoretical approach • fuzzy sets • qualifiers • vagueness • uncertainty • imprecision • graded membership • interactive sets • noninteractive sets • degree of truth • possibility distribution • system of weights • decision model • pattern matching • knowledgebank • inference engine • fuzzy reasoning • prototype • compatibility • reject space • accept space • space of inconsistency • space of uncertainty • inconsistency • true value • theoretical value • observed frequencies • statistics • parameters • inference • estimation • accuracy • inference process • conditional probability • absolute probabilities • exclusive or • compound • a priori probability • posterior probability • productive probability

1. INTRODUCTION

Knowledge representation often requires modeling of imprecision, vagueness, and uncertainty. New mathematical disciplines are being applied to this task. There are similarities and differences among possibility theory, fuzzy sets, Shafer evidence (or belief) theory, Bayes' theorem, and probability theory. All of these theories deal with reasoning and inference; they involve procedures studied in the presence of uncertainty and imprecision. This is the essence of the new mathematics.

The new mathematics focus on the *degree of truth*. They attempt to provide a measure of agreement between representations of

- the meaning of a statement and
- what is known about reality.

As Figure 10-1 demonstrates, the real world is mapped into the knowledgebank. This is done by means of one of the mathematical sciences we will be examining, expressed in the form of rules—as discussed in Chapter 12.

The new mathematics do not need to be visible to the user who queries the AI construct, though understanding them greatly improves the benefits we can derive from AI. As Philippe Smets underlined in a personal discussion, the whole system of propositions—*true* and *false*—exists *without* the human being and his brain. With the human being, the concepts of *necessity* and *belief* are also introduced.

The real world is almost synonymous with the *unknown object*. Typically, this unknown object is described by attributes used in prototypes. Its schema is initially filled by input data, and it is completed during the classification of the rules. Such work has two goals:

1. To connect to unknown facts, states, and values representing established characteristics.
2. To do the classification itself and try to detect prevailing patterns.

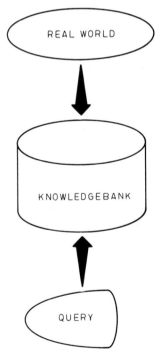

Figure 10-1. Queries are addressed to the knowledgebank, for instance, for justification of an opinion which has been given. The knowledgebank finds the documentation from its rules within the real-world environment to which it is addressed itself.

As explained in the appropriate chapters, connecting to unknown facts, states, and values can be done through induction, deduction, and abduction. For instance, deduction rules can be used to perform data abstraction, just as *fuzzy* predicates may be employed in defining premises.

The real world is populated by human beings, who have beliefs but also vagueness and uncertainty. One form of ignorance results from randomness encountered by chance. This is the field of probability theory. The probability of an event is usually known not as a real value between 0 and 1 but as belonging to an interval.

It is relatively easy to accumulate probabilities. It is hard to make out a particular case in such a way that it will stand rigorous criticism. But we do have valid tools in mathematical statistics which offer significant assistance in experimentation, estimation, validation, and the testing of hypothesis.

The problem with probability theory is that it works much better in the sciences than in qualitative reasoning applications. People are not very good at estimating probabilities. Also, qualitative estimates are sometimes meaningless; indirect methods are better. They lead to qualitative estimates and belief functions. The latter do *not* require a probability value to be within a precise interval.

Belief functions are used to model and quantify subjective, personal evaluations and estimations induced by evidence. Some types of evidence are strong enough to result in knowledge; others are fuzzy; still others are conditional: The sun will shine (*A*) if it is daytime and the sky is not clouded (*B*).

The notion *A*|*B* (*A* given *B*) is a conditional probability. It has been expressed by Bayes' theorem. At the end of the nineteenth century, Bayes devoted his life to statistics. Nearly a century later, his theorem became one of the foundations of AI constructs.

Bayesian probabilities ensure that a degree of belief can be quantified. The major axiom is the *additivity axiom,* which states that the probability of the union of two disjoint events (*A* and *B*) is the logical sum of the probabilities of each event. This approach is usually justified by axioms describing decision processes.

Nevertheless, beliefs can exist outside of any decision context. This is a *cognitive process* per se. For such a process, the *possibility theory* is instrumental. It is particularly applicable where categories are poorly defined and measurements can be sources of error.

Possibilistic logic incorporates degrees of possibility, making it feasible to reach deductions from vague propositions. Reasoning is based on fuzzy predicates expressed in the form of a possibility distribution; an example of such distribution was presented in Chapter 4. We will return to this issue later.

Fuzzy notions and beliefs per se, are noncrisp. They are not black or white, 0 or 1. They may be vague, involve uncertainty, or demonstrate ignorance. Ignorance may be due to lack of accuracy, lack of specificity of information, or other reasons. Nonetheless, the result of possibility theory implementation is the development of rational systems. The knowledge engineer and the user can implement various functions easily. They can find out experimentally the outcome of hypotheses which they are testing on the outcome of their own qualitative reasoning.

Figure 10-2 integrates the concepts just examined into a layered structure. The bottom level is the real world. It has both physical and logical characteristics. Over it we built a logical construct.

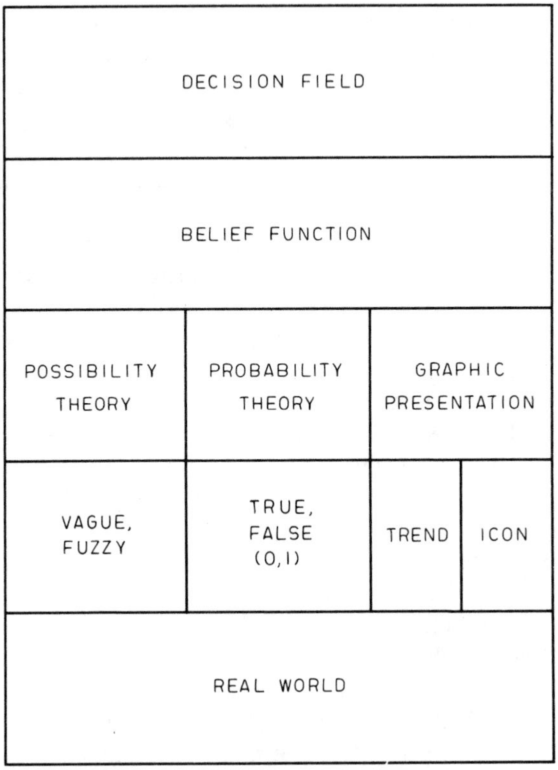

```
┌─────────────────────────────────────────────────┐
│                                                   │
│                 DECISION  FIELD                   │
│                                                   │
├─────────────────────────────────────────────────┤
│                                                   │
│                 BELIEF  FUNCTION                  │
│                                                   │
├──────────────┬──────────────┬────────────────────┤
│              │              │                    │
│ POSSIBILITY  │ PROBABILITY  │      GRAPHIC        │
│   THEORY     │   THEORY     │   PRESENTATION      │
│              │              │                    │
├──────────────┼──────────────┼──────────┬─────────┤
│              │    TRUE,     │          │         │
│   VAGUE,     │    FALSE     │  TREND   │  ICON   │
│   FUZZY      │    (0,1)     │          │         │
│              │              │          │         │
├──────────────┴──────────────┴──────────┴─────────┤
│                                                   │
│                  REAL  WORLD                      │
│                                                   │
└─────────────────────────────────────────────────┘
```

Figure 10-2. A layered approach to the infrastructure of a decision field, including the real world to which it applies.

The lower logical layer is the *simplest:* It can be expressed through a fuzzy set with vagueness and uncertainty, a decision tree (true, false; 0, 1), a trend, or an icon. The next layer involves theory and methodology: possibility theory, probability theory, or graphic presentation. Probability theory is an instance of possibility theory.

Belief functions are expressed through the use of one of the means just described. While these may be transparent to the user, they are fundamental to the mechanism. In turn, belief functions form the infrastructure on which rests the *decision field.* Let us now focus on means and tools.

2. IMPLEMENTING FUZZY LOGIC

Fuzzy logic is a logic that works with uncertainties. Though we can always put some certainty factors into an AI construct, the latter is not given a definite path to reach conclusions. The model is characterized by

- imprecision, uncertainty, and vagueness,
- a degree of truth but also of uncertainty, and
- possible logic due to an inability to calculate, incompleteness, or simply ignorance.

Fuzzy sets presuppose logical sufficiency and a necessity function, but also incomplete information or complex estimation schemes. The probability of using a certain control valve in a chemical plant depends on several factors: high temperature, pipe corrosion, pressure, and the risk of exceeding tolerance limits. Implementing a necessity function, we may test key variables to establish which ones are more discriminative, eliminating those of less importance. We may establish influencing values, but such values themselves may be vague.

"Higher than 100°C" is an ill-defined term. We know that 100°C is the boiling temperature for water, but not necessarily for other liquids. Ignorance may be due to imprecision or may be the result of it. Not all processes are of a crisp accept/reject, true/false type where a single value signals a cutoff point.

Beginning in World War II, a theory of mathematical statistics was developed to support a three-valued logic:

- accept,
- continue testing, or
- reject.

This theory can be applied to a goal-seeking, iterative search process. Fuzzy logic can be three-valued, multivalued, or infinitely valued—in contrast to the binary computer and the classical construction of computer programs.

Typical computer programs are useful in applications that require manipulation of precise data. AI constructs are designed to deal with a more realistic world in which

- information need not be manipulated precisely and
- judgment and/or evaluation can be only approximate.

By employing fuzzy logic, the program has a much greater chance of *accurately* following a perception prevailing in the real world. Available methods in fuzzy logic help interface numerical and symbolic values. They partition numerical scales into *linguistic categories*. Membership functions are *domain* and *context* dependent.

Partitioning numerical scales into linguistic categories is important, as approximate reasoning relies on linguistic variables, qualifiers, and hedges, as well as on noise words. Cost, measurement, and volume are examples of linguistic variables. Their metrics give quantitative results, although the definitions which proceed from them are often qualitative. They can be derived from indirect methods and subjective judgment.

In the past, this was considered a hindrance; today we look at this problem differently. We appreciate that indirect method of deriving probabilities, for example, give more reliable results and avoid the reduction of accuracy. By using limits, we can quantify a linguistic expression:

- Most likely: more than 90%
- Rather likely: 75–90%

- Above average: 60–75%
- Average: 40–60%
- Less than average: 25–40%
- Rather unlikely: 10–25%
- Not likely: less than 10%

This is a seven-value system. It may not be precise, but it is much more accurate than asking a manager to respond only "yes" or "no" or pressing him to reply with one probability.

Low, high, and *reasonable* are qualifiers. *Very, quite,* and *about* are hedges that can be used with qualifiers. Possibilistic estimates (such as ranges of probabilities) are still better. We don't ask the domain expert to say 73.5% or 20.2%. We ask him to use a range scale, which can be expressed in linguistic categories and quantitative measures at the same time.

A similar approach can be used with diagnostics and quality control, including causal reasons. When none of the observed properties which ultimately caused the anomalous result were themselves anomalous, the cause of the anomaly must lie somewhere in between. In other words, one of the internal components must be faulty.

Through fuzzy set implementation, hypotheses made about the number of faulty components might be better focused utilizing observations caused by the same properties. Consider the following example. The behavior of A is anomalous and needs to be explained. B, C, D, and E are observable properties, and they are all normal (Figure 10-3). So the explanation for why A is anomalous must be that there is a faulty component. But if F is also normal, it can be deduced that its hierarchical cause, namely, G, must also be normal. Therefore a possible explanation for the anomaly of A is that H is malfunctioning—but we are not sure.

Malfunctioning can be expressed in ranges. It may not be enough to hypothesize the operation of an open/closed switch. If temperature drop is the important variable, it may be due to causes which we can identify as a function of the drop. We do so in electrical

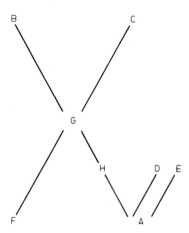

Figure 10-3. Flowchart of the interconnection of different hypotheses in the case study described in text.

engineering when we measure current and mentally create an idealized model. Fuzzy theory permits us to map this model into the machine.

Fuzzy sets help us handle an idealized abstraction. Inference permits us to deal with uncertainties. Handling *uncertain data* is an opportunity, provided that we have the means to do so. Fuzzy theory provides a method of treating essential subjective information— therefore, *ill-defined and ambiguous.*

If a process does not reflect random characteristics, and if we are not able to express our thoughts quantitatively, we should not use probability theory. But we can use

1. an *empirical approach* such as Mycin's belief/disbelief system, or
2. a *theoretical approach,* that is, possibility theory.

Ill-defined and ambiguous information is typical of human cognition and reasoning. Fuzziness defines the following state of mind:

- We may not know exactly what we want,
- But we can describe the process of a weighted decision.

The *fuzzy sets* are *qualifiers.* Their proper place in an expert system or any other AI construct is that of an intermediate layer between known modeling solutions and the system's architecture. It cannot be repeated too often: Few real-life business decisions can be encompassed in yes/no answers. The alternatives are shown in Figure 10-4.

Starting with the premise that one possible solution is always the two-valued logic, the network proceeds in two ways: toward a two-valued logic structure, exemplified through probability theory, and toward a three-state logic solution. The latter leads to *n*-state logic and its formalization: possibility theory.

Conditional (Bayesian) probabilities are an outgrowth of probability theory. Together, the Bayesian approach and possibility theory implementation are the pillars on which the fuzzy sets rest. Real-world perceptions and empirical approaches both influence the way we develop and use the notions of vagueness and uncertainty.

In general, truth is understood as conformity between a statement (or proposition) and the actual state. In contrast, with possibility theory, a *degree of truth* is a measure of agreement between the representation of the meaning of a statement and *what is actually known* about reality. This is valuable from an information systems viewpoint.

The measure of possibility is taken with reference to a statement restricting the value of variables (constraints) implicit in the statement. What can be said about the truth of a proposition depends upon the state of knowledge, which sometimes—but not always—is synonymous with matching procedures between the meaning of a proposition and the information against which the procedures are tested. The latter is supposed to represent the real world.

3. INTRODUCTION TO POSSIBILITY THEORY

The strength of probability theory rests on its theoretical foundations and on the principle of additivity. But probabilistic concepts and functions cannot handle all cases. This is the reason for the development of possibilistic functions and solutions.

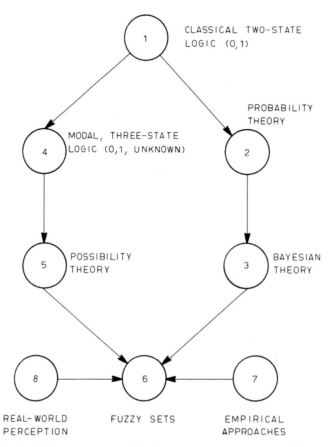

Figure 10-4. Possibility theory and probability theory have much in common but also have significant differences. Probability theory is based on two-state (binary) constructs, possibility theory on multi-state models (ternary, etc).

We have spoken of crisp vs. fuzzy sets, underlining the difference between certainty and fuzziness. There is also a contrast between vagueness (something that is not clear), uncertainty, and imprecision:

1. *Vagueness* refers to lack of sharp boundaries. Something is not clear; its meaning is uncertain. There are no clearly set boundaries of a set of objects—for instance: "the water is warm." "the weather is mild."
2. *Uncertainty* refers to data unreliability. We have collected statistics, but we don't know if they are accurate. In fact, they may be neither accurate nor precise.
3. *Imprecision* refers to the contents of information. A statement such as "The temperature is between 16°C and 24°C" is *not* precise, but it has some interesting implications. It forms the basis of a possibility distribution. Figure 10-5A shows the reason.

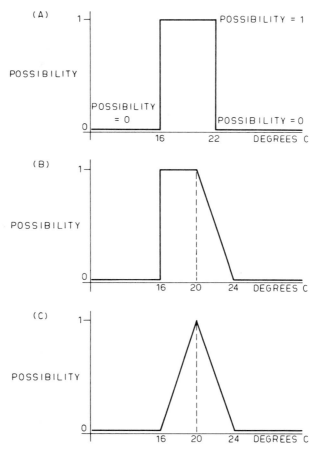

Figure 10-5. The nature of a possibility distribution is conditioned by real-world information, though the latter may be fuzzy. This figure shows three different possibility distributions.

The imprecise statement made in item 3 can be interpreted in the following manner: Any temperature below 16°C has *a possibility equal to 0*. The same is true of any temperature above 22°C. By contrast, temperatures between 16°C and 22°C have a *possibility equal to 1*.

- A possibility equal to 1 means that a certain event is possible but not certain.
- A possibility equal to 0 means that the event is impossible.

The whole concept of possibility theory rests on this premise. As stated in Chapter 4, when in science we reject, we are much more certain (sure of ourselves) than when we accept. It is only normal that a possibility equal to 1 does not mean certainty.

Now let's consider vagueness. The concept behind this word is context dependent; it is also subjective. Something is vague if it is ill-defined, hence Lotfi Zadeh's idea of *graded membership* which he elaborated with Richard Bellman in the mid-1970s.[1]

---

[1] Both Bellman and Zadeh were at the time at Stanford University.

In the previous example, someone may say, "I guess the temperature is between 16°C and 22°C," but actually, he thinks otherwise. He is rather sure that the temperature is between 16°C and 20°C, with a scaling-down possibility between 20°C and 24°C. The 22°C he mentioned is the middle range—an average value.

If we compare Figures 10-5A and 10-5B, we see that the latter represents the man's opinion on water temperature much better than the former. In the range of 20°C to 24°C, the possibility is steadily reduced until it reaches 0. Had the man thought that the only value with a possibility of 1 (certainty) was 20°C, but that there was an increasing possibility of 16°C to 20°C and a decreasing one as explained, then the possibility distribution would resemble Figure 10-5C. In essence, these are the critical possibility distributions.

This is also the way an interview with a domain expert would proceed. When we express vague predicates, we should be able to take advantage of them. People like to be imprecise, or they may have to do so. Unless we have the proper tools to exploit such a situation, imprecision is helpful neither in decision making nor in any other activity.

It is quite important to be able to express the concept that some facts are more possible than others, that is, to qualify and quantify the degree of certainty. L.A. Zadeh, R. Bellman,[2] Dempster, G. Shafer,[3] D. Dubois, and H. Prade[4] have worked on elegant theories. Unfortunately, though these theories focus on the same notions, they are not necessarily compatible. Hence the resulting AI constructs are not portable.

The elegance of possibility theory,[5] and the superiority of its qualities in contrast to those of probability theory, are demonstrated by the fact that we can express different beliefs on the same subject. This is impossible with probability theory. The more limited perspective of probability theory make the following statement contradict itself:

Diagnostic Status	
0.89	This blood sample is Type A
0.60	This blood sample is Type B
0.25	This blood sample is Type B

These are possibilites, not probabilities. It is inconceivable to express a cumulative probability of 174%. By contrast, with possibility theory, we conclude that the blood sample is Type A with 89% confidence, type O with 60% confidence, and type B with 25% confidence. Note that this is a diagnostic status, not an interpretive analysis. This example contains no recommendation about what action to take based on the conclusion. However, after the diagnosis is done, the system can go into a consultation mode whereby the user can review the answers, ask which rules the system used to reach the conclusion and so on.

The point of aggregation is, of course, crucial. Bellman and Zadeh have pointed out that the type of operator for the aggregation of fuzzy sets (in the sense of an intersection) may

---

[2] Then of Stanford University.
[3] Princeton University.
[4] Université Paul Sabatier, Toulouse.
[5] No distinction is made between possibility theory and belief function, nor are the differences elaborated. This would unduly complicate an issue which is not easy to grasp in the first place.

depend on whether the sets are *interactive* or *noninteractive,* which is sometimes interpreted as "dependent" or "independent." We will not treat aggregation in this book.

Let's draw a conclusion about what we have said regarding possibility theory. It has been shown that uncertain IF . . . THEN . . . ELSE rules can be modeled into a new mathematical theory of evidence. This rests on beliefs about compatibility relations between two or more varibales. Conditional possibilistic structures provide estimates of events; these estimates are equivalent to an expression:

- If proposition A holds, then there is a certain function which holds a degree of certainty (possibility) about compatibility relations.
- The evidence contained in such a conditional possibilistic function can be combined with beliefs in such variables, using a mathematical distribution as the basis.

This concept fits well into the framework of a qualitative approach to a multivariate system of possibilistic structures. The latter can be computationally simplified if certain topological properties are satisfied—for instance, when the overall computation can be broken down into many local computations and/or when useful results are presented in graphic form.

4. DOMAINS OF VAGUENESS AND THE RECOGNITION OF PATTERNS

We have said that the concepts of possibilistic expression and graded membership contribute to expert decisions, their mapping into AI constructs, and the development of good predicates. Even the concept of vagueness can be turned to advantage through the appropriate tools.

Let's take an example from reliability and availability. A certain configuration of a computers and communications (C+C) system marketed as a package has shown availability of 91% to 94%. The statistics in the database do not permit us to use classical probability theory for calculating the mean and standard deviation because of the vagueness and uncertainty they involve.

Uptime is influenced by the environment in which a system operates; prevailing humidity is an example. Both basic and application software have a great impact. Power variations, pollution control of the air, operator training, the know-how of maintenance engineers, and so on also affect uptime. There is no reason to believe that the availability statistics come from a homogeneous environment. In fact, the opposite is more likely to be true. Therefore, the chief engineer chose possibility theory.

As stated, the statistics indicate an availability of 91% to 94%; that is the highest frequency. All values in this range have a possibility equal to 1. But there is also a declining possibility toward 86% availability; that is the lowest frequency. Similarly, in rare cases, some C+C systems reached 97% availability (a hardware/software figure). These references are plotted in Figure 10-6.

TR stands for the domain.

This symbol indicates availability in this example and degrees of water temperature in the preceding example (Section 3).

X reflects the percent availability value.

This refers to a given system to be installed. It is unknown to everyone, including the chief engineer and the client. What both of them know is that when the client asks for an availability figure—say, x—he also wanted to know its possibility factor.

$\Pi(x)$ is the possibility function (Boolean algebra function) of X.

If we know the *possibility distribution*—which we do as Figure 10-6 documents—we can easily estimate this function. In Figure 10-6 this is done in a graphic manner.

This approach is much more accurate than saying, in response to a customer's query: "The availability is good." To emphasize, in the present example, as in many others, uncertainty refers to our partial ignorance of the truth or falsity of an information element (IE)—in this case, the homogeneity or lack of homogeneity of the backgrounds from which reliability statistics are drawn. The situation becomes clearer if we attach a grade of uncertainty to a statement, which is precisely what we did.

In the case of this C+C system, as in many other scientific, engineering, and managerial environments, there is a trade-off between imprecision and uncertainty. Though a statement may be both imprecise and uncertain, usually one of these two aspects predominates. Precision is greater than certainty in the reliability example. In a given state of knowledge, imprecise statements can be more certain than precise ones—and vice versa.

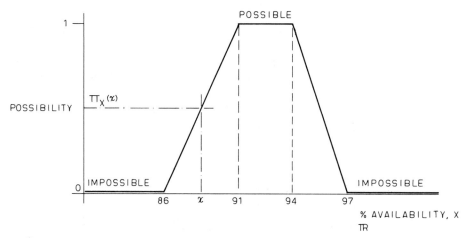

Figure 10-6. A possibility distribution is exemplified in this curve, which includes the domain (in this case, percent availability) and the necessity function, which not only divides between possible and impossible (binary approach) but also presents tonalities of gray.

An answer to the customer's query such as "92.5% availability, on the average" would have been inaccurate and imprecise, but it would have appeared certain. By contrast, an answer such as the one characterized by the possibility distribution in Figure 10-6 appears less certain, but it is accurate. The fuzzy (vague) predicate being used presents complete information. All IE values entering into this reliability evaluation are properly defined. As a result, the answer to the following queries is crisp:

- Availability less than 86%? *No.*
- Availability more than 86%? *Yes.*
- Availability less than 97%? *Yes.*
- Availability more than 97%? *No.*

Other queries too receive an accurate response:

- What is the possibility of a 92% availability? 1.
- Of 88.5% availability? 50%
- Of 87% availability? 20%

Such answers are calculated by taking values of the function

$$\Pi_X (x)$$

where x is the availability asked for in the query. It is easy to prove that

$$\Pi_X (92)\% = 1$$

$$\Pi_X (98)\% = 0$$

In an AI construct, the proper expression of the statement is a matter of knowledge representation. But the theoretical bases are solid.

It has been stated that the availability of the C+C system can be 91%, 92%, 93%, or 94%—all values having the same possibility. The inverse can also be true. We can use a *system of weights,* without expressing proportions, just by using only absolute values. The following example suggests nine criteria for purchasing a computer for desktop publishing purposes. Among them, they establish a *decision model:*

0.8 (386 microprocessor)
1.0 (Running Pagemaker) desktop publishing
0.5 (with 20 megabytes) or more on the hard disc)
1.0 (700,000 pixels or more resolution)
0.15 (light blue background color)
0.7 (easy keyboard use, standard layout)
1.0 (good local maintenance)
0.9 (ready interfacing to mainframes)
0.6 (price of the equipment)

This model also helps define trade-offs. Alternatively, weights might have been evenly distributed along the continuum of each aspect.

Fuzzy reasoning can also be used for *pattern matching* between data and premises—specifically, for the combination of different fuzzy premises. Such a model is helpful for propagating results from possibility grade to conclusion and for prototyping.

We can conceive the following system structure:

1. The *knowledgebank* is composed of frame-like objects (prototypes, templates), as well as decision rules, unknown objects.
2. The *inference engine* is designed for tree searching, with rule activation, matching, and selection at each node of the tree.
3. *Fuzzy reasoning* is selected for representation of uncertainty and imprecise knowledge, as well as for the interpretation of solutions.

The prototypes are typical objects representing their class. They provide hierarchical "part-of" links and support three types of attributes: interval, set, and structure. The construct features control slots.

As an example of applying fuzzy reasoning to prototypes, let's consider pattern matching between the *unknown object* and the *prototype*.[6] The goals are as follows:

1. *Compatibility.* The AI construct must look for compatibility between the object and the prototype by establishing similarities.
2. *Incompatibility.* Decisions by the AI system should be based on the differences between the object and the prototype.

This two-valued compatibility/incompatibility solution is vital to understanding the construct and the way it works. Compatibility/incompatibility leads to a two-sided system for solution interpretation, and is an excellent example of belief/disbelief function.

Belief/Disbelief graphs may resemble a statistical operating characteristics curve. We are faced with type I and type II errors. By and large,

- Type I error reflects an area where lack of knowledge predominates, though uncertainty may have many reasons.
- An example of type II errors is noise in the image subjected to pattern recognition.

Since anything but the *accept* quarterspace is in essence a rejection area, we conclude that rejection can be due to lack of knolwedge or to noise, rather than pure incompatibility.

This model can become more sophisticated if prototype attributes are given different importance and we account for complex criteria. However, in general, such fuzzy pattern matching allows us to quantify the similarity of objects through the use of a basically qualitative approach.

Let's repeat the fundamental notions. The basic idea of this approach is to separate *compatibility* from *incompatibility* and use a separate scale for each. We do not need to normalize to 1. Instead, we can use a two-dimensional plane for representation. Criteria for threshold can be established by various methods, such as the following:

---

[6] This is written with reference to a fuzzy set project on pattern recognition done by Catherine Granger, then at the French national research institute INRIA.

- by example,
- by judging the consequences,
- by training,
- through educated guestimates, or
- arbitrarily.

Thresholds need not be monolithic and invariant. They can be modified at the prototype level or during the operation of the system.

The range of applications is impressive. This two-scale system has been applied to projects as varied as the automatic classification of galaxies, the identification of planktons, and the diagnosis of antenna faults. In pattern recognition applications, the key problem has been the interpretation of parameters within a very large number of possible shapes.

5. DESCRIBING RULES OF BEHAVIOR: BAYES' THEOREM

Statistical tools describe the relationships between variables of interest in a study or experiment. Some of the tools state the other variables on which each pertinent factor depends, the functional relationship of each dependence, and the constants in each functional relationship. Other tools show how results are distributed around an expected or *true value*.

If we wish to benefit from the formal language of mathematics, we must have a model of the system which tells us

- which variables should be measured and
- what values to assign to the controlled variables.

However, there are gaps in this logic. First, factors are rarely studied alone. Typically they interact with each other and are analyzed in interaction.

Mathematical statistics allows us to study different factors and to combine the obtained results. This is done through statistical formulas:

1. *The addition formula.* This states the probability that at least one of two events is equal to the sum of the probabilities of each event minus the probability of the compound event.
2. *The multiplication formula.* This states that the probability that two events occur together is equal to the probability of one event multiplied by the conditional probability of the other, given that the first occurs. This is precisely what we will examine in this chapter after we consider the preconditions for proper analysis.

The second problem with mathematical logic, as discussed in preceding chapters, is that much of the mathematical statistical inference is based on the assumption that the available data are a random sample drawn from a population whose distribution approaches the normal. We have said that when the data are not obtained from a random sample or when extreme variation, trends, periodic fluctuations, discontinuities, etc., are detected, the use of nonparametric techniques becomes important.

We must always choose our tools carefully. The more powerful tools are, the greater the damage that results when they are poorly chosen or misused.

The third factor in using mathematical logic is that we should appreciate the deeper meaning of the probability of an event, that is, the number between 0 and 1. It denotes the *theoretical,* or ideal, value of the frequency of that event based on the *observed* frequencies. The theoretical and observed aspects should not be confused. This means that when we run an experiment and obtain certain numbers, these are *statistics.* They are never exactly equal to the numbers we want, that is, the *parameters.* Mathematical statistics help to bridge this gap by predicting the outcomes resulting from a set of assumptions.

- Mathematical statistics is the inductive science of change.
- Probability theory is the deductive science of chance.

Each has its role. Mathematical statistics enables us to make inferences about the nature of the underlying distribution. It provides the tools for estimating parameters based on knowledge of the outcomes of experiments.

As in any inductive science, one can never be absolutely certain that a specific cause underlies the observed effect. But the tools do permit numeric inferences and estimates. They associate with each a number which represents the extent of uncertainty in this result—which defines the extent of our confidence in our conclusion.

Fourth, the central problems of mathematical statistics are *inference* and *estimation.* We have spoken of population estimations based on samples. That is done through statistics.

We can always increase the *accuracy* of our induction by increasing *n.* Nevertheless, such an increase is often expensive and sometimes impossible. We must be concerned with the efficiency of statistical procedures—specifically with the number of trials to be done. This establishes the precision or level of significance that can be obtained with a fixed number of trials.

Problems involved in the *inference process* are both mathematical and philosophical. Furthermore, many of the tools commonly used today in this field are relatively new, though probability theory was well established by Pascal and De Laplace.

Qualitative decision processes often require conditional probability. In many cases, stochastic processes are used to orient a decision based on certain suppositions: car accidents are more probable on wet pavements; power failure is an electrical problem due to . . . ; most likely, an unbalanced treasury account is due to errors in . . .

A hypothesis is made about some event other than the one observed. Our decision process must consider a conditional probability. We have the theory to do so.

Consider a population of N balls, including N_A red balls and N_H defectives. Suppose that the event of a ball chosen at random being red and defective, is A and H, respectively. Then, from the Laplace definition:

$$P(A) = \frac{N_A}{N}, \qquad P(H) = \frac{N_H}{N}$$

If we want to find the probability of a defective ball's being red, we have to deal with a conditional probability. Out of the total population we distinguish a subpopulation of defectives, and within this subpopulation we consider the subset of reds. In probability theory, this is written as $N_{HA} \vert N_H$, where N_{HA} is the number of defective reds. Essentially, $N_{HA} \vert N_H$

is a brief way of stating that we are looking for a subpopulation N_{HA} of defective reds within the population N_H of defectives. The probability of event A, if event H has happened, is

$$P(A|H) = \frac{N_{AH}}{N_H} = \frac{P(AH)}{P(H)}$$

Stated differently, $P(A|H)$ is the *conditional probability* of A on the hypothesis H (for given H).

In statistics we often refer to *absolute* probabilities, in contrast to *conditional* probabilities. But the conditional probabilities have much weight in qualitative decisions. That is why Bayesian mathematics is so popular.

Let X be an event such that $0 \leqslant P(X) \geqslant 1$ and say that the only change from an absolute operation is that all results originally possible (with the absolute operation) which are not contained in X become impossible. One way to fulfill this requirement is to omit any outcome in which X does not occur. It then follows that the possible results of the conditional operation are the elements of X.

If each of these results is denoted by Y_j, $j = 1, 2, \ldots n$, then the probability of these results is given by $P(Y_j|X)$. Essentially, Y_j is a subset of X, or, in different terms, each Y_j is an element j of X. That is, $P(Y_j|X) = P(Y)$. This means that, for independent events, the conditional probability of Y, if X has happened, is equal to the absolute probability of Y. The conditional probability remains undefined when hypothesis H has zero probability. As an example, suppose that an urn contains r red and b black balls. Two balls are chosen at random without replacement. If the first ball is red, what is the probability that the second ball is also red? Event H (first red) can occur in $(r + b - 1)$ ways. AH (both red) can occur in $r(r - 1)$ ways. Therefore:

$$P(A|H) = \frac{(r - 1)}{(r + b - 1)}$$

Note that taking conditional probabilities of various events with respect to a particular hypothesis H amounts to choosing H as a new sample space. In order to reduce the total probability of the new sample space to unity, we have to multiply all probabilities by the constant factor $1/P(H)$.

With this modification, all general theorems on absolute probabilities can also be applied to conditional probabilities. We will return to this issue later.

Given that $P(A + B) = P(A) + P(B) - P(AB)$, if we want to find the probability of either event A or B happening, given that event H has happened, then

$$P[(A + B)|H] = P(A|H) + P(B|H) - P(AB|H)$$

Each of these conditional probabilities can be expressed as the ratio of two probabilities, for example:

$$P(A|H) = \frac{P(A)}{P(H)} \quad \text{and} \quad P(B|H) = \frac{P(B)}{P(H)}$$

In Figure 10-7A, the population is I (universe) and both H and A are sets within this population.

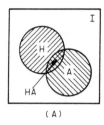 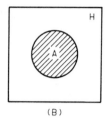

Figure 10-7. Event diagram based on the example presented in text.

In our earlier example, out of the total number of balls in the urn, some are defective, some are red, and some are both defective and red. Then we make the defective set the population of interest (Figure 10-7B). Set AH is now the only one which contains balls with attribute A.

In fact, we do not need to identify any more of this set as HA because all balls in the newly defined population have attribute H. If the same urn contained red (A) and green (B) balls, and both A, B can have attribute H, then within the population H may have had two sets, A and B.

Figure 10-8 also shows that the probability of the joint occurrence of two events can be expressed as $P(AH) = P(A|H)P(H)$. In addition:

$$P(ABC) = P(A|BC)P(B|C)P(C)$$

Conditional probabilities do not exist only for two sets. Statistical theory permits more complex solutions. We will return to this issue later.

6. PROPERTIES OF CONDITIONAL PROBABILITIES

Let A and B denote two events and A' and B' the corresponding complementary events. A' stands for not-A. Hence $A + A' = 1$, and $B + B' = 1$. In this sense, A' denotes the event that A does not occur and B' denotes the event that B does not occur—which is the sense of complementarity.

The results of n observations are tabulated in Table 10-1:

TABLE 10-1.   Distribution of Observations in Regard to Events and the Corresponding Combinations.

Events	Events		
	B	B'	Total
A	c_1	c_2	$c_1 + c_2$
A'	c_3	c_4	$c_3 + c_4$
Total	$c_1 + c_3$	$c_2 + c_4$	

Note: $c_1 + c_2 + c_3 + c_4 = n$.

- c_1 indicates the absolute frequency of the simultaneous occurrence of A and B.
- c_2 indicates the absolute frequency when A fails to occur but B occurs.
- c_3 indicates the absolute frequency when A occurs but B fails to occur.
- c_4 indicate the absolute frequency when both A and B fail to occur.

AB (or $A \cdot B$) denotes the compound event of both A and occurring. $A + B$ stands for *either* A or B occurring. We have not yet introduced

$$A \oplus B, \text{ or } A \dotplus B^7$$

This denotes that *at least one* of the two events occurs. This means AB, $A'B$, AB', or more than one.

If A and B are mutually exclusive, then the occurrence of one of them precludes the other. It follows that

$$AB = 0$$

$$A \oplus B = A + B$$

The event $A \oplus B$ is equal to the condition that either A or B occurs, which we denoted by *exclusive or*. Let's recapitulate:

AB stands for both A and B.
$A + B$ stands for A or B.
$A \oplus B$ stands for A and/or B.

These concepts and systems of notation can be extended to more than two events. From the definitions which have been given, we can deduce that

$$A \oplus B = AB + AB' + B'A$$

$$A + B = AB' + B'A$$

The corresponding probabilities are $P(A)$, $P(AB)$, $P(A + B)$, and $P(A \oplus B)$. Expressing them by means of the symbols in Table 10-1, we obtain

$$P(A) \quad = \frac{c_1 + c_2}{n}$$

$$P(AB) \quad = \frac{c_1}{n}$$

$$P(A + B) = \frac{c_1 + c_2 + c_3}{n}$$

Dividing all the numbers in Table 10-1 by n, we get Table 10-2.
Tables 10-1 and 10-2 give us the following relations:

$$P(A) + P(A') = \frac{c_1 + c_2}{n} + \frac{c_3 + c_4}{n} = 1$$

---

[7] Both signs $\oplus$ and $\dotplus$, are used in literature for exclusive or.

TABLE 10-2. **Probabilities of the Distribution of n Observations in Regard to two Events and the Corresponding Combinations.**

Events	Events	Distribution
	B B'	
A	$P(AB)$ $P(AB')$	$P(A)$
A'	$P(A'B)$ $P(A'B')$	$P(A')$
Distribution	$P(B)$ $P(B')$	

In other words, the probability of an event *plus* the probability of its complementary event equals 1.

$$P(A) = \frac{c_1 + c_2}{n} = \frac{c_1}{n} + \frac{c_2}{n} = P(AB) + P(AB')$$

This means that the probability of an event is equal to the sum of the probabilities in the corresponding row or column of the table.

The probability of at least one of the events A and B may be written

$$\frac{c_1 + c_2 + c_3}{n} = \frac{c_1 + c_2}{n} + \frac{c_1 + c_3}{n} - \frac{c_1}{n}$$
$$P(A \oplus B) = P(A) + P(B) - P(AB)$$

Hence, the probability of the occurrence of at least one of the events is equal to the sum of the probabilities of the two events *minus* the frequency of the compound event.

The probability $P(A \oplus B)$ may also be expressed by $P('B')$ as follows:

$$P(A + B) = \frac{c_1 + c_2 + c_3}{n} = \frac{n - c_4}{n} = 1 - P(A'B')$$

This means that the probability of the occurrence of at least one of the events is equal to 1 minus the probability of the occurrence of *none* of the events. This *none* is complementary to *at least one*.

Now let's consider the $c_1 + c_3$ observations where event A has occurred. These constitute a subset of the total set of n observations. The probability that an event B in this subset is denoted by

$$P(B|A)$$

is *the conditional probability of B given A,* of which we spoke in the preceding section.

The division of the first (and then the second) row of figures in Table 10-1 by the *total* number gives

$$P(B|A) = \frac{c_1}{c_1 + c_2}$$

$$P(B'|A) = \frac{c_2}{c_1 + c_2}$$

In a similar manner:

$$P(A|B) = \frac{c_1}{c_1 + c_3}$$

$$P(A'|B) = \frac{c_1}{c_1 - c_3}$$

The probability of the compound event AB can then be written

$$\frac{c_1}{n} = \frac{c_1 + c_2}{n} \cdot \frac{c_1}{c_1 + c_2}$$

$$= \frac{c_1 + c_3}{n} \cdot \frac{c_1}{c_1 + c_3}$$

which can be easily restructured in a form expressing probabilities:

$$P(AB) = P(A) \cdot P(B|A)$$
$$= P(B) \cdot P(A|B)$$

which is almost identical to what we said in the Introduction: The probability of the compound event equals the probability of one event multiplied by the conditional probability of the other event, given that the first events happens. In this, as in all preceding definitions, a *compound* event consists of two or more single events—for instance, a dice tossed twice or four cards drawn one at a time from a deck.

In its analytical detail, this is what is often called today *Bayesian probabilities,* or *Bayes' theory.* The statistical approach developed by Bayes rests on two basic premises:

1. For every entity, no matter how unlikely, there is a prior or *a priori probability* that could be true.
2. Given a prior probability about some hypothesis, there must be some *evidence* we can call on to adjust our belief.

Bayes had no definite views on this prior probability. Indeed, in the Bayesian model, it may be a very low one. It may even be zero. This, however, the theory says, does not prevent us from calculating *as if* the prior probability was nonzero.

Key in this context is the second premise on relevant evidence. If such evidence is lacking, the prior probability will remain unchanged. Given relevant evidence, this prior probability can be modified to produce a *posterior probability* of the same hypothesis. Based on the foregoing concepts, we can generalize for two events, each of several possible outcomes.

This is the sense of the equation written by Bayes in the eighteenth century— the basis of Bayes' theorem. Names have been assigned to the various components of the equation:

- The left-hand side is called the *a posteriori probability.*
- This contrasts to the *a priori probabilities* and there are also *productive probabilities.*

Bayes himself seems to have had misgivings about this theorem. However, it was considered by many others to be *the answer* to the problem of *inference.*

Given only the probability distribution of the underlying parameter—the a priori and productive probabilities—a way exists to find the probability that a particular population gave rise to the sample. The difficulty is that we almost never know the necessary distribution. In most cases, the underlying parameter is not even subject to probability.

11

Objects, Metaobjects, Metalanguages, and Metaknowledge

Keywords

objects · entities · object world · object knowledge · information elements · universal machine · table of behavior · metaknowledge · metapredicate · philosophy · active entities · relationships · encapsulation · behavior · object class · object type · sockets · uncertainty · object orientation · abstract · homogeneity · message-passing · paradigm · concurrency · reusability · dependability · maintainability · supervisory · interpreters · multiple inheritance · philosophy of AI · metadata · metalanguage · metarules · view-point · metadescription · explicit self-representation · heuristic · metadatabase · metalevels · types · class · object class · object independence · data abstraction · inheritance · object language · reflection · metatheory · class process · virtual memory · metainterpreter · continuation · demons · global object management · schema · role · controlled inference procedure

1. INTRODUCTION

Thirty-five years ago, computer applications evolved from the simple, unsophisticated world of transactional data processing. At the time, the problems were solved in a day-to-day fashion. People handled them using old notions from accounting machines. This world is now as remote as prehistory.

Research on AI forced us to face the most ancient problem of mankind—*our relation to reality.* This has had a tremendous impact on our way of thinking, requiring us to consider objects, languages, and metaknowledge.

Objects are things that exist in the real world. Actions are also regarded as objects. *Entities* are callable objects. The distinction is necessary as objects are being addressed, and as they change and act continuously.

The world in which objects exist is known as an *object world.* Knowledge in the object world is called *object knowledge.* The data managed in the usual databases are an example of object knowledge.

In the new mathematics, the word *object* has a meaning quite distinct from its meaning in ordinary language. It refers to the idea of a set of operations that take place only when precise conditions are met.

Since an object includes *information elements (IEs)* and operators, there is no essential distinction between IE and operations on IE. Figure 11-1 distinguishes between passive entities (data structures) and active entities involving operations. Because of them, one machine can emulate the work done on any other machine on both object components. Turing called this the *universal machine.*

Turing machines offered a connection between abstract symbols and the physical world. If all the information defining an automatic machine was written out, it would form a *table of behavior* of a finite size. *The table was the machine.* It could exhibit

- acts of recognition and
- acts of decision.

The most complex decisions could be built out of elementary states and positions, with reading and writing being the kernel. This brings us to the concept of language.

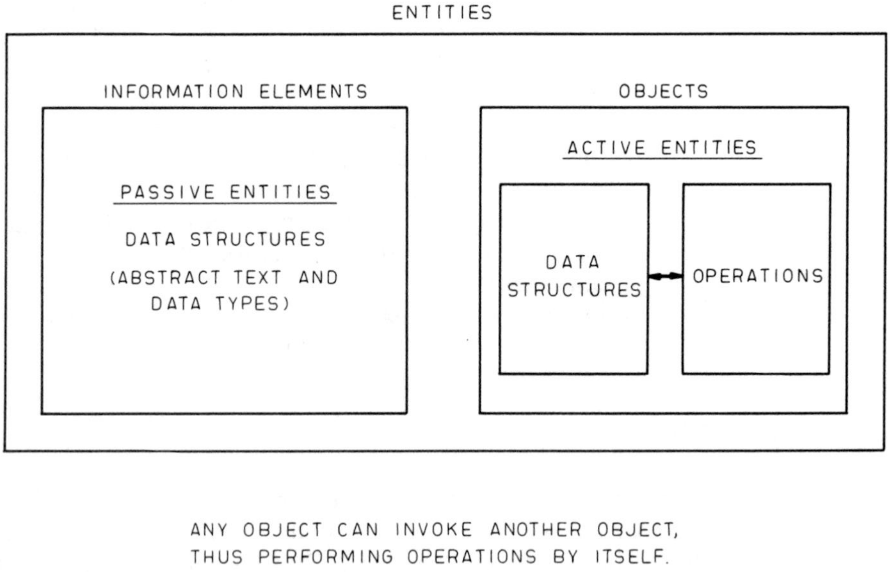

ENTITIES

ANY OBJECT CAN INVOKE ANOTHER OBJECT,
THUS PERFORMING OPERATIONS BY ITSELF.

Figure 11-1. Objects are of two types: passive entities, mainly information elements, and active entities. The latter include both data structures and instructions.

The *language which we use forms our mind*. English, German, French, Italian, Russian, Chinese, and Japanese are languages. So are Fortran, Cobol, Pascal, C, Basic, Lisp, and Prolog. Geometry, trigonometry, arithmetic, algebra, Boolean algebra, probability theory, engineering statistics, and possibility theory are also languages.

Early on, civilized mankind realized that *language is the bridge between*

- reality and
- our way of thinking.

We need language to *express* and *recall knowledge*. But there is also *metaknowledge*, the knowledge of the necessary conditions on objects and relationships between object-covering action(s):

- *Object knowledge* is a basic-level knowledge, the usual description of things. Typical logic programming is an expression of object knowledge.
- *Metaknowledge* is higher-level knowledge, just as a *metapredicate* is a higher-level predicate. A metapredicate controls the inference processing mechanism.

A metapredicate is a second-order predicate, just as a metaobject is a second-order object, above the level of the abstract data type which characterizes any object. These notions are similar to the foundation of *philosophy*.

During our many meetings, Tibor Vamos aptly remarks that since its inception, philosophy has been based on four entities:

1. reality,
2. language,
3. ways of thinking, and
4. knowledge representation.

As we work increasingly with AI and start to create the world of the twenty-first century, we must look deeply into all of these problems of men, machines, and communications. We must establish our thinking in unambiguous ways. The only way to do so successfully is to return to the fundamentals and start again.

2. OBJECTS, PATTERNS, INHERITANCE

We have said that an object is an abstract data type. It can be a segment of the database associated with type-specific operations, which define data and active entities. For instance, Smalltalk objects are *active* entities.

An object is something in the world that we try to model: a computer system, a car, a table, a logical entity.

- Some objects are rules.
- Other objects are active values.
- Still other objects are a combination of both.

Objects may be examined in isolation, but basically they are cooperative structures. Therefore, understanding objects and the way they work is practically synonymous with comprehending the way they cooperate. In turn, objects cooperate for a specific purpose: to achieve a given goal.

Objects are designed as system components. They handle *relationships* using the principle of encapsulation. The object packages:

- an entity (information element),
- the operations applying to it (procedures), and
- the message-passing capabilities.

The object is defined by its *behavior,* not its representation. An *object class* is the set of instances of an object type. In its most basic form, it is a module consisting of a number of passive entities together with the set of procedures (active entities) used to manipulate those passive entities.

As stated, manipulations are done to reach a goal. The *task of reaching a goal* is the focal point of object-oriented solutions. By contrast, the internal operations of an object are less important. They become a point of interest mainly in the sense that they contribute to the task to be accomplished.

In order to perform tasks, objects communicate; they do so according to their own designs. Coordination is necessary; without it, there will be no message patterns and call patterns—only random exchanges. A well-ordered communications system is necessary for all objects (and any other entities) constructed to accomplish some sort of work.

Messengers working within object-oriented systems can

- learn by apprenticeship and
- use visual counterparts as a mirror of system behavior,

thus leading to object behavior as objects fire their own rules. Scripts of audiovisual objects can be written within the rules of objects. In this sense, interaction of script languages with objects leads to animation.

Object semantics start with simple items—such as a bit map representation on a screen—and the specification of their operations. An important addition to the system is automatic triggering within a given domain and for given activities. This permits users to organize objects that work together into chains of objects, one acting after the other. Figure 11-2 presents an interactive approach to object-oriented systems combining office information with factory automation and knowledge representation.

Messaging is the connecting link, with message objects sent from one workstation to another, possibly through a local area network or long haul. To interact, such messages connect to one another by means of interfaces defined as *sockets.* Such interactions may be monodirectional (one way) or bidirectional.

Like all patterns,[1] those of messages and calls may be

- unstructured or
- loosely structured but relational.

---

[1] Gestalt (pattern, frame, form, appearance) theory and syndrome theory are roughly seventy-year-old concepts though they are very recent in the computer sciences.

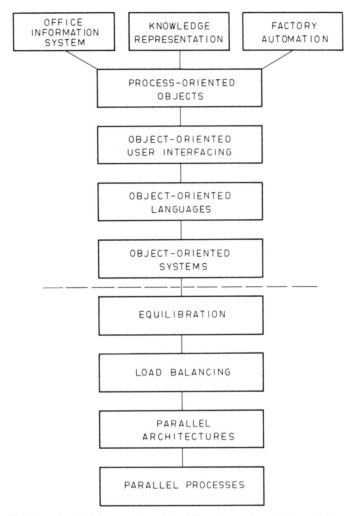

Figure 11-2. A good methodology can be useful in different types of applications. This figure integrates expert system experiences from two areas, office information systems and factory automation, into a common procedure.

We don't necessarily know how objects may be related. What we do know (by means of hypotheses) is that they are a combination of rule-based systems, semantic networks, and frames. This approach leads to new ways of knowledge engineering.

Key to this situation is similarity between patterns. If patterns are close, they are similar—but what does "close" mean? To respond accurately we need a special metric, one which combines individual and collective expertise. Such a metric may be

- noncomplementary (belief/disbelief),
- nonlinear, or
- not really statistical.

Typically, the environment is one where everything is weighted. Weighting takes place by relevance, frequencies, elapsed time, viewpoints, or principles—including a combination such as graphic representation and experimentation.

Handling uncertainties is a process related to the weight of individual items. Possibility theory is only one layer of the AI construct—more precisely, a lower layer.

The *principles* can change the measures in a transformation process. Hence it is wise to weight the weights, evaluate the measures, and provide a controlling mechanism able to ensure ordered patterns.

Ordered patterns can be achieved through higher levels of abstraction which establish a configuration of objects, defining a *scene*. Scenes can have temporal changes and aggregation(s) of changes—and event(s). Aggregation(s) of events create a history. A schema (script) is an abstraction from individual histories. Higher-level and lower-level software may be associated with objects. Examples are given in Figure 11-3.

An object can have various attributes and values associated with it by means of a property list. An attribute can stand for a descriptive property such as size, or it can represent a relationship between the described object and another object. Relationships can also be defined in terms of set memberships or predicate functions.

One object can invoke other objects, thus performing operations by itself. However, though object-oriented programming has become widespread in recent years, there are few guidelines to help us determine whether or not a system is truly object oriented.

In a sense, *object orientation is an approach* rather than a specific set of language constructs. Object-oriented solutions typically use an arbitrary programming language and still write in an object-oriented style. Nevertheless, object-oriented programming languages do exist with built-in constructs that support (or enforce) this style of programming. We will consider this subject in Section 4.

An object has an internal state. It imports and exports data and operations. It may pose a problem of concurrency.

Objects interact through indirect binding. Before interactions can occur, it is necessary to provide interrogation and synchronization facilities. Binding between modes requires invocation channels.

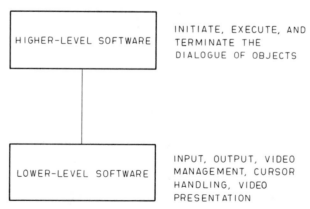

Figure 11-3. Expert systems are essentially a new type of software. This figure divides logical approaches into two layers, a higher and a lower one, each with specific goals.

While objects may be examined in isolation, they are not built that way; instead, they are components of systems. Therefore, understanding of objects requires understanding of the way in which they cooperate to accomplish given goals.

With an *object orientation,* the main concepts are as follows:

1. *Abstract* text/data types. We are interested in object behavior rather than its representation.
2. *Encapsulation* of information elements and commands.
3. *Homogeneity*/consistency. Objects can be manipulated only through their own methods.
4. *Independence* in a given environment. Each object is responsible for itself.
5. The *message-passing* paradigm (pipes) from object to object.
6. *Inheritance* (equilibration, forks). The programmer specifies the interface to an object type. This interface is the method.
7. *Concurrency* (some systems). It should be possible to add new types at runtime.
8. *Reusability* by adopting well-designed object types.
9. *Dependability* through strong type checking.
10. *Maintainability/portability* via the separation of implementation and interfacing.
11. *Metaobject* structure and control.
12. Operation under *supervisory interpreters* (demons).

Reference has been made to abstract data types, encapsulation, homogeneity, and independence. We must define inheritance beyond the level treated in Chapters 9 and 10, as many object-based and object-oriented systems use this mechanism.

In a system with inheritance, one class of objects is described as a *specialization* of another class of objects. This representation has consequences. The implementation of the new class of objects can inherit part or all of the implementation of the old class of objects which is its parent class. This saves a great deal of coding.

The new parts of the class's implementation are added to its own definition. However, because of procedural inheritance, objects of the new class can frequently be used in applications that were specifically designed to use objects of the parent class without making any modification to the application's code.

Inheritance is hierarchical and is a very inexpensive operation. *Multiple inheritance* exists in networking. In a multiple inheritance scheme, rules may be triggered according to both internal conditions and those of the universe. The latter can be thought of as a mechanism of inheritance affecting various objects: active objects controlled by users and others which are inactive, temporarily stripped of their rules.

3. THE CONCEPT OF META AND ITS IMPACT

Meta is the key to a causal connection. It can serve as a command language and provides not only linkages but also an infrastructure for the development of a layered system in knowledge representation. From developmental activities to the implementation of the resulting constructs, we need a rigorous discipline:

- *Meta* can be the foundation of such discipline.
- It can also lead toward a *philosophy of AI* which is currently either nonexistent or still in its infancy.

McCarthy has introduced the first-order theory of individual concepts and proportions. His hypothesis is that it can constitute a formal language for knowledge representation. If clauses, goals, and states are the pivotal points of self-representation, meta is both the means and the background concept.

An everyday example can better explain this concept. Let's consider data and metadata as related to a bankers' check. Figure 11-4 suggests three layers of reference:

1. The top layer is the validity limit (a monetary reference) and the validity range (timing). This is a metalevel.

Typically, bankers' checks have a printed reference: "Not beyond xxx dollars." They must also be cashed within a given period, such as one year. If not, they automatically expire and need to be reissued.

2. The middle layer, also meta, consists of the emission date, value date, debit account number, and credit account number.
3. The bottom layer (object level) includes the notion of a banker's check, normalization references, and the specified monetary value of the check.

While we use checks every day, we are not necessarily aware of the logical infrastructure on which they rest. Yet, it would not be possible to handle checks without it.

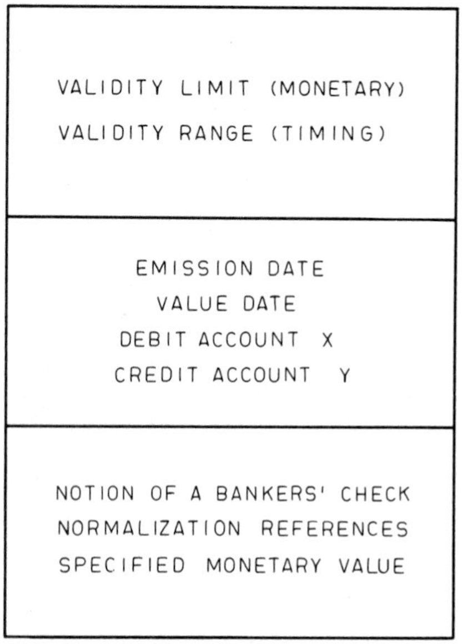

VALIDITY LIMIT (MONETARY)

VALIDITY RANGE (TIMING)

EMISSION DATE
VALUE DATE
DEBIT ACCOUNT X
CREDIT ACCOUNT Y

NOTION OF A BANKERS' CHECK
NORMALIZATION REFERENCES
SPECIFIED MONETARY VALUE

Figure 11-4. The notion of *meta* can best be expressed in a layered fashion, using as an example a banker's check. Validity limits are a metalayer over the debit/credit operation implied by the check, and the latter is a metalayer over the specified monetary value of the check.

Meta can act as the conceptual interface between a computer realization and a subject in the real world. It can facilitate conceptual modeling by providing a two-way road between the generalization and a generative way of producing instances. Patterns of some coherence and metrics of spaces or events are different though partial approaches to this problem. The same can be said about frames, semantic networks, logic programming, and learning by example.

As a conceptual interface between a man-made system (thus an artifact) and a real subject, meta is helpful in mapping and commanding instances of conceptual modeling. In turn, conceptual modeling provides a two-way road between

- generalization (hence induction) and
- a generative way of producing instances.

In this sense, *metadata* are data that describe or help to interpret other data. All DBMSs store and manipulate several kinds of metadata. For instance, a relational DBMS must know the name of each relation, the number of attributes, the name and type of each attribute, the storage representation, and the access paths for each relation.

Metadata are data about data. Their use is critical for the effective management of the data resource and in defining the best structures for logical and physical databases.

We have said that the language we use forms our mind. This is just as true of the *metalanguage*. Language constructs in AI are representation facilities performing a set of inferences that extend an explicit set of beliefs to a larger virtual set of beliefs. Such a representation facility participates in the system's reasoning activities by providing automatic inferences as part of each assertion operation.

Frame languages are particularly powerful in this regard because the taxonomic relationships among frames enable descriptive information to be shared among multiple frames through inheritance. In addition, the internal structure of frames enables semantic integrity constraints to be automatically maintained.

But not everything is positive. A key premise of knowledge system technology is that domain knowledge should be effectively used by a system and easily understood by the AI construct's enduser. These goals are achieved more effectively if domain knowledge is represented in declarative rather than procedural form. This limits the capabilities of frame systems, since they provide no direct facilities for declaratively describing how the knowledge stored in frames is to be used.

As a facilitator, the language we employ assumes a fundamental role and influences the results obtained. Since they are languages about languages, *metalanguages* act as abstractions and controls of lower-level linguistic constructs. Therefore the factors previously described are even more significant at a metalinguistic level.

The control of sequencing of rules can be expressed in terms of English-like IF . . . THEN statements. Control rules are *metarules*. Application-specific aspects of the problem can be formulated in a very high-level production rule language. In a nutshell, metarules are

- rules that affect rules and
- rules that influence the inference system.

Meta-level description in the form of an interpreter is general in the sense that *metavariables* can range over any language construct expressed at the object level. A universally quantified metavariable may be used to denote an object-level goal.

Specialization by partial evaluation is regarded as restricting the domain of metavariables (in the meta description) to constants naming object-level entities. It is also seen as instrumental in executing parts of a metaprogram which become ready for execution. Formally, the resultant program is still a meta-level program. However, it is easy to translate it back to the object level, since the same language is used for object and metalanguage. We return to this subject in Section 4.

A metalanguage can be used as the foundation of a viewpoint mechanism. A *viewpoint* is a collection of statements representing the assumptions of a theory. Multiple viewpoints provide the ability to handle different situations arising

1. from hypothetical reasoning
2. from evolution of situations over time, or
3. from reasoning about beliefs.

The ability to manufacture a *metadescription* out of any description provides a means for accessing its internal structure. Examples include interrogating the system about the concepts that are present, examining the goal structure that has been generated in the course of a deduction, and generating an explanation of the conclusion.

Metaobjects are the interpreters of objects. This higher-level layer permits a logical/physical split between metaobject and object. It creates an *excellent self-representation,* as objects can access and modify their metaobjects through tracing (inheritance, equilibration). Metaobjects assist the user in understanding the object, including its

1. functionality,
2. limits, and
3. constraints.

The metalevel is in complete control of the object level. *The linkage is heuristic.*

Not everybody agrees with this broader view of metaobjects. Some consider them as basically pieces of code sitting in slots as attributes of, say, frames. Still others see them as closely related to metadata and metarules—through them influencing the behavior of a domain-specific *rule base* and *database.* There is a tendency to consider that, without this connection, a metaobject is not really a concept by itself. In a similar manner, a *metadatabase* is not seen as an independent concept.

While the field is still under development, and therefore some definitions[2] can vary among researchers, there is agreement on the need for *metalevels.* Gödel said: "We cannot have a system unless we step out of this system and explain it." This is *the sense of the metalevel.* Let me repeat it.

If we conceptualize a system, we must go beyond the system.

We can look at three concepts in a general sense: metaobjects, objects, and tracing. The key is a connection involving *meta and the referee* (Figure 11-5). Through inheritance and equilibration, tracing affects the metalevel. The object layer can also impact on the meta, but the strong connection is meta to object (referee).

---

[2] Particularly limits of definitions.

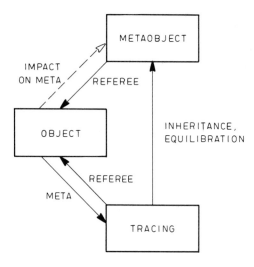

THE KEY TO OBJECT BEHAVIOR IS THE CONNECTION

Figure 11-5. As this figure shows, meta notions are most prevalent in an object-type organization. Meta, inheritance, and equilibration are three concepts on which all knowledge-based systems rest.

Meta describes only general relations. These relations are precisely what we attempt to determine for discovery and command purposes. Meta provides the framework within which constructs can exist and operate.

A general problem solver should have meta characteristics and a layered structure. When we have a metastructure, we can take *chunks of knowledge* without losing sight of the overall reference. We preserve the organization while making it possible to plan, execute, and control.

4. OBJECT-ORIENTED LANGUAGES AND OPERATING SYSTEMS

Object-oriented languages enable the programmer to create his own object *types*. Each object is an instance of some type and supports the *operations*[3] that are defined for that type.

When talking about objects, the word *class* is often used interchangeably with the word *type*. It is, however, more accurate to think of an *object class* as the set of instances of an object type. This gives a broader definition that is more applicable to real-world situations.

---

[3] Often called *methods*.

The notion of object *independence* is important. It indicates that each object is ultimately responsible for itself. Objects can be manipulated only through their methods (operations), respecting basic object-oriented concepts such as data abstraction, independence, the message-passing paradigm, inheritance, homogeneity, and concurrency. We spoke about them in Section 2. We repeat them here because of their impact on object-oriented languages.

Since the fundamental concepts in an object-oriented environment are *data abstraction* and *inheritance,* the language must permit us to specify an interface to a new object type as a collection of methods which can be invoked. The language must provide the tools to define the representation of the object's state and the implementation of the methods. The latter should be the only acceptable interface to an object.

In this sense, languages which support data abstraction but not inheritance are not fit for object representation.[4] It should be possible to add new types at runtime and to maintain an object-oriented system. For this, we need libraries of reflective behavior of objects:

- Simple objects can have compact representation.
- Complex objects call for extra memory, extra computation, and far more attention.

Another critical aspect of object-oriented programming is how much the limits can be understood and controlled by the user, who is the ultimate beneficiary and custodian of the system. This is helped by the concept of a *metalanguage* and by the careful choice of an *object language.*

According to the schema which we have defined, the metalanguage is the higher level and the object language the lower one (Figure 11-6A). One of the earliest metalanguages was the command language of the military. Another example is the system commands of the operating system and the DBMS. We will come back to this notion later.

Attention should be paid to the distinction between

1. The *metalevel,* which has complete control of the object level, and
2. The *reflective level,* starting at the object level, which decides on the next layer interaction.

Reflection is an integral part of inheritance. An example is given in Figure 11-6B, emphasizing causal connection. From object construction to reflective computation and back, connectivity resembles what we already know from subroutine linkage.

So far, in terms of our work with reflection, we are most familiar with the implementation of heuristic constructs. Reflective computation is *metatheory.* Figure 11-6C gives an example:

1. Reflecting my beliefs in the metatheory.
2. With the metatheory providing the linkage: "What I believe other people believe."
3. Thus leading (at the object construction level) to Eva's beliefs.

---

[4] For instance, Ada 2.

(A)

(B)

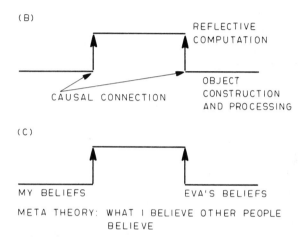

Figure 11-6. Any language can be divided into an object level and a metalayer. The same is true of all interpersonal communications.

Introspective constructs include environmental definitions and, sometimes, the text of the program. However, most work so far has been done in providing extensions to an existing language. New structures are necessary to provide a higher level of metatheory.

To recapitulate: Reflective computation is closely associated with object processing. A language that supports metatheory works as follows: From time to time, as necessary, it goes up to the higher reflective level and reflects about object processing. The critical aspects of this process are

    1. providing for self-representation,
    2. ensuring a causal connection, and
    3. programming the reflection itself.

The last can be done through reflective theories, functions, and rules. Implementation examples can be found in ESP and PSI.

In this object-oriented programming style, a type and *class process* defines

    ▪ instance predicates for controlling process status and
    ▪ class predicates for process creation and identification.

A class process in ESP has the following:

nature	with__link
	waiting-frame
attribute	ready__queue
	instance__array
activate	process
	program

On invocation, the program is pushed onto the invocation stack of the process and the instance predicate, *goal(Program)*, is called. When the goal finishes, the program is popped from the invocation stack. If the stack becomes empty, the process terminates.

A program executed by a process must be an instance of some program class which inherits the class "as program". This gives a basic framework for programs. In process activation, the goal predicate defined in each program class is automatically invoked.

Every object is shared between users and has a recovery segment. Logging/restoration is done by hardware with paged virtual memory capability. Virtual memory is a basic ingredient of this approach: we will see why in Section 5.

Solutions of this type typically follow successive software layers, as shown in Figure 11-7. They address themselves (bottom-up) to the representation of objects, recovery management, securing/saving/restoring system primitives, housekeeping, object storage/ retrieval, global object management, and global transaction handling.

The ESP-Simpos-PSI handling of object-oriented processes provides for *stream variations*. Various types of streams, with their features, are defined—for example, priority control, bounded buffer control, message-based communication facilities, channels, and ports. A channel is a message-based communication primitive useful in describing multiple-client/multiple-server interactions. Major operations on a channel are as follows:

- Send a message to the channel specifying a sender (channel) for a reply, using ":send(Channel, Message, Sender)".
- Receive a message from the channel with a sender returned, using ":receive(Channel, Message, Sender)".

A port is a message box for two-way communication based on channels. Key operations on a port are sending a message to connected ports, receiving a message from the port, connecting the port to another port, and disconnecting ports from each other.

Bounded-buffer functions are used for buffered message communication. They have two waiting queues. One is for processes waiting for messages, the other for processes waiting for buffers. The concept of semaphores is being employed.

An interrupt process is instantiated from the class *interrupt-process*. This inherits the class *process*, since an interrupt process is a special kind of process. It is resumed with an interrupt or a software trap. When suspended, it releases the processor. The interrupt handling mechanism is encapsulated in the class interrupt-process.

A boot process is the sole instance of the class *boot-process*. The latter executes the boot program inheriting the class *as-boot-program*. After initiation, a boot process goes under the control of the supervisor and acts exactly like an ordinary process. This is possible because the class boot-process inherits the class process and overrides the predicates ":create" and ":activate".

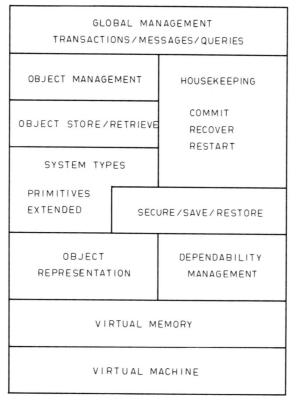

Figure 11-7. Global database management calls for object management as well as housekeeping. Object representation is a lower layer than object management but a higher one than the machine level.

As this discussion shows, an object-oriented language and operating system is not a strange construct to what we know so far about languages and operating systems. It is a construct which inherits the characteristics of programming languages and operating systems, adding to them primitives and structures which are designed to serve an object-oriented environment.

5. HARDWARE-SUPPORTED VIRTUAL MEMORY IN AN OBJECT-ORIENTED ENVIRONMENT

We have said that object-oriented linguistic constructs and operating systems inherit the characteristics of those already established by software engineering for von Neumann-type computers. They add to these characteristics features specific to the metalevel and to the lower layer of object handling. But they also require prerequisites.

Fifth-generation computers should provide these prerequisites through hardware. The reason that software for these computers is so much simpler than that required for von

Neumann-type computers is precisely this conversion to a hardware-supported capability. Excellent examples are paging and virtual memory.

The implementation of *virtual memory* for logic programming is much more significant than a virtual memory system for a traditional language for two reasons:

1. With object solutions there is no distinction between program and data. Hence, virtual memory means not only that we can have programs that occupy more memory than is actually available, but also that we can access large amounts of data represented directly in the language.
2. A relational database run under logic programming is more flexible in representing data than databases. A language like Prolog is more powerful than the best database query languages.

The power of the virtual memory/logic programming environment offers able solutions to a variety of problems and at the same time imposes further requirements. Examples of problem areas with fertile implementation domain for this approach are

1. information systems with complex interlinking files operating globally,
2. environments characterized by widely distributed, interconnected databases,
3. applications requiring systems consistency under distributed control,
4. problems requiring consistency definitions at a level below (more fundamental than) that of file consistency,
5. CAD/CAM systems with multiple simulation requirements,
6. communications aggregates with node-intense activity,
7. simulation of large organizations modeled on the basis of objects, messages, and transactions, and
8. large AI constructs built in a modular way with a variety of interconnecting capibilities—causality being the most important.

Causal connections are reflective, defined through metalevels, and requiring a *metainterpreter*. Clauses, goals, and states are the pivotal points of self-representation, as we will see in Section 6.

Causal connection means *continuation*. Figure 11-8 presents a layered structure which encapsulates in an interpretive mode source and object level programming, system programming, data, and environment.

We have defined *demons* as networkwide supervisory processes. New information is handled as follows:

- It begins with the receipt of a sensor report or message at the report monitor.
- The report is parsed and injected into the database.
- The information is then classified and routed by demons.

The process suggests possible interpretations of the information. A demon can act like an interrupt handler in an operating system. It may perform no action until (and unless) a specific situation is encountered. This approach facilitates *global object management*, which deals with multiple nodes. It brings the object(s) to user nodes and the process(es) to specialized and/or distant node(s). Then it fetches the result to the user nodes.

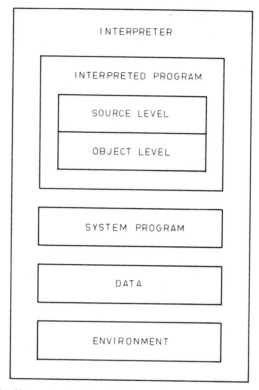

Figure 11-8. The role of interpreter is outlined. The interpreter program, basic software, data, and the notion of the operations environment are integrated within this system.

This process focuses on the issue of environmental description as well as on demons. Demons are supervisory processes. In a distributed system they operate globally. For able global object management, we must take a system approach including transactions, messages, and queries. Such a process will typically

- address itself to multiple nodes,
- account for all events (global and local),
- handle aggegation of changes,
- bring objects to the user node or processes at distant node(s), then bring the result(s) to the user node,
- require environmental description,
- abstract from individual histories,
- ensure performability, and
- call for supervisory interpreters (demons).

This is the knowledgebank management system (KBMS) structure of which we spoke in Chapter 5. An AI system, particularly a large one, cannot successfully operate without KBMS capabilities.

In a programming sense, a *schema* will define all potential objects and relations in the problem space. Around this concept, a high-level user interface can be designed and the system can operate a set of schema constraints. This allows unification with external databases.

Global schema constraints can be introduced as restrictions on the cardinality of relationships—for instance, the number of objects that can stand in that relationships to each other (one-many, and so on). A properly chosen language would avoid referring to instances of objects by means of long chains of links originating at the top of a tree. This is particularly important when AI systems become larger.

Solutions should ensure that specification of control information is kept distinct from knowledge. This reflects a natural distinction and facilitates the building of AI constructs. Knowledge elicited from an expert is more easily integrated into the knowledgebank. Control can be specified separately by the knowledge engineer.

As stated, objects are connected by relationships. The latter improve the expressive power of the system and ensure that data independence is achieved in the database. A virtual memory approach should ensure the able handling of object-oriented programs independently of their size and should support reflective capabilities.

In a global object management sense, the combination of a powerful logical language and a hardware-supported paging mechanism should make feasible agile man–machine communication. While both the developer and the enduser are affected by this process, more attention should be paid to the needs of the user. This brings us to the notion of roles.

A *role* is a system object which can be manipulated directly by a user. But a role does not correspond necessarily to one user.

- A user can have many roles.
- A role can be common to many users.

Roles belong to object types; they are objects. Individual roles are distinguished as instances of the type by giving values to particular attributes. They can also serve other purposes.

User interfaces can change among role types or classes. At the same time, the rules associated with roles can serve to authenticate users for security purposes. Different role types can have different authentication procedures.

Finally, rules enable roles to accept or originate only certain types of messages, to create other objects, and to move to object managers. Here again, a hardware-based paging mechanism can be instrumental in simplifying software development. It is sometimes necessary to structure roles to obtain role hierarchies. We can have roles which inherit properties or rules from other roles. Classical memory management approaches are inadequate for these processes. Hardware-supported virtual memory is a better solution.

6. METAKNOWLEDGE

Metaknowledge is knowledge about knowledge. *Metaknowledge differs from object knowledge:* It describes the controls on object knowledge. The value of an object is determined by the results of evaluating completed actions. Metaknowledge can be also seen as constrained knowledge.

IF <certain condition> is inconsistent
THEN <knowledge bank rejects such condition>

Metaknowledge is based on the aims and intentions of the users: AI constructs, programs, databases, developers, endusers. We can structure metaknowledge, permitting an intelligent database management system to

- contain opinions on each object and
- include concepts for managing logic databases.

As the preceding example demonstrated, *constraints* form part of the metaknowledge.
Knowledge sources usually transform entries at one level of abstraction into entries at another level. Some knowledge sources operate from the bottom up. They aggregate several lower-level entries into a smaller number of higher-level entries. Other knowledge sources operate from the top down, exploding a compound knowledge source into its components.
Metaknowledge handles knowledge about

1. representation of objects (through schemata),
2. representation functions (function templates),
3. reasoning strategies (by means of metarules), and
4. inference rules (rule description).

Through the implementation of the concept of metaknowledge we can avoid the requirement of always having to apply hierarchical structure for abstraction.
Metaknowledge helps combine metarules and metadata into one system. As Figure 11-9 demonstrates, the metaknowledge layer features concept(s), definition(s), and constraints. The lower level of object knowledge includes rules and data. Table 11-1 presents aspects of metaknowledge and the way in which they are encoded.

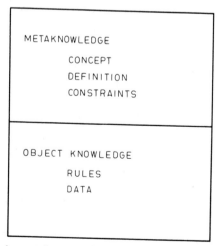

METAKNOWLEDGE

CONCEPT

DEFINITION

CONSTRAINTS

OBJECT KNOWLEDGE

RULES

DATA

Figure 11-9. Knowledge is a metalayer over data. But there is also a higher layer: metaknowledge.

TABLE 11-1. Aspects of Metaknowledge

Knowledge About	Encoded in
Representation of objects	Schemata
Representation of functions	Function templates
Inference rules	Rule models
Reasoning strategies	Metarules

Reasoning about appropriate representations is necessary in an environment in which user-defined descriptions are possible. If a model is a mechanism for problem solving through abstraction, a metaknowledge engine would try to solve problems by using the meta problemsolver. The metaknowledge used by this solver may be intuitive and pragmatic or based on metapredicates.

Metapredicates are part of the metaknowledge layer. In Chapter 3 we said that a predicate takes variables and instances as arguments. A metapredicate features <clauses> as arguments. Thus, the

Demo <clase> :=   demonstrate the inference procedure

is a metapredicate. It is an *interpreter* of logic programming that permits many control functions. We can have two or three arguments:

Demo <clause, control method>

The control method can be backward chaining, forward chaining, or a blackboard. Chaining was discussed in Chapter 8.

A metapredicate can be seen as a problem-solving, *controlled-inference procedure*. Metapredicates require a fast predicate logic. An example of a metapredicate is the Demo <clause> just mentioned. This is known as a *second-order predicate*. Its functions are to

- demonstrate the clause, deducing from the database,
- help check the redundancy of the database,
- prevent inconsistency of the database,
- assist in developing intelligent DBMS
- attain truth maintenance,
- permit the development of new functions, and
- make feasible knowledge assimilation.

Metaknowledge and metapredicates come close to embodying David Hilbert's notion of an edifice of mathematics with no contradictions based on theorems. As Hilbert realized, to do so, it is necessary to separate real mathematics from models.

From this notion we derive the concept of defining the unit edifice, which is pure mathematics, leading to a uniform theory. A meta-based system could be structured along this line, even if it addresses a given domain rather than all domains. In this case, the Hilbert approach would be sized within *that domain* and its system theory.[5] The metaknowledge that is valid for a given domain would not necessarily be applicable to other domans.

We have spoken of reflective processes. A system with metaknowledge is self-reflective, able to express its own metatheory. This implies that knowledge about the larger system, as well as knowledge about a specific domain, can be represented in the knowledgebank,. The AI construct can therefore be the object as well as the subject of the deduction process.

Metaknowledge can be used to define and activate control strategies, providing a description of the way in which a class of rules should be used to solve a specific problem or set of problems. This is important in scientific problems and also in managerial decisions which are

- personal processes, hence
- functional and situational, but also
- subject to quick change.

In these cases, the Demo <clause> can be instrumental:
° IF Rule "X" fires

then append a tupple to the fire list[6]

IF the "Why" query is entered

then display the condition for each tupple. A similar reference can be made regarding the

Simulate <clause>

This is a logic programming (guarded horn clauses, GHC) metapredicate which serves KBMS and DBMS functions. The design within the PSI project, Simulate <clause>, is important, as the Delta[7] relational database does not include rules. PSI has the rules; Delta has the facts.

It is up to the KBMS to feature knowledge, both assimilation and equilibration, based on the Demo <clause> metapredicate.

Through metapredicates, only nonredundant and consistent knowledge can accumulate in the database. This is important for a running AI processor. The intelligent system must be enabled to determine whether knowledge is consistent and nonredundant relative to existing knowledge. Metaknowledge provides the basis for this facility.

---

[5] Though the concept of meta is much closer to Gödel's ideas, there is no reason why Hilbert's uniform theory cannot be applied—provided that we carefully limit its extent within the boundaries of a properly defined system.
[6] Rule name, fact, value.
[7] The database server associated with the parallel server of the PSI engine.

12

The Inference Engine and Its Environment

Keywords

inference • inference engine • rules • frames • scenarios • logic programming • qualitative reasoning • predicate • statement • metapredicates • meta • objects • canonical • canon • table of behavior • control method • control inference procedure • consistency • flexibility • generality • additivity • explanation facility • proposition • inference mechanism • knowledgebank • global database • dialogue engine • logical motors • fact • state • values • characteristic distribution • inference process • induction • generalization • deduction • general induction rule • abduction • cause • effect • conditional probabilities • functional decomposition • abstraction • description levels • inheritance • equilibration • deep knowledge • shallow knowledge • depth of knowledge • domain of knowledge • shallow machine • deep knowledge machine • deep systems • similarity-based learning • semantic networks • conceptual dependencies • uniform processing • deductive retrieval • multiperspective • hierarchical • constraints • logic • Lisp • Prolog • simulation • kernel language • methodologies • pipes • forks • semaphores • cursors • demons • program invocation • one logical network

1. INTRODUCTION

Inference is reasoning from premises to a conclusion. The *inference engine* is the reasoning mechanism of the AI construct. Fifth-generation computers are designed as inference engines. The inference engine is a generalized reasoning and dialogue manager. It contains the strategies used to solve problems, acquire knowledge, interface with other systems, and provide explanations for the reasoning process. Each combination of the inference engine with a knowledgebank becomes a unique application. Together, they act as a model of the expertise for the specific domain.

Formal rules describe relationships. They also handle control information to focus on a specific problem solution. An important aspect of the inference engine is the representation of the expert's reasoning. This knowledge captures the application's expertise.

The inference engine is written in the form of *rules, frames, scenarios,* and *logic programming.* Rules are of the form

IF   hypothesis
THEN   Action I
ELSE   Action II

For instance:

IF   Benefits
THEN   Success
ELSE   Failure

Inference is both an act and a process. The goal is to use approximate reasoning strategies

- to arrive at a vital estimate of a situation
- while having uncertain data and imperfect rules

To do so, we have to establish connections between facts and underlying rules. They must be such that we can predict further occurrences from those already experienced. The full accomplishment of this task is the real end of the scientific effort.

But there is a difference between past scientific efforts and the newer ones focusing on AI and inference mechanisms. This difference is the focus on *qualitative reasoning.* It is a significant improvement of the scientific method, opening up new vistas in scientific achievement.

Arnold Toynbee (1889–1975) suggested that, in the past, science was successful in the degree to which it ignored those features of phenomena that are most important to human beings for all purposes except those of technology. For nontechnological purposes, Toynbee states, the translation of qualitative impressions into quantitative notations is an intellectual and aesthetic impoverishment.

The sounds we hear and the colors we see are more significant and more satisfying for us than the quantities to which they are reduced by the sciences of acoustics and optics. To a much greater degree, the same is true of our thoughts. The process of inference focuses precisely on our thoughts and translates them in a manner which can be explained to machines and processed by them. The objective is to

1. construct higher-order inferences from simple syllogisms,
2. handle knowledge instead of data,
3. ensure that a variety of qualitative problems can be efficiently solved,

4. provide a communication method convenient for users through a human window, and

5. significantly improve programming productivity by making it feasible for every user to act as a programmer through the appropriate tools: a shell or very high-level, user-friendly language.

There are constaints to this process. Some of these are technical, and we will see the reasons for them. Others relate to methodology. The way it has been done for nearly 40 years, the classical DP work pays inadequate attention to the structure–function relationship, though that relationships is fundamental to the success of a man-made system.

2. THE CONCEPT OF PREDICATES

The word *predicate* means "to proclaim, declare, or affirm." A predicate can be a verb of complete meaning; a verb and its adverbial modifier; a linking verb and its complement; or a transitory verb and its object.

To predicate is to make an affirmation or statement. We usually do this by using *first-order predicate logic;* languages such as Lisp rests on list manipulation—though, up to a point, Prolog and Lisp have the same characteristics. But there are also *second-order* predicates, better known as *metapredicates.*[1]

- A first-order predicate takes variables and instances as arguments.
- A second-order predicate uses clauses as arguments.

Sentences about beliefs, desires to know, or items of knowledge are formalized in first-order logic. McCarthy has introduced the first order theory of individual concepts and proportions as a formal language for knowledge representation. This theory is intended to avoid paradoxical conclusions.

First-order predicates have a *canonical* form. In mathematics, a trigonometric *canon* is a table that gives the values of trigonometric functions. This definition is important, as Turing considers a *table of behavior* that defines a machine completely. Every different possible table defines a machine with a different kind of behavior. In Turing's definition, there will be infinitely many tables corresponding to an equal number of machines. This approach transforms the rather vague idea of a mechanical process—as well as that of a definite method—into a table of behavior—hence, a *canonical table.*

In terms of a second-order predicate, the *demo* <clause> is an interpreter of the logic programming structure, permitting a variety of control functions. This is the function of the metapredicate. The *demo* <clause> may say: "Demonstrate the inference procedure" or "Store the intermediate stages." It can also have two or three arguments: *demo* <clause 1, control method>. The *control method* may be backward chaining, forward chaining, or a blackboard function.

As *control inference procedures,* metapredicates require a fast predicate logic—hence, a

---

[1] The concepts of *meta* and *objects* are of great importance in AI. They are discussed in Chapter 11.

fifth-generation computer. Among the functions of a second-order predicate, the following are most significant:

- Demonstrate the clause, deducing from the knowledgebank
- Help check the redundancy of the knowledgebank
- Assist in database management intelligence
- Attain truth maintenance
- Permit development of new functions
- Make knowledge assimilation feasible
- Prevent inconsistency of the knowledgebank

The issue of *consistency* is very important. The prevention of contradictions in a knowledgebank is vital for knowledge assimilation. The presence of noncontradiction under sufficient conditions to guarantee consistency must be defined in detail. If noncontradiction is detected, the knowledgebank is said to be consistent.

Predicates and metapredicates help provide a generic AI system (Figure 12-1) characterized by the following:

1. *Consistency*, hence without contradictions.
2. *Generality.* Any fact or rule can be encoded.
3. *Flexibility.* Facts, states, and values can be used in more than one way.
4. *Additivity.* The program can evolve easily, with new facts and rules being added or old ones deleted.
5. *Explanation facility.* The system's line of reasoning can be displayed and the system's response justified.

The foregoing discussion shows that predicate calculus is a way to write expressions about the world. The language of logic has evolved over thousands of years and is still being

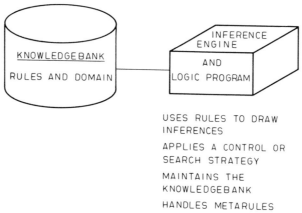

Figure 12-1. A generic AI system consists of the knowledgebank and the inference engine, the latter being the compiler of the knowledgebank. This figure identifies the key functions of the inference engine.

developed. Using logic, we can make *propositions* about the world, that is, statements that are either true or false. We can use predicate calculus for AI problem solving.

These definitions, and the characteristics they invoke, are vital, as a rule-based system is able to reason about its own search effort, in addition to reaching decisions about the problem domain. This calls for a dynamic way of structuring and involves

- *an inference mechanism* acting as the control structure for using the knowledgebank in a search for a solution to the problem,
- *a knowledgebank* containing facts and rules of the domain associated with the problem,
- *a global database* keeping track of input data, problem status, and the history of what has been accomplished so far, and
- *a dialogue engine* able to engage in intelligent man–machine communication, as well as prod, guide, extract answers, and present results.

We have said that *inference is reasoning from premises to a conclusion.* Such reasoning can be algorithmic (algebraic, differential equations, and so on); a programming structure (e.g., linear programming, vectors, matrices); Boolean logic (algebra of sets, Bayesian); a stochastic process (probability theory, statistics); rules with uncertainty (possibility theory); other rule-based systems (logic programming); or taxonomic (classification, menus, trees, frames).

It is precisely these *logical motors* which permit computers to behave in increasingly intelligent ways. Figure 12-2 gives an example of the use of possibility theory, thus

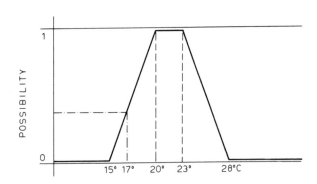

POSSIBILITY THEORY EXPRESSES
IMPRECISE FACTS AND UNCERTAINTY.

POSSIBILITY FUNCTIONS, TOO,
HAVE A CHARACTERISTIC DISTRIBUTION.

Figure 12-2. Possibility theory is *not* probability theory. This figure demonstrates the nature of a possibility distribution.

expressing imprecise facts and uncertainty. (This concept is further elaborated in Chapter 10.)

Suppose that historical values about water temperature in June on the French Riviera tend to range from 20°C to 23°C. The possibility of these values is taken to be equal to 1. However, if spring is late, temperatures of 15°C to 20°C are not impossible—with the latter having a greater possibility than the former. On the other hand, an early summer may bring water temperatures in the 23°C to 28°C range—the latter with a very low possibility.

This situation permits us to build a possibility distribution, in the form of a trapezoid, representing imprecise facts and uncertainty. If we want to know the possibility of encountering a water temperature of 17°C, we can do it by using

- the *fact,* water temperature
- the *state,* June on the French Riviera,
- the *values,* the historical temperature data,[2] and
- the *characteristic distribution* we derived from such data through possibility theory.

This example is a simple and practical implementation. A theoretical system is made up of

- concepts,
- fundamental laws, supposedly valid for those concepts, and
- conclusions to be reached by logical deduction.

Not only must these conclusions correspond to our experiences, but the system of laws itself must be described in a formal manner. This is precisely what the foregoing example demonstrated.

Like the prevailing hypothesis regarding the biological networks of brain nerve cells, possibility rules help relate incoming queries to values already stored. They can cope with information even when it is filled with errors or ambiguity. They can deal with messy information, collecting scattered facts to recognize and remember from incomplete details, much as the brain seems to do.

3. INDUCTION, DEDUCTION, ABDUCTION

The previous water temperature example demonstrates how we can deal with imperfect data. Typically, three *inference processes* help provide most of the capability we need to cope with such values. These processes are induction, deduction, and abduction.

1. *Induction* is the search of rules partly ordered in generality. For this reason, induction is often considered nearly synonymous with *generalization.*

Induction can be top-down or bottom-up. It involves redundancy and a model of generality.

---

[2] Noun, singular.

2. *Deduction* is computation in the sense in which this term is used in a typical engineering problem.

In contrast to induction, *deduction draws out the logical consequences of given statements.* For instance, the statements may be: "George is a man" and "Mary is a woman." Through the process of deduction, we can further draw on these statements to form new ones:

- "Men are mortal."
- "George is a man."
- "George is mortal."

Induction goes beyond the given evidence. Deduction merely reformulates it. According to Aristotle, *the scientist discovers by induction* and then lays out what he has learned in a deductive structure. He is thus *building a science.*

Rudolf Carnap (1891–1970) thought that the key to logical thinking is to be found in the ideas of verification and induction. For Carnap, a theory was genuinely scientific if it was roughly possible to verify it by empirical observation. To this statement, let us add that the putative scientific theory does not actually have to be true. It may turn out to be an honest scientific mistake and fail to be verified. The *general induction rule* is given in Figure 12-3.

3. *Abduction*[3] is an inverse probability. It is the technical term for the likely cause of an effect, rather than the probable effect of a cause.

Let's further explain the abduction process in the sense of a Bayesian probability. In ordinary prepositional logic, A implies B. With abduction, if B is true, then there is a strong possibility that A is true:

A/B

A is the *cause; B* is the *effect. A/B* states that the effect B is known. The *cause may be A.* Hence, first find B, the effect, and then speculate on the cause. As we will see in Chapter 13, at the end of the nineteenth century Bayes developed the theory of *conditional probabilities.*

In contrast, deduction states precisely the opposite: There exists a cause. The likely effect of it may be X. For example, because of electromagnetic theory (the cause), there is conductivity (the effect).

Table 12-1 presents a summary of induction, deduction, and abduction. Let's relate these concepts to the discussion on the inference engine. As stated in the Introduction, the general presentation of a rule is:

IF   Hypothesis
THEN   Action
ELSE   Other

---

[3] The concept of abduction exists in Aristotelian logic but not the term. The term was coined at the University of Tokyo in the AI research conducted there in connection with the ICOT project.

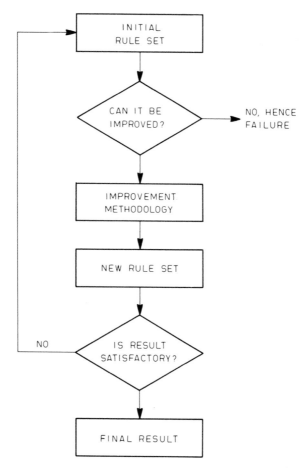

Figure 12-3. Like any other process, induction can be improved with methodology and associated procedures. This figure shows one approach.

TABLE 12-1. Induction, Deduction, and Abduction.

Induction	is generalization
	It is a *search of rules* (more precisely, space of rules) partly ordered in generality.
Deduction	is computation
	Given the cause, or causes, calculate the likely *effect*
	or
	Draw the logical consequences of a statement
Abduction	is inverse probability
	A is the *cause*; B is the *effect*.
	Given the effect B, the likely cause is A. This is the concept of Bayesian probability.

But this is only an example, not a rule about rules. The *notion* of a rule is a slippery concept, referring to things of different scale and level. These are reflected through the reasoning process we choose: induction, deduction, and abduction in this example.

In fact, rules may not even be the dominant form of representation. In addition, they are often language bound. EMycin,[4] a shell, allows simple rule description; it does not involve a pattern machine. Lisp and Prolog permit the expression of more complex structures, including pattern machines.

In short, there is no well-known standard to be used to say *"As a rule, this is a rule."* As an alternative, the concept of logical inferences is used—which is a process description approach. We have discussed three of the basic elements of reasoning. Induction, deduction, and abduction permit us to map into a machine the characteristics of human thought and reasoning—one of the AI goals. But though necessary, these three processes are not enough. We also need functional decomposition.

Functional decomposition consists of splitting up AI designs into a component hierarchy corresponding to functional modules. *Abstraction* is a way of stating design problems in a manner that allows certain critical issues to be considered early on and across the full spectrum of the design process. Abstract solutions are descriptions that stand for an equivalence class of detailed solutions. They are represented by *description levels*. The term *representation* is used in a technical sense in AI and computer science.

If a system has and can use a data structure which can be said to represent something (an object, a procedure, and so on), then the system itself can also be said to have knowledge, namely, the knowledge embodied in that representation about the physical or logical system which it maps.

Another basic process is *inheritance,* which allows a system to pass values through link or slot relations. An AI construct can provide slots with default values, for instance, to increase programming efficiency. Inheritance simplifies programming because some relations can be left implicit instead of written out in rules. We will return to this notion when we talk of *objects.*

Finally, the induction, deduction, or abduction rules we are using may contain errors or contradictions. To remove them from the AI construct, we need a process of *equilibration,* or truth maintenance. If there exist *contradictory* rules, facts, and/or values, we must adjust the knowledgebank to weed out *inconsistency.* At all times in the life of an AI construct, the knowledgebank must be consistent. Figure 12-4 demonstrates the equilibration process.

Equilibration is very important not only because, by definition, a system must be complete, consistent, and noncontradictory, but also because intelligence implies the inability of logical contradictions. It emphasizes organized behavior, not only goal setting; underlines the making of plans, not just goal seeking; and establishes survival patterns. Hence, intelligence requires proper definition, not just a simple description effort.

---

[4] This stands for "Empty Mycin" or "Essential Mycin," that is, the expert system Mycin without its knowledge bank.

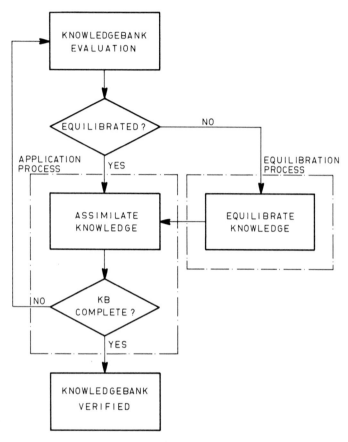

Figure 12-4. Equilibration is one of the most vital operations in expert systems. It ensures that the written rules are noncontradictory. This flow chart describes the procedure.

4. DEEP AND SHALLOW KNOWLEDGE

The incorporation of *deep knowledge* in an AI construct solves fundamental problems of classical system technology. At the same time, learning through progressive refinement can be used to gain *shallow knowledge* from experience. The learning component analyzes the system's failure to solve some problems and refines the problem-solving knowledge to cope with them. This process results in an AI system which gradually solves more problems in a more efficient way. On the other hand, for many domains, deep knowledge is easier to grasp than the shallow knowledge, particularly when the machine we are working with is not very powerful. This means that trade-offs are required.

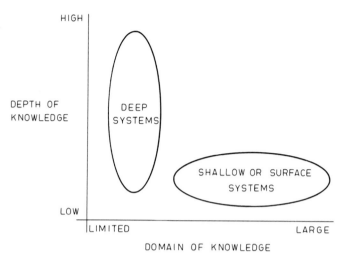

Figure 12-5. Both the depth of knowledge and the domain of knowledge can vary from nil to large. This figure shows that the two areas where work is done are often dissociated from one another—yet most projects require their convergence.

Figure 12-5 contrasts *depth of knowledge* to *domain of knowledge.* The way we define deep knowledge is practically synonymous with a rule-based system.[5] By contrast, *shallow, or surface, knowledge* indicates the ability to exploit a large domain—for instance, a global database—but no part of it in depth. In the limiting case, a shallow knowledge engine is the KBMS administering *episodic memory.*

Both deep and shallow approaches are AI constructs. However,

- The *shallow machine* is an intelligent engine for large or very large databases.

Its object is a learned search of global database environments. This is domain knowledge.

- The *deep knowledge machine* is an inference mechanism.

Expert knowledge is very important in its development. Deep knowledge is necessary for building the inference engine.

Surface (shallow) knowledge systems are typically a database of pattern–decision pairs. They support a simple control structure to navigate through the database. There is less agreement on exactly what characterizes deep systems.

Generally, deep systems solve problems of significantly greater complexity than surface systems, but this distinction is imprecise. Some surface systems support the hypothesis of *similarity-based* induction. The goal is to make decisions by looking for *patterns in data.*

---

[5] Note that this is the definition followed in the majority of cases (universities, AI laboratories and project teams, books, articles)—but not in all cases. The alternative (minority) view inverts the definitions of deep and shallow knowledge given in this textbook.

Hence, *similarity-based learning, memory-based reasoning,* and *classification* are related examples.

During our 1989 meeting Walter Van der Velde of Free University, Brussels) maintained that deep knowledge can be seen as the textbook knowledge a human expert has about his domain of expertise. He suggests that for many domains this knowledge is easy to grasp, and it is feasible to base reasoning on it. Moreover, high-quality shallow knowledge can be acquired from expertise, and convincing explanations can be based on it.

Deep-knowledge models can be used to describe and reason about a real-life system. We can develop a structural model describing the various components and their part–whole relations. A geometric model addressing the general layout and dimensions of components tends to be a deep-knowledge model. We employ this notion in Chapter 4 when we talk about *model making.*

Causality is an important concept in deep model systems. A causal model consists of a set of properties of components which are causally related. In causality, the value of one property is determined by the values of one or more other properties. Some of these properties are observable; most of them, however, are not or are observable only with difficulty.

Causal relations can easily be represented in a network where the nodes stand for the properties of the components. *Semantic networks* illustrate relationships through diagrams consisting of nodes and arcs.

- The nodes represent objects, actions, or events.
- The connecting arcs, called *links,* represent the relations among the nodes.

A link may mean that the object on one end is an attribute of an object on the other end. Alternatively, it could mean that one implies the other, or even something else that define the link to mean. This inforamtion is translated in terms of attribute-value memory structures, representing *conceptual dependencies.* These map the meaning of sentences through a small number of primitives (or basic concepts), signifying actions, states, or changes of state.

Rule learning is one of the main subjects in deep knowledge. But before rules can be outlined in detail, we have to establish their format and a method for deep causal reasoning. When we start using this approach, our goal should be to find simple rule formats and simple deep reasoning methods, subsequently building a more complex system.

Another crucial part of the AI system is its explaining/justifying component to provide *justification.* The construct must capture what happened inside the machine:

1. What rules were fired?
2. What is the risk involved in, for example, a loan decision?

One of the attractions of writing the rules is that we can give an explanation/justification leading to the explicit representation of the object. We will return to these notions later.

Deep and shallow knowledge form a cross-discipline. However, it is also true that different groups of people have different definitions because they have different aims in pursuit of knowledge, which leads them to value one kind of knowledge or one solution over another. When an approach is polyvalent, *constraints* help to tailor it to the requirements. Constraints on design are used to guide this process. These constraints can propagate both ways in the abstraction hierarchy—down from the specification and up from the limitations of the implementation technology.

Figure 12-6 repeats the general layout of Figure 12-5 but places a boundary around the bulk of engineering and managerial applications. Both deep and shallow AI constructs are necessary in typical work in these two domains, and file references are vital.

About 75% of an engineering design consists of a search of the engineering database which may be stored in the more diverse media, generally paperbound. One major engineering company had 1,300,000 different blueprints. When, in the late 1970s, they were transferred to CAD, a study found that about 300,000 of them were quite active.

Based on this experience, we might view a design engineer as walking through a space of problems to be solved through file references. Each problem is attempted *as if* it is not significantly different from those previously studied. The designer tries to use his shallow knowledge, consisting of accumulated know-how, searching rules which worked for similar problems. These rules provide guidelines but also constraints. Should this process fail, he must have a detailed understanding of the structure and underlying principles of the domain.

Having solved his search problem through constrained action and/or the acquisition of deeper knowledge, the designer should correct the causes of his initial failure to solve the problem. He can streamline his search model with experiential knowledge that has been refined to prevent the same failure in his next search.

Surface knowledge is constrained knowledge. *Deductive retrieval* is possible through knowledgebank construction. A search is more effective when a *uniform processing* environment is assured. Text, data, vector graphics, and programs must be uniformly processed. Metadata and metaknowledge are helpful in this task.

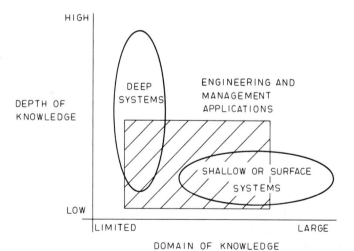

Figure 12-6. Engineering and management applications call for deep knowledge of the subject itself, as well as a broader domain of knowledge than what may be required in specialized subjects like physics or chemistry.

5. STRUCTURING A LOGICAL PROCESS

A logical process is *multiperspective.* The overall picture of the situation is constructed from elements recognized in various subsystems which may be quite diverse. A logical process is also *hierarchical,* since low-level problems are used as the building blocks of higher-level problems.

A logical, *qualitative* process is *subjective,* which makes it the antithesis of a *quantitative* process. In addition, different experts—even those believed to have the same level of expertise or thought to be of the same mind—may have different approaches in using their problem-solving skills. A may be better in lateral thinking and hence stronger in generating alternatives. B may be better in analytical/vertical thinking, and hence better in exploring a given alternative in a deep-seated.

The knowledge engineer tries to streamline some of these differences in the descriptive part of the AI construct. He does so through rules and a methodology. At the beginning of this chapter, we spoke about the concept of

Demo <Clause>

The use of metapredicates ensures that only nonredundant and consistent knowledge can accumulate in the knowledgebank. This is important for a running process. The intelligent system can tell whether knowledge is consistent and nonredundant, relative to existing knowledge, through rules, facts, states, and values. The use of metapredicates helps to guarantee the proper transition between past knowledge of algorithmic calculus and the coming implementation environment of facts, states, and values where *soft data* dominates. Figure 12-7 exemplifies this situation and dramatizes the difference between *observation* and *prediction,* expressed in successive steps.

Logical constructs elaborate a manageable transition between observation and prediction. In the hierarchy of perception/cognition skills that we examine, perhaps the first and most fundamental is the capability of detection. In detection situations, all available sensory data are focused on answering a single yes-or-no question: "Is it or isn't it?"

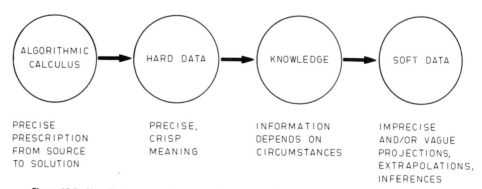

Figure 12-7. Algorithmic approaches act on hard data to uncover underlying knowledge. Heuristics also act on data, particularly where imprecise or vague information is the rule.

The next most fundamental skill in AI work is the mapping of perception and/or knowledge in a form which can be explained to the machine. As described in this chapter, this focuses on logic and logical description.

Logic is the tool for describing situational calculus. *States* present boundaries for facts. A *fact* is true in a given state within which it can have values.[6] *Predicates* relate facts to a given state. *Actions* are functions describing a transition from state to state.

We have spoken about *rules* and how they can be used in logical representation. Indeed, the inference engine is a high-level interpreter of rules. In contrast the better-known mathematical model is, in general, a simulation of real entities.

The knowledgebank contains rules. In general, with fewer than 100 rules we have a simple system; with 100 to 500 rules the system is of average complexity; with 500 to 1,000 rules, it is fairly sophisticated. That is the situation today in the majority of cases.[7]

Thousands of rules indicate great complexity and require significant skill. We do not yet have the technology to develop and control such systems. Nor do we have the necessary computer power in logical instructions per second (LIPS) to process them—though this situation will change with fifth-generation computers.

Another issue which is not very well resolved is the *size of rules:* How many conditions and how many actions should there be for each rule? Rules can always be made bigger, and hence all-inclusive, or smaller by inserting rules representing intermediate states. Rule size is a function of the level of detail at which an AI system represents its concepts. To a large extent, it is determined by the knowledge engineer—hence, of the AI construct's designer.

We have also referred to frames, scenarios, and logic programming. Though this is not the appropriate place to elaborate in detail on these terms, a well-rounded discussion on the subject of inference requires us at least to define them.

Frames help organize knowledge in ways that make it easy to describe and explain inferences. They map closely associated objects and events that are connected through routing like menus.

Scenarios describe the AI construct in an accurate but fluid form. They are frame-like structures that use stereotyped situations to represent knowledge in a particular context. They are unique in having a time orientation, as they are concerned with sequencing cause and effect. One of the best scenarios I have seen explains to the computer what it means "to be a restaurant." Whenever the system has queries about the service functions and layout of a restaurant, it refers to this scenario.

Scenarios can and should be networked. It cannot be repeated too often that the value of AI systems is almost never in stand-alone applications. There is a continuous process from algorithms and calculus to knowledge and inference. Nowhere is this better demonstrated than in *simulation.*[8] Simulation plays a key role in logic programming. A second-order predicate is

Simulate <Clause>

---

[6] We used these concepts in Chapter 5 when we discussed knowledgebanks.
[7] These figures are not compatible with those in my book *Applying Expert Systems in Business,* (McGraw-Hill, New York, 1986–87). They have been revised upward due to accumulating AI experience.
[8] We defined and discussed simulation in Chapter 4.

It is a metapredicate that permits us to link to KBMS/DBMS functions, intelligent CAD, experimentation, and existing data processing/word processing applications. Simulate <Clause> permits us to go from the real world to the model. It makes it feasible to obtain experimental results, and it helps map a model solution into the real world through inference.

Inference engines typically come with a *kernal language* and its translators. Software and hardware act as cooperative problem-solving mechanisms. In of PSI, which we considered in Chapter 3, the kernel logic programming language was developed in a number of versions, starting with the so-called kernel language zero (KL-0) based on Prolog. This extends Prolog by incorporating features for

- program structuring,
- relational database interfacing,
- parallel programming, and
- data type checking.

Languages must be supplemented by *methodologies*. These have to be flexible and heuristic, exploiting unanticipated paths, providing for chaining of rules, and able to handle dynamic structures.

As emphasized in Chapters 1 and 2, methodologies for AI are still under development. Theoretical work in laboratories is revealing the landscape of AI and helping to manage this landscape. The aim is to facilitate software development.

The importance of methodologies is underlined by the fact that the use of inference engines is either increasing in many computing converts to AI or will soon be what we now call AI. As explained in other chapters, we are interested in methods that provide results or examples of behavior that are characteristic of human intelligence. But this definition is too general. By contrast, an inference engine approach tends to be specific.

6. FUNCTIONS AND ROLES OF THE OPERATING SYSTEM

We have spoken of fifth-generation computers and inference mechanisms, indicating that the one is made for the other. But we have also implied that native system commands are necessary to interface between the application and the machine.

Section 6 of Chapter 9 described PSI. ICOT developed an operating system, Simpos, for the PSI engine. Projected in the image of Unix, [9] Simpos' capability is growing. It features

1. a *kernel*, similar to that of Unix,
2. *pipes, forks, semaphores, cursors,* and *demons,* and
3. an *object-oriented* language, ESP, in which Simpos has been written.

Simpos is a programming and operating system—hence, an *environment*—developed as a systems software and prototype providing a good programming environment for PSI and

---

[9] See D.N. Chorafas, *Fourth and Fifth Generation Languages*, Vol. II: *Which Unix?* McGraw-Hill, New York, 1986.

featuring an object-oriented approach to logic programming. This object-oriented approach provides both a modular programming framework and the concept of states with objects. Its encapsulation and inheritance mechanisms facilitate changes to and extensions of the system.

An *object* is a building component in Simpos. It is defined externally by a set of operations which the object accepts to achieve *given goals*. Internally it is implemented by a set of Prolog clauses and slots.

- Clauses define what the object should perform when it accepts an operation.
- Each of the slots holds a value or an object which represents the state or structure of the object.

While the object orientation is new, Simpos' similarity to Unix not only *employs existing knowledge* but also *permits transitory solutions,* using an interface/interpreter. It also permits us to develop simpler AI constructs on less expensive supermicrocomputers running under Unix. These are portable to PSI engines through the interface/interpreter.

Although objects were discussed in Chapter 11, it is proper to define them briefly here. *Objects* are abstract data types associated with specific operations. Thus, an object includes both

- information elements and
- the operations on them.

Objects exist in the real world and can have various attributes. Actions can also be regarded as objects. Values can be associated with an object by means of a property list.

In Simpos, a set of objects which behaves in the same manner is defined as a *class*. A template of objects of the same class is given by a class definition, and an instance (object) is defined from this template.

An inheritance mechanism is provided to define a new class, associating it with existing classes. If a class inherits other classes, this class has externally all the operations of those classes defined in itself. We often use this concept in the examples presented in this text, though this statement was not explicitelly made.

A *demon* predicate makes object-oriented programming with multiple inheritance easier and more effective. Suppose that a demon predicate is defined in a component class which a certain class inherits. When an operation on the object of this class is called, the demon will be also called implicitly. There is no need to call the operations explicitly. Two types of demon calls are supported:

- *before demons* and
- *after demons.*

A before demon is called before the primary predicate of the main class. An after demon is called after the primary predicate.

While Simpos is not a universal solution for all AI-oriented operating systems, it is a good reference. It is also a valid example of an *environment* which includes both logic programming and operating system features.

NEC developed for CHI, its fifth-generation computer, a complete environment organized in five layers, as demonstrated in Figure 12-8. From top to bottom, it includes

- an interpreter/compiler library,
- exception processing/information management,
- process management/memory management input/output management/host interface, and
- linguistic support.

The linguistic support chosen can make or break the fifth-generation computer. In the ICOT project, a kernel language, KL-0, was developed with object-oriented features added to Prolog. The personal sequential inference machine (PSI) and its basic software were built through KL-0 and its successor, ESP. As stated in Chapter 3, ESP is an object-oriented programming language.

Simpos is written in ESP. Thus the kernel language is the focal point around which software and hardware have been developed. Logic programming covers

1. computer architecture,
2. new programming styles,
3. programming language semantics, and
4. database semantics.

Database semantics are treated in Chapter 5, where a distinction is made between *intentional* and *extensional* databases.

In Simpos, a process is an active entity which executes a program. A process can be in one of the four states: *running, ready* to run, *suspended,* or *dormant.*

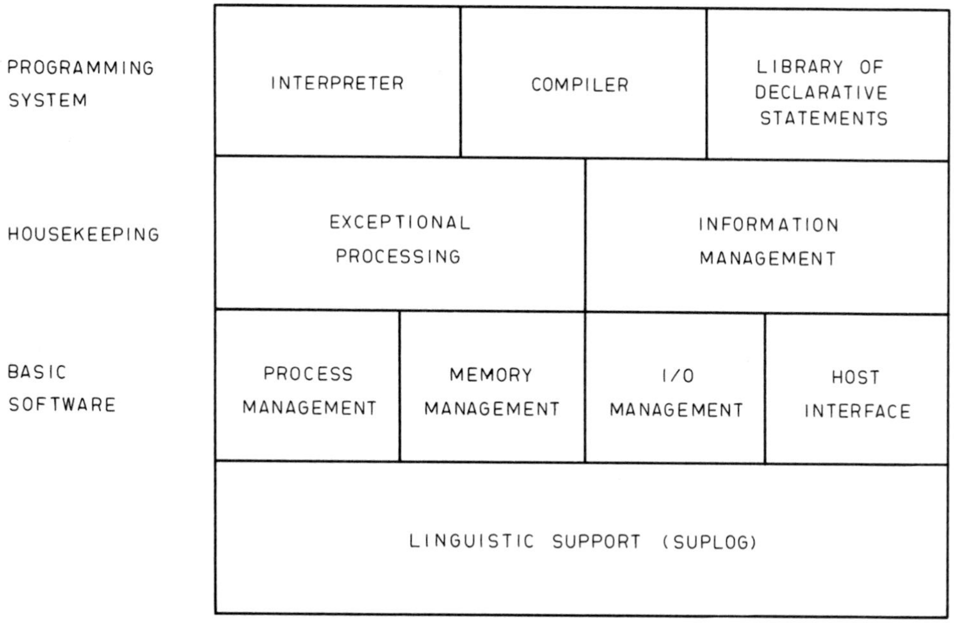

PROGRAMMING SYSTEM	INTERPRETER	COMPILER	LIBRARY OF DECLARATIVE STATEMENTS
HOUSEKEEPING	EXCEPTIONAL PROCESSING	INFORMATION MANAGEMENT	
BASIC SOFTWARE	PROCESS MANAGEMENT / MEMORY MANAGEMENT	I/O MANAGEMENT / HOST INTERFACE	
	LINGUISTIC SUPPORT (SUPLOG)		

Figure 12-8. Any AI computer requires a solid software environment. This figure presents the software system designed by Nippon Electric for the CHI machine.

- A running process is currently executing a program on a processor.
- A ready process is a queue wating to be run.
- Suspended processes are not in the ready queue.
- Dormant processes are not managed by the supervisor.

A process is an object which accepts operations to control its state. Some processes in the system are allocated to interrupt task handlers, such a traps, device managers, and the garbage collector. These interrupt processes are dispatched not by the supervisor but by the PSI hardware. The hardware also activates a boot process when the system is bootstrapped.

The program indicates what a process should perform. But unlike classical programming, a Simpos program is an instance of a program class. When many processes execute the same program independently, each process is given a program instance of the same program class. Such programs share the code but have a different set of instance slots. The entry of the main program is defined as an instance predicate of the program.[10]

After being instantiated, a program is given to a process to be executed. This step is called *program invocation*. To keep track of program invocations, a process has an invocation stack onto which is pushed an invoked program.

Simpos features a layered structure. From top to bottom, it consists of the following:

1. *A programming system* with facilities for coordinating/interpreting/editing/debugging, as well as librarian functions.
2. *An operating system* featuring three sublayers:
   - Input/output media, including windowing, filing, printing, and networking.
   - Supervising, handling the processing pool, streaming, and timing.
   - A kernel concerned with processing and memory management.
3. *Hardware* functionality.

The environment ensures an *interactive* facility through the best tools, featuring full computer assistance, and with a development capability always online. The goals are end-user convenience, greater professional productivity, change in the infosystem culture, fast development times, and high-quality software. In problem-solving terms, the objectives are to

1. construct higher-order inference from simple syllogisms,
2. handle knowledge instead of data,
3. ensure that a variety of problems can be solved efficiently,
4. provide a system convenient for users, and
5. significantly improve programmer productivity.

In a network operating system now under development, the main functions are user-directed service facilities. Among them are

---

[10] The following paragraphs show the results of a meeting held at ICOT, as well as concepts expressed in a paper by Takashi Hattori, Norihiko Yoshida, and Takumi Fujisaki, published by ICOT, Tokyo, 1986.

1. security,
2. virtualization,
3. virtual network characteristics,
4. network transparency, and
5. network control.

On a networking basis, various types of streams with additional features are defined. Priority control, bounded buffer control, message-based communication facilities, channels, and ports are part of the primitives. A channel is a message-based communication primitive useful in describing multiple-client/multiple-server interactions.

Network virtualization means that network systems and various resources over them should be integrated effectively and appear uniform to network users. The *one logical network* concept is an example of network system virtualization.

Network control facilities correspond to kernel functions at the operating system level. They include recovery, restarting, reconfiguration, and so on. Kernel functions proper to communication systems are adaptive for routing or flow control. They are similar to load balancing or thrashing in computer operating systems.

Other software-based services corresponding to operational management functions are error detection, error correction, use and failure statistics, accounting information, and so on. The network operating system must also provide for interconnection to a variety of services, the most important being file servers in a distributed database, as the following chapter shows.

13

The Knowledgebank and the Database

Keywords

knowledgebank • rules • facts • states • values • domain • objects • microdomain • memory-based reasoning • idea database • siutation-action • databases • heuristics • intentional database • extensional database • rule base • rule interpreter • knowledge • data • soft data • hard data • conventional database • logic database • constraints • extensional database • intentional database • database server • parallel model • global database • relational databases • metaknowledge • object knowledge • multimedia • inference engine • episodic memory • domain structures • rule predicates • episodes • text animation • program animation • networking construct • idea-search • search strategy • quality of search • select from where • conceptual query • vague queries • conceptual approach • interacting • relational DBMS

1. INTRODUCTION

An AI system consists of two fundamental parts: the knowledgebank and an inference engine. We spoke of the inference engine in Chapter 4. The *knowledgebank* is a repository of *rules* and of information made up of *facts, states,* and *values* about the *domain* to which the system is addressed. The knowledgebank also includes definitions and methodologies.[1]

We have said that *a domain is a set of values.* In general, a set of operators does not need to be specified. But we have defined, *objects,* suggesting that an object includes both

---

[1] For a discussion of methodologies, see Chapters 7, 8, and 9.

information elements and operations, being identical to a *microdomain* when operators are included.

Rules associated with a domain control the interactive assimilation of new knowledge. Rules may also manage the domain information or guide a process of *memory-based reasoning* in a context of recorded episodic information. An *idea database* requires simple rules of the following form:

IF	A text mentions a conceptual unit anchored in <Argument>
THEN	Start in-depth processing of that package
ELSE	Skip an otherwise irrelevant reference

Episodic memories require very large computer power[2] by today's standards. Given the difficulty of building and maintaining a large knowledgebank, and the fact that existing processors are rather slow, the typical domain of expertise is narrow. Sometimes broader coverage is achieved by using a relatively shallow set of relationships between, for example, facts and relations. Another constraint is the rather limited knowledge representation languages that currently exist.

The domain of knowledge is local to the problem. However, as AI constructs grow, we have to expand the domains' perspectives. To explain this concept more clearly, let us assume that the domain consists of cube design and production. A cube has dimensions A, B, and C. The following *facts* are in the knowledgebank:

Fact 1: notion of the cube.
Fact 2: notion of measurements and metrics.
Fact 3: definition of dimensions and tolerance.
Fact 4: unit of measurement (for instance, millimeter).
Fact 5: dimension A and its tolerances.
Fact 6: dimension B and its tolerances.
Fact 7: dimension C and its tolerances.

States are also in the knowledgebank. In this particular case, they include Shift I, Shift II, and Shift III. The values are in the database. They represent actual dimension measurements corresponding to facts and states.

The importance of the knowledgebank is underlined by the fact that in present AI work emphasis is on the role specific and detailed knowledge rather than on reasoning methods. The first successful application of this approach was the Dendral program at Stanford University, a long-term collaboration between chemists and computer scientists for automating the determination of molecular structure from empirical formulas and mass spectral data.

The key idea is that knowledge is power; experts often know more facts and heuristics about a domain than less well-informed problem solvers. Such a collection of facts and heuristics is therefore highly valued. In a way, as the opening paragraphs of this chapter stated, the task of constructing knowledgebanks becomes the limiting factor in AI develop-

---

[2] Memory-based reasoning applications have been successfully done on the Connection Machine, but this equipment features 2,500 to 10,000 MIPS.

ment. It is no surprise that much of the applied AI research in the last decade has focused on techniques and tools for knowledgebank organization and management.

Domain knowledge must remain dynamic. As shown in Figure 13-1, having defined the purpose of the domain, we must look at the knowledgebank and its rules, as well as the approach to be taken in using them. This influences the global database perspectives and, in turn, is influenced by the control strategy we have adopted.

An ossified knowledgebank is little better than a textbook. This alternative is continuous dynamic updating, pruning, and readjustment of the system. The system will also probably have to be completely reorganized from time to time simply because of the mass of new knowledge that has been added to it. However, because few AI systems have been in continual use in real environments, the problems associated with this task have not really been faced.

Flexibility and *dynamic updating* are the keywords. *Hypertext* solutions can be instrumental, as they are able to solve two thorny problems: provision of agile man–machine interfaces and user-transparent database/knowledgebank access. Both are vital in an interactive environment.

A number of announcements (SuperCard, Hypercard, etc.) create applications with custom menus and dialogue boxes, and support multiple window types (resizable windows) as well as icons, cursors, and color look-up tables (cluts), the last being directly imported and exported. At the enduser level, hypertext approaches support online reference to the scripting language and include a range of commands as well as extensions. They offer feature control of color palettes for special effects, preserving colors in imported graphics.

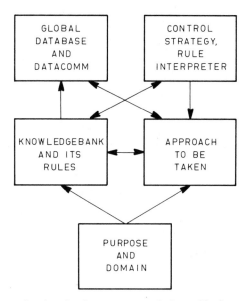

Figure 13-1. The approach to be taken in expert system design and implementation is affected by a number of considerations, key among them being purpose, domain, global database, control strategy, and the type of knowledgebank to be built.

Nothing prevents us from fully exploring the use of hypertext modules in a knowledge bank-oriented sense, integrating with other AI constructs and providing for user-actuated, dynamic management of the knowledgebank. We must realize that we need to use intensively the best tools at our disposal rather than reinventing the wheel.

2. KNOWLEDGEBANKS
VS. DATABASES

Knowledge-based systems provide facilities beyond the databasing capabilities we have become familiar with over the last thirty years. They make feasible the creation of knowledgebanks whose know-how can be employed to ensure new system capabilities. Furthermore, know-how-dependent processes are useful for solving problems related to a class of objects.

The most popular approach to representing the domain knowledge needed for an AI system is production rules, also referred to as *situation-action* rules. These are the IF . . . THEN . . . ELSE rules we discussed in Chapter 4. Rules are invoked by pattern matching with features of the task environment. They may or may not appeal to the global database.

There is only a thin line separating the rules in a knowledgebank from the domain facts it contains. This is due to the fact that the power of the AI system lies in the specific knowledge of the problem domain, with potentially the most powerful systems being the ones containing the most knowledge. And *facts can be as much a matter of knowledge as of rules.*

Another real-life concept affecting this situation is that AI constructs reflect expert know-how. An expert usually has many judgmental or empirical rules for which the available evidence provides incomplete support. In some cases, the expert does not distinguish clearly between the rules he establishes and follows and the facts in his mind.

When we contrast a database to a knowledgebank, we see that a primary distinction between them can be expressed in two simple sentences:

- *Databases* have a predetermined structure.
- *Knowledgebanks* consist of a set of rules and unstructured, even isolated, facts.

The paths by which facts are related in a knowledgebank are determined ad hoc, as needed to solve a particular problem. This characterizes a *heuristic* search in contrast to a structured approach, whether probabilistic or deterministic.

But the knowledgebank also has a methodology, the latter implying a rigorous discipline. In a sense, because of its rules and methodology, a knowledge-based system acquires a fourth dimension, beyond the three already provided in classical computing by databasing/ data communications/data processing.

Table 13-1 compares the contents of a knowledgebank to those of a database. Figure 13-2 groups the main components of the knowledgebank into three classes:

- facts and states for the domain,
- rules, and
- methodologies.

TABLE 13-1. Contents of a Database and of a Knowledgebank.

Knowledgebank	Database
Facts and states	Information elements—hence
Relations between information elements	values—subject to:
Decision rules	Input
Methodologies	Updating
Consistency control	Retrieval
Propagation actions	
Dynamic extensibility	

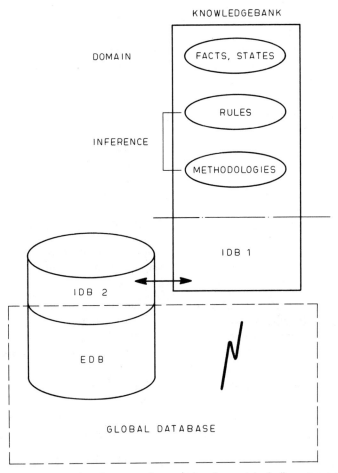

Figure 13-2. The quality and performance of an expert system rest basically on two entities: its knowledgebank (including the domain and inferences) and the global database it can access.

IDB stands for *intentional database,* EDB for *extensional database.* These are concepts we will elaborate in Section 3.

The rules in the knowledgebank are instrumental in reaching conclusions. The calculations and extrapolations that the expert system does may employ probabilistic reasoning, algorithmic approaches, or heuristic patterns. As stated earlier, rules should be kept dynamic. Their strength lies in the lessons learned while the system is in use.

The design of an AI construct, and therefore of the knowledgebank, starts with working principles. Typically, it involves the convergence of many disciplines, allowing the user to challenge and examine the reasoning process underlying the system's answers. When domain knowledge is stored as production rules, the knowledgebank is often referred to as a *rule base* and the inference engine as a *rule interpreter.* An AI system differs from conventional computer programs in several important respects. One of the more visible is in the way

- *knowledge*-type inquiries
- *data*-type inquiries

are made. The *database* implies quantitative references and precise queries. We know—or at least we should know—what we want.

Using a knowledgebank, we have only an *idea* of what we *might* want, whether this is expressed in qualitative or quantitative terms. Subsequently, the AI system uses its know-how to provide us with answers. Table 13-2 emphasizes this process by underlining critical aspects of man–information communication. Both the query and the contents of the database are examined.

- Queries to classical databases are crisp. The contents of such databases are also crisp and precise.

Crisp means *true* or *false*—no fuzzy set, no partial answer, no unknown information. Data processing chores of the 1950s and 1960s, as well as management information systems of the 1970s, had databases of that type. The same is true of DSSs and of information centery applications of the 1980s. This has been the general situation.

The early expert systems applications maintained the crisp character of queries but changed the nature of the database contents. The latter have been characterized as *crisp but imprecise.* They contain unknown and partial information. They may be crisp, but they are imprecise.

This situation, too, has changed. AI implementations during the 1980s had databases which were vague or stochastic. At times, such databases contained more text than data.

TABLE 13-2. Query Types and Database Contents.

Query Type	Database Contents
Crisp	Crisp and precise
Crisp	Crisp but imprecise (unknown, partial)
Crisp	Vague or stochastic
Vague	Precise
Vague	Vague

Vagueness refers to ill-defined words. In terms of data, vague is approximations, or *soft data* developed from inferences and projections, in contrast to *hard data,* which result from measurement values.

In the future, many AI applications will operate in the information environment which has just been explained. Others will be characterized by vague queries, though the database contents will be precise. Still others will feature both vague queries and vague databases.

We will return to these notions later in this chapter when we talk about *idea databases.* At this point, let us make sure that the differences between knowledgebanks and databases is clear:

> ▪ *Conventional databases* are organized in a way that assumes that anything that is not in the database is false.

This is not true of the knowledgebank. No knowledgebank has ever made such a claim.

> ▪ *Knowledgebanks* can start working with a reasonable endowment of rules. Their contents will both grow and change during implementation. But while the rules must form a system which is complete and noncontradictory, many possible rules and facts may still not exist.

When Carnegie Mellon University (CMU) completed R1 (the Vax configuration expert system) for DEC, it had approximately 500 rules and it worked. Subsequent restructuring at CMU brought it to 800 rules. Since its 1982 operation and maintenance by DEC, it has grown to 5,000 rules—at least this was the last count stated in a DEC meeting.

Further, even when a knowledgebank has been completed, it is not yet ready to be run. We must first use the compiler to translate it into optimized language statements so that it will be accepted by the system. It is advisable not to underestimate the work needed in this area. The compiler may accept the knowledgebank on some occasions without error messages, but the resulting compiled knowledgebank file may cause the system to abort during a session, requiring a rerun.

Such compilation is typically done interactively, and the session proceeds through a series of questions. Responses tell the system how to go about searching for an answer to the problem to be solved. As developers, and subsequently as users, we should also be able to request help at any time during a session by typing a question mark in response to a query.

Finally, as designers, we should also have a fully transparent environment to work with. This way, we can focus on the selection, organization, and formulation of the knowledge components.

3. INTENTIONAL AND EXTENSIONAL DATABASES

Now that we have established the difference between knowledgebanks and databases, we will return to the term *database* in order to explain the concepts *intentional* and *extensional.* We will do so by returning to the PSI engine of ICOT, presented in Chapter 3, and its operating system Simpos, discussed in Chapter 4.

A *logic database* (knowledgebank) defines the meaning of objects and the semantic relationships between objects. *Knowledge* is expressed by

1. rules (*intentions*),
2. facts (*extensions*), and
3. constraints.

We referred to *constraints* in Chapter 4 and said that they are critical to logical constructs. They are restrictive conditions on the validity of

- the object knowledge and
- the associated actions.

Descriptions of constraints must cover state changes caused by actions, including worlds, environments, times, metrics, conditions for changes, actions before and after the change occurs, and patterns of given coherences.

The role of constraints in AI work is not always fully appreciated in a way that is commensurate with its contributions. Yet not only is this subject vital, but there is an engineering precedent for it.

Several constraints can enter the design of a physical product, such as an internal combustion motor. These constraints include weight, resistance to vibration and shock, space/volume, and revolutions per minute. Still another example is *tolerances*. Since tolerances have minima and maxima, the concept of constraint is applicable to both physical and logical constructs. *Constraints* extend before and after the action in the database.

In Chapter 11, we also introduced the concept of *meta* and said that a higher layer in a hierarchical structure implies control of and constraints to those layers below it. This, it will be recalled, led to the concepts of first- and second-order predicates. These concepts integrate into Figure 13-3, which includes the following:

- An *extensional database* as the bottom layer. This includes facts and their derivates: states and *values*—hence, data.
- An *intentional database* as the next higher layer (IDB 1). Intentions are rules—hence, the first-order predicate reference.
- An *intentional database*, IDB 2, as a still higher layer. This contains second-order predicates.
- At the top level, the *deep* knowledge of the inference engine—a third-order predicate.

Note that IDB 2/EDB and deep knowledge/IDB 1 are designed in separate boxes. The reason is that IDB 2/EDB is the *database server*, which may be either central or distributed. The ICOT project is developing a hardware engine for it called *Delta.*

Deep knowledge/IDB 1 is the AI-enriched WS, which will surely be distributed. These two layers constitute the PSI engine, which we examined in Chapter 3.

The connecting link between PSI and Delta is a linguistic construct. ICOT works on further developments to Prolog. As already stated, GHC (guarded horn clauses) is a parallel processing version of Prolog which has gone through the intermediate stage of Kernel Language 1 (KL-1).

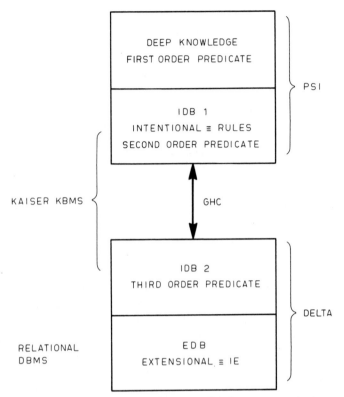

Figure 13-3. Future databases will be organized into layers. This figure presents the Japanese model developed in connection with the New Generation Computer Project. The upper two layers reside in the PSI engine. The lower two layers are located in the specialized database computer. Connectivity is ensured through GHCs.

This approach is a full *parallel model* for AI implementations. The parallel model links several

- inference processors,
- complete engines, and
- secondary memory devices

in a network. The processor is an inference machine, and the engine is a unification entity. The network and (physical) hierarchical memory are logically integrated. In some solutions, the physical hierarchical memory is placed between the primary memory (within the processor) and the secondary (hard disc, optical disc) memory. In others (e.g., the foregoing example), it is fully distributed through file servers, which are attached in a local area network or connected long haul.

The function of distributed memory is to store temporal resolution relative to knowledge-bank retrieval and provide shared access capabilities for processors. The challenge is to do so while gaining speed. As stated in Chapter 4, we gain speed if we

TABLE 13-3. Transition in the Information Sciences.

From:	To:
Relational database	Knowledgebank
Analysis of results	Explanation of results
Applications generator	AI generator
Descriptive language	Natural language

1. reduce the number of instruction accesses and
2. eliminate most of the data accesses.

This process must be ensured by the operating system (Simpos in the case of PSI), but also by the proper KBMS. In the ICOT project, this is the role of Kaiser. The extensional database is served through a DBMS. *Oracle* and *Ingres* have been chosen for this purpose.

Table 13-3 outlines the transition which has taken place in the information sciences: From hierarchical databases we have moved to networking and from there to relational databases. From relational databases we have gone to knowledgebanks. Along with the other changes identified in Table 13-3, the new landscape has significant differences from the old one.

The general schema is given in Figure 13-4. The user of the WS needs to access the *global database*. This is the aggregate of all databases in the system, whether intentional or extensional. Access is obtained through the human window. The global database is searched through a surface expert system (Esystem). But the implementation is specific to a domain and involves deep knowledge. Frontending is provided by other AI constructs to classical computer applications.

The critical feature which distinguishes queries made in this environment from other forms of computer-based access is the ability to extract substantive information from both the intentional and the extensional databases. This contributes effectively to the construction of an appropriate AI utility model. The described system possesses three capabilities:

1. It is able to encode and store information about previously completed operations in an accessible manner.
2. Based on current knowledge of ongoing AI work, it is able to determine what items in its knowledgebank are relevant and how they relate to the current problem.
3. It can utilize the retrieved rules, facts, and values in a way which facilitates the construction of further useful and valid AI models.

Furthermore, if the database is relational and the field structure corresponds exactly to predicates and relations, then there will be no interface problems in querying. This is taken care of by predicate logic, and the reference is valid even if the database structures are quite arbitrary.

Having defined the system in both an intentional and an extensional context, we can now add some remarks on its implementation. First, the fundamentals. The aim of *logic databases* (knowledgebanks) with

1. *intentional (rule)*

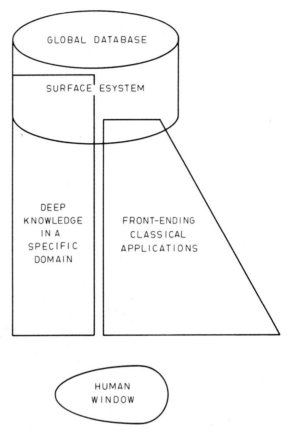

Figure 13-4. In a hybrid approach, the global database would be served by a surface expert system which will be accessed through the deep knowledge modules in specific domains and the frontend via classical data processing applications.

characteristics is to ensure global database access. This is not achieved by relational database structures what have a different goal. However, intentional constructs are linked to *relational databases* through

   2. Extensional features (facts, states, values).

Hence, knowledgebanks and databases are not conflicting. They are complementary.

  The extensional database has only an instance of the data. It cannot rule on the intentional database, but the inverse is true since the intentional database includes *conceptual* facts (rules).

  Logic engines must use both intentional and extensional databases. Logic programming should include *intention* and *extension* knowledge (Prolog does so). This context can be extended in a networking sense. IDB 1 is in the inference engine. EDB 2 is part of the database server. In the inference machine, IDB 1 is associated with the user application programs. *Metaknowledge* and *object knowledge* ensure knowledge management. IDB 2 is the knowledge management layer of the database server. It contains rules for shared user knowledge management and control knowledge (metaknowledge). The relational database system in the extensional database is integrated into the logical programming language. Knowledge and data are treated in the same manner.

4. KNOWLEDGEBANK MANAGEMENT

We have said that a *knowledgebank* contains *facts* and *rules*. Facts have states and values. Rules are longer-lived. Facts (or assertions) are medium-life information. Values are short-lived; they can change rapidly during the course of user interaction.

As longer-term information, rules direct the AI construct on

- how to generate hypotheses from what is presently known or
- how to create new facts.

How does this approach differ from conventional database methodologies? The answer is clear. Because of its intentional characteristics, a *knowledgebank is creative.* Information in a *database is normally passive.* It is either there or it is not. In addition, in a knowledgebank the facts are active. The rules it contains try to fill in the missing information, and *they ask* the user for new facts. Logic management, data management, and dialogue management constitute the expert system implementation (Figure 13-5). However, the knowledgebank itself should be managed. That is the reason for a KBMS.

Knowledgebank management software administers rules and facts and assesses large external databases which function like libraries to the inference functions. The inference

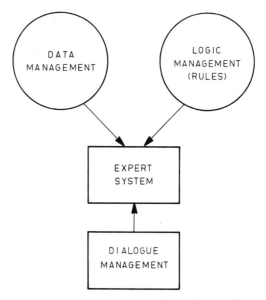

Figure 13-5. Both data management and logic management contribute to the accuracy of an expert system construct. Instrumental in its success is good dialogue management.

functions correspond to library users, and the large distributed databases correspond to the libraries. Knowledgebank management software ensures

- knowledge representation systems,
- knowledgebank design and maintenance support,
- large knowledgebank systems.
- experimental knowledge acquisition systems, and
- the management of distributed database systems.

Knowledge bank management software may even provide the aggregate with a certain level of learning functions. Universal knowledge can be arranged as an ensemble of knowledgebanks which are the components of the KBMS.

Within this aggregate, a special systems knowledgebank may include specifications for the system itself, such as a processor specification description, an operating system specification description, a language manual, a program module component containing frequently used programs, a computer architecture component, and perhaps a VLSI technology design component. Knowledgebank management hardware or software can be projected to support the corresponding knowledge representation and associated large-scale database software.

This solution should focus both on *multimedia* (text, data, graphs, image, voice) for communications purposes and on *storage*. Multimedia storage, often called *multibase* storage, typically comprises central (high-speed) computer memory, magnetic disc storage, tape files and optical discs. Five areas offer fertile applications fields for optical storage in a computing and data processing environment:

1. Unloading the magnetic disc storage of mainframes dedicated to *transactional* data processing.
2. *Managerial* decision support and information center-type operations.
3. Substitute for *tape handling:* mounting and dismounting.
4. *General archiving* as an alternative to a variety of media ranging from tape libraries to microforms.
5. *Special applications* in fields connected to departmental computing where rear-end solutions can be valuable.

In the example we considered in Section 3, optical or magnetic disc storage will be located in the extensional database. Its content will typically be multimedia: text, vector graphics,[3] data, voice, and other images. To manage the extensional database, we need IDB 2—hence, a KBMS. But since we also have IDB 1, we conclude that the KBMS occupies two out of five levels of the layered structure we have seen. Let's bring it back to memory:

1. In the top layer were user program(s). This is the inference engine.
2. The next layer was the intentional database. This is a KBMS (IDB 1).
3. The middle layer was occupied by the horn clauses interface, a linguistic construct for parallel processing.

---

[3] See also Chapter 15 on CAD.

4. A KBMS (IDB 2) was the top layer for the database server.
5. The lowest level was the relational database program (EDB).

Among the functionality criteria of a KBMS we distinguish the range of supported rear-end facilities, the free-form database access capability (idea processor), the management of facts and states, the administration of the rule base, protected mode operations, access to and coordination with very large databases, and operations in an environment of distributed databases, each run through a relational DBMS.

Simulate <Clause>

is a metapredicate which serves KBMS and DBMS functions. Its contribution is important, as relational database management does not include rules. In the case of PSI/Delta, the KBMS (Kaiser) features knowledge assimilation and equilibration. This is based on the Demo <Clause> metapredicate.

AM, the first expert system (written by Douglas Lenat) with self-learning characteristics, is a good example of the role of a KBMS in *knowledgebank organization*. To organize the knowledgebank, AM uses elementary ideas in finite set theory. Heuristics is employed

- for generate new mathematical concepts by combining elementary ideas, and
- for discarding bad ideas.

However, these claims have been strongly critical in *Artificial Intelligence* magazine, in an issue which appeared some three years ago, and no real answer has been given.

The knowledgebank of R1 was structured around the properties of some 400 Vax components. There were rules for determining when to move to the next subtask based on the system state. There were also rules for carrying out partial configurations. We have said that XCON, the successor to R1, has grown to include 5,000 rules. A KBMS has been necessary for knowledgebank organization and administration.

The knowledgebank of EL employs rules that represent general electrical principles, make conjectures, and decide what to forget when contradictions occur. SYN, and MIT Esystem which uses the propagation ideas of EL, contains in its knowledgebank electrical laws. KAS takes a different approach. Its rules focus on

- inference networks for expressing judgmental knowledge,
- semantic networks for expressing the meaning of the propositions employed in the rules, and
- taxonomic networks for representing basic knowledge among the terms of the domain.

There is also knowledge of various mechanisms employed in Prospector for representing and using know-how, as well as consistency rules. The latter form a KBMS context.

Such functionality goes well beyond the now classical DBMS function of a data description language, data manipulation language, data dictionary, database housekeeping operations, routines for retrieving information about a dataset, and routines for modifying dataset records. It requires more than database security functions and programs for interactive applications or routines for checking the validity of interactive input.

In addition, existing DBMSs are *passive*. They respond only when invoked by a user.

Therefore, they cannot provide effective access to diverse types of information. The result is that without KBMS

1. applications suffer unacceptable retrieval errors and delays, particularly in a distributed database context,
2. information is not always compiled from a variety of sources, as it should be to meet inference requirements, and
3. processing primarily regards only limited kinds of knowledge—yet we need able supports for object types, relationships, and constraints.

Let's conclude with the statement that the *knowledgebank* and the *inference engine* are the two key architectural components of AI. They are part of a *knowledge management* discipline. The *theory of knowledgebanks* includes

- knowledge representation,
- knowledge models,
- recursive data models,
- object-oriented models,
- knowledge indexing, and
- knowledge transformation.

Knowledge management involves constructs and languages, constraints in representation, and the administration of rules, as well as metadata management and the able handling of extensible data dictionaries.

5. EPISODES, DOMAINS, RULES, AND IDEA DATABASES

There exist three approaches to AI solutions: *episodic memory, domain structures,* and *rule predicates.* Rule-based systems are the classical approach, the first generation of AI constructs. Episodic memory is only now coming into existence in connection with powerful fifth-generation computers. Domain structures fall between the two extremes of

- a database of episodes and patterns, and
- representations of deep knowledge.

The expert system with deep knowledge has its problem-solving structure compiled into it. The domain model is addressed to data searching within the range of problems it handles. It contains no data and/or rules alien to the domain.

Episodic memory is characterized as an *establish-refine* type. It registers *episodes* in the sense of facts/states/values, which are neither ordered nor sorted. They occur in a flat database, and hence in a relational organization. Episodes stored in an episodic memory will be accessed by very powerful computers on the basis of a certain pattern—for instance, *underlining concepts* on a representative page presented through the human window—and then by asking the computer to "search all other pages which include this concept."

Note that we talk of concepts, not keywords. Keywords are preestablished, and hence inflexible. They also require not only significant preparatory work but also a prior decision on which keywords might be significant in future usage. Underlining of concepts is done ad hoc based on current requirements. It is a dynamic approach which also eliminates much of the preparatory work. That is how *idea databases* work.

For practical purposes, the scales are reversed. With classical computers, efficiency is

- 98% a function of database design and
- only 2% a function of the means by which the query is generated.

Idea databases change this frame of reference. Efficiency becomes embedded in the means by which the query is generated—hence the KBMS, the DBMS, and the fifth-generation computer.

Another contribution of intelligent databases is *text animation.* Animation represents information contained in large chunks of text in the form of a knowledgebank. This knowledgebank is used to drive a computer-based consultation. Based on these premises, the Microelectronics and Computer Development Corporation (MCC) is actively working on a fifth-generation computer/AI project for *program animation.* This imaginative project will allow analysts and programmers to overfly their construct on a three-dimensional video presentation. In this manner, through computer animation, they will be able to examine the functionality of every node and to operate the programming system before it is released.

In spite of its sophistication, an idea database requires *simple software.* The search is done by massive computer power. A program for an idea database will look like this:

```
IF          an unknown text token occurs in text,
THEN        check all properties tentatively assigned to it.
AND         compare the property sets to the token
AND         select the property set whose similarity is maximal.
AND         assign the self slot of the token same filler contained in the
                selected property set.
AND         present the set.
```

This is precisely the opposite of underlining a wanted concept. The goal is to exclude alien text tokens.

Figure 13-6 suggests a way in which an idea database construct will be executed. The work is done by the knowledgebank. Analysis, evaluation, and execution are supported by metaknowledge and object knowledge. A human window provides the man–information interface. The rest consists of execution control and resource management.

An *idea database* (idea processor) is *free-form,* which means that information is viewed in a semiorganized manner

- in a way that corresponds to real-life folders and piles of papers.
- rather than through the irrationally regimented structure of current database and file managers.

Idea databases have much to do with messaging and communications. Links can be substantially enhanced if metadata concepts characterize the implementation.

In a free-form idea processor, a *networking construct* directs the propagation of information through a web of nodes. Each link connects two nodes: the *antecedent* and the *consequent.* A node may be the antecedent/consequent of zero, one, or more other nodes.

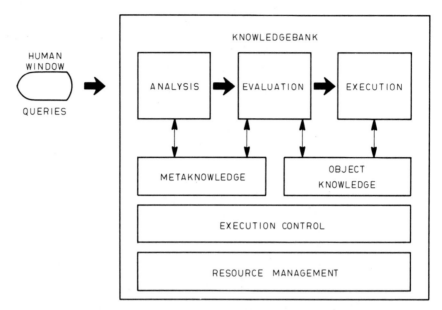

Figure 13-6. This diagram identifies the components of the knowledgebank. It also highlights the role of metaknowledge and object knowledge.

Connections between nodes are specified by experts based on their domain knowledge; that is what we call *free form.*

This example demonstrates why a hypercube architecture, such as the Connection Machine, is the proper one for the idea database. In Chapter 3 we spoke about a five-digit number of processors, one at each node and with nonaddressable, high-speed memory. This is precisely a hardware networking image. It corresponds, bit by bit, to the software search image defined in the preceding paragraph.

The implementation of new idea databases is based on episodes. The same is true of *memory-based reasoning* and the work done by David Walz and his colleagues at Brandeis University. While the two approaches are not precisely the same, they are very similar. They both contrast to the work done via similarity-based learning—that is, the generation of rules. They also differ from explanation-based and case-based reasoning, since they do not depend on having a strong domain model.

Key to memory-based reasoning is *recall from memory.* The theory is simple and appealing:

- Rather than being a preliminary to the generation of rules,
- the objects in storage should be the basis of reasoning.

The problem with memory-based reasoning is computational speed for parallel *idea search* (events, objects, entities, metafiles) in large databases. However, as stated on several occasions, new parallel fifth-generation architectures feature speeds at the GIPS level.

The process of memory based reasoning involves two phases:

Phase I consists of hypothesis formation.

The system selects, from a large database, past situations similar to the current situation that the user wishes to understand. It is important that the database be large.

Phase II examines the hypothesis suggested by the returned instance.

The support of each hypothesis is examined using *Bayesian* theory. On the Connection Machine, this is done at a rate 200 times faster than that of the largest available mainframe. A 10-gigabyte memory can be managed by fresh, complete comparison every minute.

The pivotal point of memory-based reasoning is its *search strategy.* Five approaches constitute the search strategy, each employed as the best fit. Written in increasing order of sophistication, these are Boolean queries, simple queries, relevance feedback, speed document search, and memory-based reasoning through idea search.

One of the important assets of memory-based reasoning is the *quality of the search.* The parameters measuring this quality are

- *precision,* the proportion of retrieved documents which are relevant,
- *recall,* the proportion of relevant documents in the *entire database* which are retrieved,
- *ease of use,* including how quickly a user can learn to employ the system, and
- *short response time,* a critical factor for interactive searching.

These goals must be achieved in a free-form structure. They have been reached on the hypercube implementation. But, as cannot be repeated too often, free structure means intelligent approaches to solutions and very powerful machines.

6. ENSURING AN INTELLIGENT QUERY FACILITY

It took two decades of computer usage, the development of the DBMS, and the increasing use of real-time data processing to obtain a reasonable query language. Honeywell's DM IV, based on Codasyl's IDS II DBMS, was one of the first products on the market. IBM's SQL came thereafter, and with it, the *select from where* discipline was established.

Valid as they may have been in their time, the query languages of the 1970s today seem archaic. Even the implementation of some expert system constructs for query purposes does not give valid results compared to idea databases and memory-based reasoning.

What we now tend to call first-generation AI systems base their explanations on a backtrace of the heuristic rules that were needed to find a solution. yet the path followed to reach the solution often differs from a convincing rational argument as to why the solution is valid. This is particularly so if a lot of heuristic knowledge was used in the reasoning process.

There have also been problems with knowledge acquisition which affect query response quality. Finding heuristic rules is not always easy. Experts typically take a long time to come up with solid suggestions about the methods and procedures they use. The rule set seems never complete; at times, it also shows inconsistencies across experts or even within the mind of the same expert.

By contrast, second-generation AI systems have access to a deeper understanding of the search space. They are capable of formulating a more convincing explanation which goes beyond the mere recall of which rules fired. As such, they constitute a major advance in AI technology. Second-generation AI constructs start to exhibit learning behavior in the sense that they are capable of acquiring new heuristic rules. This learning capability is extremely valuable in implementing intelligent queries.

Many tasks supportable by expert systems can be envisioned for an intelligent query implementation: search for documents, pattern matching, discovery of design failures, diagnosing faults or failures, monitoring, servicing, repairing, and so on. In all these example, the *conceptual query* is the cornerstone. For example:

"Find all pages, including the Concept I underlined," or

"Find reports that contain a table with a caption about sales."

The new theory treats *retrieval as inference* and assigns two types of attributes:

1. *Exact match:* keywords, data, author.
2. *Partial match:* text string, graphics, audio, image.

Partial march involves uncertainty in the retrieval process, and hence, plausible inference. We spoke of this when, in Table 13-2, we associated *vague queries* with either precise or vague contents in the database. Vague queries must be handled through a plausible inference; this framework applies to entire document searches.

Our tools must change because the nature of users' queries has changed. Fifteen years ago, queries were extremely simple, typically transaction oriented. Operating in realtime, the teller asked for the last deposit or for the balance in a client's account. Queries became more complex when messages and management information were added to the database (Figure 13-7).

Today queries, particularly management queries, are analytical. The user accesses many databases with diverse data structures (i.e., text structures). He wants answers from files which are not even remotely compatible. He does not want mere statistics; he is after comparison and critical tests. Furthermore, he is seeking a subsecond response time.

There are good reasons for uncertainty in querying. Recent research documents that with certainty, only very limited goals can be satisfied. *Partial match* attributes are based on the probability or possibility of a match. They can have preferred and acceptable attributes with different levels of importance: high, medium, low. One approach is to associate quantitative references with these qualitative levels and then compute the overall score for a document. The cornerstone of this methodology is *plausible inference.*

To summarize: Contrary to the so far dominant theory about certainty in queries and in database search—as well as the need for crisp information—new findings suggest that certainty is the wrong method. What we are really after is a *conceptual approach* which includes vagueness and imprecision but can lead to a very high performance capability. Retrieval should be made with

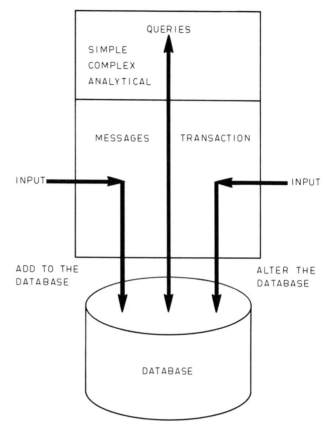

Figure 13-7. The database is typically enriched by both transactions and messages. Queries exploit the contents of the database and can be assisted by expert systems.

- greater semantic content,
- freedom in querying, and
- ad hoc, free-form approaches.

The advantages of this approach are an improvement in the quality of management information, resulting in better productivity and greater accuracy. Partial matching gives superior results. Text retrieval techniques were the first to be developed using plausible inference.

In any search, we must estimate how likely it is that the retrieval approach will achieve its goal. While, as stated, this introduces uncertainty in querying and retrieval, current research indicates that with certainty only very limited goals can be satisfied. The developing office document retrieval theory specifies the following properties for a query language in office environments:

1. *Incomplete specification of assertions.*

The query/retrieval system should use its knowledge of document structures, text/data types, and associated predicates to allow incompletely specified queries. An assertion such as

About <report, text>

is incomplete because the report can contain data, such as images or tables, for which this predicate is not valid.

The system should be able to translate this predicate into a valid query. It should include tools for application development and for integrating data, sound, and pictures, according to a standardized formal structure that guarantees document interchange between different systems. This is the goal of the office document architecture (ODA).[4]

2. *Flexible specification of assertions.*

This calls for predicates able to specify queries (such as *about*) and facilities for handling uncertainty, such as *range queries.* User-defined predicates are also appropriate. If the documents contain attributes with images, predicates such as *looks like* may be defined by a person doing searches on images.

Furthermore, flexible specifications must allow the interchanging of documents between systems of different vendors and between different devices in a system. This makes it necessary to define a standard way of describing the contents of the document.

In conclusion, the concept of idea databases has entered the implementation phase. AI techniques are used in interpreting queries. At the same time, the industry as a whole is very close to using natural langauge for queries with

- a minimum amount of structure or
- no structure at all.

Episodic memory is one of the solutions. Everything is in the global memory. Authorized multiple users, *interacting* with one another and with the knowledgebank, can employ an intelligent recall capability while maintaining version control. This cannot be done with the more conventional relational type DBMSs. It requires KBMSs and applications based on plausible inference. These are also helpful in specifying the distinction between databases and knowledgebanks.

---

[4] Developed by ISO, ODA is supported by a growing number of American and European companies. In *Esprit,* ODA has been selected and is being implemented in a number of projects. The office document architecture is discussed in Chapter 15, section 5.

14

Implementing Multimedia Databases

Keywords

engineering database • *real-world model* • *information elements* • *distributed database* • *multimedia database* • *media* • *data* • *fiber optics* • *knowledge representation techniques* • *object-oriented languages* • *global database* • *a priori* • *system-wide view* • *network bandwidth* • *database bandwidth* • *processing bandwidth* • *human windows* • *AI* • *temporal relationships* • *base technology* • *kernel technology* • *integration technology* • *kernel* • *object oriented* • *service-level integration* • *conceptual model* • *cognition* • *conceptual modeling* • *logical representation* • *symbol system* • *alphanumeric characters* • *figures* • *images* • *audio* • *operations* • *display* • *structured approach* • *procedural approach* • *whole text* • *office document architecture* • *declarative approach* • *logical structure* • *physical layout* • *specification of assertion* • *query specification* • *document compilation* • *WYSIWYG* • *workspace definition*

1. INTRODUCTION:

An *engineering database* is the *real-world model*. It is a properly designed and coordinated aggregate of *information elements* managed in a uniform way. This is typically done by means of

- The Database Administrator (DBA), and
- Database Management Systems (DBMS) residing in each machine.

The information elements contained in the database should be defined and designed in a coherent and comprehensive manner. *Comprehensive* means by both men and machines. They should be available for authorized access by users: men, WS, hosts, basic, and applications software. Accessibility must be assured through communications media.

An engineering database must be regularly calibrated and updated. It should be supported by services such as recovery, restart, and security. It should be possible to network many engineering databases together into a *distributed database* (DDB) whcih may span over a continent or even the world.

A new concept is *multimedia databases* (MDB). It can be explained in a two-tier manner. In a physical sense, multimedia databases are defined as traditional data plus a form of voice (audio, sound), image, icons, and vector graphics.

More importantly in a logical sense, multimedia databases are object oriented. They support data structures (essentially text structures) and integrate documents for storage, retrieval, presentation, and exchange. The logical and physical definitions integrate into the context of *media*. This defines the universe in which symbols are materialized, both physically and logically.

Figure 14-1 suggests a relation between functionality and connectivity for data, image, and voice. The focus of convergence is the physical layer, but the process is assisted by the outer physical layer. The latter also includes management responsibilities, as we will see when we talk about the DBMS.

The study of multimedia databases requires an architecture around whcih database management will be built. The architecture should also define interfaces to existing systems, including agile user interfaces (human windows).

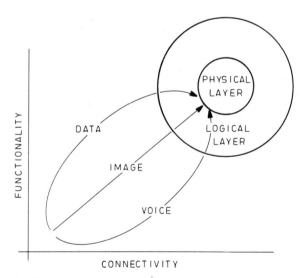

Figure 14-1. Multimedia solutions make sense if they operate online and are characterized by a high degree of functionality and connectivity. The bases of the system is not the physical layer but the outer logical layer, which reflects the results to be gained.

Object-oriented multimedia databases provide

1. a unified view of information elements in different media and
2. the ability to integrate their components into one multimedia conceptual model.

Relations among the kinds of objects being supported are defined through operators of the type IS-A, A-KIND-OF, or IS-PART-OF. Using the same command name, we can concatenate different types of operations.

Prior to discussing multimedia databases, it is necessary to explain what the term *media* means in the database context. Like *data, media* is a singular noun. The latin word *medium*[1] has been widely used in the field of communications to indicate communication means. However, the sense is not the same in database environments.

The term *multimedia database* was first used at the ninth Very Large Databases (VLDB) Conference, held in Florence in the late 1970s. Since 1985, the Japanese Ministry of International Trade (MITI) has earmarked a significant budget to develop multimedia DBMSs that include *fiber optics*—both discs and networks. Solutions will require *knowledge representation techniques* and *object-oriented languages*.

2. A MULTIMEDIA DATABASE ARCHITECTURE

Conceived as polyvalent, flexible structures, multimedia databases are open-ended and extensible. They feature a multimedia DBMS[2] and basically are managed through relational principles, but require both intentional and extensional database constructs, which we have already discussed.

Distributed and multimedia databases lead toward the concept of a *global database*. In its implementation, the global database is an aggregate of databases containing objects—and therefore both information elements and commands. All objects are encapsulated, callable entities and are pertinent to the global database structure.

- from the microfile level at the personal WS
- to the central text and database warehouse.

Therefore, global databases cannot be successfully implemented (if they can be implemented at all under current technology) without a strategic plan for end-user computing and for the management of central resources. The plan should be made beforehand not after we have been forced to develop a standard when we find that we cannot support or maintain the diverse sets of information elements throughout the organization.

The establishment of a system integration plan is just as important, since the way

---

[1] There is also the latin word *datum*. Both *datum* and *medium* have Greek origins—$\delta\varepsilon\delta o\mu\varepsilon\nu\alpha$, $\mu\varepsilon\sigma\alpha$, respectively. In Latin, the plural forms of *datum* and *media* are *data* and *media*. In information science usage, *data* and *media* are singular forms.
[2] Which is being projected but is not yet available.

computer systems communicate leads to integrated or nonintegrated approaches. There is nothing worse than a database system which

- is incomplete and inaccurate;
- features tools that are weak, hard to use, and have no common user interface;
- contains applications which are hard to develop and maintain.

The overall result is multiple incompatible systems that run stumblingly throughout many departments and many different functional areas. For a while, they are expensive and ineffective; eventually, they become a disaster.

This situation underlines the reasons for architectural implementation, which affect six types of resources:

1. The *systemwide* view, which in the past was applications oriented but today should be applications independent. At this level, the architectural concept serves as the integrator.
2. A *network bandwidth* permitting real-time transmission of multimedia information elements not only under normal conditions but also under peak workload, worst-case conditions.
3. A *database bandwidth* able to handle the large volume of bit streams necessary for future storage, ranging from vectorized raster images to other graphics, text, data, and voice. For a while, the terabytes will become the unit of measurement. Then this, too will become too small.
4. *Processing bandwidth.* The clocked nature of real-time voice, image, text, and data connections requires that the application be able to schedule itself, and hence use ample resources. GIPS will be necessary not only for processing but also to meet the timing requirements for servicing the ongoing connections.
5. *Human windows.* In Chapter 8 we defined this term and described its characteristics. The enormous amount of interactivity required by man–machine systems has many implications, including the transformations associated with the various input/output devices tuned to provide the highest granularity of information.
6. *AI constructs,* some acting deep knowledge engines focusing on a given domain; others operating as intelligent database managers; still others managing presentation elements, which consist of vectorized images, graphics, text, data, and voice information elements; and, finally, able to synchronize the channels with no loss of interactivity due to delay.

Another major requirement for the support of generic multimedia applications is a mechanism which permits an application to determine and transmit the *temporal relationships* between the information elements from different media. This affects the scheduling of the application. It also forces document architectures that wish to use multimedia systems to provide for this temporal information. The same can be said about multifunctionality, as shown in Figure 14-2.

We have said that multimedia information is traditional data plus information elements in

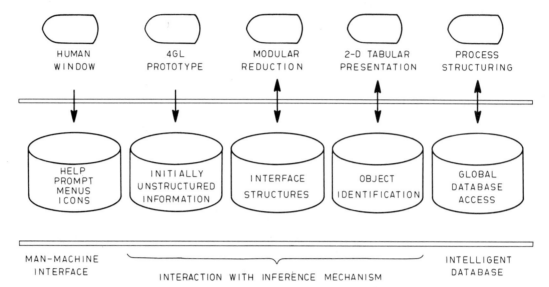

Figure 14-2. From man–machine interfaces to intelligent distributed databases, results are provided by the interaction with the inference mechanism.

the form of voice, images, icons, and vector graphics. The usage of multimedia information in computer systems is very recent. To a considerable extent, it focuses on document type applications.

Yet, the need for system architecture that includes multimedia applications is already evident. System definition includes database management that leads successfully to multimedia implementation. Modern engineering design work and managerial applications demand database systems able to incorporate multimedia information elements stored in diversified supports for information processing.

Multimedia data often include nonformatted and complex information elements such as text, figures, images, and voices. Hence, multimedia database systems should feature integration and management tools able to handle different types of information elements stored in various media:

- alphanumeric databases,
- figure and image databases,
- voice, sound, and audio databases, and so on.

Currently, there are very few database systems of this nature, mostly in preliminary and experimental stages. They are being promoted for a variety of fucntional reasons and technical facilities. Hence, we must prepare for them by developing suitable system architecture and system integration.

A DBMS able to manage text, data, figures, image, and voice, integrated into one aggregate to overcome heterogeneity, is beyond today's level of technology. Therefore, as we will see in the next section, several research projects currently focus on different

DBMSs—one per media. Research projects on multimedia DBMSs typically involve three layers:

1. *Base technologies* for text, data, graphs, image, and voice.
2. *Kernel technology* which is largely object oriented.
3. *Integration technology* with knowledge representation at the base.

A text DBMS, figure DBMS, image DBMS, and voice DBMS are the partial solutions. The *kernel* will be object oriented because object concepts are suitable for handling multimedia. The system architecture must ensure that system integration is achieved in a distributed sense. Without such support, we can neither organize nor manage even single-media databases.

Furthermore, our work in the multimedia domain should have insight. We must overcome the heterogeneity of media; this will not be done through brute force. One way to achieve the new environment is to follow the transition in logical constructs (operating system DBMS) which has taken place and learn from it. A complementary approach examines the physical media on which the coming multimedia databases will rest.

Since multimedia applications are meant to enhance communication, they must be able to adapt to the man–machine interfaces, databasing, processing, and networking environments in which they are embedded. The goal of their application is to maximize interactivity while maintaining critical temporal and operational constraints.

At the networking level, a substantial amount of effort is required in the area of physical integration. The primary motivation is to amortize the cabling plant costs of an organization over voice, video, and data services. The compromise effort is known as Integrated Services Digital Netowrk (ISDN). It is too narrow a bandwidth, and it has no place in a multimedia system.

The solution at the processing level is fifth-generation computers. They are designed as inference engines and have one to several orders of magnitude greater ower than von Neumann-type machines. This power is measured in

- LIPS, logical instructions per second (typically, KLIPS),
- FLOPS, floating point operations per second (mostly KFLOPS or MFLOPS), or
- MIPS, millions of instructions per second (and, more recently, GIPS).

Databasing is increasingly dependent on optical media. We will talk about suggested approaches in the following section. The fudnamental aspects of man–machine interfaces were discussed in Chapter 8.

3. VOICE-LEVEL INTEGRATION

The solutions to be developed for the implementation of multimedia databases, and the architecture to be chosen, should support *service-level integration*. Typically, this is a logical layer resting largely on AI capabilities. Media that are only physically connected merely provide an illusion of the appropriate characteristics.

To achieve *system-level integration,* the architecture should ensure a standard way of looking at interactive, real time applications. Its acceptance will depend upon its ability to describe the applications in general while providing enough of the basic structure necessary to assist implementers in their efforts.

We have spoken about the three levels of reference: the base, kernel, and integration technology. Each level focuses on the database as the model of the real world and an aggregate of information elements. In database design, the real world will first be translated into a *conceptual model.* This is typically done in two steps:

- *Cognition,* realized by the acceptor(s), followed by
- *Conceptual modeling,* the perception of the real world.

The conceptual model represents how the database designer recognizes the data structure of the real world. As we know from experience with classical database design and administration, this will be translated into another form: the *logical representation.* To represent the real world as a conceptual model, we must describe our perception through a *symbol system:*

1. *Alphanumeric characters* are an example, but they are not the only one.

Alphanumeric characters are generally the predominant type of information element used in an office environment. But other data types, such as pictures, images, charts, and sound, are also needed to enhance the presentation. Frequently used forms often contain text, figures, and data. Hence, the following distinctions are necessary.

2. Another symbol system is *figures,* including graphs, line drawings, and plane and solid figures.

Still other symbol systems frequently encountered in our thinking are

3. *Images,* including paintings, carvings, photographs, films, and video images—but also vectorized raster images (as discussed in Chapter 15).
4. *Audio,* such as voice and other sounds.

Voice-level integration is one of the technologies under development. It includes encoded speech, voice storage and retrieval, voice recognition, speech synthesis, and language translation, as we will see by the end of this section.

5. A *combination* of these media.

The congitive problem centers on how to recognize the real world. The problem of the logical representation follows, leading to model construction. The higher layer addresses itself to integration. At the level of the cognition process, the knowledge and intelligence of the accepter may vary. This is as true of voice as of other symbol systems. Hence, conceptual models constructed for cognition purposes may differ. Only in terms of digitization will they look the same:

For multimedia systems, we require general-purpose, enduser-oriented document managers, but also able solutions to cognitive problems of presentation and manipulation.

Needed contributions include enabling modalities such as voice annotation of graphics and text:

- speech command augmentation of menu selection by a mouse,
- touch and speech command in a put-that-there mode, and
- hypertext, nonsequential document handling (see the next section).

Solutions must be both user friendly and cost effective. If a page consists only of text and data, it can be stored as ASCII data in a file. If it also contains other types of data, then we have two options:

1. Store the entire page as an image.

In this case it is necessary to store even the text as image data, which has enormous storage requirements.

2. Identify this page as consisting of a set of primitives, some of which may be text and the rest of other data types.

If solution 2 is chosen, certain pictures or logos may be used on more than one page. Hence we should develop a way of organizing and integrating these primitives into a page.

We also need a method of link together various pages corresponding to a document. Documents of any type have to be stored and retrieved in an organized manner. All this points to the need for a multimedia document management solution.

In considering the evolution of databases, we often forget that the breadth of information which can be stored in a computer has increased tremendously because of advances in digital representation of real-world objects. In the past, an object, such as a map or voice recording, could not be stored in a computer database because of the inadequacy of computer input, storage hardware/software, and output. Today it can not only be stored but also altered, merged, sorted, and transmitted over networks.

This is a logical extension of three major advances: CAD, word processing leading to document handling, and new support media (including associated technologies), such as optical discs and digital recording.

Since optical discs are still an emerging technology, we have to choose a system that is likely to be stable over a long period of time. We also have to provide for integration of optical discs into our operations—a difficult task because of the lack of standards. As stated earlier, physical integration alone does not guarantee the success of an optical disc used as file server. It is also necessary to make the write-once feature transparent to the user. Such problems can be approached, studied, and solved. But first, we need to focus on them.

Human speech can be stored in many different formats, the selection depending on the required quality of the reconstructed audio signal. Encoded speech with higher intelligibility requires higher data-encoding rates and therefore greater memory storage requirements. The types of speech coding are

- source modeling (Vocoder),
- parametric methods, and
- waveform coding.

Encoding rates vary from 2,400 bits per second (BPS) of speech for linear predictive coding to 64,000 BPS for pulse code modulation. At these rates, 18,000 to 480,000 bytes of storage would be required for a one-minute voice note unless compression techniques are applied.

Information can be stored as normal text information and speech synthesized by using text-to-speech hardware and software. The speech produced is not high in quality, but the amount of storage needed for each second of speech is very low. An advantage of using speech synthesis for audio output from a computer is that the content of spoken text messages can be easily searched. By contrast, searching recorded audio messages for word patterns is not easy.

Voice recognition is the process of recognizing patterns within the digitized speech signal and consists of two parts:

- speech recognition and
- speech understanding.

Speech recognition searches for patterns in the incoming speech which match those of stored templates. It can be divided into speaker-dependent/speaker-independent and isolated-word/connected-word systems. Speaker-dependent approaches identify spoken words only from a single speaker, having been trained to recognize his words. Speaker-independent systems identify selected words spoken by any speaker.

Isolated-word systems require a discrete pause between spoken words; connected-word systems do not. Speech understanding attempts to improve the accuracy of speech recognition by using information on the context of the spoken passage.

From voice mail to real-time language translation, the importance of speech handling is rapidly increasing. It is an integral part of multimedia applications as well as of service-level integration. Like image, voice is a vital component of compound electronic document implementation. Furthermore, the design of multimedia document-handling systems is steadily evolving.

At the service level of implementation, we need to support new media, such as input/output devices with functions such as speech recognition, speech synthesis, polyvalent presentation, and graphics. One of the basic requirements is a framework of classes to represent captured objects at the user's request, giving the user the ability to add messages.

The system must also provide build-in abstraction for requests and message presentation, as well as appropriate multimedia message protocol(s). Figure 14-3 follows the path from presentation of the request to spatial and linear representations of information elements. From the presentation level to storage management, the system ensures that the storage devices show where an information element is at the time of a request.

The logical form provides an approach to multimedia integration. This is executed largely through AI constructs. When we talk about handling multimedia information, our aim is not just to store the real-world object and allow the user to make changes to it. Our primary goal is to understand the function of this object and use the computer system to execute this function effectively.

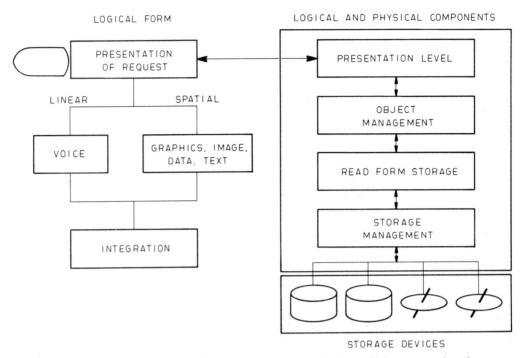

Figure 14-3. Any integrative approach is characterized by a logical form which uses a number of physical and logical components, including an array of storage devices, both magnetic and optical.

4. HYPERTEXT RESEARCH AND TEXT UNDERSTANDING

Hypertext is an approach to information management in which data is stored in a network of nodes connected by links. Such nodes can contain multimedia: classical data, text, image, graphics, audio, video, source code, or other forms. They are meant to be viewed and manipulated interactively.

Hypertext solutions involve issues, systems, and applications. Among the issues are cognitive aspects of using and designing hypertext systems, supporting collaborative work, management of complexity in large information networks, and strategies for effective use of hypertext—as well as legal issues: copyrights, royalties, and social implications of various solutions.

Hypertext systems focus on database constructs, virtual memory, abstract machines, intelligent database engines, database management, and multimedia support. Solutions may feature distributed systems, include querying and searching, imply uncertainty in searching, and promote agile user interfaces. Hypertext applications include

- CAD
- technical documentation,
- electronic publishing,
- electronic encyclopedias,
- the authoring of books and articles,
- medical and legal information,
- interaction tools for education,
- scholars' workbenches,
- information analysis, and
- knowledge acquisition.

The preparation and submission of reports is an example of how hypertext is implemented. A report consists of information elements, operations, and display elements:

- *Information elements* may be of single media or multimedia.
- *Operations* are of the type sort, merge, group, insert, or delete; they may also be more sophisticated.
- *Display elements* have a characteristic title, heading(s), format, columns, and rows.

Operations can take place both before and after displays. Sophisticated operations executed in a multimedia environment make advisable the use of AI constructs. "Before" and "after" displays are important references, as many users don't know in advance what information they want until they see it.

Classical report writers provide for format control, a report heading, a page heading, column titles, subheads, content lines, subfooting, recap lines, page footing, and report footing. Speech, image, and gesture dynamics go beyond this and require a top-level command language.

Every placement and movement of an item on a video form has consequences in the multimedia database. The immediate interface is the area where these resources are managed by direct manipulation through natural combinations of, for example, voice, image, text, and probably gesture. Different approaches elaborated for report generation have in common one or more of the following:

- a command file,
- structured English,
- form specification,
- expert system assistance, and
- interactive multimedia.

More sophisticated solutions address the issue of text understanding. This involves natural language parsing and structural models reflecting both theoretical and empirical conditions.

Figure 14-4 shows the basic organization of a text analysis system followed by a current project. The knowledge sources are the

1. cultural layer,
2. constituent structure (hierarchical),

3. factual knowledge,
4. rule knowledge, and
5. semantic structure.

It has recently been established that the cultural layer is very important in expert test manipulation. This is true of systems ranging from language translation to test understanding by computers.

The constituent structure is an empty shell. Factual and rule knowledge are embedded in intermediate layers. Knowledge information is provided by the semantic structure.

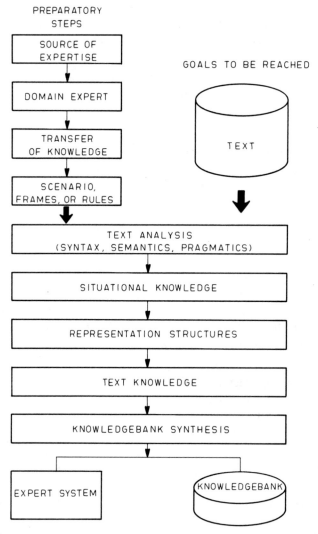

Figure 14-4. This diagram comes from a project on the automation of text handling through the use of expert systems. It identifies the necessary sequential steps, as well as their nature.

Two approaches are typically followed in research on text understanding:

- structured and
- procedural.

The *structured* approach focuses on syntax, semantics, and pragmatics. Followers of this approach usually choose a serial solution, which is clearly delineated under central control. The *procedural* approach centers on a thematic progression pattern that exploits text coherence phenomena. This method tends to parallel the distributed control structure.

Research on text understanding is becoming relevant to expert system designers, since the automatic synthesis of knowledgebanks through text analysis directly attacks the knowledge acquisition bottleneck. However, such research is still in its infancy. Analysis of the requirements of text understanding shapes a theory in terms of cooperating, lexically distributed processes.

Text understanding requires a system architecture that supports parallel interactions among the knowledge sources. Corresponding grammar specifications have to meet

- elaborated communication requirements of the distributed organization of linguistic knowledge in terms of word experts and
- text structure requirements based on appropriately tuned text grammars, leading to automatic acquisition of knowledge through text analysis.

Although practical results are not expected prior to the mid-1990s, text analysis looks promising. It is one of the major components of multimedia database implementation. It can also be seen as a more sophisticated layer over current breakthroughs in document-handling technology, as well as language translation.

Commonsense knowledge has also been used to reduce ambiguity in prepositional phrase modifiers. This method is employed in preference to strategies which appeal to the meaning of the preposition. It is combined with information about verbs and nouns drawn from

- the text under study, and
- generic databases.

This approach aims to establish which syntactic structures generated by a semantically naive parser are plausible in a common sense.

One of the problems with text-understanding systems is that synatactic rules alone produce numerous ambiguities, many of which are not semantically possible or likely interpretations. At the same time, some syntactic ambiguities correspond to possible semantic ambiguities. A commonsense disambiguation method assigns constituency for prepositional phrases according to commonsense preference. The only ambiguities which remain are those that are semantically plausible.

Another research field connected to modern text-handling solutions is user interfacing for text proofreading, using AI approaches. One project focuses on structure and other high-level primitives, examining text as a sequence of characters and attempting to develop flexible text management capabilities.

Current solutions stress morphological, syntactic, and semantic procedural approaches. What is missing is tools for the retrieval and manipulation of sentences and paragraphs—

including a conceptual text model containing as much information as possible. The proof-reading knowledgebank can contain integrity constraints.

One project focuses on keywords in context, permitting users to extract and order objects. Organization is layered in the form

- whole text,
- paragraphs,
- sentences,
- segments, and
- words,

with *whole text* being the topmost layer. Predicates are associated with each level, helping to structure an approach which avails itself of text formatting.

Another project centers on a sequence of images. In a logical representation, components such as words and paragraphs are stored as paradigms, creating a document-handling structure. We will return to this issue in the following section.

Figure 14-5 integrates the various approaches referred to *as if* they were parts of a global project on text understanding. It is important to keep in mind the difference between text and common data handling.

Common data handling in classical databases does not have a natural structure. Text has characters, words, lines, sentences, paragraphs, section headings, chapters, and relational schemas. Formatting can be made more orderly; that is the purpose of the office document architecture developed by the International Standards Organization (ISO).

5. OFFICE DOCUMENT ARCHITECTURE

Office document architecture involves both office document models and the concept of *uncertainty in retrieval.* Uncertainty is related to the query rather than to the document base itself. As established by ISO office document architecture, documents have

1. types
2. logical layout, and
3. structures.

The OSI reference model is supported in many projects and has made possible the *laboratory* demonstration of interfaces, bridges, and gateways linking devices from different manufacturers. Office document architecture is a multimedia document interchange standard.

The term *document* refers to the user-created information flowing through and between offices. Documents include messages and other kinds of information not necessarily thought of as documents in the past. The solutions we are after should cover all document-related activities. Increasingly, such solutions include AI concepts. In engineering and business environments, system studies should focus on document interchange between separate office systems connected through a network.

Type/layout/structure definitions are constrained by standards. These include standards

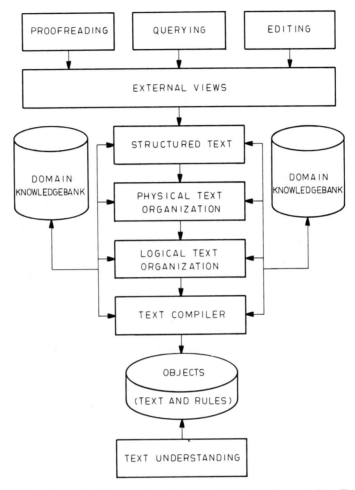

Figure 14-5. Another text handling example particularly oriented to querying and editing. The ultimate goal of this research project is text understanding.

describing the range of document structures permitted by the standard; the relationships between logical and layout views of a document; and means for ensuring that the standard is enforced.

Emphasis is placed on a *declarative* approach. The office document architecture calls for

1. *logical structure,* that is, manuscript content;
2. *physical layout structure*—how a document is organized into pages, and so on; and
3. *the relation between logical and physical structures.*

The information flow resulting from document exchange is handled through a network. Whether dealing with voice, image, text, or data, a network involves a combination of interconnected terminals, processes, and users. This includes the equipment, software, and human activity aimed at moving information between points where it may be

- generated,
- processed,
- stored/retrieved, and
- employed.

This makes the network a collection of services. Such services are useful in creating, revising, distributing, filing, and generally handling documents. Since any organization has dissimilar office systems, the system architecture should ensure that they communicate easily with one another in a universally comprehensive manner. This is the function of the office document architecture.

As Section 6 demonstrates, the devices attached at the ends of the network are equally important. They have to be polyvalent, multifunctional WSs, supporting network ports but also uniform formatting and presentation services (Figure 14-6). The system architecture should help us define compatible devices.

A network interconnecting office systems can bring great gains in productivity. We definitely need a uniform structure for information that is interchanged between offices. Such a structure must be able to

- convey any document, regardless of its content,
- from one office system to another,

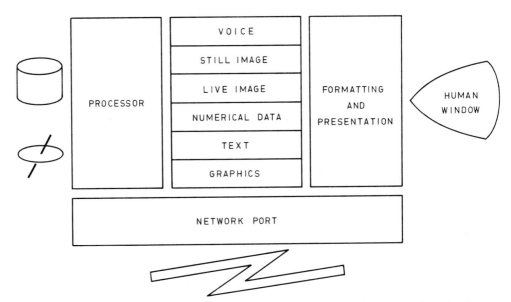

Figure 14-6. A multifunctional WS requires expert systems able to manipulate the layers of functional reference shown in this figure. A key to successful implementation is homogeneous formatting and presentation throughout the company.

As well as communicate the intent of its creator or sender as to how it should be processed. Therefore, the architecture must also be flexible, interfacing to diverse resources, and extendible to accommodate new requirements.

Rules must also be established to ensure that different office systems interpret documents uniformly and act upon them in a comprehensive manner. Formats must be defined that are compatible among dissimilar office systems, thus giving all attached office systems an identical understanding of the data streams originating, received, or exchanged.

In parallel with this effort, the now developing office document retrieval theory should be used to specify the properties of the query language in office environments. Three points must characterize this language:

1. *Incomplete specification of assertions:* about Report, Text
2. *Flexible specification assertions*: range of queries; look-alike solution.
3. *Relating assertions about different views of documents,* calling for manipulation language associated with multimedia models.

In all cases, *query specification* must ensure an able interface for the specification of query predicates and associated uncertainty. *Uncertainty is a very important part of retrieval.*[3]

Able approaches to document retrieval are related to *document compilation.* Compilation is a multistage process that consists essentially of a translation of the form

$$\text{Lexical} \rightarrow \text{Syntactics} \rightarrow \text{Semantics} \rightarrow \text{Pragmatics}$$

Important is the definition of necessary operations between logical and physical structure—the levels at which the office document architecture addresses itself.

A further key aspect is interactive form development. It rests on the bases of document design:

- databases,
- messages,
- queries, and
- transactions.

Interactive screen design can be done from fields and/or from text. For instance, transaction logic design requires data source access, editing, validation, formatting, prompts, default values, browsing, and chained lookup.

These characteristics identify a new domain of research that assumes availability of a basic technological infrastructure. The latter should provide a well-defined interface to the applications domain. The application domain per se is characterized by a wealth of problems that can be solved economically and effectively only if they are explored in the context of an architecture rather than piecemeal.

In this new field of research, few solutions are available. One of the better ones is *what you see is what you get (WYSIWYG).* It requires invertible transformation including the

---

[3] See also the discussion of the mathematics of uncertainty in Chapter 10.

relation between logical and physical parts. This is often obscured by classical algorithmic descriptions, and by some algorithmic approaches that are neither linear nor interactive.

Among the problems with WYSIWYG implementation are:

- demand evaluation,
- the WYSIWYG range within a document,
- use of bidirectional semantic pointers for updates, and
- links from the referencee to the referenced part and vice versa.

The data-driven evaluation of the demand for documents must be invisible on the screen. User requirements must be met in a parametric manner, as most will be ad hoc. This is particularly true of the WYSIWYG requirements of design engineers and managers.

The main challenge is to develop heuristic approaches and a generic architecture for applied information systems. Global user requirements must be integrated as those regarding flexibility, performance, continuity, security, transparency, renovability, extendibility, and low cost, as well as ways of overcoming heterogeneity. In this context, the knowledge engineer and the information engineer should specify user organizations' information management requirements in terms of largely predefined

1. models of behavior,
2. architectures and functional tools, and
3. properly structured inference engines and knowledgebanks.

A document-oriented knowledge system handles knowledge in an integrated manner, using a global representation. However, each piece of information can be handled independently, as message systems may request. Message systems typically deal with fragments of information into which messages may be separated. The context and location of each fragment are important. The whole purpose of the message is communication and integration into the distributed multimedia database.

6. WORKSPACE DEFINITION AND THE ENDUSER

Distributed multimedia databases are now being implemented for the enduser. It is precisely for the enduser that we develop system architectures, plan for voice-level integration, focus on text understanding, and adopt an office document architecture. The success or failure of these endeavors will be judged by the answer to one question: *How much did we help the enduser in his work?*

The enduser works at *his* WS, into which is mapped *his* workspace. Thus we need a *workspace definition*. The workspace contains

- problem definition, and
- status.

Knowledgebanks, the global database, and communications provide

- domain knowledge,
- concurrency of access,

- distributed operations,
- security, and
- reliability.

The inference engine of a WS

- has deep knowledge and
- ensures elimination of inconsistency in information.

This summarizes what we have spoken about in Chapter 13 and in the first five sections of this chapter.

There are few solutions to the problem of able workplace support, even though WSs have been available for about ten years. However, important hardware and software products, now under development, will be available in the 1990s.

The whole culture of WS implementation is changing. Up to now, enduser functions depended on centralized data processing for support. As a result, costs were high and innovation was deemphasized. Emphasis is now being placed on fostering innovation, developing new architectural concepts, and implementing natural languages through AI at the WS level.

To foster innovation, our goal should be to develop a computer environment that will be suitable through the year 2000. Current projects assume that both the system architecture and the operating system will have interactive, realtime characterisitics to facilitate multiple communication or to implement the solution. An example is efficient document creation and editing connected to interactive graphics. At MIT, Project Athena includes an architecture of eight layers, which are as follows from top to bottom:

8. pictures/images
7. drawings
6. properties of materials
5. structural drawings
4. construction codes
3. financial analysis
2. planning and evaluation (PERT) chart
1. geotechnical data

Most exciting architectures are relatively weak in support of these functional areas. A new architectural solution has to be developed to incorporate them and allow advanced design features for the future. Part of this architectural solution is optical disc technology that stores pictures and images, thus serving the higher layer.

In Project Athena, the architecture under development supports secure direct access from all dedicated processors, enabling them to efficiently store, retrieve, and manipulate documents in their own storage media (optical, magnetic) and in networked database servers. Hence, currently available architectural functions have to be greatly extended and enhanced.

At the same time, *natural language implementation through AI* is a top-priority software project—including language translation. Project Athena focuses on the ability to sustain a discourse in multiple languages. Other functions include

- reading foreign newspapers;
- videotext-based, three-dimensional presentations—for instance, navigating in finding an apartment; and
- analysis of voice spectrograms.

Some of the WS-based natural language subsystems are currently being pilot tested. *The system goal is coherence,* that is, accommodating heterogenous hardware but using

- One operating system.

Different operating system options have been examined; 4.2 BSD has been chosen because it has valid functions.

- One DBMS.

Ingres has been adopted for implementation.

- Standard network protocols.

TCP/IP is the current choice. At the time of this writing, there has been no decision on LU 6.2, DIA/DCA, X.400, and ISO/OSI migration. However, Ingresnet is used for remote database access, helping to implement immediately a distributed database environment.

- A small set of languages.

C, Lisp, and Fortran have been retained as fourth-generation languages, supported by those in the Ingres constellation: Quel, Equel, Vifred, RW, and ABF.

- Standardized data representations: graphics, equations, vector fields.

Project Athena has adopted GKS as the two-dimensional standard. No three-dimensional standard has been chosen.

Because of its multifunctional interests, Project Athena provides a comprehensive picture of the future support services necessary for WS implementation. The documentation of the choices being made is valid and can serve as a frame of reference.

In terms of the philosophy of implementation, compound electronic documents and electronic publishing are the keys to user orientation. Currently available compound electronic document routines can create text, tables, maps, bar and pie charts, and other graphics illustrations. They are then transmitted electronically to similar WSs at remote sites.

In terms of software development, the most recent high-technology issues are

- application generators and
- computer-aided software engineering (CASE).

Like CAD, CASE is an ambiguous term. In its narrower sense, it usually refers to graphic aids for program design, as opposed to the older programming/coding tools. In its broader sense, it refers to tools which take graphics-based designs and provide finished programs. This is a technology under development.

The goal is to incorporate expert system capabilities in CASE. Rule-based programming is potentially the greatest advance since the change from batch to online processing. Figure

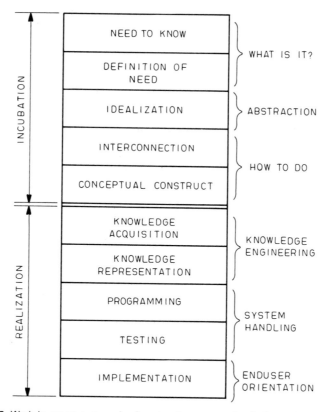

Figure 14-7. Work in expert systems involves two large areas: incubation and realization. Each consists of successive layers, which are identified in this figure.

14-7 outlines 10 production-oriented layers, but it must be emphasized that tools are necessary but not enough. Successful implementation involves a combination of foresight, training, momentum, product quality, and direction.

Application generators, also known as *application development systems,* generate complete sets of programs without procedural code. They are oriented to fourth-generation languages and are usually associated with relational DBMSs.

- Program code generators,
- report program generators,
- query languages, and
- screen design programs

may be part of a system or may be free-standing application generators. They are all software productivity aids.

The major objective of application generators is to increase the productivity of professional programmers and endusers. Basic requirements of application generators are to

- have a short learning curve,
- interface with the current systems and files,
- support both batch and online environments, and
- provide adequate documentation.

Like all complex software, application generators must be selected systematically, matching the tools to specific application needs. *Prototyping*[4] of applications is one of the more important uses of generators. Prototypes may be

- sample screens,
- functional models, or
- evolutionary systems.

Other features of application generators include fast and ready implementation, ease of maintenance, ability to impose standards, and an integrated development process that is transparent to the complex systems environment.

When the proper implementation perspective is maintained, application generators are useful in specific areas. There are also areas in which they are less effective. They are superior for enduser programming of systems that are more complex than spreadsheets. They are inferior for production applications with complex file interactions.

Fourth-generation programming tools are popular with endusers because they require no support from professional programmers and relatively little training. They also produce end products with few errors, and are self-documenting and easy to modify.

Application generators sacrifice operating efficiency for general usefulness. Endusers do not care if the computer efficiency is high. They simply want the online systems benefits and the ability to prototype and modify at will. Finally, at this moment, they need the service.

---

[4] See also Chapter 4.

15

Computer Aided Design¹ Enriched by AI

Keywords

> *uncertainty in retrieval • raster scanning • optical recognition • interpretation • CAD geometry • data capture • parametric design • COM • micrographics • WORM • threshold • mean value • gradient • noise • white threshold • black threshold • data examination • data modification • segmentation • teaching mode • post processing • editing • multimedia • paragraph • figure • model • search facility • indexing • video frames • semantic knowledge bank • web of links • image processing • document images • committing • concurrent access • laser disc • image manager • laser printer • workflow software*

1. INTRODUCTION

Classical computer-aided design (CAD) solutions are enriched through AI to support the processing of documents during product development, manufacturing, sales, and maintenance in the field. CAD/AI presupposes that existing documents are in a digital form. This is true of technical drawings, product specifications, contractual clauses, and maintenance directives, as well as other types of information.

The contribution of AI starts very early in the CAD process to enable fast digital

---

¹ The term *computer-aided design* is used in the sense of computer-aided *engineering*—not drafting. Since it is an established term, there is no reason to change it every few years.

conversion and computerized storage of a large amount of graphics, drawings, images, and art for immediate retrieval in the design process. It also permits

- easy interactive graphic update and design work to be performed on a WS,
- the merging of graphics and text into structured documents, and
- verification and production of documents on multimedia.*

An engineering WS enriched through AI is shown in Figure 15-1. The workspace contains the problem description and status. The knowledgebank and communications provide for domain knowledge, concurrency of access, distributed operations, security, and reliability. The inference engine of a workspace

- has deep knowledge and
- ensures resolution of the inconsistency of design information.

For engineering workplaces and also for WSs of any type, during the next five years the overriding issue will not be the operating system, which more or less settles on Unix, but

1. interactive screens and graphics, and
2. querying, reports, and analysis.

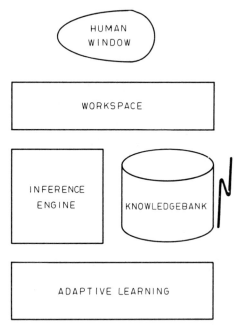

Figure 15-1. A WS enriched through expert systems is composed of the workspace (domain) to which it is applied, the knowledge bank, the communications discipline, and the inference engine. The human window is an integral part of it. Eventually the same will be true of an adaptive learning module.

---

* See Chapter 14.

The software of these two fields is the focus on new investments. Such software will become increasingly rich in AI constructs.

In terms of interactive screens, the need is technical and involves human interfaces, menu generators, graphic writers and other graphics tools, forms managers, screens builders, and screen manipulators. The basic requirement for querying and analysis is organizational, though technical aspects are important in two ways:

- the provision of the proper equipment (AI constructs, software and hardware solutions);
- the mathematical infrastructure necessary for design puroses, as well as for document retrieval.

As we will see in Chapter 17, the latter rests on expert systems implementation. The evolving office document architecture focuses not only on office document models but also on the concept of *uncertainty in retrieval*. As explained in Chapter 10, uncertainty is related to the query rather than to the document base itself.

The new era of CAD promises to be quite different from the one we now know. It will feature multiple representations of software architecture for comprehension and completeness; support an automated verification and testing environment; ensure control of work flow; look after heuristic and algorithmic efficiency; guarantee global and local variable usage; and provide for interfaces as well as for good administrative procedures.

One of the disadvantages of current CAD is the lack of reliable means of determining internal consistency except by personal inspection. There is no valid support for automatic analysis in establishing formal evaluation criteria based on test requirements and simulation. As a result, extensive reviews have been necessary to ensure completeness and consistency—but without the benefit of user input. Such reviews have been typically done in plain English, but the use of English for specification and control is ambiguous, subject to varying interpretations.

In an automated system such as CAD, plain English needs to be supplemented with additional representation. AI constructs provide it by transcribing English requirements into a formal representation. Automated verification can be done at this level. An embedded expert system will allow traceability.

Other AI constructs will make feasible multiple representations of the requirements for comprehension and completeness—for instance, a Petri net-type control flow graph for machine representations. This approach permits the development of multiple specifications. It also provides tools for ensuring consistency, compatibility, and completeness, thus making possible an open-ended system architecture.

2. SOLUTIONS TO THE INPUT PROBLEM IN A CAD ENVIRONMENT

Two serious problems have affected classical CAD and have impeded implementation. One is the incompatibility of CAD solutions offered by different vendors, underlying the importance of an open system architecture. The other is the input into CAD of several hundred thousands engineering designs that are still active in major manufacturing organizations.

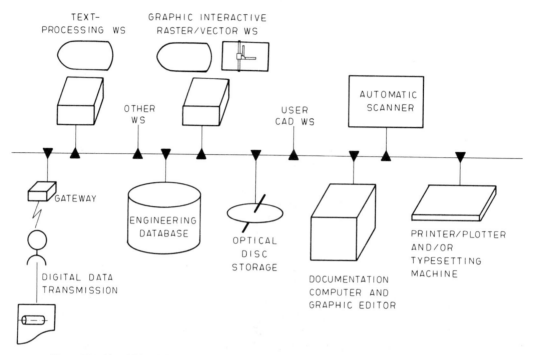

Figure 15-2. Many WSs will be attached to a network whose kernel includes the engineering database (optical disc storage being an integral part of it), gateway(s), automatic scanner, printer/plotter, and other components, as shown in this figure.

Other documents must be brought into CAD and can benefit from automated solutions, but the input of old drawings is the greatest challenge. Until this problem is solved, and in a fully automatic manner, a dichotomy is bound to exist within engineering:

- half CAD,
- half manual.[2]

The result is half-baked approaches. The interest in establishing and applying automatic input methods is thus evident. Figure 15-2 presents a system overview. Let's see how it works.

In terms of input, the basic principle is the *raster;* scanning, storage, and editing are the output. At the scanner, originals are automatically translated into pixels. Graphic information is raster compressed in the engineering database and made available for instantaneous retrieval.

Graphic information is updated in raster form on the WS. When desired, it can be output on raster plotting media. New technology permits us to avoid the time-consuming, quality-reducing conversion of scanned data into line art and vectors, shading and symbols.

---

[2] Even computer-run operations, which are not online, interactively managed through multifunctional design WSs are largely *manual.*

There is no reason for manual and photographic cleaning, rescaling, or merging of text and graphics. The mass storage of paper copies can be slowly weeded out. The transfer of documents can be simplified and the quality improved. These results can be obtained through intelligent machines.

A full conversion process is typically divided into phases. *Scanning the drawing* is the first phase. It converts the physical drawing into an electronic raster (pixel) image that is reviewed at a scan WS. Next the in *optical recognition and interpretation* phase, handwritten or standard CAD-generated dimensions are read automatically from a scanned engineering drawing. The process recognizes normal, dashed, toleranced, and limit characteristics.

A dimension is recognized, interpreted, and verified. It is then automatically entered into the engineering database. The *creation of CAD geometry* is the next phase of the drawing conversion and checking process. It occurs at either a conversion or a scanning WS.

Guided by the system, the user then *indicates regions of the drawing to be defined as views:* traces over scan data representing geometric elements such as lines, arcs, circles, ellipses, and splines; and indicates which geometric elements are attached to the previously recognized dimension text.

In the following phase, the operator *indicates the elements to be dimensioned,* adding notational information to the drawing. Subsequently, a geometry management system *creates a precise, complete design description* from the previously entered data.

- Rectification functions derive the size and location of the geometry from the dimensions,
- pointing out inaccuracies or inconsistencies to the user and
- regenerating the part to the corrected specifications.

Dimensions are stored with precision.[3] All necessary calculations are performed by the system.

The last phase consists of *drawing output.* The contents of the engineering database may be output to a plotter, optical disc, magnetic disc, or magnetic tape or transmitted over the network.

AI, automatic scanning, and variational geometry must be brought together to develop these geometry management processes. This is considered to be the kernel of the next generation of CAD systems.

After examining the technologies, the structure of the industry, its products, typical current applications, and likely future developments, it can be said that intelligent CAD systems (and image management) will affect virtually every major industrial organization. Managing

- the externally acquired information,
- the internally generated information which is already in technical archives, and
- the newly generated technical information

is vital to maintaining the organization's competitive position.

---

[3] Some systems support 15 or more significant digits.

As the preceding description of the conversion process shows, the principle is simple. Once a technical document is placed in a storage device, it becomes an electronic image. The management of this resource can be automated. This includes editing, combining, enlarging, reducing, inserting, storing, displaying, transporting, and reproducing it in other documents or forms.

AI constructs and parametric design approaches also help to customize software to specific users' needs and applications, but the most important contribution is *raster data capture*. The first experiences suggest that this is the simplest level of scanning and digitizing drawings for storage and retrieval purposes. It is also the lowest level.

For the time being, raster data capture is limited to pictorial displays. But newer approaches are able to do away with part of this limitation. Assisted by AI, the raster-stored drawing will soon be able to be transferred directly to a conversion system when required for CAD use. This approach permits low-cost drawing storage and conversion to a CAD-usable format when required.

The overall activity of rule-based systems can be thought of as a series of repetitions of a recognize–act format. This represents the control scheme of a system and is managed by an interpreter. Data examination consists of comparing antecedent patterns with recent elements in working memory. Antecedent patterns may be

- simple strings,
- complex graphs, or
- code which can inspect working memory elements.

AI software directs the process of deciding what subset of rules and data elements should be considered. The cycle consists of comparing, matching, scheduling, and executing. Matching consists of searching selected rules and comparing their antecendent patterns against selected data. While this might be done through classical software, it is a very time-consuming process. Heuristic selection can improve overall efficiency and lead to knowledgebank organization.

The scheduling mechanism decides which rules with matched antecedents should be fired in the current cycle. It accounts for redundancy, ambiguity, or error in data and for incomplete or erroneous rule antecedents. The scheduling mechanism itself may be implicit or may be explicitly implemented as a set of metarules. All of this is important because, in the automatic input of engineering designs, the hard part is finding the relevant features and combinations of features.

At the engineering WS level, the queries posed by the designer are subject to analysis, evaluation, and execution (Figure 15-3). Both metaknowledge and object knowledge are used. A similar process is applicable at the stage of automatic document capture, with queries posed and answers given by the system itself.

The conversion expert system can create accurate, checked engineering database designs from paper and from microfilm drawings. It provides CAD representations which may even be more accurate than the original drawings. Many originals contain errors or ambiguities due to engineering changes and incomplete or inaccurate data. These will be flashed out by the system. Thus drawings can be readily verified and transferred to CAD.

Errors are often left in an engineering design because of inadequate checking. The checking of designs made on paper is difficult and time-consuming. Ironically, design

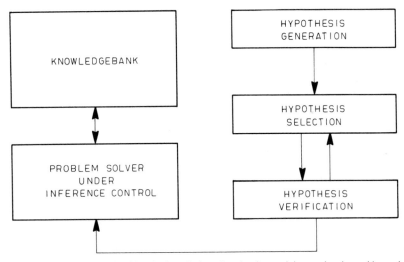

Figure 15-3. The knowledgebank has both analysis and evaluation modules serving the problem solver and testing hypotheses.

checking is more difficult when we use CAD, unless errors are found by expert systems. An expert design checker helps to eliminate conflicts in dimensioning and identify lack of compliance with design logic, finding dimensional inconsistencies between various views of a drawing.

Error avoidance is based on error detection and correction. Expert systems-ensured accuracy reduces possible field failures, which are very expensive.

An AI-assisted geometry management process can also be helpful in making engineering changes. For example, if a dimension on the drawing is changed, the system will redraw the geometry accordingly. This reduces the time a draftsmen would spend converting the engineering change into a new drawing.

As a rule, conversion systems must be able to interpret the geometry and notation of drawings adequately. They should ensure complete design definitions even from complex dimensioned input. Expert systems should be used as tools in the checking process, a function to be implemented in any automated CAD environment.

Agile user interfaces must be specifically projected for drawing conversion, creating a system that leads operators to create an intelligent CAD part from an existing drawing in the most efficient way. Such interfaces must be polyvalent, as input may be from different types:

- scanning of a physical drawing;
- reading of an electronic representation of a drawing; or
- new CAD designs.

No matter what the input source has been, the output must be either a complete, accurate representation of the original drawing or a corrected version of it. In terms of execution, as stated, some implementation models distinguish between the *scan task* and the *conversion task*. Tasks which can be performed on the conversion station may also be performed on the scan station. But scanning itself may only be done on the scan station.

3. MANAGING ELECTRONIC IMAGES

In Section 2, we discussed the phases of conversion that constitute automated document production. In an engineering environment, the term *document* includes not only technical drawings but all types of manuals, illustrated parts catalogues, field and service documentation, procedure descriptions, and catalogues with art, illustrations, photos, and graphics combined with text or parts lists. Documents may be sets of drawings and production support information or other materials to be used in field services and maintenance tests.

The goal is to enable the conversion of a large number of drawings, illustrations, graphics, and other types of art into a compressed digital form usable in CAD. The procedure we have explained is based on input and storage of graphics and text in a structured format on direct access media for instantaneous retrieval by CAD WSs. This permits easy update and creation of graphics, stored on a computer directly in a scanned and digitized form, without the need to convert back to line art. It also makes feasible the output of easily obtainable verification and production documents. The stated steps are as follows:

- Convert graphics into a raster (pixel) representation, using automatic scanning techniques.
- Update and design on a raster image through raster and vector design.
- Display the techniques and output on raster devices such as a CAD WS, printer/plotter, typesetter, and so on.

Scanners have resolutions varying

- from 5 dots per millimeter (100 dots per inch)
- to 40 or 50 dots per millimeter (1,000 dots per inch).

The price of scanners generally increases with increasing resolution. After scanning, designers can edit the image using CAD-like or raster editing functions.

Optical character readers, image scanners, laser printers, improved telecommunications, and optical digital mass storage, are physical components. The biggest challenge is not just to access the documents and images electronically but to understand the information flow: who must see it, who needs to see it, who creates it, and who can benefit from it.

If the trend in the technology of electronic image management includes an increase in hardware capabilities and lower processing costs, the most significant advance is the addition of AI. State-of-the-art developments permit *parametric design* together with an *expert drafting* system which checks the accuracy of the drawings.

In a parametric design system, dimensions can drive the geometry. For this reason, AI-enriched solutions are able to turn sketches or inaccurate geometry into accurate, checked geometry. Users may create engineering databases either from a scanned image or from sketch input, generating accurate engineering files automatically from the sketch.

Drawings in raster and other CAD formats are handled by the appropriate drawing management system. We have spoken of the conversion of existing paper drawings into

CAD databases. Different solutions can be used in image management systems. Some incorporate past technologies—for instance, *computer output to microfilm (COM)*.

For nearly two and a half decades, COM has been an essential part of information management. This technology was particularly valuable during the transition to a completely electronic approach. The COM process is part of *micrographics*. Older technologies are microfiche and microfilm. They continue to coexist with advanced information and image management, at least until the mid-1990s.

But microfiche, microfilm, and COM have been superseded by newer systems supporting fully electronic image management. Using *write once read many times (WORM)* optical systems, image information is stored in digital records run by computers; eventually, this system will eliminate most microform approaches.

In managing fully electronic images, formalisms become very important. They should be developed over a range of applications, including

- data capture of drawings, illustrations, photos (print raster), and art through a digitized procedure;
- text processing, linking online text to document handlers and multimedia databases;
- interconnecting to CAD systems and plot interfaces; and
- document output generation on different media and in different scales, utilizing recording procedures as well as telecommunications (standard telephone, satellite and TV transmission).

In the AI-based solutions now entering the market, the costly and time-consuming activities of classical manual document preparation can be eliminated or drastically reduced. There is no need for inking or tracing of pencil illustrations and graphics. The system accepts pencil drawings as originals. Nor is there a need for manual paste-up of graphics to incorporate text.

The editing capabilities of an expert system allow conversion of scanned and digitized graphics and drawings into a vector representation. This enables updating of graphics on a CAD system and easy use of textures, shadings, signs, and symbols.

The emerging facilities go well beyond already available zooming, windowing, and rescaling:

- size reduction,
- enlargement,
- rotation and
- translation.

They ensure positioning and copying of graphics of different types and sources, allowing automated composition, pagination, and final master output. Such systems are professional. They are also very expensive and should not be confused with desktop publishing systems, which have very limited capabilities.

Companies that have many drawings in paper or microfilm format are interested in electronic image management systems. So are firms facing drawing quality degradation and loss of information. Unfortunately, manual conversion of drawings into CAD is a long, expensive, uninteresting task.

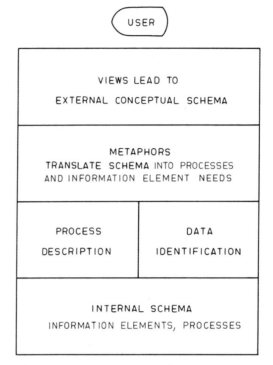

Figure 15-4. A layered approach identifies the components leading from an external conceptual schema to an internal schema in the database.

Once the system is in place, it can be used for several purposes. For example, some of the existing drawings may not be drawn to scale; this problem can be corrected with expert system support. The system can also handle engineering change orders and can help to maintain an accurate database.

The interactivity of the engineering designer with the intelligent CAD system is shown in Figure 15-4. The designer works with an external conceptual schema. Metaphors translate this schema into processes and information elements—hence, into objects. There is AI-directed

- process description and
- data identification.

Mapped into the internal schema can be multimedia information elements supported by corresponding processes.

Electronic image management enables immediate access to the latest version of a drawing; the networking capability makes feasible the rapid transfer of drawings throughout the organization; digital data can be stored without any loss of information. Editing, copying, and output of drawings can be done much more rapidly with AI-supported capabilities.

The need for preparatory work should never be underestimated. Software modules help do the conversion in an accurate and productive manner, but they do not correct procedural failures or management errors. The AI construct checks for completeness and consistency of the dimensions of a part. It does not tell management how to administer the product development cycle.

4. VECTORIZATION OF THE RASTER IMAGE

The first major advantage of raster image vectorization is an application adaptive concept through software. A process based on gray value images enables the use of a gradient in gray tone and gray tone averages instead of only threshold values.

Bridge and gap filters (within lines, between lines); smooth, clean edges and borderlines; and contrast differentiation can be handled. A gradient in gray tone is adaptive to discrepancies in materials, light, and sensors. Contrast differentiation permits color filtering through color filter contrast improvement.

Raster image vectorization employs an interactive algorithm and parameter selection with graphic feedback. Lines are guaranteed within original line widths. Data reduction capabilities are handled through band smoothing—specified maximum deviations from the original center line. Post processors are controlled by flexible parameters, thus permitting current knowledge to be used. Both interactive and background batch solutions can be applied, the former being the preferable approach.

Vectorization permits geometry management, promoting user- and application-adaptive software approaches. It makes feasible the application of raster technology to line art as well as symbol conversion. Data structures can differ between geometric elements.

The process gets its name from the definition of lines as *vectors*. An AI classification process is the reasoning mechanism. It extracts the center of a line like its skeleton, creating a gray value raster file, and then subjects the findings to a *verification* program (raster analysis).

Key to this procedure is the existence of an intelligent binary conversion mechanism. Another basic mechanism is raster compression for storage efficiency. Figure 15-5 demonstrates the milestones, starting at the optical scanning level.

In the filtering of binary images, an equal-density method with one or two thresholds can be used. A gradient maximum, average value, gap filter, and bridge-tag-edge filter are employed.

An AI classification process focuses on the selection of appropriate vectorization, representation, and classification parameters. Line-area and pixel approaches are employed. This is followed by intelligent raster pixel reduction to create a connected raster grad (the skeleton of the binary image).

Line following through the raster grad, smoothing, and the handling of points, areas, and nodes is the next stop. The resulting data structure will be stored in the system's database. It can be subset to post processing.

Raster image vectorization can handle surfaces and lines. AI approaches provide flexibility for the production of vectorized data:

> ▪ A *threshold* method is valid with good-quality originals when no fine details are required.

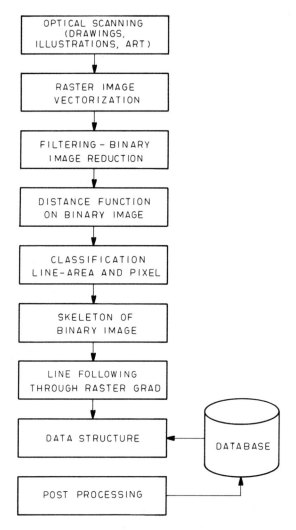

Figure 15-5. An optical scanner enriched with an expert system hopes to break the bottleneck which has existed in CAD. This figure shows the steps involved in such a process.

- The *mean value* approach is used when the line quality is poor (frayed edges, etc.).
- Breaks in lines and frayed edges may make advisable a *gap filter* solution.
- A *gradient maximum* is preferred when lines are very close together.

For vectorization purposes, the gradient maximum method employs a *noise* threshold which is less than the difference between the *white* and *black* thresholds. The chart looks like a quality control chart with axes: scan width and gray value. The white and black thresholds are plotted against the gray value, with an uncertainty area between them. For all pixels between the two thresholds, a mean value of the neighbors is calculated:

IF element $\leq$ (mean $-$ noise) THEN line element (1)[4]
IF element $\leq$ (mean $+$ noise) THEN not a line element (0)

The task is to find the lowest value of the four preceding elements. IF there are none, THEN there is no line element:

IF element $\leq$ (noise $-$ lowest value) THEN line element (1)
IF element $\leq$ (noise $-$ lowest value) THEN not a line element (0)

Possibility theory can be useful.[5] It is a rule-based system with antecedents. A distinguishing feature is the clear separation of

  1. *data examination,* the search for significant patterns, from
  2. *data modification.*

The use of antecedents focuses on the examination of data. A debugging process in the vectorization of raster images would consist of finding the rule where the deviation occurred and determining whether it occurred because a rule fired when it was not supposed to or because the action taken was inappropriate.

We have said that the gradient maximum method for raster scanning employs two thresholds: white and black. The mean value approach uses three thresholds: white, noise, and black, with the noise line being the mean value. The pixel will be 1 if the gray value is less than the mean value of the eight neighbors.

In Chapter 10 we spoke of pattern recognition. The vectorization of raster images is based on pattern recognition and involves four distinct but interconnected processes:

- segmentation,
- learning to recognize,
- post processing, and
- editing and control.

Segmentation interfaces between vectorization and the production of a segmented pattern vector image which has been processed and analyzed. It isolates symbols for further recognition from a vector image file. The criteria used are width, gray value, length, curvature, number of breakpoints, curves, nodes, size, and parametized interval combinations.

One of the AI fields that is still experimental is that of self-learning mechanisms: The system *learns to recognize* by being taught—through the designer—new symbols to be used during automatic pattern recognition. Symbol perception is based on a segmented vector image file and a learned symbol library managed by the expert system.

---

[4] Pixel 1 vs. pixel 0.
[5] See Chapter 10.

The *teaching mode* defines symbols for the library by features and tests to be performed in recognition. This helps define a complete set of features that separate symbols. The recognition mode uses the symbol library to identify symbols and can work in both batch mode and interactively. Both AI and the symbol library are vital system components.

The strategy is to look for situations which take the form of patterns in input or memory. The system responds by activating appropriate pieces of code to cause action: recognizing a symbol or pattern, activating a device, or providing output information.

Symbols and patterns in the library can be examined as chunks of knowledge. Each symbols is structurally independent. It has some intrinsic meaning in the system. Reactions are activated by perceived patterns compared against data in working memory.

Teaching the system takes the form of incremental explanation. The operator helps the construct understand what the real world knows. Thus knowledge can be added to the library in small, meaningful modules.

As the expert system becomes more learned, and therefore more sophisticated, it can know (and understand) not only relevant features but also combinations of features. This is important in following situations that might occur.

A priori knowledge of every detail of every possibility is not necessary. The library does not have to specify all possible cases. The system will cope with uncertainty through its deep knowledge engine and the application of possibility theory.

The designer should use a natural language interface[6] to communicate with the inference engine and the knowledgebank. The reasoning methods are based on the mathematics of uncertainty. Symbols and patterns are the facts. The knowledgebank library grows through successive system implementations.

Two more phases are necessary. The goal of *post processing* is to convert an attribute of a symbol based on attributes of other symbols—for instance, a length to a line. The goal of *editing* and control is to correct the results of previous activities interactively, as well as to assign names to symbols, edit curves, and so on.

An expert system helps to convert raster data back into geometric elements with their specific meanings, like symbol, point, line, arc, and polygon. This geometry data will be loaded into classical CAD systems to be used in specific applications.

Solutions use current knowledge characterizing the specific drawing as much as possible. This requires structured adaptive software that allows maximum use to be made of the scanned information. AI constructs are instrumental in providing the needed support.

5. AN ELECTRONIC PUBLISHING ASSISTANT

Real electronic publishing solutions are *multimedia*. Like any system, electronic publishing is composed of subsystems and components, including vectorization of raster images and text handling.

---

[6] See Chapter 8.

At the subsystem level, good solutions are now available for electronic publishing. The problem is their interconnection. In other words, while individual companies have developed valid solutions for limited domains, the necessary companywide architecture and system integration are still missing. Until they are developed, we cannot really talk about eliminating paper, but we can automate important parts of the engineering and manufacturing processes—particularly if we employ AI concepts.

For the reasons just stated, the present section rests on a supposition: that the integration has been accomplished and an electronic publishing assistant is made available. The kernel of this assistant is an AI construct.

The electronic publishing assistant is a complex network of information and know-how. The text it manipulates, including *paragraphs* and *figures,* is hierarchically structured, and text elements are individually accessed through various mechanisms, including memory-based reasoning, keywords, an index, a table of contents, and a table of figures.

The electronic publishing assistant's *methods* correspond to algorithmic or heuristic approaches. For instance, there are algorithms for computing the minimal paths of a system given by its network and heuristics modeled by a search function or Markov chain. There is a resulting series of *models* reflecting the mathematical structures in reference.

There are details transparent to the user, who is provided with cursor control functions such as right, left, upward, and downward, first character on the page, first character of the next sentence, next row, and so on. Also visible to the user is control action from the keyboard (format, row advance, row distance, character distance, frame, and print from the display selected, as well as tabulator and layout functions, center text, high/low positioned letters and numbers, border equalization, reformatting, pagination, and repagination).

The expert system assists in setting up alternative *layouts* as desired. Each one is given a name, which can be inserted at any point in the document any number of times. A simple layout may consist of

- margins,
- paragraph spacing,
- indentation,
- type of justification,
- type size and typeface,
- number of columns,
- interlinear spacing,
- page size, and
- worde spaces.

Layouts can be freely copied between documents, as can tabulations, headers, and foorters. Complex layouts are characteristic of compound electronic documents which integrates text, data, image, graphics (and eventually voice); therefore multimedia.

The user has available a graphic mode (line art, diagrams) and text manipulations, including text definition for operation, insertion, deletion, moving, searching, mark and exchange notions, automatic page numbering, table/text merging, and footnotes.

An expert system provides *search facilities* that allow the user to search for a group of letters or words either behind or in front of the cursor's position, with a space being treated like any word delimiter. This text can be replaced, changed, or deleted every time it occurs or waits for user confirmation each time it is found. Typefaces or type sizes can also be searched for, allowing the user to make changes to them.

Primitives are available for frame and header definitions for graphics, art, and illustrations for multicolumn pages and overlapping text and graphics. There is store display content including codes and references for selected parts; storage cataloguing, and indexing, as well as typesetting codes and control.

Interactive operations are controlled from the text terminal. Data exchange is done in both directions, with the system enriching user input with information from its memory and providing an error report when input errors are found. The spelling thesaurus is on an optical disc. It is used to provide a rich online vocabulary, thereby significantly increasing the user's productivity and the quality of the text.

Full *indexing* facilities allow the user to mark words or phrases, which can be extracted to form an automatically alphabetized index with page numbers. Running headings and footings can be used, with the option of alternating left and right for odd- and even-numbered pages. Any number can be defined within a document; these numbers may be positioned flush left, centered or flush right. Page or folio numbers can be included.

An integrated raster image editing system constitutes the core of interactive graphics color WS (over 1 megapixel resolution). One offering supports 256 colors simultaneously and features raster and vector refresh capability. Engineering workbenches are equipped with a data tablet, a digitizing table, trackball function, and an alphanumeric keyboard.

Apart from the classical editing functions, the software manages *video frames,* each frame corresponding to an animation of a selected subject. One example is a movie showing the different steps in the manufacture of a machine currently under redesign for performance improvements. Similarly, at the designer's request, the WS can provide

- examples of field usage,
- selected quality histories, and
- malfunctioning situations detected and presented by the expert system.

A *semantic knowledgebank* helps the designer select the appropriate chapters in the machine's history or apply the appropriate methods to a model. This knowledgebank contains interrelated objects. Some objects are static, as in a classical textbook. Others are dynamic.

To consult the knowledgebank and database, the design engineer is provided with an AI-enriched system of authoring/consultation tools: human window functions, editors, browers, knowledgebank compilers, and interpreters. Also available is an authoring shell and a consultation shell, each with its tools, as well as an intelligent tutoring system incorporating semantic knowledge of subjects, providing both flexibility and guidance.

The design system works interactively, editing and updating scanned illustrations, drawings, art, photos, and graphics stored in its memory or in databases it is permitted to access. Access is controlled by authorization, write/read protection, and identification code. Prompts and a help file are available at any stage. The user can modify the eye position—above/below/right/left/closer/farther/aperture—by using a simple menu.

Symbols, image macros, and standard parts within graphics or parts of a graphic are stored separately in raster form or optionally in vector form in a symbol library for direct keyword access, display, and manipulation. At the designer's request, images of

- illustrations,
- drawings, or
- graphs

to be manipulated interactively on the display are automatically represented by a window/ grid structure. Realtime image zooming, scaling, translation (shift), and rotation are performed and displayed. A verify function is provided to save the master and working images. The same is true of automatic realtime rerastering of images to fit selected windows into the display pixel memory sector.

A technical documentation generator assists in the development of new documents from other existing documents and the automatic indexing of words and sentences. There is a teachable style-checking system, a rule-based incremental parser, and an expert system-assisted document inspection facility.

Both image and text become executable programs with interactive debugging capabilities. Pointers to the database are attached to every character for immediate retrieval and analysis. The same is true of all figures, diagrams, and images.

The system permits merging of different raster and vector images from various sources. For isntance,

- elements of a library are copied into a displayed image,
- parts of images are copied together, and
- a vector stroke-represented image is mapped onto a raster image.

It is feasible to do text editing in a selectable orientation in raster images using a standard alphanumeric keyboard and a font library. The same is true of geometric definition of new elements such as points, lines, areas, and ellipses with changing line thickness or line types, utilizing background construction line grids. It is also possible to do vectorization and vector/stroke representation of elements of selected areas within an image. This is done in realtime.

A color graphics toolkit ensures that all standard graphics functions are adapted for the color screen: colored triangles, circles, rectangles, lines, and strings in any loaded font. Color map control is assigned to individual windows. The system keeps track of which window has control of the map, as well as spectral, hue, gray, inverted gray, intensity, and other characteristics. Color map manipulation is done through shifting up or down animation and through transfers to and from arrays. An AI construct assists in easy interfacing with other applications.

An automatic report generator contains a relational DBMS, which also handles complex relations between objects, including indirect pointers through some fields, default values, and back pointers. There is embedded knowledge regarding how a report should be put together according to the type and goals of the report.

The database is implemented using object-oriented programming. It handles multiple strategies, accesses distributed storage, generates a file which is then sent to the formatter, and features a kernel which is application independent.

The screen hard copy system allows users to dump a portion of the screen to a local or remote laser printer or plotter. It automatically reroutes output to a file if a printer is not available: makes hard copies of windows or arbitrary regions of the screen: centers output on the page, permitting both upright and sideways printing; and signals the user upon completion of transfer to the printer.

The knowledgebank for this electronic publishing assistant may be divided into one or more sections, each concerned with one self-contained aspect of the application. The ability to decompose a large or complex knowledgebank into a set of well-defined sections greatly simplifies workbench design, development, and subsequent maintenance.

Using the sectioning facility, it is possible to make the system reflect the inherent structure of the knowledge of the application domain. Each section of the knowledgebank will typically contain a number of multimedia information elements (image, graphs, photos, tables, data, text), each of which may be displayed either unconditionally or when some specified condition is met.

A thesaurus of references to other knowledgebank sections permits the contents of the referenced section to be accessed and applied. Each section reference is either unconditional or dependent upon some specified condition which is met.

A *web of links* allows for direct connection between

1. engineering WSs among themselves (every designer having his own).
2. the engineering WS and the global database,
3. the engineering WS and the supplier WS and mainframes,
4. the engineering WS and the manufacturing WS,
5. both the engineering and manufacturing WSs to the sales WS,
6. both the manufacturing WS and sales WSs to field WSs for maintenance feedback, and
7. the engineering WS and the quality control WS, the quality database, reliability statistics and field maintenance findings.

There is no file exchange problem, AI constructs having achieved full compatibility and portability among all of these levels of reference. (This full-fledged file transferability is the greatest challenge and unsolved problem.[7] Both local area networks and long-haul networks are used—the former at a transfer rate of 100 MBPS or better to account for the massive bit transfer requirements.

6. OPTICAL STORAGE AND IMAGE PROCESSING

The computer-assisted publishing systems generally available today are largely PC based. In this present chapter, the PC is conceived of as a WS to a larger system, with an impressive storage capacity. It is an implementation of the optical disc technology.

Figure 15-6 outlines the layout of the *image processing* system, including local area network connectivity. Functionality is based on four activities:

---

[7] See also D.N. Chorafas (in collaboration with Steve Legg), *The Engineering Database,* Butterworths, London and Boston, 1988.

1. scanning
2. indexing
3. committing, and
4. distributing.

The page scanner digitizes, compresses, and stores the information. Different types of scanners can be used online to the system—for instance, a manual unit handling DIN A4 and A5; a universal with automatic feed for A3 documents; and a mixed document scanner.

As the preceding sections have emphasized, in an engineering environment scanners must accept technical drawings with good resolution. The object is to capture the images of documents and store them in digitized form. An input WS enters keyed data and text. All the information is subsequently indexed for easy retrieval.

The process with simpler document entry stations involves capturing a facsimile image. *Document images* can then be viewed immediately for quality on an image display. Each

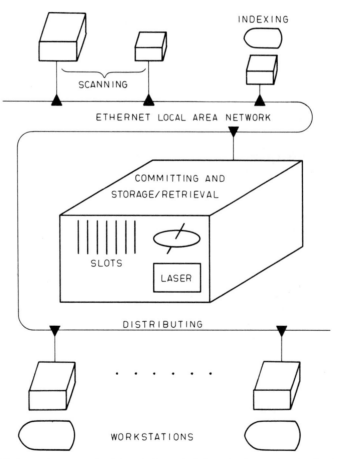

Figure 15-6. A complete network of input WSs, optical disc juke box, and professional WSs. All components of the system are interconnected through a local area network, in this case Ethernet.

document may be stamped sequentially so that the paper original can be archived sequentially if it has to be retained for legal reasons.

One or more WSs can be used for indexing purposes. Indexing permits subsequent searches through keywords. It can be done for whole documents and/or windows. In one implementation, up to 223 indexing fields are available (not to confuse with 239 characters per field, as stated later).

Short of available computer power permitting users to employ memory-based reasoning, indexing criteria must be established by the user organization. They may include, for instance, the customer name, customer number, and other references. Filing can be accomplished automatically under any number of file folder names, in a manner similar to the system in which paper documents are copied and filed in different folders.

Typically, it is possible to index in several different ways. For instance, for individual documents, one type of software supports over 16,380 document categories with different index files, allowing 239 characters per field.

Each indexing category can use the same index field defined for another category. File folders can be used as a complete document image, data and text filing structure. In most commerical offerings, because of compression, no disc space is wasted for index fields that are left blank.

As an option, the database may reside in a mainframe rather than in the filing system itself. When documents contain information that must be entered into a mainframe, the system allows simultaneous image display and data entry through a window. The proper procedural design is therefore necessary to decide on alternatives and implement them.

Once indexed, text, data, and images can be accessed on demand by the end user's WS, or they can be put under program control and assigned to move automatically from one desk to antoher. Since information is treated in the same manner, filing, retrieval, display, and all other system functions can operate consistently, regardless of the type of information or its source.

Committing is the process of writing on the optical disc. Currently the WORM technology is used. Committing takes place after the document number and document class (folder) have been allocated through the indexing process. This permits users to work with predefined parameters: number of pages, input by scanner type, selected resolution, and so on.

In one offering, the read/write laser unit is in the juke box, which supports up to 64 discs of 12-inch diameter.

- Under current storage density of 2.6 gigabytes per disc, this provides 166.4 gigabytes of storage.
- It will be increased to 512 gigabytes as single density reaches 8 gigabytes.

Forthcoming are bigger laser disc juke boxes with 200 discs. Most importantly, up to eight juke boxes can be clustered together. Even with 64 slots and 2.6 gigabytes per disc, a cluster provides 1.33 terabytes[8] of storage. This immense capacity can have an unquestionable impact on information systems applications.

---

[8] Trillion bytes.

Each enduser WS attached to a local area network can call pages on the optical disc for review, interrogation, or updating. Updating which will be done by the server, concerns the indexing of information on a magnetic disc—not an optical disc. Since many WSs may access the documents stored on an opitcal disc, *concurrent access* is ensured. In fact, a major benefit of an advanced imaging system is concurrent access.

In a procedural and an organizational sense, the impact of optical disc storage/retrieval is self-evident. Traditional media such as paper or microfilm are available to only one person at a time. By contrast, with storage in digital form, optical disc systems allow multiple users to view the same information simultaneously. Thus, image systems facilitate parallel processing and significantly shorten the information handling time.

Another benefit is workflow improvements. Such improvements may be the most dramatic benefit associated with an optical disc system.

The pacing and sequencing of work in a manual paper processing operation are usually controlled by batches, based upon time of receipt. Yesterday's work is processed in total before today's work is begun. In an optical system, the computer can be used to prioritize incoming work and control the workflow from station to station.

In addition to pacing the workflow, the automated document system provides significantly better clerical productivity. Additional benefits come from the ability to transmit information, simplifying the transportation of documents between WSs and eliminating queuing time at the WS.

Electronic transmission virtually eliminates the information float, thus significantly reducing the processing time. Still another benefit of optical systems is integration, at least within an office building or factory.

Since the image exists in digital form, it can be displayed simultaneously, using a split screen or windowing, with a data or text application. The whole process is supported by software that permits the optical disc and the electronic publishing system to produce original, near-typeset-quality documents—business letters, reports, and manuals,—created on a WS and printed on laser printer.

The user has editorial control to write, edit, cut, paste, and move blocks of text. Each document is organized into components and pages. Each can have its own unique format: margins, tabs, and so on. However, the lower-cost electronic publishing systems have quality problems and size thresholds. Large books or complicated manuals cannot be automatically formatted to standards. In general, supported functionally includes the following:

1. *Text and forms generation software* that handles custom-designed forms and letters.
2. *Computer output to laser disc,* which does for an optical disc system what COM does for a microfiche system.
3. *Document entry software,* which controls high-speed scanning, compression, display, and index entry checking.
4. Image management software, which handles indexing optical library management, and backup.
5. WS software, which supports windowing, text editing, images, retrieval, zooming, and rotation.

6. *Laser printer software* for images, multifont text, graphics, and data.
7. *Workflow software,* which manages and automatically routes document images throughout an office environment.
8. *Mainframe communications software,* particularly for support of the more popular protocols and emulation.

Access time for optical disc storage is acceptable for secretarial chores but not for managerial applications. Access time for unmounted optical discs is 15 seconds and for mounted discs 7 seconds. If the information is in a cache, access time is less than 1 second. This, however, is the exception.

One of the most important areas for optical disc implementations is archiving, including the enormous tape archives of larger organizations and paper archives. One offering permits 50 to 60 magnetic tapes to be dumped to one side of the optical disc.

Technical data tend to indicate that this is a safe procedure in terms of quality of information. Artificial aging shows that optical discs can survive for at least 10 years; by comparison, magnetic tapes must be refreshed much more frequently. Other applications areas, too, are open for careful study.

16

Robotics and Artificial Vision

Keywords

robots • stationary robots • mobile robots • androids • motion • action • system architecture • system integration • factory aggregate • computer vision • document processing • vision systems • low-level vision systems • high-level vision systems • touch sensing • inspection • quality control • pattern recognition • processing • interpretation • set of symbols

1. INTRODUCTION

Natural language understanding, voice recognition, image processing, object modeling, geographic patterns, and artificial vision systems are among the foremost areas of AI implementation. AI constructs have been successfully used to identify images and sounds. Artificial vision and hearing are useful in guiding robots, as well as in military surveillance.

Robots are composite entities. The latest generation exhibits intelligent physical behavior. Robots may be

- *stationary,* such as assembly-line arms, or
- *mobile,* designed for autonomous tanks.

A robot typically integrates systems from varied AI disciplines: vision, natural language, problem solving, expert system behavior, and planning. An application of hypothetical reasoning is a planning application—for example, the types of plans that a robot may have to construct in order to accomplish a desired end.

Planning issues both require and impose communication and cooperation standards between subsystems more demanding than those the latter would encounter in solving a problem alone. This emphasizes the need for robot intelligence.

Robot intelligence is one of the most attractive and least clearly defined subjects. Psychologists and biologists study perception, cognition, learning, and other aspects of intelligent behavior in natural organisms. Research ranges from humans down to the most primitive animals and insects. But the results are not yet conclusive.

AI is very important in robotics, as robots and robotic systems are becoming vital performers in many manufacturing systems. It is important to know not only what robots can do but also how to improve their intelligence. Only then can we plan the utilization of robots.

The descriptions of concepts, mathematical tools, and methodologies in the earlier chapters of this book is a prerequisite to intelligent robotics implementation. The use of intelligent robot systems in industrial applications requires a background ranging from the detailed knowledge of key system components to the architecturing of the entire aggregate.

Intelligence comprises perception, cognition, evaluation, projection, and other information processing skills that enable a system to develop autonomously. While many of these skills may be possessed even by lower life forms, others, such as language, abstract symbol construction, and formal manipulation, are employed extensively (as far as we know) only by humans and man-made artifacts.

Through modeling and reasoning, robots equipped with AI constructs can assimilate the differences between observation and expectation. According to cognitive scientists, structural features are more important than accurate dimensions in deciding object statuses such as the search for objects. For object recognition, robot sensors provide information on the objects to be recognized by analyzing the observed data using a priori knowledge. For example, using object recognition and status identification techniques, a computer system for multi-modal matching (which plays a vital role in human information processing) has been developed for autonomous mobile robots. The matching processes collaborate by sharing the same model, therefore, improving the efficiency and reliability of mobile robots. These robots can then do the matching themselves at a practical speed.

Knowledge representation structures employed by a robot's AI construct, in conjunction with the robot's senses, form models which can be subsequently manipulated. Such models may reflect the robot's external environment, as well as its physical configuration and internal state. To be employed in an able manner, such representation structures must be complete, allowing all important aspects of the situation to be permanently represented. It must also be adaptable so that the stored information is used efficiently. An efficient structure is one that is matched with available processing capabilities, ad hoc situations. Only then can robots be considered intelligent.

We are on the threshold of a change in the universe comparable to the transition from nonlife to life. In Chapter 1 we spoke about a projection that by the year 2000 a machine of nearly human complexity will be available; and by the year 2050, we will have intelligent man-made systems more powerful than humans by one or two orders of magnitude. Though these are somewhat remote projections, they help identify a possible timetable reflecting the development of *androids*.

2. ROBOTICS: A POSTINDUSTRIAL PERSPECTIVE

The word *robot* means different things to different people. Its meaning varies as a function of time, culture, level of technology, and implementation. Earlier, the definition of a robot was limited to a machine performing one specific task that can be programmed (and reprogrammed) to do a variety of jobs. An alternative definition stressed the aspect of programmed multifunctional manipulators. Neither of these definitions necessarily included AI. Yet, AI researchers have been working on ways to add intelligence to these machines in the forms of vision, tactile sense, planning, and learning.

One way to classify robots is to divide them into three main groups:

1. industrial multifunctional manipulators,
2. android robots, and
3. automated environments (factories).

Another classification also considers three groupings but uses different criteria: microrobots, midrange robots (midrobots), and macrorobots. We will examine this reference.

Considered from the original industrial viewpoint, a robot is a reprogrammable, multifunctional manipulator. It is designed to move and/or manipulate material, parts, tools, and specialized devices. It does so through variable programmed motions, with the aim of performing a variety of tasks. This definition was formulated by the Robot Institute of America (now called the Robotic Industries Association) after lengthy consideration and discussion. Every noun and adjective in it is packed with meaning, and it is designed to describe practical, working, and economically productive robots.

If off-the-shelf manufacturing and other industrial robots are our primary interest, this definition sets the proper focus. But it emphasizes robot *motion* rather than general robot *action*, indicating that this definition does not adequately capture the rapid evolution of practical robot senses or the developing robot's intelligence.

The now classical robot applications range from high-precision equipment required for tasks ranging from fine mechanics to heavy duty; from manipulators to transporters, welders, and assembly robots. All of them have been important steps toward an automated factory, but the landscape is changing. Robots are taking on a new character: the ability to imitate humans. Arms and legs are now equipped with basic intelligence functions. Robots have acquired perception and cognition. They are hearing and speaking.

Some robots follow instructions from a human voice and are capable of moving toward a group of objects, selecting the right one and carrying it to a designated place. Sophisticated robots are used for assembling electronics parts. At its plant in Osaka, Sumitono Electric Industries has capitalized on the fact that the robot perceives objects with two movable eyes made of 300,000 optical fibers, differentiating shapes and sizes through image recognition technology. A carbon-fiber arm can grip and carry objects weighing up to 1 kg (2.2 lb). Its legs are equipped with an optical character-reading device which permits the robot to follow written instructions and to detect objects in its path.

Even rudimentary AI constructs can give a robot the logic and memory capability necessary for sensory feedback and coordination. More sophisticated solutions enlarge such intelligence, providing for autonomy and practical usefulness in imaginative applications.

There are intriguing scenarios about humans living with robots and using them to advantage in factories and farms, as well as in weapons systems. Robots are beginning to meet us where we live. As defined by one specialist, the aforementioned class of microrobots includes smart microwave ovens that cook, test food, and tell time; computerized fuel/ignition systems that adapt to and monitor engine conditions; and cameras that sense light, move shutters, and talk to the human photographer.

These are microprocessor-based engines that are rapidly acquiring new capabilities and finding many niches. They add intelligence and adaptability to personal tools and household appliances. They are also beginning to be linked together in communicating networks, forming more sophisticated devices and higher robot organisms.

Today there is a great deal of emphasis on autonomous intelligent vehicles. They are considered to be the true test of sixth-generation computers by the year 2000. But there is no real reason why all robots should move. Some will perform better if they remain stationary but online. One example is AI-enriched private and public branch exchanges; another is AI-based systems for foreign exchange operations.

There is a consensus, however, that the days of dumb machines are drawing to a close. This does not only refer to the current world, which has mainly nonmobile industrial robots with manipulator arms preprogrammed to perform a repetitive action. It extends to all machines including telephone exchanges.

Fixed, semi-intelligent robots have been used mostly in the metal-working sector of industry, particularly in automobile production. They are cost efficient in hazardous or boring jobs like spray painting, welding, and loading and unloading machine tools. Robots have been utilized for three important reasons:

- They can go where people cannot go, for example, into nuclear reactors.
- They are precise and consistent, turning out products of uniformly good quality.
- They fit well into high-technology environments ranging from the disc drive to assembly plants of semiconductors.

These are examples of midrange robots. However, the more complex the job becomes, the more we need robot intelligence. Adapting to an evolving technology, robot manufacturers have to add vision, pressure, and tactile sensation capabilities to industrial robots.

In earlier years, robots worked without the benefit of any sensory input. Today a vision component makes such robots more flexible by performing a scene analysis. Different researches have identified some of the capabilities that vision systems should provide for robots. They include *location*—such as objects on a conveyer belt and topological or geological features: *orientation,* so that the object may be grasped correctly; and *identification,* to determine which of many objects is the desired one.

These developments lead to an evolutionary definition of robots and robotics: AI-enriched, computer-based systems that interact independently with the world through their own senses, intelligence, and actions. In less *than a decade,* the word *independence* will have to be outlined in this definition. Though independent robot action is today a matter of degree (and of some controversy), the autonomous, intelligent vehicle will be the hallmark of sixth-generation computers.

A different way of making this statement is to note that computer evolution is proceeding in three major steps:

1. automation and data processing
2. expertise (knowledge-based), and
3. autonomy.

As previously stated, many consider that the real future of robots lies in computer autonomy. Such engines are not yet available, but they are an objective to which enormous resources are dedicated.

From exploration of the oceans and outer space to mining, there exist bright prospects for autonomous robots. Intelligent, autonomous robots will not only open frontiers in the realms of weapons and warefare; they will have an enormous impact on everyday life, both creating and responding to technological challenges. If effectively addressed, the development of androids can proceed on a scale that will reshape our planet—for better or for worse.

While intelligent, autonomous vehicles still belong to the class of midrange robots, macrorobots will become more important. An example is the ongoing effort in many countries to build a completely automated factory that will require only two or three people (and eventually none) to run it.

The significance of intelligent robotics goes far beyond that of momentous technological advances such as the transistor. It is now a new computer technology, and surely not the ultimate computer form. We have already said that telecommunications will profit from this trend—and will also be a major contributor to its realization.

3. FROM FACTORY PLANNING TO INTELLIGENT ROBOTICS

Industrial robots were once considered a machine tool, programmed to manipulate parts or other tools in a sequence of motions. We have seen why this concept is no longer true. The trend in robotics has a postindustrial perspective with many different facets.

Worldwide, the tendency in building robots is to use new materials: high-strength, low-alloy steels, plastics, and composites. Vendors are noting that compact, lightweight and streamlined robots with strength equivalent to that of the larger, heavier models of the present will become more prevalent. There is also a growing trend away from hydraulically driven robots and toward the development of greater sensory capability and AI constructs.

While these developments are both important and interesting, they are not enough. As we often fail to appreciate, it is not sufficient to produce AI-enriched robots made of new materials, regardless of how intelligent they may be. We must also be able to fit them into their intended environment and ensure their integration.

This indicates the need for another kind of knowledge engineering—that of large and very large systems. Presently, there are few experts in this profession. Until the number of experts increases, robots will be underutilized and badly utilized. Industries have become aware of this fact; some auto manufacturers are even talking about projecting the "factory of the past."

If AI is to become a pillar of manufacturing in the postindustrial era, knowledge engineering has to attack the problem of large-scale systems. Big systems are not small systems that have outgrown their original size. Big systems have totally different requirements in terms of

- planning,
- designing,
- implementing, and
- controlling.

System architecture and *system integration* should become keywords in engineering design. They can both profit handsomely from AI[1] and knowledge-based systems. We can use AI to project networks. We can integrate AI with CAD, manufacturing, engineering, and plant layout. We can build factories, transport systems, and intelligent buildings which integrate robot technology with system engineering concepts. But in these tasks, the key element will be the knowledge engineering designer—not just the intelligent robot.

We are also interested in studying, developing, and designing robots with increasing intelligence and learning functions, particularly the types of AI applications that enable robots to learn from experience and determine how to perform unfamiliar tasks on their own. Research in robotics aims to transform the machines of today, first into engines with common sense and then with full intelligence.

Commonsense robots are already able to cope economically with errors and shortcomings in the world environment for which they have been designed. By 1993 it is expected that intelligent robots will be able to make their own detailed plans from loosely defined instructions, working in more hostile environments than the factory. This will be the third robot generation.

Robotics research over the next ten to fifteen years is seen not only as one of the most demanding areas for engineers but also as providing a breathing space that will allow society to decide how it will live in the twenty-first century. This, too, is a subject which requires high-caliber knowledge engineers, psychologists, sociologists—and politicians.

A narrowly conceived engineering view will be doomed to failure. Given the magnitude of the challenge, narrow views are not only insufficient but also counterproductive. Because robots will be increasingly used for broader tasks in industrial and business automation, it is important to know what they can do *within an environment*—not just on their own. We must learn the limitations of their capabilities and how to plan their usage. Efficient approaches will be based on modeling robot behavior, prototyping automatic plant formation, identifying unsolvable and poorly solvable problems, and acquiring feedback knowledge for robot design.

With robot dexterity and intelligence at a premium, perception, decision, and action have

---

[1] See also D.N. Chorafas, *System Architecture and System Design,* McGraw-Hill, New York, 1989.

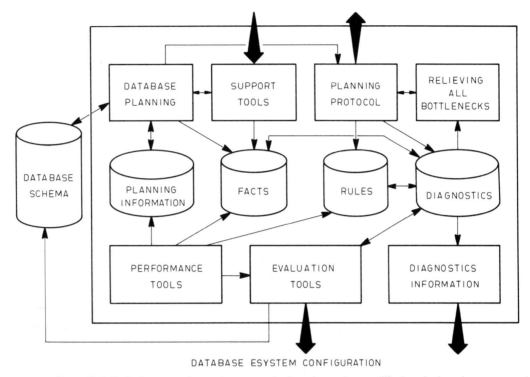

DATABASE ESYSTEM CONFIGURATION

Figure 16-1. Basically, system integration means database integration—a difficult task given the incompatibility of present-day databases and DBMSs even within the same organization. This figure presents the schema of an integration project which uses AI.

to be studied and implemented in a way which integrates well with the operational environment. This means developing databases as well as AI constructs (shallow expert systems) able to exploit the database. Figure 16-1 presents an expert system configuration for communicating databases.

To emphasize this last point: Robots are not intelligent just because they incorporate micro-processors and AI constructs. Intelligent robots require access to distributed communicating databases, which themselves should exhibit AI-type characteristics. There are also other prerequisites.

Sophisticated image analysis requires computing at a speed unattainable at prices industry will accept today. In decision making, the limits may lie within the supervisory computer because of the complexity of the robot's three-dimensional working environment. But new technologies, such as hypercube architectures, can help break the number-crunching bottleneck.

In action, limitations range from accuracy, reliability, and wear to the risk of catastrophic events such as collisions in the workplace. There have been instances of robots painting other robots rather than the car on the production line. To meet these challenges, the design trend is no longer toward the universal robot (as was once confidently expected) but toward a number of generic types tailored to perform repetitive tasks such as spot welding, gluing, and assembly. (Review the definition given at the beginning of Section 2.)

When we talk of implementation in a dynamic environment, both computer speed and robot speed are at a premium. In terms of speed, current robots are far too slow to compete with dedicated machinery such as that used in the textile industry. The arms of future robots must achieve high speed and stiffness. But speed, while a requirement for many types of work, is not enough.

The technology of artificial machine vision,[2] an area that has as many detractors as supporters, is gaining momentum. No longer simply a useful technology in search of a market, artificial vision appears to have gained users' acceptance. While we are still in the process of forecasting the future of this industry, we can say that it will be one of great importance for both inspection and gauging applications—as well as for robot guidance.

Machine parts recognition, automatic visual inspection, imaging devices, and camera model(s) are some of the visual sensing technologies. The class of image segmentation typically include edge detection and thresholding. Shape description calls for heuristic approaches, mathematical shape descriptions, and syntactic shape analysis. Recognition methods involve template matching, decisions, and structural and syntactic solutions.

This environment has come a long way from the early days of industrial robots, which were characterized by an emphasis on robot hardware. As robots have become accepted in integrated manufacturing, the importance of added features (as well as of sophisticated software) has grown. This further underlines our emphasis on factorywide (generally, systemwide) knowledge engineering.

Robot motion, analysis of sensory information, and interaction with other automation hardware components and databases call for advanced tools—and for programmable approaches. For a robot to perceive and recognize its environment, an efficient vision system becomes very important. To follow the direction of this research, we must understand both the motivation of robot vision and its mechanics. Only then can we successfully develop the major parts of a vision system and their integration.

These factors are part of the emerging infrastructure of research required to develop the intelligent robot. This can be visualized from different angles, including the following:

1. Robot design and manufacture, from the integration of machine intelligence to sensor and motor action.
2. One of the three major elements of any robotic system: its program, manipulator, and dynamic devices.
3. Integration capabilities, including robots in upstream and downstream operations.
4. The overall aspect of a system enriched with intelligence—down to the minute details.

"God is in the detail" said Mies Van der Rohe. Unless and until we have done our homework, we will not get good results. Not only will the investment in robotics fail to pay off, but the whole project will end in dissatisfaction and infighting.

---

[2] See also Section 5.

Knowledge engineering should both appreciate and attempt to solve these problems. Taking the manufacturing environment as an example, doing our homework means decomposing a sheet metal air conditioning unit into features to which we can assign a value in functional terms and a cost related to the robotics used to make it. Here the goal must be to identify those components which are expensive to manufacture but are not commensurately valuable to the customer.

Once we focus on the key elements and their detail, programs will need to be written, including three-dimensional modeling with simulators. Programmability can be either simple (mechanical programming, pick-and-place) or sophisticated. The latter is:

- changeable
- adaptable, and
- reflective of a knowledge engineering approach.

Programmability must also respect interfaces—within the robot, with other robots, in the workspace(s) defined by the environment, and with the eventual user.

We must not only explore the state of the art but also follow the future directions of software development in all aspects of robotics. This leads from realtime control systems and low-level algorithms through applications programming for the overall factory organization. Properly planed work will be done in interaction with design, engineering, and manufacturing databases, for reasons previously discussed.

4. TOWARD DISTRIBUTED ACTIVE ROBOTS

Robots that walk, talk, and exhibit human-like behavior are still not practical. The most common kind of industrial robot today is not as glamorous as science fiction imagines, yet certain science fiction ideas are playing an increasingly important role in manufacturing.

Robot actions are performed in all areas where software runs in realtime: reacting to inputs from the environment and controlling effectors that interact with the environment or parts of it—whether this involves people or other systems. An active intelligent machine system has a purpose which determines design choices.

A robotics factory has engineering, databasing, data processing, and communications requirements in generating control information from the sensed data. The implementation of robot controls calls for the development and realtime use of hardware and software, including both numeric and nonnumeric (logical) expressions. The computer's ability to do the calculations is not in doubt. The problem lies in our ability to perceive things. This is the function, outlined in the preceding section, of the system integrator.

Interaction with the environment calls for the right perspective in information exchange. The relevant four layers in a factory environment are shown in Figure 16-2. From the bottom up, they are

- source data collection,
- process control,
- robotics, and
- factory aggregate.

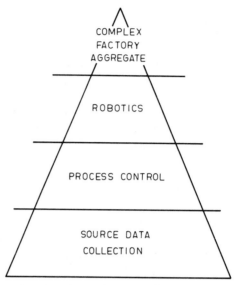

Figure 16-2. Vertical integration involves a layered structure from source data collection to the complete aggregate. This figure comes from a manufacturing application.

Source data collection and process control are the two technologies we know best, the areas where we have accumulated the greatest experience. The *factory aggregate* level, which integrates robotics and office automation capabilities, still has few experts and few manufacturers who are able to fill the gaps. There exists, however, a growing body of knowledge in robotics.

Implementation experiences are more successful when robots do not attempt to be everything to everyone, but instead focus primarily on their particular area of expertise. It is important to understand the difference between customized and modularized systems; in the latter, the components are basically the same, but the configuration may differ from system to system. A vendor should be able to supply a particular type of system more than once, even though the environment may be different.

The best way to attack the problems of modularity and adaptability is to return to the fundamentals. The major subsystems are

- sensors,
- effectors,
- robot intelligence,
- control action, and
- power/drive components.

The components of a robot include

- links,
- joints,

- motors,
- gearboxes,
- microprocessors, and
- software.

Links, joints, motors, and gearboxes are hard to model precisely. We must think of mass, weight, inertia, stiffness, tolerances, flexible coupling and noise—but also of availability and life cycle. These represent many constraints on few components.

Prototyping is helpful in designing for modularity. It also permits to experiment on clean interfaces. As stated in Chapter 4, valid approaches to prototyping consider the big picture first and then focus on the details of subsystems, applying the concepts of modularity and experimentation to key features.

From the viewpoint of the sensors, it is necessary to study the AI implications. By combining AI with advanced sensing units, we obtain smart sensors—a major research goal. Smart sensors can be used for image processing, high-speed factory inspection, inertial guidance, and other tasks.

Sensory modes include position (direct, indirect) and tactile capability for the robot itself (finger: force, area, wrist) and fit into the work space. Remote sensing may involve electromagnetic characteristics (both imaging and nonimaging) as well as acoustical ones.

Internal state sensing will typically support position, velocity, acceleration, force, the corresponding signal processing, the resulting servo controls (analog and digital), and adaptive control. External state sensing calls for the ability to handle

1. geometric variables, both nonvisual and visual,
2. dynamic variables,
3. proximity, force/torque, and tactile variables, and
4. data formatting, computation, and task context.

Video cameras, proximity sensors, and tactile sensors are examples of external sensors that might be found on robots. Sensor reference controls include information and its computation; task models; transformations from external to internal states; structuring and programming of sensor-referenced controls; and performance stability. All of these are open to prototyping.

Few robots in operation today incorporate external sensors, but color image acquisition is a basic functional component of computer vision. Image display is the other vital component. The display of reconstituted raw image data and pictorial results is important.

A general-purpose robot will have 6 degrees of freedom. It will be able to move the end of its arm to a specific point in space and will have three more articulations at the wrist in order to orient the end effector for the job being performed.

Robots of the future will have little resemblance to those of the past. Much of the early robot equipment was hydraulic, featuring stiffness and strength. However, it was slow and nonlinear; collisions were difficult to control; there were fluid restrictions. As the characteristics of robots changed, stiffness and strength, which were formerly advantages, became liabilities.

We now talk about different robots altogether. Emphasis is placed on the ability of the device to be under central software control—particularly when enriched with AI. Mobil robotic applications, for example, focus on four abstraction levels:

- the task to be done,
- in-room navigation,
- next-to movement (from object to next object), and
- at-the-job movement (software and motor command).

A developing design trend is to separate the mechanics from central intelligence while incorporating AI constructs into actuators and sensors. This results in a *distributed active system.*

But radical changes in machine design demand more time. They also call for global solutions—not just approaches at the machine level. Rather than trying to robotize a conventional piece of equipment, such as an earth-moving tractor, by adding sensors and computer intelligence, it will be more rational to reevaluate the tasks now performed by conventional machinery. Some of them will be combined and eliminated; others will be largely revamped.

New departures in engineering design call for more imaginative solutions within the environment, leading to new technical solutions. Today we do not have the technology to built complex system aggregates with distributed intelligence—but we have the ability to move toward them.

From process control to telecommunications, robots have no physical arms or legs. Intelligence is provided by software which monitors, decides, and controls the activity with which it has been entrusted. In this sense, the whole telephone network can be viewed as a robotic universe within which other telecommunications robots can communicate.

It is no accident that for SL-1 and its descendant private branch exchanges (PBX), Northern Telecom develops 500 new software modules per year. To build its new Hicom PBX, Siemens has spent 75% of its development budget on software, though the hardware development costs were also significant.

PBXs are the gateways to factory automation. The communications link is fundamental to any intelligent robotic device. But like any system, the telecommunications universe requires specific engineering and design. It is an active system in which events occur at various times. Services are provided by the telephone network on a contention basis. The communications universe itself consists of practical solutions to problems of information theory. The realtime nature of the network and the contention for the use of available resources create challenges which are not always faced in the best manner.

5. IMPLEMENTING
COMPUTER VISION

Computer vision,[3] *machine vision, artificial vision,* and *AI vision* are practically synonymous terms. They describe the technology of analyzing and identifying the contents of a scene from images of that scene. This has many major applications in areas such as the following:

---

[3] The term *computer vision* is preferred because it avoids frequent repetitive use of the word *artificial.*

1. *Industrial robotics:* automated visual inspection, vision for robot guidance.
2. *Document processing:* character recognition, computer understanding of drawings and maps.
3. *Medicine:* automated blood cell counting, tumor detection on radiographs.
4. *Other areas:* remote sensing, cartography, reconnaissance, and so on.

Sensors are at a premium for perception and AI constructs for cognition. A variety of algorithms for computer analysis of images have been developed over the past few decades. As the power of computers continues to increase, more and more of these algorithms are finding practical applications, provided that there is guidance as to how they can be used.

In Section 3 we said that, to be successful with robot applications, we must understand both the motivation of robot vision and its mechanics. Visual sensing and image segmentation techniques must be described. Shape description and recognition methods, the interpretation of three-dimensional scenes, and shape analysis techniques must be developed.

Vision systems are not monolithic, and their sophistication is increasing. The so-called *low-level vision systems* are not knowledge based in the current sense of the term. They are not equipped with rules so that they can be used flexibly in unanticipated ways. But they do measure various features of images and, in some cases, they can be efficiently implemented with robotic hardware.

High-level vision systems employ AI reasoning techniques. They are able to cope with ambiguities. They can handle some ad hoc situations and expand in other directions. *Touch sensing,* like vision, is a form of image processing. And, like vision, it makes use of image enhancement, analysis, and identification.

There are two- and three-dimensional computer vision systems. Both have proved relevant to most manufacturing and assembly processes, but they are just beginning to work on the factory floor. For instance, sensing technology uses visual data from television cameras to help inspection, identify parts, or increase guidance or control in the manufacturing process.

Yet, as the preceding sections have stated, while technology keeps evolving more and more rapidly, industry is faced with the monumental task of applying it in a practical manner to solve specific manufacturing and assembly problems. In this sense, the most common mistake is underestimating how much work this requires—and how much skill.

An implementation area of great importance is *inspection* and *quality control (QC)*. In industry more money is being allocated on inspection than on manufacturing, in its strict sense, and artificial vision is the key to automation of the inspection process.

Problems are far from being solved. A successful laboratory demonstration of new computer vision techniques only means that half of the job has been done. The burden of working out the application often falls on the manufacturing engineer and the plant manager. They should be assisted by knowledge engineers. Management, which only cares about buying technology, is not very interested in knowing the tedious details of how to make this technology work properly.

Applications engineering is the vital link. I underline this notion in particular because it is not properly appreciated. Yet, this is a *vital part* (if not *the* vital part) of knowledge engineering. It is also a basic responsibility of management, even if this is not often appreciated.

Attention to detail has as many implications for management as it has for engineering. Clear-eyed industrial management is moving away from macrostructures, previously used to provide economies of scale, toward microstructures as AI becomes the key operator. When we exercise insight and foresight, high technology—and computer vision is an exchange—acts as a flywheel of change in industry.

While the mathematics of computer vision are an exciting scientific subject and a prime field of AI research, even the most imaginative solutions will be of no avail unless they are enriched with an applications perspective. There is a world of difference between developing computer vision and implementing it. That is what many new companies with brilliant AI research people did not understand—and they went under.

Knowledge engineers are needed *both* in AI research side and in implementation. Direct interaction with the real world is one of the primary challenges of AI. To a limited extent, computer vision has already achieved the input part of this goal, with systems delivering expert levels of performance in restricted domains. But how good are the applications? Do industries recover their capital and make a profit?

AI systems work in demanding environments that are

- rich in data,
- subject to many types of error,
- computationally very intensive, and
- online to other applications, some of them classical, others advanced.

Understanding the AI principles behind such systems is not only very interesting scientifically, it is also critical for assessing their utility, flexibililty, and future potential. The same is true of the business principles and the other interconnected engineering disciplines that enter the system and make up the total environment.

Let's take two examples. The first is aerial recognition. How much detail a camera can see is determined by:

$$\text{diameter of resolution patch} = \frac{\text{height}}{\text{focal length}} \times \text{diameter of a pixel}$$

$$s = \frac{h}{f} d$$

It is a matter of resolution. Whether a satellite can identify, for example, a silo site depends on the diameter of the smallest detail—the resolution patch it can see. This is determined by its height, the focal length of its optics, and the size of the picture elements (pixels) of its film or electronic detector (Figure 16-3).

In 1973, a year after the signing of the SALT I treaty, American satellites spotted what looked like the excavation of silos for a powerful new intercontinental ballistic missile in northern Siberia. This was a violation of the new treaty, and the Nixon administration protested to the Soviet Union. Keep watching, the Russians replied. As the work continued, satellite observations showed that these were not missile silos; they were underground command posts (which were permitted by the treaty).

Some satellites are equipped with special types of radar to obtain images at night and to penetrate cloud cover. These are known as *synthetic aperture radars* (*SAR*). After the radar's waves are bounced off the ground, they are tricked electronically into perceiving that

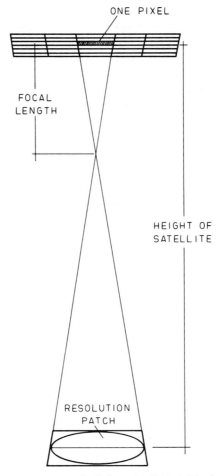

ONE PIXEL

FOCAL
LENGTH

HEIGHT OF
SATELLITE

RESOLUTION
PATCH

Figure 16-3. The resolution patch of a satellite is determined by its height, the focal length of its optics, and the pixels of its film or electronic detector.

the satellite's receiving antenna is as long as the distance the spacecraft has traveled during that interval.

In radar systems of this sort, the amplitude and arrival time of each reflected wave must be briefly stored. Then all the pulses returning from a given point on earth must be added up electronically. Complex computational capability is carried on board the satellite, which makes it possible to send back pictures in real time.

In both cases, pattern recognition is only part of the job. It is the total system which provides the shield of surveillance, not the components alone—no matter how powerful and sophisticated these components may be. To be modernized, the total system needs AI constructs as much as its most complex component does. It also needs architectural design.

In the surveillance system, large phased-array radars on the ground and on ships monitor the maneuverings of satellites. The latter are also observed with very large optical telescopes installed on Maui in Hawaii and in Florida. They also monitor the testing of missiles and aircraft, as well as the trajectories of ballistic missile reentry vehicles.

A well-architectured global system ensures that activities taking place deep inside foreign territory can be observed by radars on the periphery of that territory. Then they are handled in an expert manner by over-the-horizon radar that seems to defy a physical law: that all radio waves travel in a straight line.

The second example of an AI system comes from an office environment. At the beginning of this section, we said that document processing—including character recognition, as well as computer understanding of documents and maps—is one of the important areas of artificial vision. When we deal with image processing services, the primary capability sought is the ability to input hard copy

- letters,
- memos,
- documents,
- graphs, and
- pictures

into databases. The main interest is in printed text and is oriented to optical character recognition (OCR) equipment. However, there is also the need to handle images such as handwritten signatures and technical drawings. Advances in image processing point to developments that will handle all these needs in one device.

One of the main factors that impeded the proliferation of CAD was the problem of integrating old drawings into the CAD-supported engineering database. When nearly a dozen years ago we introduced CAD, in one company I have been working with, we were confronted with the problem of manually converting about 1,300,000 old drawings. Twenty-five percent of these drawings was still active. The problem had no feasible solution, so it was necessary to work with two incompatible reference files. But this problem it can be solved with pattern recognition if AI approaches are not restricted to the devices alone. An engineering wide view is necessary.

6. PATTERN RECOGNITION

If robotics is just beginning to bloom, then computer vision is still in the seedling stage. But the prospects are encouraging. Behind this statement is the wide domain of possible employment of computer vision.

The basic element of computer vision is *pattern recognition*—that is, the investigation of technical and mathematical aspects of automatic *processing* and *interpretation* of patterns. This requires the transformation of a sensor signal into a suitable symbolic description. Typically, the format of a sensor signal is a sequence of sample values (integers).

Patterns may be images, sequences of images, or continuous speech. The format of a symbolic description depends on the application and its requirements. Examples include the analysis and classification of the whole pattern; a complete symbolic description, naming relevant objects and relations; and a protocol of changes with respect to a prior recording of the same environment or focal point.

Pattern recognition transforms an array (or subarray) of data into a *set of symbols*. The translation is

$$\text{data} \rightarrow \text{symbols}$$

This requires the recognition of objects (or words), the segmentation of images (and speech), and the matching of structures. The last should then be processed through knowledge engineering, with the aim of transforming one symbolic structure into another. Hence:

$$\text{symbols} \rightarrow \text{symbols}$$

On this process depend image and speech understanding, reactions to sensor signals, and analysis and reporting of surveillance situations.

Visual sensing techniques, for instance, include imaging devices and a camera model. Typically, the direct readings in a gray-level mosaic are of no inherent interest. These readings are produced both by objects and by those objects' immediate environment, particularly when they contain random fluctuation or noise, which affects sensor readings.

For most perceptual tasks, an AI construct must filter out environmental effects, deriving an image which accurately reflects underlying objects. A common task of perceptual programs is to construct a map of distance or depth from the sensor to the surfaces in its environment, as explained in the satellite example (Section 5). This is done using readings of a gray-level brightness mosaic as the starting level.

For living organisms, depth-from-brightness mapping is accomplished primarily by binocular imaging (stereopsis). Two separate eyes look at an identical scene, registering slightly different images because of their slightly different perspectives. The amount of this difference (parallax) is greater for points that are closer than for those that are farther apart.

Stereopsis is the measurement of distance, and hence form, from the disparity between the images in the two eyes. For a living organism, stereo information is sufficient to interpret depth. The task of the knowledge engineer is to write a heuristic program or algorithm that can see a random-dot stereogram in the same way. There is evidence about how the human brain does the calculation.

Computer vision takes an approach which involves signal-related factors: imaging hardware, AI constructs, thresholds, edge detection, and region analysis. Methods like searching and planning are used in the unification of edges and in the literal focusing of attention. Heuristic methods are exploited, including mathematical shape descriptors, syntactic shape analysis, recognition solutions, and scene interpretation. Three general methods are usually employed:

- bit-by-bit comparison,
- feature inspection, and
- generic property verification.

Among the major approaches in pattern recognition are

- template matching,
- decision-theoretic (statistical), and
- structural/syntactic approach.

A key strategy is elimination. The computer lists all the possible ways to interpret a single spot on an image. It then eliminates the ones that are incompatible with the possible interpretations of other spots, given certain assumptions. For instance, a spot on a surface cannot be facing right and its neighbor left if there is no dark-light boundary between them. Knowing the source of the illumination, the AI construct works out which way the brightest parts of the image must be facing. Assuming the objects to be smooth, it then works out the direction in which each other part of the image is facing. Finally, it compares the result with a stored mathematical representation (template).

The computational approach to vision depends on a big assumption: that the brain contains a library of objects that can be compared against the stimuli it receives from the retina. Optical illusions suggest that this assumption is correct. Many of them seem to work only because the brain is intolerant of ambiguity. It prefers to see a familiar object even when it is looking at an unfamiliar shape.

At the higher levels of vision where surfaces and objects are perceived, we need a derivation of world knowledge using more sophisticated algorithms. At the still experimental cognitive level of vision, we talk of knowledge representations and indexing schemes used for object and spatial relation models and for robotic navigation.

A pattern recognition system usually consists of several modules for performing specialized transformations on data. Often, more than one module is available to compute the same types of results (regions). During processing, alternative and competing results may be obtained.

Suppose that we wish to design an active compliance device which utilizes force sensory feedback information to control a robot arm in fine motion. It should incorporate pattern recognition methods for force surveillance and guidance control, permitting the manipulator to improve its performance in fine motion.

The approach will utilize pattern recognition and control techniques, learning from past experience in the insertion process. The goal is force feedback control. The device will include at least two subsystems:

- force recognition
- guidance and control.

In terms of features extraction, the objective is to select a valid number of features from the measurement space to represent each of the control regions. Optimization is necessary, as too many features will slow down the process and too few will result in inadequate representation. They may also lead to incorrect recognition.

The goal of the following phase—classification of features and partitioning of control space—is to identify the hand's control region accurately. This identification is based on the extracted features. Another goal is to retrieve the feedback gains to serve the robot.

A number of questions have to be answered: Into how many control regions should we partition the control space? What is the percentage of recognition error of the control regions? The confidence intervals? The effect of noise? The permitted error? Both vagueness and uncertainty are present. Hence, in this connection, the AI compatibility/incompatibility model (we considered in Chapter 10) is very useful. In fact, it has been developed for pattern recognition applications.

The guidance and control module has some or all of the following selection tasks: identifying the transformation to be carried out next; using a particular module to carry out the transformation; and choosing a subset of results for further processing. These choices are usually known as the *processing sequence*.

- When the same processing sequence is selected for all (or nearly all) patterns of a field of problems, this sequence may be specified in the system structure. It can be hardwired.
- When the processing sequence is different from pattern to pattern, then dynamic control strategies are necessary. An AI construct is an asset.

The AI solution is superior, as fixed processing sequences do not give satisfactory results for complex patterns. Images, image sequences, and continuous speech are themselves dynamic. Able solutions require designing, planning, scoring, and searching activities, where knowledge engineering is of prime importance.

In the case of robot arm control, the overall goal is to design an adaptive control mechanism for manipulation. It should be able to track a desired position trajectory as closely as possible at all times. It should do so over a wide range of manipulator motions and payloads, with feedforward and feedback components. The same is true of expert system capabilities.

This example helps document the reasons for the surge in interest in pattern recognition. It is due to requirements which range from weapons systems to industrial situations. Solutions are helped by technological advances, not only in electronics but also through research on human perception. They are enhanced by the fact that there exist many common aspects among a variety of different applications.

17

Polyvalent Information Networks for Business and Industry

Keywords

criteria for networks • logical layers • one logical network • network control center (NCC) • reliability • security • protocol • asynchronous • binary synchronous • header • trailer • packet switching • multimedia • diagnostics • intelligent modems • automated solutions • cost effective • service differentiation • multimedia support • electronic banking • infrastructure • automation • office work • electronic teller • client's profile • liquidity risks • operating risks • fraud risks • multimedia applications • dynamic model • design implementation • information center • static model • any-to-any connectivity • infrastructure • network • configurer • cost of network • network performance • topology • presentation

1. INTRODUCTION

Data communications systems were originally designed to be dedicated to a single application. Terminals were bought and installed for specific purposes, and computer programs were written with these terminals in mind.

Data communications and databasing systems for a given area of implementation were often developed independently of each other. The result was many incompatible terminals, transmission systems, and protocols. The rules used to manage storage, retrieval, and flow of data were incompatible; so were the software and the equipment.

This situation was characteristic of computers and communications approaches during the 1960s and the early 1970s. Even thereafter, with distributed information systems, computer professionals at data processing centers concentrated on getting a few major applications up and running. Attempts to integrate all subsystems into one compatible, homogeneous aggregate were frustrating.

Staff members were used to keep existing programs running, and little effort was spared for the problems of consistency. By the late 1970s, however, management was beginning to appreciate the complaints of users who had to deal with multiple terminals on their desks. At the same time, new economic and technical factors were making integration an important topic. Microprocessor technology had improved to the point where the cost of intelligent WSs had declined sharply. PCs began to replace dumb terminals.

Attention now focused on the way to design and apply networks so that maximum use could be made of their resources. *Criteria for networks* were established and alternatives evaluated by comparison to these criteria. The following are the most important:

1. *Pipe capacity* at multiples of megabits per second (MBPS) going beyond 1 gigabit per second (GBPS).

The choice of transmission capacity is a function of the applications environment, user requirements, multimedia, communicating databases, and economics.

2. *Logical layers,* preferably all seven of ISO/OSI, plus an eighth layer to provide *one logical network* into which several physical networks can be integrated.

A major part of the logical structure is the *network control center (NCC).* In at least one of the better network architectures, NCC functionality represents 40% of the code.

3. *Reliability.* Reliability is not an ability. It is the probability that a given system will operate over a projected time and without failure under established environmental conditions.

The more our daily business is assisted by computers and communications, the more reliable should be the systems and their components. A systemwide availability rate of 99.9% for hardware and software is an attainable goal.

4. *Security.* Since we depend more and more on networks, we must utilize transport media which are secure and protected.

Not only must transactions and messages be encrypted, but access policies should be established with authorization and authentication prerequisites.

There are other design criteria for networks. They include the bit error rate (BER), transmission capacity without blocking (Erlang), modems and bus interface units, digitization, flexibility, and expandability. A recent addition to the requirements list is the use of AI constructs. They can be helpful in network design, operation, and maintainability.

2. SOLUTIONS WITH AI-ENRICHED MULTIMEDIA COMMUNICATIONS

Data communications originated in the late 1950s and early 1960s. In 1958, the first point-to-point transmission of computer data took place between Andrews Air Force Base and NATO headquarters (SHAPE), then located in Orleans, France. It was a magnetic tape-to-magnetic tape transmission—hardly exciting by today's standards, but it did open a new vista.

At about the same time, efforts to connect teletype terminals to a computer were less successful. But in 1963 the concept of the frontend processor (FEP) was developed at Dartmouth College. This made it feasible to connect to a computer a dozen terminals, and then a few dozen, up to the 60,000, 80,000, and 150,000 terminals featured by current networks.

Whether the connecting line(s) was point-to-point or multipoint (multidrop), early attachments were made to mainframes which themselves were centralized. The mainframe played the role of three engines in one. It performed

- Data communications (with the help of FEP),
- Data processing, and
- Databasing (with or without a DBMS).

The concept of a network as a self-standing entity with a structure and a mission developed between 1967 and 1969 with Arpanet. This is the dominant approach used today. Arpanet also introduced a new protocol designed for packet-type communications. A *protocol* is a set of conversions establishing a rule of conduct in communications. The terminals, WS, and hosts using the same protocol can exchange information with one another. Otherwise they need interfaces or may not even connect at all.

The earliest protocol developed and used with teletypewriters was of the *start/stop* type. It derived its name from the fact that each character being transmitted had a start and a stop bit. It was also known as an *asynchronous* protocol from the type of communication taking place. Though the start/stop mode is an inefficient way to interconnect, it is also the least expensive at the terminal level. Therefore, it is still the most widely used form today.

By the mid-1960s, *binary synchronous* communications protocols (BSC, bisync) began to be implemented. They featured a *header* part and a *trailer* part. The header contained housekeeping information (where from, to, etc.). The trailer was used for error control. BSC was a character string protocol. *Packet switching* (the Arpanet development) is typically a bit string with an improved header and trailer and a longer message. The now popular CCITT Recommended Standard X.25 is a packet switching protocol.

As computers shifted toward the role of communicators rather than calculators, their mission and architecture changed. As Figure 17-1 suggests, it first moved from principally switching to storing (databasing), and then from storing to networking.

There was also a parallel change in the communications domain; it was greatly enlarged and acquired new perspectives. From the time of Alexander Graham Bell, the goal of telephony[1] has been voice transmission. But in the 1960s, the basic orientation changed to voice and data—though voice was and still is the dominant part.

By the mid-1980s, the focus of interest was on an integrated carrier: voice, text, data, and image—that is, a *multimedia*. This change is significant to applications of AI. We will see why.

---

[1] The term *telephony* is a composite of two Greek words: *tele* stands for long distance, *phony* for voice.

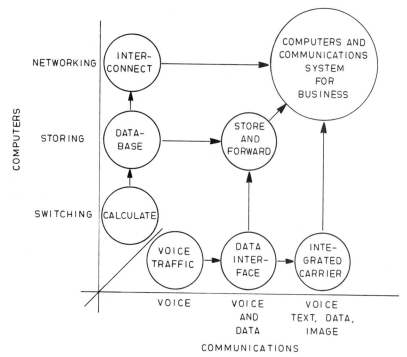

Figure 17-1. Computers and data communications started as two separate domains. Today they constitute one integrated system for business and industry.

Every time we refer to multimedia networks, the background factors are as follows:

1. Communications designers must project these networks.
2. System architects and system integrators must use them effectively.
3. Telecommunications engineers must monitor, control, and maintain them.

All three areas of activity can be enriched by AI. Let's examine the reasons one by one.

The Introduction described four basic design criteria: pipe capacity, logical layers, reliability, and security. What can AI do for them?

Pipe capacity is no longer at the 70-baud level. It is not even at the 9.6 kilobit per second (KBPS) level, which is more than two orders of magnitude higher. By now these are old standards.

With local area networks, where broadband transmission rates can be 400 megahertz (MHz)[2] and beyond, we use fairly complex bus interface units (BIU). The same is true of baseband transmission of, say, 1 MBPS or 10 MBPS. But there the BIU is simpler.

---

[2] Megahertz is a frequency modulation (analog) measure of capacity. KBPS is a digital transmission measure.

BIUs are programmable devices that can be considered small computers providing the connectivity from WS and host to pipe capacity. They feature buffers, control transmission, administer protocols, and detect collisions and errors. Expert systems can be of great assistance to a BIU, as each of these functions can be better served through heuristics than through procedural programming.

The seven layers of ISO/OSI have had no AI assistance so far. But requirements have changed with the eighth layer to be designed and implemented in order to permit transparency between layers—that is, one logical layer.

Just as, in the 1960s and 1970s, protocols became prominent, AI is today not just the better way but the only way to achieve effective connectivity among incompatible networks. It is also a valid approach for

- avoiding the extensive reprogramming required to match a growing variety of incompatible terminals and communications links, and for
- permitting the use of an open vendor policy in order to profit from the savings resulting from tough market competition.

These are services a system architecture should support in a way which is fully transparent to the enduser and reasonably transparent to the computer professional. While eighth-layer protocols like MAP. TOP, and CAN[3] aim to achieve the same goal, the results obtained so far show that our old concepts about what a protocol is and does are not good enough for the future.

Reliability is another key design variable which can benefit significantly from AI. The implementations in this domain range from network design (preoperating the system) to supervision, quality histories, and *diagnostics*. In fact, diagnostics is one of the most fruitful implementation fields for expert systems.

Figure 17-2 presents an intelligent network structure with emphasis on diagnostics, damage evaluation, and dynamic reconfiguration. The inference engine and domain knowledgebanks support the network administration and online testing subsystems. Further, the adopted telecommunications access solution features an expert system able to engage a user (man or machine) in dialogue to establish authentication.

The preceding example alos underlines the role an expert system can play in security and protection. Properly written, it not only permits security standards to be implemented but also supervises to determine whether these standards are being observed. The results obtained allow these security standards to be refined.

Also, when we talk of network usage, a basic measure is the bit error rate (BER), which reveals the quality of the line. BER is expressed in errors per so many thousand bits. An error rate of

- 10^{-2} is a disaster. On the average, it means one error every 100 bits.
- 10^{-4} is bad enough; 10^{-4} to 10^{-5} is what is known as *voice quality lines*.
- 10^{-7} or 10^{-8} is what the telephone companies offer for data quality lines.
- 10^{-11} or 10^{-12} is what is really needed.

---

[3] By General Motors, Boeing, and Bank of America/IBM, respectively.

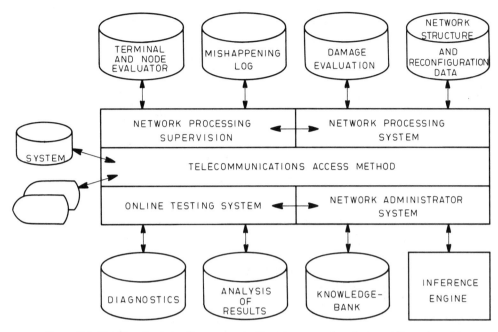

Figure 17-2. The future lies in intelligent networks. These have a number of prerequisites and consist of several interactive components, as shown in this figure.

It is not easy to improve the systemwide quality of transmission because large parts of the telecommunications plant are old (lines, switches, transmitters, receivers, interfaces). But *intelligent modems* with forward error correction capabilities can obtain a BER about two orders of magnitude lower. Thus, here too, AI has a role to play.

3. NETWORKS FOR ELECTRONIC BANKING: AN EXAMPLE OF GOALS AND SOLUTIONS

There is no better way to demonstrate an implementation perspective than by doing. For this reason, we will follow a case study on network development in the banking industry.

Banks depend greatly for their future business on computers and communications. During the 1980s, they invested heavily in networks. Over the last few years, a second focus of financial institutions has been AI. These investments in computers and communications by the financial sector are designed to promote innovation, reach the client online, improve the quality of service, increase managerial productivity—and, at the same time, lower costs. Banking was once a labor-intense industry; now it is technology intense. Among the top product problems faced by dynamic banks are the following:

1. Able *online handling of new types of products,* for instance, combined deposits and securities.

2. Fully *automated solutions* oriented to simpler products. The aim is low-cost production and distribution.
3. *Cost-effective* handling of very large volumes of transactions, which result from the bank's role as financial intermediary.
4. *Service differentiation* by client group. Typically, 20% of clients account for 80% of profits.
5. Steady development of the *bank's infrastructure,* to face present and future problems.
6. *Automation* or all *office work* beyond the levels currently achievable with classical computers.
7. Fast expansion of *electronic banking* with *multimedia support.* The network must operate 24 hours per day.

There are two basic reasons why the network of a financial institution must work around the clock. One relates to retail banking, the other to wholesale and interbanking transactions.

Automated teller machines (ATMs) and point of sale (POS) equipment are examples of retail banking implementations. ATMs permit direct debiting, thus cutting manual costs. But direct debiting must be done online.

Direct debiting and online approaches promote self-service banking, further cutting clerical costs. In turn, the bank ensures 24-hour operations to improve customer convenience and service. Thus computers and communications networks supporting 24-hour banking are a competitive investment.

But self-service in banking also imposes requirements. The client has been accustomed to talk to the teller. Many clients resist the cold appearance of a machine which they do not consider to be user friendly. We can overcome this resistence by turning the ATM into an *electronic teller,* endowing it with

1. an expert system which can communicate interactively with a client, prompt and help him, and
2. an optical disc capability actuated by the client or the expert system—hence, multimedia.

The optical disc can show a prerecorded discussion with a banker, who explains the service; demonstrates animated images to make certain points; presents alternative possibilities; and helps the client find his way. It is a demonstration of multimedia.

At the other side of the client service equation—wholesale banking—a focal point is investments. Another important service is loans to medium-sized and large companies. A bank's loans portfolio is responsible for 65–75% of its revenues. The bank's potential earnings capacity is strongly related to its lending activities, but lending can also be risky. Major factors determining a loan policy are

1. The quality of the company asking for a loan,
2. The condition of the economy and of the industry the company is in, and
3. the diversification or hedging undertaken by management to spread the risk.

Commercial loans are highly leveraged. Relatively small loan losses, or nonperforming loans, have a tremendous impact on the institution's earnings—and its viability. But first-class loan officers are in short supply. Hence the assistance expert systems can give is highly appreciated.

Let's assume a network of branches belonging to *our* financial institution, each with its loan officers. There are written directives on the conditions for loans, but these directives are not always followed. A computers and communications network can help in the execution of loan policies, particularly if its features expert system support.

One of the first modules to be established through AI assistance is the definition of a *client's profile*. Typically, 40 to 60 rules—hence, a simple expert system—will suffice to establish such a profile, particularly if coupled with shallow expert systems exploring public databases for information regarding this client firm: its credibility, loan profile, dependability, and financial health. AI modules would focus on loan and investment risks, for instance:

1. *Liquidity risks* as a function of cash drains exceeding current cash and secondary reserves;
2. *Operating risks* in reference to potential losses in carrying out day-to-day activities (e.g., inefficiencies, administrative errors, bad cost decisions, poor marketing);
3. *Fraud risks* due to dishonest activities of the company's personnel and others in the environment; and
4. *Fiduciary risks* associated with improper discharge of trust activities.

In the past, even with computers, loan information pertinent to a given branch office stayed there. Only the larger loans beyond the branch's responsibility were sent to headquarters for clearance. By contrast, a networking approach permits corporatewide information exchange and database accessibility.

A global database accessible by all authorized users, both men and machines, improves the quality of service and, in particular, enhances management control. Through the able use of electronics, we can add value to the product we bring to the market, thus hitting the third layer in Figure 17-3, above software and hardware.

In fact, we can do more than provide value-added services by bringing *solution selling* under perspective. The most lucrative clients to a bank today are the wealthy clients— whether corporations or private individuals. Those clients are also the most demanding. Therefore banks have to do much better than their competitors.

Banking management is also asking for immediate technology-based solutions to respond to increasingly stringent government requirements. For years, for example, customers at many banks have complained that when they deposit checks, those funds may not become available for two weeks or more. Meanwhile, depositors are often unable to pay bills on time, or the checks that they write bounce because of insufficient funds.

A new law enacted by Congress in mid-1987 stipulates that banks must clear checks drawn on local institutions within two working days, while out-of-state checks must clear after six business days. In 1990 those intervals will be further reduced, to one and four days, respectively. Networking solutions are necessary to provide an answer to this requirement.

Office automation is no longer confined to the office. The new goal is *the automation of services to customers*. The office functions per se are only an intermediate step toward this goal. Banking procedures have this in common with high-technology engineering. They are

```
┌─────────────────────────────────────────┐
│                                           │
│            AI  TECHNOLOGY                 │
│                                           │
│   PROBLEM-SOLVING  FUNCTIONALITY          │
│   INFERENCE  ENGINE                       │
│   KNOWLEDGEBANK  MANAGEMENT               │
│   INTELLIGENCE-ENRICHED  PROGRAMMING      │
│                                           │
├─────────────────────────────────────────┤
│                                           │
│              SOFTWARE                     │
│                                           │
│   COMMUNICATIONS  SOFTWARE                │
│   RELATIONAL  DATABASE  MANAGEMENT        │
│   GUARDED  HORN  CLAUSES                  │
│   LOGIC  PROGRAMMING                      │
│                                           │
├─────────────────────────────────────────┤
│                                           │
│              HARDWARE                     │
│                                           │
│   KNOWLEDGEBANK  ENGINE                   │
│   PARALLEL  INFERENCE                     │
│   SEQUENTIAL  INFERENCE                   │
│   VLSI                                    │
│                                           │
└─────────────────────────────────────────┘
```

Figure 17-3. There are three layers in AI technology. The top layer is characterized by problem-solving functionality. The middle layer is software, and the bottom layer is hardware.

very complicated. To attack their nonautomated component in an able manner, AI will be very much needed.

This still unautomated part of banking—as in other industries—accounts for 70–75% of all operations. We will return to this issue in Section 5, where we will suggest solutions which can bring good results.

4. COMMUNICATING DATABASES FOR ONLINE BANKING: A CASE STUDY

The Introduction stated that banks are well ahead in high technology. In fact, they compare favorably to the most advanced organizations worldwide in terms of their ingenuity in implementing computers and communications technology. There are several reasons for this situation.

1. *The sheer weight of large numbers.*

In the Western world, the banking public has greatly increased as a percentage of the population. Many people have more than one account. Also, for the reasons stated earlier, banks actively promote online operations to the bank's database by clients.

2. *Current and projected profits from online operations.*

The better-organized banks are able to make a profit on online services, though others still lose money, particularly on PC and mainframe connections by clients—but no more on ATMs. Still, PC and mainframe access to the bank's database is seen as having a longer-term payoff because of new service offerings.

Being ahead in the implementation of high technology, some of the financial institutions point toward possible developments in new paying services to compete with nonbank banks.[4] Cash management is an example at the wholesale level; retail customers can make fund transfers between accounts by using PCs.

Figure 17-4 presents the conception and structure of an integrated banking system. It

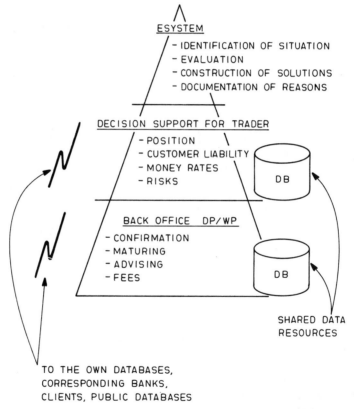

Figure 17-4. The conception and structure of an integrated system, whether in banking or in manufacturing, can be seen as a series of layers. This example comes from the financial industry.

---

[4] For instance, brokerage houses and department store chains.

TABLE 17-1. Terminalization of Banking Functions.

	1980 (%)	1985 (%)	1990 (%)
Self-service	3	10	60
Central departments	10	20	70
Back office	30	45	80
Front desk	60	80	100

includes both domestic and overseas networks, each addressing the branch offices in its area. Both connect to the main office. Local area networks are widely used. The central information file (CIF) is security protected but accessible online. Corporate clients also access online the bank's information resources.

   3. *The general acceptance of online systems* that financial institutions consider to be solidly integrated into their way of doing business.

Some of the money center banks (and certain smaller banks as well) have made great strides in the use of computers and communications. The banking industry is becoming increasingly attuned to online systems and the technology of the electronic banking services behind them.

Table 17-1 presents statistics (for 1980 and 1985) on the terminalization of banking functions in three areas: self-service, central departments, and back office and front desk. The growth is impressive, even if the 1990 projection is somewhat optimistic.

To summarize the current status of online banking: The range of supported services is well rounded, but while the financial sector is advanced in the implementation of computers and communications, banks differ in terms of their investment priorities. Table 17-2 outlines the primary issues regarding investment priorities at four different institutions.

TABLE 17-2. Investment Priorities of Leading Banks.

	Investment Priority
Bank A	* Extensive network
	* Expert systems applications
	* PC-to-mainframe interconnection
	* Mainframe-to-mainframe interconnection
	* Optical disc implementation
Bank B	* High level of security/protection
	* Fully automated, low-cost solutions aimed at midrange clients
	* Database computers (rear-end)
	* Multimedia networking
Bank C	* Convert at least 65% of the remaining batch system to an online system
	* Significantly expand electronic banking for clients
	* AI-supported dealer system (new generation just installed)
	* Optical disc implementation (current application is personnel files; will expand this area of interest)
Bank D	* Very-high-level advances in information systems for customers
	* Extensive networking
	* AI implementation beyond current applications (loans, investment advising)

The types of problems outline in this table, and their diversity, suggest that each bank follows a different strategy in going beyond the simpler online solutions and to a new-generation system. This leads to the next key point:

4. For the leading financial institutions, the use of *AI* and the projected employment of *fifth-generation computers* is not a vague notion but a concrete plan.

While currently the larger AI projects are at the prototype level, smaller WS-type implementations of expert systems have gone beyond the prototype and are in full application at several banks. This is not surprising, as AI tools are viewed as means to solutions. Hence, a string commitment is being made in this direction.

Expert systems in banking are presently promoted through three channels: by personnel within the bank itself, by consultants, and by computer manufacturers. The leading financial institutions show that work in AI is well launched and fairly successful.

But there are also problems confronting the most advanced financial institutions precisely because they steadily push technology to its limits. Key problems identified in Table 17-3 are faced by Banks A, B, and C.

5. The implementation of *distributed, communicating databases* and the need to manage them through shallow expert systems.

In the middle to late 1970s, industry moved beyond distributed data processing to distributed databases. This was as true in banking as in engineering, manufacturing, and merchandizing. But in the 1970s, databases were small by today's standards. Ten years ago, 50 megabytes of online storage constituted a large database. Today many of the larger organizations have more than 1 terabyte of online storage. Thus, in ten years, the size of the online database has been multiplied by a factor of 20:

- The size of the online database will grow much faster during the next decade as *multimedia applications* are implemented.
- Users' requests for online access will grow and a *dynamic model*[5] will domi-

TABLE 17-3. Top Product Problems faced by Leading Banks.

	Problems
Bank A	* Agile online handling of new types of products (e.g., combined deposits and securities)
	* Fully automated solutions oriented to simpler products (low-cost production and distribution)
	* Very large volume of transactions
Bank B	* Service differentiation by client group
	* Uniform level of service within each client group
	* Fast expansion of electronic banking with multimedia support
	* Steady development of the bank's infrastructure
Bank C	* Joint projects in cash management service
	* Automation of all office work, beyond the levels currently achievable with classical computers
	* Management of distributed, communicating databases and AI assistance in this task

[5] See also Section 5.

nate system design, with managerial requirements showing the fastest increase.

- Reliability, security, recovery, a low error rate, and the other criteria we have considered will be further emphasized, imposing stringent requirements on *design and implementation.*

Reflecting on ongoing, successful online applications, Figures 17-5A and 17-5B differentiate between the classical central information file for transaction-type applications and the management information file (MIF). The latter is the database of the *information center,* which directs its services to managers and professionals.

While the CIF is the source database for transactions, the MIF is the kernel for messages and queries. We have differentiated between these two classes of operations and have suggested their growing importance in meeting the information requirements of managers and professionals.

Figure 17-5B details the subjects covered within the information center perspective. They range from electronic mail and time management to expert system support for management decision. This figure also identifies those subjects which occur in the transactional area of implementation. All of them have to be handled online. The same is true of direct client service, as suggested in Figure 17-5A.

These factors help exemplify what we expect from distributed, communicating databases and why the AI connection is so important. AI is a key factor in

- coping with increased complexity,
- solving the problems of concurrency control,
- improving availability,
- dealing with recovery management, and
- obtaining fast enough diagnostics to provide for a fail soft outcome.[6]

In a complex environment such as this, a transaction, message, or query must be either committed or aborted. No partial result should remain. Furthermore, information elements in distributed databases are often replicated, and replicated databases require multiple copies of objects, as well as internal and mutual consistencies. We need powerful automatic mechanisms to cope with this challenge; AI is the answer.

5. ORGANIZATIONAL INFORMATION AND EXPERT SYSTEM SUPPORT

If we look back over the history of mankind, we learn that *Homo sapiens* began to use spoken language about 43,000. B.C. Written language took almost forty centuries to develop; the approximate starting date is 3500 B.C.

---

[6] A system fails softly if it continues operating at a reduced capacity due to failures at some local modes or linky.

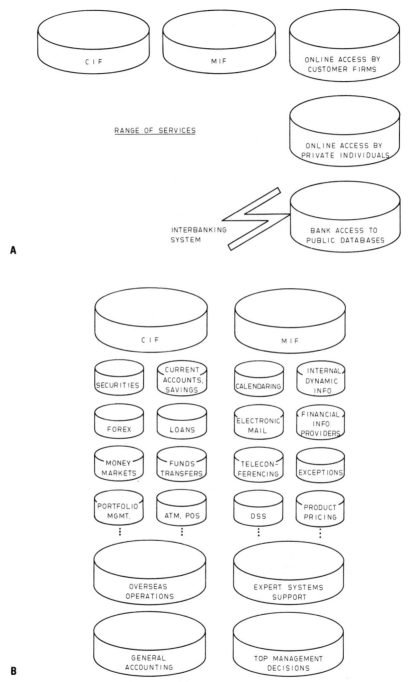

Figure 17-5A,B. A range of services must be supported interactively, with all facilities being online and networked. This figure identifies the components of the central information file (CIF) and the management information file (MIF). Expert systems support is everywhere.

In the Hellenistic era in Alexandria, books were written on papyrus through the dedication of a group of writers, but the book as we know it today had to await Gutenberg's (1397–1468) discovery of the printing press. Hence bookmaking dates to 1450. Mail service is believed to have started about 1800. The Rothschilds made their fortune out of pigeon-paged express mail, having been the first to be informed of Napoleon's defeat at Waterloo.

The telegraph was the first practical application of electricity, just as expert systems are the first practical application of AI. The telegraph dates back to 1836. Alexander Graham Bell (1847–1922) invented the telephone in 1876. Like the mail and the telegraph, the telephone tremendously enhanced communications.

Other important discoveries also date to the nineteenth-century and focus on the *office*. The typewriter dates back to 1890 and the vertical file cabinet to 1895. The early Twentieth-century saw the development of the calculator (1905), the copier (1920), and the microfilm (1925). The goal of each one of these discoveries was to improve office productivity and the quality of the work.

This has also been the initial aim of office automation: the improvement of office worker productivity. Over the last fifteen years, this goal has been approached through enhancement of tools (early 1970s to mid 1980s). Beginning in the early 1980s, emphasis was placed on the need for integration of simple systems, and by the late 1980s, attention focused on integrated *multimedia* systems.

Like all human enterprises at their beginning, such efforts were not too successful. Experience makes us suspect a *missing link*. It is time to take a fresh look and to ask critical questions. The first questions that come to mind are:

- Why did office automation not *really* take off?
- Have we reached the limits of office automation?

These are the wrong questions. They are not generic enough and therefore do not allow for a new departure. Generic questions are of the following kind:

1. Why does the office exist?
2. What are the key ingredients in an office envinronment?
3. What is being done in the office?
4. Can we do this work in a different manner?
5. Which are our alternatives?
6. Which are the objectives to be achieved?

The office exists to process messages and transactions, to respond to queries, and to manage the archives. This is just as true of a banking environment as it is of engineering or any other profession.

The key ingredients in an office environment are people:

- their heuristics and
- their knowledge.

This *defines the role of AI assistance:* the use of human knowledge and human heuristics in designing the office system and then automating it.

After we strip off the scientific shell and apply software engineering approaches, it becomes apparent that expert systems are nothing more (and nothing less) than a new, advanced programming technology. The essence of machine intelligence is to provide expert assistance and to automate the 70–75% of essential business operations which are still manual.

AI-based expert assistance is one of the two pillars on which our future competitiveness rests. The other is a dynamic model of interconnection. It is based on networked computers and communications devices plus able expert system–supported human interfaces. As Figure 17-6 suggests:

- A *dynamic model* is bidirectional, with three key commands: *plan, execute,* and *display.*
- A *static model* is undirectional. Its basic commands are *copy* and *move.*

Dynamic interconnection must be able to remember where it came from. In addition, the network should provide *any-to-any* connectivity. Bidirectional linkage requires an *infrastructure* and a large amount of storage. AI-supported, unidirectional linkage is simpler.

Because of our greater dependence on communicating databases and DSSs, the modern organization (banking, insurance, manufacturing, distribution) faces the challenge of managing very complex aggregates of people, software, and machinery. Computers and communications will store, transport, and present vast amounts of text, data, graphics, image, and voice messages.

- These will refer to *our* clients, markets, products and services, competitors, and suppliers.

DYNAMIC MODEL

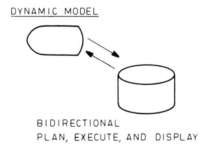

BIDIRECTIONAL
PLAN, EXECUTE, AND DISPLAY

STATIC MODEL

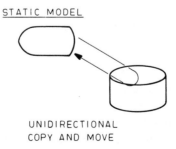

UNIDIRECTIONAL
COPY AND MOVE

Figure 17-6. It is not enough for a solution to be interactive. It should also be bidirectional, with the computer-based expert system providing prompts, help, and advice.

- They will talk about their habits, backgrounds, preferences—and the profit-ability of *our* operations.

A new challenge we now face is how to use this information to discover new business opportunities. Even when we have the information, it will take quite a while to learn how to use it properly. Hence, it is wise to implement AI to help us do this job.

While more classical software and hardware components will hae a significant role to play in terms of functionaility and throughout, we need machine intelligence to handle and distill increasing volumes of text, data, and other information elements transmitted over carriers and handled by computers.

We also need computer and communications networks to carry such information volumes from origin to destination. Networks must cover a broad range of services, to be supported at different organizational levels, at whichever layer each service belongs. A *network* is

a well-defined collection of services,
- the way to provide instantanuity in operations,
- an intelligent carrier ensuring effective information interchange,
- the means to tie together systems and components,
- a controllable structure (through an NCC).

The knowledge network of a company able to live with the technology of its time is a good paradigm of expert system application in the knowledge engineering domain. Complex financial networks of the type shown in Figure 17-7 cannot be made through time-honored methods even if the word *host* stands for many networked mainframes, maxis, minis, and supermicros—that is, for the traditional form of distributed information systems which is now fifteen years old.

New approaches are necessary, and in these, knowledge engineering will have a major role to play. Each design phase and each person's task must be clearly stated:

- Good methodology calls for life cycle design.
- Valid design approaches account for expansion, restructuring, and AI en-hancement.
- Steady design reviews and quality inspection reduce errors in early stages.
- Heuristics and simulation offer the possibility of using models for data flow and control flow.
- Quantitative measures are necessary but not enough. We also need quality metrics.

The metrics would help monitor development progress reports on quality and bring in evidence of ongoing productivity. One project run on this basis demonstrated a twofold increase in productivity and a significant improvement in quality.

Most importantly, able and reasonably lasting information system solutions require a commitment by the entire organization. They call for rigorous development methods, uniform development processes, and uniform high quality.

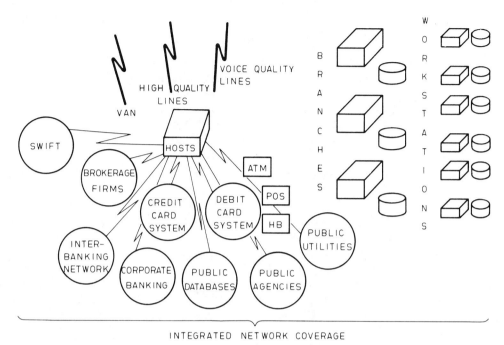

Figure 17-7. An integrated network includes online, transparent access to all supported applications areas, which may involve hundreds of branches and thousands of WSs.

6. NETWORK DEVELOPMENT WITH AI ASSISTANCE

The discussion in Sections 1 to 5 demonstrated the complexity of services to be supported through a network. We have spoken of communicating databases; online transactions, messages, and queries; organizational perspectives; multimedia communications; and the wisdom of having AI assistance in developing, implementing, operating, and maintaining networks.

When we design a network to serve the requirements of an organization, we must first define these requirements

- in a qualitative and quantitative sense
- for a current (next five years), a foreseeable (five to ten years), and a more distant (about fifteen years) time frame.

These are prerequisite—conditioned by requirements, technology, and cost—in making a decision on the characteristics of the network, as follows:

1. The system architecture we will choose,

2. The network architecture (commodity software) we will employ, and

3. The technology we will use.

These factors will help determine network structure and functionality. To take an example, PBXs based on fifth-generation computers and inference engines, and enriched with AI constructs for simultaneous translation will serve a multilingual environment, with everyone connected to the system speaking his own language—the difference made up by realtime voice translations executed through the PBX.

Natural language processing and automatic simultaneous translation will give considerable advantages to the organization which applies this technology first. This is an excellent example of the competitive headway to be gained and the business opportunities to be exploited.

Further, PCs with inference capabilities and AI constructs can act as intelligent agents, providing agile human interfaces. A new generation of operating systems, written for them, will support heavy functions that have been common in conventional large-scale operating systems but not on PCs—for example, load balancing and optimum resource allocation.

Consequently, networks connecting various types of computing resources and knowledgebanks will evolve and over time become popular. However, such networks will require AI assistance to be designed. There is, of course, no reason why we should not use AI constructs immediately in network design. This is the procedure demonstrated in the following pages.

Let's suppose an expert system written to assist in network design past the requirements specification phase. We will call it the *Configurer*. It is intended to help designers solve topological configuration problems and can be used as an integral part of network design work.

The Configurer is composed of several modules, some of which are employed as a research system to deepen our understanding of the design problem. Hence, its contribution is much broader than design. It is also an example of the benefits to be derived from the implementation of AI in networking.

This expert system construct[7] is intended to serve as a tool for the expert network designer, addressing the problems encountered in such work. It includes expertise on how to do network design which, prior to its development, was largely in the form of rules of thumb, as in all engineering projects.

The Configurer expresses its expertise through heuristics which have been shown, over the course of many years and many network designs, to generate reasonable topologies. In this sense, AI captures the collective knowledge of network designers. Once this is done, a second important design goal can be reached, making the system sufficiently modular so that:

- new tariffs,
- different network devices, and
- alternative protocols and design techniques can be easily added to the system.

---

[7] The reference is based on an expert system designed and implemented by Bolt, Beranek, Newman, in Cambridge, Massachusetts, for network design and configuration.

The need for the addition of tariffs, devices, and protocols has been addressed through AI. A third important design goal is an experimental solution to a complex of network design problems.

The intelligent design system must organize the information about the network so that it is accessible to the network designer when needed. At the same time, unnecessary information should be hidden so as not to confuse the network designer.

Newly added modules to the expert system feature a knowledgebank consisting of the configuration rules of packet switches and packet assembly/disassembly (PAD). They generate, as output, a detailed packet switch or PAD configuration, specifying boards, racks, cabling, and power. These same modules also provide a list of parts (bill of materials) and the prices for each part.

Throughout the implementation, interaction between the user and the system is mostly menu driven. The system provides two displays:

1. *A black-and-white display featuring a number of different panels.*

A command panel contains a menu of algorithms and mathematical models which the user can invoke. A variety of tabular reports, for example, on network delays and line utilizations, can be summoned by the user and displayed in the report panel. A status panel reflects summary information on the equipment in the network design.

2. *A color display which serves different purposes.*

Network maps are shown on the color display. In addition, the color display contains a number of graphs which track the progress of the network design. For example, one graph plots the *cost of the network* as the design evolves. Two other graphs display values of *network performance* measures for each *candidate topology*. By monitoring these displays, the network designer can ascertain that he is really making progress in finding better solutions.

Not surprisingly, much of the effort in the development of the Configurer has gone into the presentation of information to the designer. To meet this goal, innovative techniques have been developed for man–machine interfacing. A major problem in designing large networks is caused less by the complexity of the design than by the presentation of this complexity to the human user.

An example is density of lines and nodes. The expert system communicates its results through simplified maps. New maps can be made in which the network is untangled by moving objects around on the screen. Other maps are invoked, magnifying regions of the network. These maps are not purely passive displays. By employing the correct commands, the designer can edit any of them and thereby modify the design. Maps can also be buried, so that they are no longer in view, and made visible again when needed.

Network objects are represented by simple icons. When a network object is pointed to, its name appears on the color display. Thus, the names of objects do not obscure the designer's view of the network. If more information is needed about the network object than its name, this too can be obtained by pointing at the object and invoking the appropriate menu item—for example, the names of all objects which are homed to a packet switch.

Through a feature called *presentation*, an object can be asked to present itself. In this case, a detailed English language description of the network object is displayed. In general, a network object can be manipulated—described, moved, or deleted—by pointing to it on the map or by pointing to its name in any report.

For example, the designer is presented with information about a packet switch by pointing to its icon. This information may include the names of attached PADs.

Information about a given PAD can be obtained by pointing to its name on the list of devices attached to the packet switch. This new information includes the identities of the terminals attached to the PAD. By pointing to the name of a terminal in this list, the user can obtain information about that terminal.

Through the command panel, the designer is able to invoke many heuristics to solve each phase of the topological design problem. For instance, a number of clustering heuristics are available for packet switch placement. Commands available for backbone design are those heuristics which have been demonstrated to be useful to network engineers.

Finally, to help with requirements definition, another expert system module, the *Specifier,* allows the user to express what is asked for by the network. The user can do so in words that he himself understands, helped by a natural language interface for the specification of loads, topologies, protocols, devices, and tariffs.

In this sense, the Specifier provides input to the network's topological design system. Its action is intended to facilitate the specification of user traffic in a network. This significantly increases the designer's productivity, since most of the time devoted to network design is spent specifying requirements.

Subsequently, the Configurer takes as input a description of a network topology. As stated, topology projections detail for each network component the number of devices connected to the component and the types of interfaces required by each device. Expert assistance has been the dream of everyone who has worked with computers during the last four decades. It now seems to be on its way to realization.

Appendix

Training the Knowledge Engineer

This book has demonstrated the high level of expertise required by knowledge engineers. Intelligence costs money. Knowledge engineers are expensive; they are also scarce. But those who are in the profession must be of high quality.

Universities are under steady pressure to develop programs for training knowledge engineers. At DePaul University in Chicago, for instance, the demand for AI training was so great that the school instituted a thirteen-week program for computer professionals who want training in AI techniques. What should be taught in such a course?

- The concepts and tools of AI.
- The role of the knowledge engineer.
- The best implementation perspectives.

These issues have been thoroughly discussed throughout this book. But let us summarize here the essence of a training program in AI.

1. The *fundamentals:* What is AI? How has science been awakening through mathematics? What is the role of fifth-generation computers? How can we construct an inference engine? How effectively can we build its environment? What are the constituents of the knowledgebank? How do the knowledgebank and the database compare to and collaborate with one another?

These are the subjects treated in Part One of this book. They are introductory. They touch on humanities and aim to create a broader background.

Fifth-generation computers, knowledgebanks, and databases are discussed at the beginning on purpose. As a first practical application of non-von Neumann computers, the personal inference engine leads to a *major cultural change*. This can be attested to by the implementations which have already started.

- Technology transfer and
- computer literacy

are basic processes in putting this cultural change into effect. Computer literacy is relative. One may be quite literate in classical computers but not necessarily literate in fifth-generation computers.

2. The *functions, duties,* and *responsibilities* of the knowledge engineer: first, the professional perspective; then the knowledge acquisition processes and tools; knowledge assimilation; knowledge presentation; and the subjects of prototyping and shells.

Part Two of this book focuses on the functions of the knowledge engineer. It explains knowledge acquisition, starting with interviews with domain experts and proceeding to other solutions. Descriptive approaches are necessary; the analysis of written procedures can be helpful. The student or trainee has to be led through the successive steps.

The subject of knowledge assimilation for Esystems development should definitely be part of the course, including the process of inference; logical constructs and hybrid constructs; and global database organization. It is not sufficient to know about databases. The student should learn about knowledgebanks, multimedia databases, and global databases.

The trick is to maintain clear ideas and precise notions without falling into the trap of thinking that the knowledge of basic tools will come as a matter of course. As with time, financial resources, space, and competence, there is a shortage of imagination in the workplace. Many people are not capable of envisioning (much less appreciating) a different way of doing anything.

Where a shortage of imagination exists, there is often a surplus of problems like user resistance, obstructionism, myopia, or simply indifference. The proper teaching makes a difference—and so does practical work.

There is no better subject for a workshop than knowledge representation. This includes

- domain definition,
- prototyping, and
- rule writing.

The student must also be trained in internal and external testing, the practical implementation of the expert system kernel, and the development of value-added modules, as well as the integration of the AI construct he is writing with existing applications software on data processing, databasing, and data communications.

I would advise students to learn to use a shell by doing a few simple expert system problems. This should be done prior to studying deeper theoretical subjects. We can even emulate an expert system utilization by defining case studies.

1. writing production rules of the IF . . . THEN . . . ELSE type or
2. developing a frame-based solution which can be easily explained on the spot.

This will give the student the sense of an AI application. Chances are that the workshop will also suggest the need for more theoretical bases. Since the latter require greater involvement and attention, the motivation created through the workshop will be of help.

In developing theoretical bases, a good way to start is with the history of *analytical* and *conceptual* thought. This can include underlining the dominant role that astronomers played in computing: from the analog men who built Stonehenge through Kepler, Laplace, and Gauss. This approach creates perspectives and teaches lessons.

The Ballistic Research Laboratory at Aberdeen was the brainchild of a World War I celestial mechanics expert. The specifications for ENIAC, the Mark IV, and the IBM relay calculators were written by the theoretical astronomer who ran the IBM installation there during World War II.

The theoretical bases today are, of course, different, but the processes of the inquisitive human mind have not changed. Today we talk of objects, rules, and knowledge, but also of metaobjects, metarules, and metaknowledge. The concept of *meta* is critical in all AI work.

Further, an AI program must focus on qualitative reasoning. Qualitative models achieve flexibility by representing the domain entities and their interrelationships explicitly. The student must also be taught that in problem domains, the assumptions underlying such models change periodically. Hence, it is necessary to synthesize and maintain qualitative models in response to these changing assumptions.

Possibility theory contains rules that are synthesized into qualitative models, including the entities and relationships relevant to the domain. Experience demonstrates that this approach is useful in explaining and generating expert behavior. It offers the ability to support decision making in a problem domain—which, after all, is the objective of expert systems.

Part One introduces and then discusses methods and tools. It explains how to use them and underlines the great importance of agile, friendly man–machine interfaces. This is the scope of the *human window*.

After being taught the methodology and the tools, the student should be asked to return to the results of the first workshop and identify areas for improvement. Both productivity and quality should be closely monitored, leading the student to suggest better solutions.

Practical examples with valid solutions are also given in Part Two. Chapter 14 underlines the growing importance of *multimedia,* where AI is the pivotal point. Chapter 16 focuses on applications in manufacturing and robotics. Chapter 17 deals with AI implementation in networks, with the banking industry taken as a case study.

Such a program is evidently ambitious. It will take time, skill, and patience to teach it well. How long should the training of knowledge engineers take?

This textbook is introductory. Its teaching typically requires one quarter or semester, depending on the density of the course. But this book is not the whole training program.

Table A-1 outlines a program for knowledge engineers that I designed for a leading organization. Depending on the background of the participants, it requires four and a half to seven and a half months full time.

Apart the formal training in classroom sessions, there should also be an apprenticeship period of between six months and year. Apprenticeship is productive time working as an assistant to a knowledge engineer.

These estimates are based on the assumption that the candidate have a valid background as a starting condition. This means a university education and four or five years of professional experience, though not necessarily with expert systems.

TABLE A-1. Curriculum for Knowledge Engineers.

(The range is conditioned by the background. A larger time estimate provides a common denominator.)

	Days
A. Theoretical basis	
1. Probability theory, bayesian processes, operating characteristic curves	3–15
2. Logic and thinking in logic	2–3
3. Uncertainty, possibility theory, fuzzy sets	4–10
4. Conceptual modeling	1–3
5. Patterns, classification	4–5
6. Frames, Petri nets, Semantic nets (through shells, including teaching of shell)	4–6
7. Machine learning aspects	1–2
	19–44
B. Logic programming	
1. Linguistics, then Prolog, Lisp, or OPS 5	10–15
C. Practical experience	
1. General features of a prototype (Mycin and descendants)	4–5
2. Knowledge acquisition (including case studies and examples)	5–7
3. Knowledge representation, rapid prototyping, self-explanation	3–5
4. Rule-based systems, production systems, exercises	3–6
5. Methodology	2–3
	17–26
D. Systems background	
1. Macroengineering system architecture, system integration	3–6
2. Microengineering, DSS, integrated software, graphics, desktop publishing	3–6
3. Databases and data communications	3–6
4. Human windows (through the shell)	3–6
	12–24
E. Applications	
Experience acquisition, case studies	
Domain-specific examples, what and why in selection as a function of the application	
(Domains: banking, law, networks, CAD and manufacturing, technical diagnostics, geology, medicine)	
Total	10–15
F. Learning by Example	
Visits to organizations with esystems, both written and operating.	
Esystem-oriented report on results	
Total	10–15
G. Selection Criteria	
1. Identification of lessons learned from visits	2–3
2. How to select packages, software, equipment	3–5
	5–8
H. Cognitive science	
1. Theoretical background in cognition/perception	3–5
2. Applied experimental psychology	2–3
	5–7

TABLE A-1. Curriculum for Knowledge Engineers. *(Continued)*

	Days
I. Project management	
From contracting to planning, administering, and controlling	
1. Principles of project management	2–3
2. Project coordination and administration	2–3
3. Design reviews	2–3
4. Interfaces for hybrid systems	2–3
	8–12
Summary by chapter	
A. Theoretical basis	19–44
B. Logic programming	10–15
C. Practical experience	17–26
D. Systems background	12–24
E. Applications	10–15
F. Learning by example	10–15
G. Selection by criteria	5–8
H. Cognitive science	5–7
I. Project management	8–12
	100–166

Thus, depending on the person's background between 4.5 and 7.5 months of very intensive training are necessary, followed by Participation in a couple of Esystem projects as an "assistant to" (Apprenticeship)

Note 1: *Objects* will be taught in Part B (logic programming).
Note 2: A range of other subjects, including neurophysiology and behavioral sciences, may also need to be added. The time will depend on the background of the trainee. Alternatively, these subjects can be taught in an extended *lifelong training program.*

By contrast, a university program would be addressed to the junior, senior, or graduate level. Typically, it would involve much more mathematics:

- probability theory,
- statistics,
- experimental design,
- statistical tests,
- Bayesian rules,
- possibility theory.

But the knowledge acquisition and knowledge representation components need not be greatly enlarged, though

- frames,
- semantic networks,
- Petri nets,

- scenarios, and
- production rules

should constitute part of the curriculum. Workshops and laboratory sessions are most advisable. I have given the documentation and the reasons. The *learning and execution capability should be judged by the results obtained.*

Bibliography

Akers, M.D., Grover, L.P., Blocher, E.J., and Mister, W.G. "Expert Systems for Management Accountants." *Management Accounting,* 67, 9, 1986.

Aleksander, I., and Burnett, P. *Re-inventing Man.* Penguin Books, Harmondsworth, Middlesex, England, 1984.

Alexander, T. "Why Computers Can't Outthink the Experts." *Fortune,* 110, 4, 1984.

Arciszewski, T., Mustafa, M., and Ziarko, W. "A Methodology of Design Knowledge Acquisition for Use in Learning Expert Systems," *International Journal of Man-Machine Studies,* 1987.

Atkinson, C., and Schneider, M.L. "A Business-oriented Methodology for Expert Systems Development." Proceedings Commercial Expert Systems in Banking and Finance. Gottlieb Duttweiler Institute, Ruschlikon, Zurich.

Barr and Feigenbaum. *The Handbook of Artificial Intelligence,* Vol. 1. Pitman Books, London, 1981.

Barr and Feigenbaum. *The Handbook of Artificial Intelligence,* Vol. 2. Pitman Books, London, 1982.

Berry, D.C., and Broadbent, D.E. "Expert Systems and the Man–Machine Interface." *Expert Systems,* 3,4, 1986.

Biswas, P., and Majumdar, A. "A Multistage Fuzzy Classifier for Recognition of handprinted Characters." *IEEE Transactions on Systems, Man and Cybernetics,* SMC-11(12), 1981.

Blanning, R.W. "Management Applications of Expert Systems." *Information and Management* (the Netherlands), 7,6, 1984.

Boden, M.A. *Artificial Intelligence and Natural Man.* Basic Books, New York, 1977.

Boose, J.H. "Uses of Repertory Grid-centered Knowledge Acquisition Tools for Knowledge-based Systems." Proceedings of the Second Knowledge Acquisition for Knowledge Based Systems Workshop, Banff, Alberta, 1987.

Bratko, I., and Lavrac, N., eds. *Progress in Machine Learning.* Sigma Press, Wilmslow, England, 1987.

Breiman, L., Friedman, J., Olshen, R., and Stone, C. *Classification and Regression Trees.* Wadsworth and Brooks, Monterey, CA, 1984.

Breuker, J.A., and Wielinga, B.J. "Techniques for Knowledge Elicitation and Analysis." Report 1.5, Esprit Project 12, Laboratory for Experimental Psychology, University of Amsterdam, 1984.

Brule, J.F. *Artificial Intelligence, Theory, Logic and Application."* Tab Books, Blue Ridge Summit, PA, 1986.

Burstein, M.H. "Incremental Learning from Multiple Analogies." In A. Prieditis, ed., *Analogica,* Pitman, London, 1988.

Campbell, J.A. "Applications of Artificial Intelligence within the ESPRIT Programme." In W. Brauer and W. Wahlster, eds., *Wissenbasierte Systeme.* Springer-Verlag, Berlin, 1987.

Carbonell, J.G. "Learning by Analogy: Formulating Generalized Plans from Past Experience." In R.S. Michalski, J.G. Carbonell, and T.M. Mitchell, eds., *Machine Learning: An Artificial Intelligence Approach,* Vol. 1. Tiaga, Palo Alto, CA, 1983.

Carbonell, J.G. "Derivational Analogy: A Theory of Reconstructive Problem Solving and Expertise Acquisition." In R.S. Michalski, J.G. Carbonell, and T.M. Mitchell, eds., *Machine Learning, An Artificial Intelligence Approach,* Vol. 2. Morgan Kaufmann, Los Altos, CA, 1986.

Cercone, N., and McCalla, G. "Artificial Intelligence: Underlying Assumptions." *Journal of the ASIS.*

Charniak, E., and McDermott, D. *Artificial Intelligence.* Addison-Wesley, Reading, MA, 1985.

Chorafas, D.N. *Applying Expert Systems in Business.* McGraw-Hill, New York, 1987.

Cognitive Science. Special Issue. "Connectionist Models and their Applications." 1,9, 1985.

Cox, L.A., and Blumenthal, R. "KRIMB: An Intelligent Knowledge Acquisition and Representation Program for Interactive Model Building." *Proceedings of the IEEE Conference on Knowledge Acquisition,* Reading, MA, 1987.

Davis and Lennat. *Knowledge Based Systems in Artificial Intelligence.* McGraw-Hill, New York, 1981.

Dawson, P., Buckland, S., and Gilbert, N. "Expert Systems and the Public Provision of Welfare Benefit Advice." Presented at the British Sociological Association's Annual Conference, Leeds, England, 1987.

Debenham, J. "Knowledge Based Design." *The Australian Computer Journal,* 17,1, 1986.

DeWitt, P.E. "Fast and Smart." *Time,* March 28, 1988.

Dietterich, T., and Michalski, R. "Inductive Learning of Structural Descriptions." *Artificial Intelligence,* 16,3, 1981.

Doyle, J. "A Truth Maintenance System." *Artificial Intelligence,* 12, 1979.

Dreistadt, R. "An Analysis of the Use of Analogies and Metaphors in Science." *Journal of Psychology,* 68, 1968.

Evans, J.R. "Creative Thinking and Innovative Education in the Decision Sciences." *Decision Sciences,* 17, 1986.

Evans, T.G. "A Program for the Solution of a Class of Geometric Analogy Intelligence Test Questions." In M. Minsky, ed., *Semantic Information Processing,* MIT Press, Cambridge, MA, 1968.

Falkenhainer, B. "An Examination of the Third Stage in the Analogy Process: Verification Based Analogical Learning." *Proceedings of the IJCAI,* Milan, 1987.

Falkenhainer, B., Forbus, K., and Gentner, D. "The Structure Mapping Engine." *Proceedings of the IJCAI,* Milan, 1986.

Feigenbaum and McCorduck. *The Fifth Generation.* Michael Joseph, 1984.

Feldman, P., and Fitzgerald, G. "Representing Rules Through Modelling Entity Behavior." *Proceedings of the Fourth International Conference on Entity Relationship Approach,* October 1985.

Fikes, R.E., and Nilsson, N.J. "Strips: A New Approach to the Application of Theorem Proving to Problem Solving." *Artificial Intelligence,* 2, 1971.

Fodor, J., and Pylysnyn, Z.W. "Connectionism and Cognitive Architecture: A Critical Analysis," *Cognition,* 1988.

Forbus, K. "Qualitative Process Theory." *Artificial Intelligence,* 24, 1984.

Forbus, K., and Gentner, D. "Learning Physical Domains: Towards a Theoretical Framework." In R.S. Michalski, J.G. Carbonell, and T.M. Mitchell, eds., *Machine Learning: An Artificial Intelligence Approach,* Vol. 2, Morgan Kaufmann, Los Altos, CA, 1986.

Forsyth, R. "BEAGLE: A Darwinian Approach to Pattern Recognition." *Kybernetes,* 10, 1981.

Forsyth, R., and Rada, R. *Machine Learning.* Ellis Horwood, Chichester, England, 1986.

Fried, L. "Expert Systems Enter the Corporate Domain," *Management Technology,* 1985.

Ganz, J. "Artificial Intelligence: "Man's Quest to Duplicate Human Thinking," *Careers,* 1988.

Gaschnig, J., Klahr, P., Pople, E., Shortliffe, E., and Terry, I.A. "Evaluation of Expert Systems: Issues and Case Studies." In Hayes-Roth, Waterman, and Lenat, eds., *Building Expert Systems.* Addison-Wesley, Reading, MA, 1983.

Gentner, D. "Structure-Mapping: A Theoretical Framework for Analogy." *Cognitive Science,* 1983.

Gentner, D. "Metaphor and Structure Mapping: The Relational Shift." *Child Development,* 59, 1988.

Gentner, D., and Landers, R. "Analogical Reminding: A Good Match Is hard to Find." *Proceedings of the International Conferences on Man, Systems and Cybernetics,* Tucson, AZ, 1985.

Gick, M.H., and Holyoak, K.J. "Schema Induction and Analogical Transfer." *Cognitive Psychology,* 15, 1983.

Goldsmith, T.E. "Decision Making and Cognition: An Artificial Intelligence Perspective," *Production Systems, Expert Systems.*

Graham, N. *Artificial Intelligence.* Tab Books, 1979.

Greiner, R. "Learning by Understanding Analogies," *Artificial Intelligence,* 35, 1988.

Greiner, R. "Learning by Understanding Analogies." In A. Prieditis, ed., *Analogica.* Pitman, London, 1988.
Grossberg, S. "A Theory of Visual Coding, Memory, and Development." In E.L.J. Leeuwenberg and H.F.J. Buffart, eds., *Formal Theories of Visual Perception.* Wiley, New York, 1978.

Harmon, P., and King, D. *Expert Systems for Business.* Wiley, New York, 1985.

Hart, A. *Knowledge Acquisition for Expert Systems.* McGraw-Hill, New York, 1988.

Hayes-Roth, eds. *Building Expert Systems*. Addison-Wesley, Reading, MA, 1983.

Heaton, C. "Knowledge Acquisition for an Intelligent Instructor's Aid in a Flight Simulator." Unpublished M.Sc. dissertation, Brunel University, 1986.

Hendrix, G.G., Sacerdoti, E.D., Sagalowicz, D., and Slocum, J. "Developing a Natural Language Interface to Complex Data." *ACM Transactions on Database Systems*, 3, 1978.

Hertz, D.B. "Artificial Intelligence and the Business Manager." *Computerworld*, 17,43, 1983.

Hertz, D.B. *The Expert Executive*. Wiley, New York, 1988.

Hesse, M.B. *Models and Analogies in Science*. University of Notre Dame Press, Notre Dame, 1966.

Hilgard, E.R., and Bower, G.H. *Theories of Learning*. Appleton-Century-Crofts, New York, 1966.

Hinton, G.E., and Anderson, J., eds. *Parallel Models of Associative Memory*. Erlbaum, Hillsdale, NJ, 1981.

Hofstadter, D. "The Copycat Project. An Experiment in Nondeterministic and Creative Analogies." AI Laboratory memo 755, MIT, 1984.

Hofstadter, D. *Metamagical Themas*. Basic Books, New York, 1985.

Hofstadter, D. and Mitchell, M. "Concepts, Analogy and Creativity." *Proceedings of the Canadian AI Conference*, 1988.

Holland, J.H. *Adaptation in Natural and Artificial Systems*. University of Michigan Press, Ann Arbor, MI, 1975.

Holland, J.H., Holyoak, K.J., Nisbett, R.E., and Thagard, P. *Induction: Processes of Inference, Learning and Discovery*. Bradford Books/MIT Press, Cambridge, MA, 1986.

Holsapple, C.W., and Whinston, A.B. *Business Expert Executive*. Richard D. Irwin, Homewood, IL, 1987.

Holyoak, K.J. "Analogical Thinking and Human Intelligence." In R.J. Sternberg, ed., *Advances in the Psychology of Human Intelligence*. Erlbaum, Hillsdale, NJ, 1983.

Holyoak, K.J., and Koh, K. "Surface and Structural Similarity in Analogical Transfer." *Memory and Cognition*, 15, 1987.

Holyoak, K.J., and Thagard, P. "A Constraint Satisfaction Approach to Analogue Retrieval and Mapping." In *The International Conference on Thinking*, Aberdeen, Scotland, 1988.

Humpert, B. "Expert-System Applications in Finance Planning." Paper presented at Information Networks for Electronic Banking, Second Conference on Advances in Communications-Based Information Systems for Financial Institutions, London, April 11–13, 1988.

Humpert, B. "PEOPL: An Application of an Expert System for the Programmed Evaluation of Personnel." Dept. of Computer and Information Science," Purdue University, Indianapolis,

Indurkyha, B. "A Computational Theory of Metaphor Comprehension and Analogical Reasoning. Ph.D. thesis, Boston University, 1985.

James, M. *Artificial Intelligence in Basic*. Newnes Technical Books, 1984.

James, M. *Classification Algorithms*. Collins Technical Books, London, 1985.

Jansen, J. "Applying Software Engineering Concepts to Rule-Based Expert Systems." Technical Report TR-FC-88702. CSIRO, Australia Division of Information Technology, 1988.

Jansen, J., and Compton, P. "The Knowledge Dictionary: A Relational Tool for Maintenance of Expert Systems." Technical Report TR-FC-88-01. CSIRO, Australia Division of Information Technology, 1988.

Johnson, T. *Expert Systems in Banking and Securities.* Ovum Publications, London, 1988.

Kastner, J.K., and Hong, S.J. "A Review of Expert Systems." *European Journal of Operational Research* (the Netherlands), 18,3, 1984.

Katz, B. "A Three Step Procedure for Language Generation." AI Laboratory Memo 599, MIT, 1980.

Keane, M. *Analogical Problem Solving.* Ellis Horwood, Chichester, England, 1988.

Keane, M., and Brayshaw, M. "The Incremental Analogy Machine: A Computational Model of Analogy." *Proceedings of the European Workshop on Learning,* Pitman, London, 1988.

Kedar-Cabell, S. "Analogy—From a Unified Perspective." Laboratory for Computer Science Research M1-TR-3. Rutgers University, 1985.

Kedar-Cabelli, S. "Towards a Computational Model of Purpose Directed Analogy." In A. Prieditis, ed., *Analogica,* Pitman, London, 1988.

Kidd, A., ed. *Knowledge Elicitation for Expert Systems: A Practical Handbook.* Plenum Press, New York, 1986.

Kling, R.E. "A Paradigm for Reasoning by Analogy." *Artificial Intelligence,* 2, 1988.

Kolodner, J.L. "Reconstructuve Memory, A Computer Model." *Cognitive Science,* 7, 1983.

Kolodner, J.L., and Simpson, R.L. "Problem Solving and Dynamic Memory." In J.L. Kolodner and C. Riesbeck, eds., *Experience, Memory and Reasoning,* Erlbaum, Hillsdale, NJ, 1987.

Koslov, A. "Rethinking Artificial Intelligence." *High Technology Business,* 1988.

Kruzweil, R. "What Is Artificial Intelligence Anyway?" *American Scientist,* 73, 1985.

Koton, P. "A Medical Reasoning Program That Improves with Experience. In *Proceedings of SMAMC (IEEE),* 1988.

Koton, P. "Reasoning About Evidence in Causal Explanations," *Proceedings of the AAAI,* 1988.

Langley, P. "Data-Driven Discovery of Physical Laws," *Cognitive Science,* 5, 1981.

Langley, P., Simon, H., Bradshaw, G., and Zytkow, J. *Scientific Discovery: Computational Explorations of the Creative Process.* MIT Press, Cambridge, MA, 1986.

Lakatos, I. *Proofs and Refutations: The Logic of Mathematical Discovery.* Cambridge University Press, Cambridge, England, 1976.

Lakoff, G., and Johnson, M. *Metaphors We Live By.* University of Chicago Press, Chicago, 1980.

Lawler, R., Du Boulay, B., Hughes, M., and Macleod, H. *Cognition and Computers.* Ellis Horwood, Chichester, England, 1986.

Lenat, D. "The Nature of Heuristics," *Artificial Intelligence,* 19, 1982.

Lenat, D. "Eurisko: A Program That Learns New Heuristics and Domain Concepts." *Artificial Intelligence,* 21s(1) and (2), 1983.

Leonard-Barton, D., and Sviokla, J.J. "Putting Expert Systems to Work." *Harvard Business Review,* 1988.

Lewis, J. "How Smart Is Artificial Intelligence?" *Microtimes,* 1986.

Linden, E. "Intellicorp: The Selling of Artificial Intelligence." *High Technology,* 1985.

Lipkin, R. "Making Machines in Mind's Image." *Insight,* 1988.

Longbottom, B.W. "Artificial Intelligence Means Business." *ICP Business Software Review*

Marr, D. *Vision.* Freeman, New York, 1982.

Medawar, P. *Induction and Intuition in Scientific Thought.* Methuen, London, 1969.

Michaelsen, R., and Michie, D. "Expert Systems in Business." 29,11, 1983.

Michaelsen, R.H., et al. "The Technology of Expert Systems." *Byte,* 1985.

Michalski, R., and Chilausky, R.L. "Learning by Being Told and Learning from Examples." *International Journal of Policy Analysis and Information Systems,* 4, 1980.

Michel, C., Botti, G., Fieschi, M., Joubert, M., Casanova, P., and San Marco, J.L. "Validation d'une Base de Conaissance . . .: etude en aveugle." *Proceedings of the Avignon 1986 Workshop on Expert Systems and Their Applications,* 1, 139. Agence de l'Informatique, Paris, La Defense, 1986.

Michie, D., ed. *Introductory Readings in Expert Systems.* Gordon & Breach, 1982.

Michie, D. *On Machine Intelligence.* Ellis Horwood, Chichester, England, 1986.

Michie, D., and Johnston, R. *The Creative Computer.* Penguin Books, Harmondsworth, Middlesex, England, 1985.

Miller, D. *A Pocket Popper.* Fontana Press, Glasgow, Scotland, 1987.

Miller, G.A., Fellbaum, C., Kegl, J., and Miller, K. "WORDNET: An Electronic Lexical Reference System Based on Theories of Lexical Memory." Technical Report 11, Cognitive Science Laboratory, Princeton University, 1987.

Minsky, M., and Papert, S. *Perceptrons: An Introduction to Computational Geometry.* MIT Press, Cambridge, MA, 1969.

Mitchell, T. "Version Spaces: A Candidate Elimination Approach to Rule Induction." *International Joint Conference on AI,* 5, 1977.

Mitchell, T. "Generalization as Search." *Artificial Intelligence,* 18, 1982.

Mitchell, T., Keller, R., and Kedar-Cabelli, S. "Explanation Based Generalization: A Unifying View." Computer Science Dept. ML-TR-2, Rutgers University, 1988.

Monaco, C. "The Difficult Birth of the Typewriter." *Invention and Technology,* Spring/Summer 1988.

Naylor, C. *Build Your Own Expert System.* Sigma Technical Press, Manchester, 1983.

Negoita, C.V. "Management Applications of Expert Systems." *Human Systems Management* (the Netherlands), 4,4, 1984.

Nguyen, T., Perkins, W., Laffey, T., and Pecora, D. "Checking an Expert Systems Knowledge Base for Verifying Consistency and Completeness." *Proceedings of of the Ninth International Joint Conference on Artificial Intelligence,* 1985.

Nilsson, N.J. *Principles of Artificial Intelligence.* Tioga, Palo Alto, CA, 1980.

Ohlsson, S. "Restructuring Revisited: II: An Information Processing Theory of Restructuring and Insight." *Scandinavian Journal of Psychology,* 25, 1984.

Olson J.R., and Reuter, H.H. "Extracting Expertise from Experts; Methods for Knowledge Acquisition." *Expert Systems,* 4,3, 1987.

O'Shea and Eisenstadt, eds. *Artificial Intelligence: Tools, Techniques and Applications.* Harper and Row, 1984.

Owen, S. "Heuristics for Analogy Matching." In B. DuBoulay, D. Hogg, and L. Steels, eds., *Proceedings of the ECAI '86,* Elsevier, North Holland, 1987.

Oxman, S.W. "Expert Systems Represent Ultimate Goal of Strategic Decision Making." *Data Management,* 1985.

Parsaye, K. "Acquiring and Verifying Knowledge Automatically."

Parsaye, K., and Chignell, M. *Expert Systems for Experts.* Wiley, New York, 1988.

Partridge, D. *AI: Applications in the Future of Software Engineering.* Ellis Horwood, Chichester, England, 1986.

Passmore, J. *A Hundred Years of Philosophy.* Penguin Books, Harmondsworth, Middlesex, England, 1968.

Pearl, J. *Heuristics.* Addison-Wesley, Reading, MA, 1988.

Polya, G. *How to Solve it.* Doubleday, New York, 1945.

Popper, K. *Conjectures and Refutations,* 4th ed. Routledge and Kegan Paul, London, 1972.

Pylyshyn, Z., and Demopoulous, W., eds. *Meaning and Cognitive Structure.* Ablex, Norwood, NJ, 1986.

Quinlan, J.R. "Discovering Rules by Induction from Large Collections of Examples." In D. Michie, ed., *Expert Systems in the Microelectronic Age.* Edinburgh University Press, Edinburgh, 1979.

Quinlan, R. "Semi-Autonomous Acquisition of Pattern-Based Knowledge," *Machine Intelligence,* 10, 1982.

Rhines, W. "Artificial Intelligence: Out of the Lab and into Business." *Texas Instruments, Journal of Business Strategy,* 6,1, 1985.

Richardson, K. "Knowledge-Based System Verification and Validation as Related to Automation of Space Station Subsystems." NASA Ames Research Workshop, 1986.

Roberts, B., and Goldstein, I. "The FRL Manual." AI Laboratory Memo 409, MIT, 1977.

Roesner, D. "Schemata for Understanding of Argumentation in Newspaper Texts. In L. Steels and J.A. Campbell, eds., *Progress in Artificial Intelligence.* Ellis Horwood, Chichester, England, 1985.

Rosenblatt, F. *Principles of Neurodynamics.* Spartan Books, New York, 1962.

Rowe, A.J., and Bahr, F.R. "A Heuristic Approach to Managerial Problem Solving." *Journal of Economics and Business,* 1969.

Rowe, A.J., et al. "Management Use of Artificial Intelligence." In *Applied Expert Systems—Trends and Issues.* Elsevier, 1988.

Rowe, N. *Artificial Intelligence Through Prolog.* Prentice-Hall, Englewood Cliffs, NJ, 1988.

Rumelhart, D.E., and Abrahamson, A.A. "A Model for Analogical Reasoning." *Cognitive Psychology,* 5, 1973.

Rumelhart, D.E., McClelland, J.L., and the PDP Research Group. *Parallel Distributed Processing: Explorations in the Microstructure of Cognition.* Bradford Books/MIT Press, Cambridge, MA, 1986.

Russel, S.J., and Davies, T. "A Logical Approach to Reasoning by Analogy." *Proceedings of the IJCAI,* 1986.

Russel, S.J. "Analogy and Inductive Reasoning." Ph.D. thesis, Stanford University, 1986.

Samuel, A. "Some Studies in Machine Learning Using the Game of Checkers, part II." *IBM Journal of Research and Development,* 1967.

Schank, R. *Dynamic Memory: A Theory of Reminding and Learning in Computers and People.* Cambridge University Press, Cambridge, 1982.

Schank, R.C., and Abelson, R.P. *Scripts, Plans, Goals and Understanding.* Erlbaum, Hillsdale, NJ, 1977.

Schank, R., et al. "The Quest to Understand Thinking." *Byte,* 1985.

Shannon, R. "Expert Systems and Simulation." *Simulation,*

Shanteau, J. "Psychological Characteristics of Expert Decision Makers." Dept. of Psychology, Kansas State University, Manhattan, KS.

Shortliffe, E. *Computer-Based Medical Consultations: MYCIN.* Elsevier, 1976.

Simon, H., Langley, P., and Bradshaw, G. "Scientific Discovery as Problem Solving." *Synthese,* 47, 1981.

Sklansky, J., Wassel, G. *Pattern Classifiers and Trainable Machines.* Springer-Verlag, New York, 1981.

Skorstad, J., Falkenhainer, B., and Gentner, D. "Analogical Processing: A Simulation and Empirical Corroboration." *Proceedings of the AAAI,* 1987.

Sleeman, D., and Brown, J.S. *Intelligent Tutoring Systems.* Academic Press, New York, 1982.

Slocombe, S., Moore, K.D., and Zelouf, M. "Engineering Expert Systems Applications." *Expert Systems '86,* Brighton, 1986.

Sober, E., ed. *Conceptual Issues in Evolutionary Biology.* Bradford Books/MIT Press, Cambridge, MA, 1984.

Stansfield, J.L., and Greefeld, N.R. "PlanPower—a Comprehensive Financial Planner." *IEE Expert,* fall issue, 1987.

Sternberg, R.J. "Component Processes in Analogical Reasoning." *Psychological Review,* 85, 1977.

Sternberg, R.J. "Inside Intelligence." *American Scientist,* 74, 1986.

Stewart, S.D., and Watson, G. "Applications of Artificial Intelligence." *Simulation,* 1985.

Taggart, W., and Robey, D. "Minds and Managers . . ." *Academy of Management Review*

Tait, J.I. "Generating Summaries Using a Script-Based Language Analyzer." In L. Steels and J.A. Campbell, eds., *Progress in Artificial Intelligence*. Ellis Horwood, Chichester, England, 1985.

Ten Dyke, R.P. "Outlook on Artificial Intelligence." *Journal of Information System Management*

Tenenberg, J. "Planning with Abstraction." *Proceedings of the AAAI,* 1987.

Thagard, P. *Computational Philosophy of Science*. Bradford Books/MIT Press, Cambridge, MA, 1988.

Toda, I. "On the Future of AI." *ICOT Journal,* 1987.

Tourangeua, R., and Sternberg, R.J. "Understanding and Appreciating Metaphors." *Cognition,* 11, 1982.

Trelease, R.B. "The Forth Wave in AI." *AI Expert,* 1987.

Turban, E. *Decision Support and Expert Systems*. Macmillan, New York, 1988.

Turban, E., and Mock, T.J. "Expert Systems: What They Mean to the Executive." *New Management,* 3,1, 1985.

Uhr, L. *Pattern Recognition*. Wiley, New York, 1966.

Vogel, C. *Génie Cognitif*. Editions Masson, Paris, 1988.

Waterman and Hayes-Roth, eds. *Pattern-Directed Inference Systems*. Academic Press, New York, 1978.

Weiss and Kulikowski. *A Practical Guide to Designing Expert Systems*. Chapman & Hall, 1984.

Welbank, M. "A Review of Knowledge Acquisition Techniques for Expert Systems." British Telecom Research Laboratories, Martlesham Consultancy Services, 1983.

Wielinga, B.J., Breuker, J.A. "Interpretation of Verbal Data for Knowledge Acquisition." In T. O'Shea, ed., *ECAI '84: Advances in Artificial Intelligence*. Elsevier, 1984.

Wielinga, B.J., and Breuker, J.A. "Models of Expertise." *Proceedings of the ECAI 1986*.

Winston, P.H. *Artificial Intelligence*. Addison-Wesley, Reading, MA, 1977.

Winston, P.H. "Learning and Reasoning by Analogy." *Communications of the ACM,* 1980.

Winston, P.H. "Learning New Principles from Precedents and Examples." *Artificial Intelligence,* 19, 1982.

Winston, P.H. "Learning by Augmenting Rules and Accumulating Censors." In R.S. Michalski, J.G. Carbonell, and T.M. Mitchell, eds., *Machine Learning, An Artificial Intelligence Approach,* Vol. 2. Morgan Kaufmann, Los Altos, CA, 1986.

Wolstencroft, J. "A Long Review of Models of Reasoning by Analogy." UCL/EQUUS Internal Note, to be supplied with the documentation for the October 1988 project review, 1988.

Wong, S.K.M., Ziarko, W., and Ye, R.L. "Comparison of Rough-set and Statistical Methods in Inductive Learning." *International Man–Machine Studies,* 24, 1986.

Zadeh Lotfi, Fu and Tanaka, eds. *Journal of Fuzzy Sets and Their Applications to Cognitive Decision Processes*. Academic Press, New York, 1975.

Index

Index